Investing For Canadians For Dummies, 2nd Edition

Eric and Tony's 20 Immutable Investing Laws

1. **Saving is a prerequisite to investing.** Unless you have wealthy, benevolent relatives, living within your means and saving money are prerequisites to investing and building wealth.

2. **Know the three best wealth-building investments.** People of all economic means make their money grow in ownership assets — stocks, real estate, and small business — where you share in the success and profitability of the asset.

3. **Be realistic about expected investment returns.** Over the long-term, 9 to 10 percent per year is about right for ownership investments (such as stocks and real estate). If you run a small business, you can earn higher returns and even become a multimillionaire, but years of hard work and insight are usually required.

4. **Think long-term.** Because ownership investments are riskier (more volatile), you must keep your long-term perspective when investing in them. Do not invest money in such investments unless you plan on holding them for a minimum of five years, and preferably a decade or longer.

5. **Match the time frame to the investment.** Selecting good investments for yourself involves matching the time frame you have to the riskiness of the investment. For example, for money that you expect to use within the next year, focus on safe investments, such as money market funds. Invest your longer-term money mostly in wealth-building investments.

6. **Diversify.** Diversification is a powerful investment concept that helps you to reduce the risk of holding more aggressive investments. Diversifying simply means that you should hold a variety of investments that don't move in tandem in different market environments. For example, if you invest in stocks, invest worldwide, not just in the Canadian market. You can further diversify by investing in real estate.

7. **Look at the big picture first.** Understand your overall financial situation and how wise investments fit within it. Before you invest, examine your debt obligations, tax situation, ability to fund your RRSP, and insurance coverage.

8. **Ignore the minutiae.** Don't feel mystified by or feel the need to follow the short-term gyrations of the financial markets. Ultimately, the prices of stocks, bonds, and other financial instruments are determined by supply and demand, which are influenced by thousands of external issues and millions of investors' expectations and fears.

9. **Allocate your assets.** How you divvy up or allocate your money among major investments greatly determines your returns. The younger you are and the more money you earmark for the long term, the greater the percentage you should devote to ownership investments.

10. **Do your homework before you buy an investment.** You work hard for your money, and investments cost you to buy and sell. Investing is not a field where acting first and asking questions later works well. Never buy an investment based on an advertisement or a salesperson's solicitation of you.

11. **Keep an eye on taxes when choosing investments.** Take advantage of tax-deductible retirement plans and understand the impact of your tax bracket when investing outside tax-sheltered retirement plans such as an RRSP.

Investing For Canadians For Dummies, 2nd Edition

Cheat Sheet

12. Consider the value of your time and your investing skills and desires. Investing in stocks and other securities via the best mutual funds is both time-efficient and profitable. Real estate investing and running a small business are the most time-intensive investments.

13. Where possible, minimize fees. The more you pay in commissions and management fees on your investments, the greater the drag on your returns. And don't fall prey to the thinking that "you get what you pay for."

14. Don't expect to beat the stock market averages. If you have the right skills and interest, your ability to do better than the investing averages is greater with real estate and small business than with stock market investing. The large number of full-time, experienced stock market professionals makes it next to impossible for you to choose individual stocks that will consistently beat a relevant market average over an extended time period.

15. Don't bail when things look bleak. The hardest time, psychologically, to hold on to your investments is when they're down. Even the best investments go through depressed periods, which is the worst possible time to sell. Don't sell when there's a sale going on; if anything, consider buying more.

16. Ignore soothsayers and prognosticators. Predicting the future is nearly impossible. Select and hold good investments for the long term. Don't try to time when to be in or out of a particular investment.

17. Minimize your trading. The more you trade, the more likely you are to make mistakes. You also suffer increased transaction costs and higher taxes (for non-retirement plan investments).

18. Hire advisers carefully. Before you hire investing help, first educate yourself so that you can better evaluate the competence of those you may hire. Beware of conflicts of interest when you consider advisers to hire.

19. You are what you read and listen to. Don't pollute your mind with bad investing strategies and philosophies. The quality of what you read and listen to is far more important than the quantity. Find out how to evaluate the quality of what you read and hear.

20. Remember the highest-return, lowest-risk investments: your personal life and health. They're far more important investments than the size of your financial portfolio.

WILEY

...For Dummies®: Bestselling Book Series for Beginners

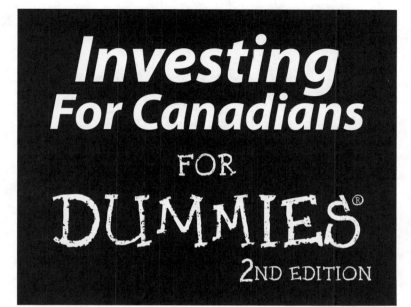

Investing
For Canadians

FOR

DUMMIES®

2ND EDITION

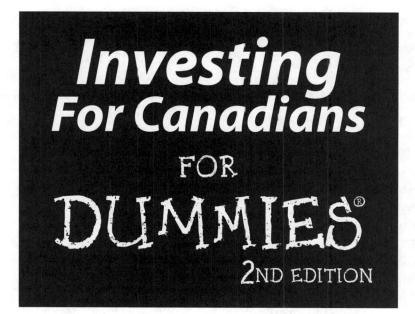

Investing
For Canadians
FOR
DUMMIES®
2ND EDITION

by Eric Tyson and Tony Martin

John Wiley & Sons Canada, Ltd

Investing For Canadians For Dummies®, 2nd Edition

Published by
John Wiley & Sons Canada, Ltd
6045 Freemont Boulevard
Mississauga, Ontario, L5R 4J3
www.wiley.ca

National Library of Canada Cataloguing in Publication

Tyson, Eric (Eric Kevin)

Investing for Canadians for dummies / Eric Tyson and Tony Martin. — 2nd ed.

Includes index.

ISBN 0-470-83361-0

1. Investments. 2. Investments—Canada. I. Martin, Tony (Tony M.). II. Title.

HG4521.T97 2004   332.6   C2004-904386-2

Printed in Canada

4 5 TRI 09 08

Distributed in Canada by John Wiley & Sons Canada, Ltd.

For general information on John Wiley & Sons Canada, Ltd., including all books published by Wiley Publishing, Inc., please call our warehouse, Tel 1-800-567-4797. For reseller information, including discounts and premium sales, please call our sales department, Tel 416-646-7992. For press review copies, author interviews, or other publicity information, please contact our marketing department, Tel: 416-646-4584, Fax 416-236-4448.

For authorization to photocopy items for corporate, personal, or educational use, please contact The Canadian Copyright Licensing Agency (Access Copyright). For an Access Copyright license, visit www.accesscopyright.ca or call toll free 1-800-893-5777.

About the Authors

Eric Tyson

Eric Tyson is an internationally acclaimed and best-selling personal finance author, lecturer, and advisor. Through his work, he is dedicated to teaching people to manage their money better and to successfully direct their own investments.

He earned a bachelor's degree in economics at Yale and an M.B.A. at the Stanford Graduate School of Business. An accomplished freelance personal finance writer, Eric is the author of numerous best-selling books including For Dummies books on Personal Finance, Mutual Funds, Taxes (co-author) and Home Buying (co-author) and is a syndicated columnist. His work has been featured and quoted in hundreds of national and local publications, including *Newsweek*, *Kiplinger's Personal Finance Magazine*, *Los Angeles Times*, *Chicago Tribune*, *The Wall Street Journal*, and *Bottom Line/Personal*, and on NBC's *Today Show*, ABC, CNBC, PBS's *Nightly Business Report*, CNN, CBS national radio, Bloomberg Business Radio, National Public Radio, and Business Radio Network. To stay in tune with what real people care about and struggle with, Eric still maintains a financial counseling practice.

Tony Martin

Tony Martin is a nationally recognized best-selling personal finance writer, speaker, and commentator. Tony's focus is on providing Canadians with the means to understand the world of personal finance and the tools to better manage and grow their own investments.

Tony has produced both television and radio programs about personal finance. He is the co-author, along with Eric, of the national bestseller *Personal Finance For Dummies For Canadians*. He also writes the popular and widely read Me and My Money column that has appeared in the *Globe and Mail*'s Report on Business for many years, and which keeps him in touch with the real-life investment concerns and conundrums of Canadians. His work has appeared in numerous other publications, including *The Financial Post*, *Readers' Digest*, *ie: Money*, and *Canadian Business*, and he has reported or appeared on ROB TV, CBC Television, TVOntario, CBC Radio, as well as numerous other TV and radio stations across the country.

Dedication

Actually, before we get to the thank yous, please allow us a *really* major thank you and dedication.

This book is hereby and irrevocably dedicated to our family and friends who ultimately have taught us everything that we know about how to explain financial terms and strategies so that all of us may benefit.

Author's Acknowledgments

Behind every good book (and we trust, dear reader, you think that this one qualifies) is a great project editor, or in this case, great project editor*s* — thank you, Marcia Johnson and Michelle Marchetti, for your enthusiasm, insights, and attention to detail.

Eric sends his thanks also to Tina Sims for all her fine editing and to Andy Lewandowski and Justin Wells for additional editorial and research help, and we both are grateful to all of the fine folks in Production for making this book and all the charts and graphs look great! Thanks also to everyone else who contributed to getting this book done and done right.

Also, a tip of Eric's cap to the fine lot of technical reviewers who helped to ensure that he did not write something that wasn't quite right. In the U.S., this important job was well handled by Chris Wheaton. For the previous editions, this book benefited from the wise input of Bob Bingham with Bingham, Osborn and Scarborough; Ray Brown, residential real estate guru, fellow author, sometimes mentor, and always great pal; Ed Wholihan, McKinsey & Co. management consultant extraordinaire; Ken Fisher, investment manager and most informed stock market historian; Al Gobar, real estate investing guru; small-business professor Pam Autrey of the University of Texas; and Dennis Ito, Bob Taylor, Madelyn O'Connell, and Marilyn Wilson from KPMG Peat Marwick LLP. Thank you, one and all!

Tony would like to thank financial planning whizzes Warren Baldwin of TE Financial, Peter Volpe from Integra Capital, and Doug Macdonald of Macdonald Shymko & Co. Ltd. for their insights, comments, and review, as well as Gena Katz, chartered accountant and gracious explainer of tax matters in plain English. Thanks also to the fixed income folks at Scotia Capital Markets for their great stats. As well, a tip of the hat to Joan Whitman, whose easy-going professionalism helped bring the first edition of this book to life. Finally, we're grateful for the sharp eye and good taste of Karen Alliston for her thorough and thoughtful copy-editing.

Publisher's Acknowledgments

We're proud of this book; please send us your comments at canadapt@wiley.com. Some of the people who helped bring this book to market include the following:

Acquisitions and Editorial

Associate Editor: Michelle Marchetti

Developmental Editor: Kelli Howey

Copy Editor: Karen Alliston

Production

Publishing Services Director: Karen Bryan

Publishing Services Manager: Ian Koo

Project Manager: Elizabeth McCurdy

Project Coordinator: Robert Hickey

Layout and Graphics: Pat Loi

Proofreader: Susan Gaines

Indexer: Belle Wong

John Wiley & Sons Canada, Ltd.

Bill Zerter, Chief Operating Officer

Robert Harris, General Manager, Professional and Trade Division

Publishing and Editorial for Consumer Dummies

Diane Graves Steele, Vice President and Publisher, Consumer Dummies

Joyce Pepple, Acquisitions Director, Consumer Dummies

Kristin A. Cocks, Product Development Director, Consumer Dummies

Michael Spring, Vice President and Publisher, Travel

Suzanne Jannetta, Editorial Director, Travel

Publishing for Technology Dummies

Andy Cummings, Acquisitions Director

Composition Services

Gerry Fahey, Executive Director of Production Services

Debbie Stailey, Director of Composition Services

Contents at a Glance

Table of Contents

Introduction

By 2000, when the first edition of this book was published, more and more investors were piling into technology (especially Internet) and name-brand stocks. Fewer and fewer market analysts were warning about stock market corrections. Here is what we said in the prior edition of this book:

> Internet stocks aren't the only stocks being swept to excessive prices relative to their earnings at the dawn of the new millennium. Various traditional retailers announced that they are opening Internet sites to sell their goods, and within days their stock prices doubled or tripled. Also, leading name-brand technology companies such as Dell Computer, Cisco Systems, Lucent, and PeopleSoft traded at P/E ratios in excess of 100. Companies in other industries like investment brokerage firm Charles Schwab, which expanded to offer Internet services, saw its stock price balloon to push its P/E ratio over 100. As during the 1960s and 1920s, name-brand growth companies soared to high P/E valuations. For example, coffee purveyor Starbucks at times had a P/E near 100.

> What we find troubling about investors piling into the leading, name-brand stocks, especially in Internet and technology-related fields, is that many of these investors don't even know what a price-earnings ratio is and why it's important. Before you invest in any individual stock, no matter how great a company you think it is, you need to understand the company's line of business, strategies, competitors, financial statements, and price earnings ratio versus the competition, among many other issues. Selecting and monitoring good companies takes lots of research time and discipline.

> Also, remember that if a company taps into a product line or way of doing business that proves highly successful, that company's success invites lots of competition. So, you need to understand the barriers to entry that a leading company has erected and how difficult or easy it is for competitors to join the fray. Also, be wary of analysts' earnings and stock price predictions. As more and more investment banking analysts initiated coverage of Internet companies and issued buy ratings on said stocks, investors bought more shares. Analysts, who are too optimistic (as shown in numerous independent studies), have a conflict of interest because the investment banks that they work for seek to cultivate the business (new stock and bond issues) of the companies that they purport to rate and analyze. The analysts who say buy, buy, buy all the current market leaders are the same analysts who generate much new business for their investment banks and get the lucrative job offers and multimillion-dollar annual salaries.

In late 1999 and 2000, we also wrote numerous columns for newspapers, magazines, and Web sites warning investors about the perils that await those who, in the pursuit of greed, sought to get rich quick. As this book goes to press in 2004, the times, of course, have changed. Some investors with poorly diversified portfolios lost nearly everything, and some who borrowed money to buy stock lost everything. Many Internet companies have gone bankrupt, while most others have had stock price plunges of 70 or 80 percent or more. The seemingly solid name-brand companies like Cisco Systems, Dell, Lucent, PeopleSoft, Starbucks, and Charles Schwab have generally gotten clobbered or gone nowhere for several years.

With the stock market boom in the 1990s and the subsequent volatility and plunges, the media's coverage of stocks and the overall market continues to mushroom. More magazines and news programs are devoted to investing and the markets than ever before. Unless you live in a log cabin in the wilderness without access to television, radio, the Internet, or printed publications, you can't escape the rising tidal wave of investment coverage.

When stocks were rising, more people came into the investment markets for the first time. There's certainly a good side to that: Unless you have benevolent, loaded relatives, you should take an interest in securing your financial future. That said, especially in the 1990s, we found increasing numbers of people spending much time (too much in our opinion) researching, tracking, and monitoring their investments. Many of those investors who suffered the worst losses in the market decline at the beginning of this decade headed to the exits, vowing to never return. That's a mistake. The real error these investors made was in chasing after hot sectors and not being properly diversified.

With all the increased interest in and coverage of the investment world, you may think that investing times have changed. To a large degree, things haven't changed all that much. Investments that were considered lousy years ago — products with high fees and commission — generally are still lousy today.

The best investment vehicles for building wealth — stocks, real estate, and small business — haven't changed. And, you still need money to play in the investment world. Like the first edition of *Investing For Canadians For Dummies,* the second edition of this best-seller includes complete coverage of these wealth-building investments as well as other commonly used investment strategies, such as bonds. Here are the biggest changes in this edition:

✔ **Completely revised and updated.** We've freshened up the data and examples in this book to provide you with the latest insights and analyses. Wondering whether there's a way to invest in stocks without exposing yourself to much risk? Considering whether now's the time to invest in real estate or asking yourself what the heck a REIT is? Confused about how recent tax law changes should affect your investment strategies? You can find the answers to these questions and many more in this edition.

✔ **Investing resources section.** With the explosion in Web sites, software, publications, media outlets, and many other information sources offering investing advice, you're probably overwhelmed about how to choose among the numerous investing research tools and resources. Equally problematic is knowing whom you can trust and listen to and whom you need to ignore. In this new edition, we explain how to evaluate the quality of various investment tools and resources, and we provide tips for whom to listen to and whom to tune out.

How Real People Build Wealth

We know from working and talking with real live people of modest and immodest economic means that they increase their wealth by doing the following:

✔ Living within their means and systematically saving and investing money, ideally in a tax-favoured manner

✔ Buying and holding stocks, ideally through the best mutual funds

✔ Building their own small business or career

✔ Investing in real estate

That kind of investing is what this book is all about. Equally, if not more, important, we help you understand and choose investments compatible with your personal and financial goals.

You don't need a fancy university or graduate school degree, and you don't need a rich dad or mom. What you *do* need is a desire to read and practice the many simple yet powerful lessons and strategies in this book.

How This Book Is Organized

Seriously, this stuff isn't rocket science. You see, we wrote this book hoping that you gather enough information in these subject areas so that you won't need to hire a staff of financial advisers and overseers.

By all means, if you're dealing with a complicated, atypical issue, get quality professional help. But educate yourself first. As you'll discover from the mistakes that others have made, hiring someone is dangerous if you yourself are financially challenged. If you do finally decide to hire someone, you'll be much better prepared by educating yourself, and you'll be more focused in your questions and better able to assess that person's competence.

This book helps you fill gaps in your investment knowledge. It's structured so that you can read it cover to cover or simply dive into particular sections that most currently interest you. Here are the major parts:

Part I: Investing Fundamentals

Before you can confidently and intelligently choose investments, you need to be able to cut through the lingo and jargon and get to the heart of what investments are and are not and how they differ from one another. In this part, we explain what rate of return you can reasonably expect to earn and how much risk you need to take to get it. This part also details how investments best fit into your specific financial goals and situation.

Part II: Stocks, Bonds, and Bay Street

We know that you probably don't want to trade in your day job for one where you'd wear a three-piece suit and need to know on which page of the daily *Wall Street Journal* you can find yield curves. But you *do* need to understand what the financial markets are and how you can participate in them without suffering too many abrasions and lacerations. We explain what stocks and bonds are all about and how to best buy them and build your fortune.

Part III: Real Estate

We all need places to live, work, and shop, so it makes sense that real estate can be a profitable part of your investment portfolio. Intelligently buying and managing real estate is harder than it looks, which is why this part covers lots of territory. We show you the best ways to invest in real estate and provide a crash course in mortgages, landlording, buying low, selling high, taxes, and more.

Part IV: There's No Business Like Small Business

There's nothing small about the potential profits you can make from small business. You can choose the way to invest in a small business that matches your skills and time. If you aspire to be the best boss you've ever had, here you can find the right ways to start your own business or buy someone else's small business. Or maybe you'd like to try your hand at spotting up-and-comers but don't want to be on the front lines — try investing in someone else's small business.

Part V: Investing Resources

Click your radio or television on, crack open a magazine or newspaper, or go Web site surfing, and you quickly discover that you can't escape investment advice. Surprisingly, each new guru you stumble upon contradicts the one who came before. Before you know it, although you've spent an avalanche of your valuable free time on all this investment stuff, you're no closer to making an informed decision. In fact, if you're like most people, you find yourself even more confused and paralyzed. Fear not! In this important part, we explain why many experts really aren't experts and why most of them try to make the world of investing so mysterious. We highlight the best resources to use and experts worth listening to.

Part VI: The Part of Tens

These shorter chapters build your investment knowledge further. You find advice about topics such as overcoming common psychological investment obstacles, tips for investing in a down market, and points to ponder when you sell an investment.

You'll also be pleased to know that this book has a super-useful index. If you're the kind of reader who jumps around from topic to topic instead of reading from cover to cover, you'll be pleased that the index highlights the pages where investing terms are defined.

Icons Used in This Book

Throughout this book, icons help guide you through the maze of suggestions, solutions, and cautions. We hope you find that the following images make your journey through investment strategies smoother.

In the shark-infested investing waters, you'll find creatures that feast on novice waders, ready to take a bite out of a swimmer's savings. This icon notes when and where the sharks may be circling.

If you see this icon, we're pointing out companies, products, services, and resources that have proven to be exceptional over the years — in other words, resources that we would or do use personally or would recommend to our friends and family.

We use this icon to highlight an issue that requires more detective work on your part. Don't worry though; we prepare you for your work so that you don't have to start out as a novice gumshoe.

We know this is something your parents always told you that promptly flew out your other ear, but this icon indicates something really, really important — don't you forget it!

Skip it or read it; the choice is yours. You'll fill your head with more stuff that may prove valuable as you expand your investing know-how, but you risk overdosing on stuff that you may not need right away.

This icon denotes strategies that can enable you to build wealth faster and leap over tall obstacles in a single bound.

This icon indicates treacherous territory that has made mincemeat out of lesser mortals who have come before you. Skip this point at your own peril.

Part I
Investing
Fundamentals

In this part . . .

Like a good map or aerial photograph, this part helps you see the big picture of the investment world. Here, we explain the different types of investments, which ones are good and bad for a variety of circumstances, what returns you can expect, and how to make wise investing decisions that fit with your overall financial situation.

Chapter 1

Investment Choices

· ·

In This Chapter

▶ Defining investing

▶ Understanding why simple strategies are best

▶ Seeing how stocks, real estate, and small business build wealth

▶ Comprehending the role of lending and other investments

· ·

*I*f you have been successful in accumulating some money to invest, con-gratulations! You've accomplished a feat that the majority of people in the world haven't yet done. If you decide to move to the next step — actually investing some of that money — you've come to the right place. Investing For Canadians For Dummies, 2nd Edition, is your one-stop investment reference guide and counsellor, ready to prepare you for the thrilling and rewarding world of investing.

In many parts of the "developing" world, life's basic necessities — food, clothing, shelter, and taxes — gobble all of people's meagre earnings. In "advanced" countries, like Canada and the United States, most people save little, if any, money despite considerably higher incomes. In recent years, Canadians saved less than 3 percent of their take-home income, yet people in other industrialized countries, such as Japan, Germany, and Switzerland, save two to three times this amount! Although some Canadians do struggle for basic necessities, more people consider just about everything — eating out, driving new cars, hopping on an airplane for vacation — a necessity. We've taken it upon ourselves (using this book as our tool) to help you recognize that investing — that is, putting your money to work for you — is a necessity. If you want to accomplish important personal and financial goals, such as owning a home, starting your own business, helping your kids through uni-versity, retiring, and so on, you must know how to invest well.

It has been said, and too often quoted, that the only certainties in life are death and taxes. To these two certainties we add one more: being confused by and ignorant of investing. Because investing is a confusing activity, you may be tempted to look with anxiety-ridden eyes at those people in the world who appear to be savvy with money and investing. Remember that all of us start with the same level of financial knowledge — that is to say, with none. *No one* is born knowing this stuff! The only difference between those who know and those who don't is that those who *do* know have invested their time and energy acquiring knowledge about the investment world.

Some of the people you think are investing wizards are, in fact, investing fools. Many professional athletes, movie stars, and business big shots have made easily avoidable investing blunders, losing significant money through bad investments and flawed investment strategies. These wealthy people (and their advisers) made investment decisions that they could've and should've avoided.

Investing: Saving for Rainy (and Sunny) Days

Before we discuss the major investing alternatives, we want to start with something that's quite basic, yet important. What exactly do we mean when we say "investing"?

Investing means that you have money put away for future use. If you put your money in your mattress, you've chosen an investment — one that pays no interest and is subject to theft and fire! Many people chose to invest their money in their mattresses during the Great Depression in the early 1930s. Why, you ask? Banks were failing, and the stock market fell off a cliff. Therefore, during the Great Depression, the mattress was a reasonable place to invest. (Although many people didn't know it then, an even better place to invest their money was in government-backed bonds that appreciated in value as inflation ebbed.)

Investing involves the process of making choices. Whether you place your money in the bank, a mattress, or a relative's business, you ultimately have to decide where to invest it.

Some people invest some, or even all, of their money in things out of default or for reasons that don't match their current and long-term best interests:

✔ Perhaps you hold your money in a "parking place" until you figure out what to do with it. Today, the equivalent of the Depression-era mattress is a bank account. When most people receive money, it goes into their local bank account where it may sit for years on end earning little if any interest.

✔ Perhaps a broker or financial adviser who was more interested in his profits than yours sold your investments to you. Many people hold investments that they don't understand, and the investments may not be appropriate for their financial situation and goals. Perhaps you're already a student of the investing school of hard knocks and have lost money on poor investments ravaged by high commissions and fees.

✔ Your current investments may be based on your previous circumstances. Although your situation may change slowly from year to year, it may differ greatly from where you were five or ten years ago. Maybe you bought investments that made sense for you when you were in a much higher or lower tax bracket. Perhaps your investment holdings require too much time to track and monitor.

✔ You inherited your investments. What made a good investment for your parents, grandparents, or other relative doesn't necessarily make sense for you, and who says that what they held is a good investment? You can love a person and honour her memory yet still be analytical and practical about the investments that she left you.

This book, beginning with this chapter, helps you understand your best investment options so that you may begin to choose and construct a *portfolio* (collection of investments) that fits your financial situation and goals.

Millionaires Keep It Simple

We often find there's a misconception that in order to accumulate significant wealth, you need to do something complicated and out of the ordinary. The truth is that by following time-tested and simple principles and investment strategies, you can earn healthy returns and achieve financial independence — just as George, a client of Eric's, did.

The first and only time that Eric met with George was at his home. George kept a ledger of his investments on a sheet of paper that was faded and smelled old.

George was a millionaire, although you'd never know it. George's home furnishings can best be described as Spartan— probably from the years of family pets and children running around the house. The stuffing of his living room couch was falling out, and he had a Philco television set that was probably black and white.

Despite the fact that George never came close to earning a six-figure salary, he was able to retire at the age of 50. George didn't have any advanced degrees in business or any other subject, and he never went to university. He accumulated his wealth the old-fashioned (and best) way — through hard work, savings, and common-sense investing.

In his 20s and 30s, George worked overtime to come up with the necessary cash to buy a couple real estate properties. He's owned real estate ever since. George also took about 10 percent of each pay cheque and invested it in stocks.

George also didn't follow any gurus to divine the right time to sell or trade his investments. He did some homework, bought sound investments, and turned, so to speak, into an investing couch potato. "After all my time, trouble, and work to save up the money and then choose an investment, why would I want to sell it?" George asks. That's an excellent question that trigger-happy traders, especially those who predominate in the world of Internet trading, may ask themselves too late in life. Buying and then holding sound investments minimizes trading costs, taxes, and anxiety.

George hired Eric to get an opinion on whether his portfolio was properly balanced and what mutual funds he should invest in, given his tax situation. George agreed that meeting with Eric for advice and reading a couple of books on investing made the best use of his time, money, and educational needs. You see, George was also smart enough to realize that consultants cost money and that you can find out a lot on your own if you get pointed in the right direction!

While Eric talked with George, the telephone rang, and after he said hello, he waited to find out who called with all the anticipation of a young child in line at an amusement park. Then his eyes really lit up as he realized it was his granddaughter and she would soon be visiting.

George is a wealthy person in many ways. Nearly 80, he possesses great health and appears to have lots of friends and family. He enjoyed his career working in a manufacturing environment. George also served his country in World War II and earned a medal.

In addition to being with his close-knit family and friends, he spends his time volunteering and travelling. Although George has significant financial wealth and the ability to save and invest wisely, he says of his money, "I know that I can't take it with me."

You, dear reader, can accomplish what George did. The first step for you on the road to wealth is to read and internalize the simple yet powerful strategies in this book.

So Many Investment Options — So Little Time

Literally tens of thousands of different investments exist. There are thousands of stocks, bonds, mutual funds, and other vehicles. Unfortunately for the novice, and even for experts who are honest with you, knowing the name of the investment or company is just the tip of the iceberg. Underneath each of these investments lurks a veritable mountain of details.

If you wanted to and had the ability, you could make a full-time endeavour out of analyzing financial statements and talking to business employees, customers, suppliers, and so on. That's why you must be realistic and selective about the investments that you choose. Your time on this earth is limited, after all.

We don't want to scare you away from investing just because some people do it on a full-time basis. Making wise investments need not take a lot of your time. If you know where to get good information and you purchase quality, managed investments, you can leave the investment management to qualified experts and thereby free up your time for the work you're best at and for fun stuff.

 An important part of the "making wise investments" process is knowing when you have enough information to do things well on your own versus when you should hire others to help you. For example, investing in foreign stock markets is generally more difficult to research and understand compared with domestic markets. Thus, hiring a good money manager, such as through a mutual fund, makes more sense when investing overseas than going to all the time, trouble, and expense of trying to pick your own individual stocks.

We're here to give you enough information to help you make your way through the complex investment world. In the following sections, we clear a path so that you can identify the major investments and understand what each is good for.

Building wealth through ownership investments

 If you want your money to grow and you don't mind a bit of a roller-coaster-type ride from time to time in your investments' values, ownership investments are for you. With these investments you own a piece of a company or other assets (such as stock, real estate, or a small business) that have the ability to generate revenue and, potentially, profits.

Not surprisingly, the champions of wealth around the globe gained their fortunes largely through owning a piece (or all) of a successful company that they (or others) have built. Take the case of Bill Gates, founder and chief executive officer of Microsoft — and college dropout. Microsoft is the world's largest producer of personal computer software.

Every time you — and millions of other people — buy a personal computer with one of these Microsoft software packages, or simply buy or upgrade a Microsoft software program, Microsoft makes more money. As the largest stockholder in the company, Gates (along with other Microsoft shareholders) stands to make more money as increasing sales and profits drive up the stock's price. Microsoft's profits and stock price have skyrocketed several thousand percent since the company first issued shares back in 1986.

In addition to their own businesses, many well-to-do people have built their nest eggs investing in real estate and the stock market. And, of course, some people come into wealth the old-fashioned way — they inherit it. Even if your parents are among the rare wealthy ones and you expect them to pass on big bucks to you, you need to know how to invest your money intelligently. Investing like the big boys and girls is a smart move, as long as you understand and manage the risks.

If you understand and are comfortable with the risks and take sensible steps to diversify (don't put all your eggs in the same basket), ownership investments are the key to building wealth. In order to accomplish typical longer-term financial goals, such as retiring, the money that you save and invest needs to grow at a healthy clip. If you dump all your money into bank accounts that pay little if any interest, you're likely to fall short of your goals.

Not everyone needs to make his money grow, of course. For example, suppose you inherit a significant sum and/or maintain a restrained standard of living and work your whole life simply because you enjoy doing so. In this situation, you may not need to take the risks involved with a potentially faster-growth investment. You may be more comfortable with *safer* investments, such as paying off your mortgage faster than necessary. Chapter 3 helps you think through such issues.

The stock market

Stocks are an example of an ownership investment, because they represent shares of ownership in a company.

If you want to share in the growth and profits of companies like Microsoft, you can! You simply buy shares of their stock through a brokerage firm. However, just because Microsoft makes money in the future, there's no guarantee that the value of its stock will increase. In fact, the value of your Microsoft stock can decrease. But at least the next time you call Microsoft and fork over $50 for technical support, you'll have some small satisfaction knowing that you indirectly profit.

Some companies today even sell their stock directly to investors, allowing you to bypass brokers altogether. You can also invest in stocks via a stock mutual fund, where a fund manager decides which individual stocks to include in the fund. (We discuss the various methods for buying stock in Chapter 6.)

The stock market is a fine way to build wealth. In fact, Thomas has used the stock market to build his wealth over the years. At the age of 75, he is the proud owner of a portfolio worth more than $1.2 million. Thomas worked for 30 years as a pressman for a newspaper and retired in his early 50s. At the time he retired, he was making about $9,000 per year. "I never had a college education but always made sure to save and invest money each month and watch it grow," says Thomas.

You don't need a B.A., M.B.A., M.D., or Ph.D. to make money in the stock market. If you can practise some simple lessons, such as making regular and systematic investments and investing in proven companies and funds while minimizing your investment expenses and taxes, you'll be a winner.

However, we don't believe that you can consistently "beat the markets," and you certainly can't beat the best professional money managers at their own, full-time game. This book shows you time-proven, non-gimmicky methods to make your money grow in the stock market as well as in other financial markets. (We explain how in Part II.)

Real estate

People of varying economic means also build wealth by investing in real estate. Owning and managing real estate is like running a small business. You need to satisfy customers (tenants), manage your costs, keep an eye on the competition, and so on. Some methods of real estate investing require more time than others, but many are proven ways to build wealth.

John, who works for a city government, and his wife, Linda, a computer analyst, have built more than $2 million in investment real estate *equity* (the difference between the property's market value and debts owed) over the past three decades. "Our parents owned rental property, and we could see what it could do for you by providing income and building wealth," says John. Investing in real estate also appealed to John and Linda because they didn't know anything about the stock market, so they wanted to stay away from it. The ability to use *leverage* — making money with borrowed money — with real estate also appealed to them.

John and Linda bought their first property, a duplex, in 1971, when their combined income was $20,000 per year. Every time they moved to a new home, they kept the prior one and converted it to a rental. Now in their 50s, John and Linda own seven pieces of investment real estate and are multimillionaires. "It's like a second retirement, having thousands in monthly income from the real estate," says John.

John readily admits that rental real estate has its hassles. "We haven't enjoyed getting calls in the middle of the night, but now we have a property manager who can help with this when we're not available. It's also sometimes a pain finding new tenants," he says.

The income from John and Linda's rental properties allows them to live in a nicer home than they could otherwise afford. Overall, they figure they've been well rewarded for the time they spent and the money they invested.

Ultimately, to make your money grow much faster than inflation and taxes, you must absolutely, positively do at least one thing — take some risk. Any investment that has real growth potential also has shrinkage potential! You may not want to take the risk, or have the stomach for it. Don't despair: We discuss lower-risk investments in this book as well. You can find out about risks and returns in Chapter 2.

Small business

We know people who have hit investing "home runs" by owning or buying a business. That's because most people work at running their business full time, thereby increasing their chances of doing something big financially with it. If you invest in individual stocks, by contrast, you're likely to work at it part time, competing against professionals who invest practically around the clock.

A decade ago, Calvin set out to develop a corporate publishing firm. Because he took the risk of starting his business and has been successful in slowly building it, today, in his early 40s, he enjoys a net worth in excess of $5 million and can retire if he wants. But even more important to many business owners — and the reason why financially successful entrepreneurs such as Calvin don't call it quits after they've amassed a lot of cash — are the non-financial rewards of investing, including the challenge and fulfillment of operating a successful business.

Sandra has worked on her own as an interior designer for more than two decades. She previously worked in fashion as a model and then as a retail store manager. Her first taste of interior design was redesigning rooms at a condominium project. "I knew when I did that first building and turned it into something wonderful and profitable that I loved doing this kind of work," says Sandra. Today her firm specializes in the restoration of landmark hotels, and her work has been written up in numerous magazines. "The money is not of primary importance to me . . . my work is driven by a passion . . . but obviously it has to be profitable," she says.

Most small business owners (ourselves included) quickly point out that the entrepreneurial life is not a walk through the rose garden (although it does have its share of thorns). Emotionally and financially, entrepreneurship is sometimes a roller coaster. In addition to the financial rewards, however, small business owners can enjoy seeing the impact of their work and knowing that it makes a difference. Combined, Calvin's and Sandra's firms created dozens of new jobs.

Not everyone needs to be sparked by the desire to start his or her own company to profit from small business. You can share in the economic rewards of the entrepreneurial world through buying an existing business or investing in someone else's budding enterprise. We talk more about evaluating and buying a business in Part IV of this book.

Generating income from lending investments

The other major types of investments include those in which you lend your money. Suppose that, like most people, you keep some money in your local bank — most likely in a chequing account, but perhaps also in a savings account or guaranteed investment certificate (GIC). No matter what type of bank account you place your money in, what you're doing is lending your money to the bank.

How long and under what conditions you lend money to your bank depends on the specific bank and account that you use. With a GIC, you commit to lend your money to the bank for a specific length of time — generally anywhere from six months to five years. In return, the bank probably pays you a higher rate of interest than if you put your money in a bank account offering immediate access. (You may demand termination of the GIC early; however, you'll be penalized.)

As we discuss in more detail in Chapter 8, you can also invest your money in bonds — another type of lending investment. When you purchase a bond that has been issued by the government or a company, you agree to lend your money for a predetermined period of time and receive a particular rate of interest. A bond may pay you 5 percent interest over the next five years, for example.

Lending investments are all the same in that, instead of directly sharing in the ownership of a company or other asset, such as real estate, you lend your money to some organization that in turn invests it for their own profit. If you lend your money to Bell Canada through one of its bonds that matures, say, in ten years, and Bell Canada triples in size over the next decade, you won't share in its growth. Bell Canada's stockholders and employees reap the rewards of the company's success, but as a bondholder, you don't.

Many people keep too much of their money in lending investments, thus allowing others to reap the rewards of economic growth. Although lending investments appear safer because you know in advance what return you will receive, they aren't that safe. The long-term risk of these seemingly safe money investments is that your money will grow too slowly to enable you to accomplish your personal financial goals. In the worst cases, the company or other institution to which you're lending money can go under and stiff you for your loan.

WARNING!

The double whammy of inflation and taxes

Bank accounts and bonds that pay a decent return are reassuring to many investors. Earning a small amount of interest sure beats losing some or all your money in a risky investment.

The problem is that money in a savings account, for example, that pays 2 percent, is not actually yielding you 2 percent. It's not that the bank is lying — it's just that your investment bucket contains some not-so-obvious holes.

The first hole is taxes. When you earn interest, you must pay taxes on it (unless you invest the money inside an RRSP, in which case you generally pay the taxes at a later date, when you withdraw the money). If you're a moderate-income earner, you end up losing about a third of your interest to taxes. Your 2 percent return is now down to 1.3 percent.

But the second hole in your investment bucket is even bigger than taxes: inflation. Although a few products become cheaper over time (computers, for example), most goods and services increase in price. Inflation in Canada has been running in the neighbourhood of 3 percent per year. Inflation depresses the purchasing power of your investment's returns. If you subtract 3 percent for the "cost" of inflation from the remaining 1.3 percent after payment of taxes, we're sorry to say that you lost 1.7 percent on your investment.

To recap: For every dollar you invested in the bank a year ago, despite the fact that the bank paid you your 2 pennies of interest, you're only left with less than 99 cents in real purchasing power for every dollar you had a year ago. In other words, thanks to the inflation and tax holes in your investment bucket, you can buy less with your money now versus what you could have a year ago, even though you've invested your money for a year.

Cash equivalents

Cash equivalents are any investment that you can quickly convert into cash without any cost to you. Of course, the cash in your wallet qualifies as a cash equivalent. With most chequing accounts, for example, you can write a cheque or withdraw cash by visiting a teller — either the live or the automated type.

Money market mutual funds are another type of cash equivalent. Investors, both large and small, invest hundreds of billions of dollars in money market mutual funds because the best money market funds produce higher yields than bank savings accounts. The yield advantage of a money market fund almost always widens when interest rates increase because banks move about as fast as molasses on a cold winter day to raise savings account rates.

Many bank savers sacrifice this yield because they think money market funds are risky — but they're not. Money market mutual funds generally invest in ultra-safe things such as GICs, government-issued Treasury bills, and commercial paper (short-term bonds) that the most credit-worthy corporations issue.

Another reason people keep too much money in traditional bank accounts is that the local bank branch office makes the cash seem more accessible. High-interest savings accounts and money market mutual funds, however, offer quick ways to get your cash. You can generally call or write and request that your money be mailed or wired to you, or have it transferred to your bank account.

By all means, keep your chequing account at the local bank so that you can write smaller cheques to pay your cable television, phone, and utility bills. Having local access to an ABM for fast cash withdrawals is also a plus. But move that extra money that's dozing away in your bank savings account, for example, into a high-interest savings account or higher-yielding money market mutual fund! Even if you have just a few thousand dollars, the extra yield more than pays for the cost of this book. (See Chapter 8 to find out more about money market funds.)

Steering clear of futures and options

Suppose you think that IBM's stock is a good investment. The direction that the management team is taking impresses you, and you like the products and services that the company offers. Profits seem to be on a positive trend; everything's looking up.

You can go out and buy the stock — suppose that it's currently trading at around $100 per share. If the price rises to $150 in the next six months, you've made yourself a 50 percent profit ($150 – $100 = $50) on your original $100 investment. (Of course, you have to pay some brokerage fees to buy and then sell the stock.)

But instead of buying the stock outright, you can buy what are known as call options on IBM. A *call option* gives you the right to buy shares of IBM under specified terms from the person who sells you the call option. You may be able to purchase a call option that allows you to exercise your right to buy IBM stock at, say, $120 per share in the next six months. For this privilege, you may pay $10 per share.

If IBM's stock price skyrockets to, say. $150 in the next few months, the value of your options that allow you to buy the stock at $120 will be worth a lot — at least $30. You can then simply sell your options, which you bought for $10 in this example, at a huge profit — you've tripled your money.

Although this talk of fat profits sounds much more exciting than simply buying the stock directly and making far less money from a stock price increase, options have two big problems:

- ✔ If IBM's stock price goes nowhere or rises only a little during the six-month period when you hold the call option, the option expires as worthless, and you lose all — that is, 100 percent — of your investment. In fact, in our example, if IBM's stock trades at $120 or less at the time the option expires, the option is worthless.

- ✔ A call option represents a short-term gamble (in this example, over the next six months) on IBM's stock price. When you buy a call option, you're not investing in IBM as a long-term investment. IBM could expand its business and profits greatly in the years and decades ahead, but the value of the call option hinges on the ups and downs of IBM's stock price over a relatively short period of time. If the stock market happens to dip in the next six months, IBM may get pulled down as well, despite the company's improving financial health.

The way that most individuals use them, *futures* are similar to options in that both are types of gambling instruments. Futures deal mainly with the value of commodities such as heating oil, corn, wheat, gold, silver, and pork bellies. Futures have a delivery date that's in the not-too-distant future. (Do you really want bushels of wheat delivered to your home? Or worse yet, pork bellies?) You also can invest with just a small down payment — around 10 percent — toward the purchase of futures, thereby greatly leveraging your "investment." If prices fall, you need to put up more money to keep from having your position sold.

Our advice: Don't gamble with futures and options. The only real use that you may (if ever) have for these *derivatives* (so called because their value is "derived" from the price of other securities) is to hedge. Suppose that you hold a lot of a stock, for example, that has greatly appreciated and you don't want to sell now because of the tax bite. Perhaps you want to postpone selling the stock until next year because you plan on not working in order to move into a lower tax bracket. You can buy what's called a *put option,* which increases in value when a stock's price falls (because the put option grants you the right to sell your stock to the purchaser of the put option at a preset stock price). Thus, if the stock price does fall, the rising put option value offsets some of your losses on the stock you still hold. Using put options allows you to postpone selling your stock without exposing yourself to the risk of a falling stock price.

Precious metals

Over the millennia, gold and silver have served as mediums of exchange or currency because they have intrinsic value and cannot be debased the way that paper currencies can by printing more money. These precious metals are used in jewellery and manufacturing.

As investments, gold and silver perform well during bouts of inflation. For example, from 1972 to 1980, when inflation zoomed into the double-digit range in Canada and the United States and stocks and bonds went into the tank, gold and silver prices skyrocketed more than 500 percent.

 Generally over the long term, however, precious metals are lousy investments. They don't pay any dividends, and their price increases just keep you up with, but not ahead of, increases in the cost of living. Although investing in precious metals is better than keeping cash in a piggy bank or stuffing it in a mattress, the investment returns aren't nearly as good as bonds, stocks, and real estate.

Collectibles

Collectibles are a catchall category for antiques, art, autographs, baseball cards, clocks, coins, comic books, diamonds, dolls, gems, photographs, rare books, rugs, stamps, vintage wine, writing utensils, and a whole host of other items. Although connoisseurs of fine art, antiques, and vintage wine wouldn't like their pastime being compared to old playing cards or chamber pots, the bottom line is that collectibles are all objects with little intrinsic value. Wine is just a bunch of old mashed-up grapes. A painting is simply a canvas and some paint that at retail would set you back a few bucks. Stamps are small pieces of paper, less than an inch square. Baseball cards — heck, when we were kids we used to stick these between our bike spokes!

We're not trying to diminish contributions that artists and others make to our culture. And we know that some people place a high value on some of these collectibles. But true investments that can make your money grow, such as stocks, real estate, or a small business, are assets that can produce income and profits. Collectibles have little intrinsic value and are thus subject to the whims and speculations of buyers and sellers. Here are some other major problems with collectibles:

- **Mark-ups are huge.** The spread between the price that a dealer sells and then buys the same exact object back from you is often around 100 percent. Sometimes the difference is even greater, particularly if a dealer is the second or third middleman in the chain of purchase. So at a minimum, your purchase must typically double in value just to get you back to even. And that may take 10 to 20 years or more!

✔ **Lots of other costs add up.** If the mark-ups aren't bad enough, with some collectibles you incur all sorts of other costs. If you buy more expensive pieces, you may need to have them appraised. You may have to pay storage and insurance costs as well. And, unlike the mark-up, you pay some of these fees year after year after year of ownership.

✔ **You can get stuck with a pig in a poke.** Sometimes, you may overpay even more for a collectible because you don't realize some imperfection or inferiority of an item. Worse, you may buy a forgery. Even reputable dealers have been duped by forgeries.

✔ **Your pride and joy can deteriorate over time.** Damage from sunlight, humidity, temperatures that are too high or too low, and a whole host of vagaries can ruin the quality of your collectible. Insurance doesn't cover this type of damage or negligence on your part.

✔ **The returns stink.** Even if you ignore the substantial costs of buying, holding, and selling, the average returns that investors earn from collectibles rarely keep ahead of inflation and are generally inferior to stock market, real estate, and small business investing. (However, if you factor in the huge mark-ups on buying and selling these collectibles, the returns don't even keep up with inflation.) Objective, collectible return data are hard to come by. Never, ever trust such "data" that dealers or the many collectible trade publications that boast of hefty annual returns provide.

The best returns that collectible investors reap come from the ability to identify, years in advance, items that will *become* popular. Do you think you can do that? You may be the smartest person in the world, but you should know that most dealers can't tell what's going to rocket to popularity in the coming decades. Dealers make their profits the same way as other retailers do: from the spread or mark-up on the merchandise they sell. The public and collectors have fickle, quirky tastes that no one can predict. Did you know that Beanie Babies, Furbies, Pet Rocks, or Cabbage Patch Kids were going to be such hits?

You can find out enough about a specific type of collectible to become a better investor than the average person, but you're going to have to be among the best — perhaps the top 10 percent of such collectors — to have a shot at earning decent returns. To get to this level of expertise, you need to invest hundreds if not thousands of hours reading, researching, and educating yourself about your specific type of collectible.

Nothing is wrong with *spending* money on collectibles, but we don't want you to fool yourself into thinking that they're investments. You can sink lots of your money into these non-income-producing, poor-return "investments." At their best as investments, collectibles give the wealthy a way to buy quality stuff that doesn't depreciate.

If you must buy collectibles, here are some tips to keep in mind:

✔ Collect for your love of the collectible, your desire to enjoy it, or your interest in finding out about or mastering an area, not because you expect high investment returns, because you probably won't get them.

✔ Keep quality items that you and your family have purchased and hope that someday they're worth something. Keeping these quality items is the simplest way to break into the collectible business. The complete sets of baseball cards Eric gathered as a youngster are now (30-plus years later) worth hundreds of dollars to, in one case, $1,000!

✔ Buy from the source and cut out the middlemen whenever possible. In some cases, you may be able to buy from the artist.

✔ Check collectibles that are comparable to the one you have your eye on, shop around, and don't be afraid to negotiate. An effective way to negotiate, after you decide what you like, is to make your offer to the dealer or artist by phone. Because the seller isn't standing right next to you, you don't feel pressure to decide immediately.

✔ Ask the dealer who thinks the item is such a great investment for a written guarantee to buy back the item from you, if you opt to sell, for at least the same price you paid or higher within five years.

✔ Use a comprehensive resource to research, buy, sell, maintain, and improve your collectible, such as the books by Ralph and Terry Kovel or their Web site at www.kovels.com.

Chapter 2

Risks and Returns

. . . .

In This Chapter

▶ Determining risks

▶ Reducing risk while earning decent returns

▶ Figuring out expected investment returns

▶ Determining how much you need your investments to return

. . . .

A mother covers her young daughter in sunscreen and makes sure she's wearing a wide-brimmed hat before going outside in the summertime. That same mother leaves the child — fully protected from the sun's rays — to play unwatched with a relative's dog, which bites the child.

A man passes up eating a hamburger at a picnic because he heard that it's possible to contract a deadly *E. coli* infection from eating improperly cooked meat. The next week, that same man hops in the passenger seat of his friend's car and doesn't bother putting on his seatbelt. Minutes later, the car is struck head on and the man is fatally injured.

We're not trying to depress or frighten anyone. However, we are trying to make an important point about risk — something that we all deal with on a daily basis.

First things first: Risk is in the eye of the beholder. Many of us base our perception of risk, in large part, on our experiences and what we've been exposed to. Many people fret about relatively small risks while overlooking much larger risks.

Sure, the odds of developing skin cancer are greater if you're regularly exposed to the sun's rays without protection, so it's logical for the mother to clothe her child in protective clothing and regularly apply sunscreen. However, the mother completely overlooked the significant risk posed by allowing a small child to play with a dog.

Likewise, a risk of an *E. coli* infection from eating poorly cooked meat exists, so the man who was leery of eating the hamburger at the picnic had a legitimate concern. But that same man got into the friend's car without properly protecting himself by using a seatbelt and placed himself at far greater risk of dying in that situation than if he had eaten the hamburger. About 3,500 people die in automobile accidents each year in Canada, and not wearing a seatbelt greatly increases the odds of serious or even fatal injuries should you crash.

Risks: Education Conquers Fear and Ignorance

Wherever you turn, risks exist; some are just more apparent than others. Many people also misunderstand risks. With increased knowledge, you may be able to reduce or conquer some of your fears and make more sensible decisions about reducing risks. For example, some people who fear flying don't understand that, statistically, flying is much safer than driving a car. The reason? When a plane goes down, it's big news. Dozens and sometimes hundreds of people, who probably weren't under the influence or engaging in otherwise reckless behaviour, perish. Meanwhile, the media seem to pay less attention to the handfuls of people who die on the road every day. Statistically, you're approximately 40 times more likely to die in a motor vehicle than in an airplane.

This doesn't mean that you shouldn't drive or fly, or that you shouldn't drive to the airport. You may, though, consider steps you can take to reduce the significant risks you expose yourself to in a car. For example, you can get a car with more safety features, or you may bypass riding with reckless taxi drivers whose cars lack seatbelts.

Although some of us like to live life to its fullest and take "fun" risks (how else can you explain mountain climbers, parachuters, and bungee jumpers?), most people seek to minimize risk and maximize enjoyment in their lives. You'd be mighty unhappy living a life that sought to eliminate all risks, and you likely wouldn't succeed anyway.

Likewise, if you attempt to avoid all the risks that investing involves, you won't succeed, and you likely won't be happy with your investment results and lifestyle. In the investment world, some people don't go near stocks or any investment that they perceive to be volatile. As a result, such investors often end up with lousy long-term returns, and they expose themselves to some high risks that they overlooked, such as the risk of inflation and taxes that erode the purchasing power of their money.

You can't live without taking risks. Risk-free activities or ways of living don't exist. You can minimize but never eliminate risks. Some methods of risk reduction aren't palatable because they reduce your quality of life. Risks are also composed of several factors. In the sections that follow, we discuss the various types of investment risks and methods you can use to sensibly reduce these risks while not missing out on the upside that growth investments offer.

Market value risk

Although the stock market can help you build wealth, most people recognize that it can also plunge quite a bit — 10, 20, or 30 percent or more in no time. After peaking in 2000, Canadian and U.S. stocks, as measured by the major large-company indices (for Canada, the TSX composite, and for the U.S., the S&P 500 index), dropped about 50 percent by 2002. Stocks on the NASDAQ, which is heavily weighted toward technology stocks, plunged more than 76 percent from 2000 through 2002.

In a mere six weeks (from mid-July 1998 to early September 1998), large-company Canadian and U.S. stocks plunged about 20 percent. In just under three months, a broad measurement of companies traded on the Toronto Stock Exchange fell by almost 27 percent. During the same period, an index of smaller-company U.S. stocks plunged 33 percent. If you had invested $5,000 during this time period, your investment may have shrunk to $4,000 or less. Similarly, those who invested $50,000 saw it shrink to $40,000 or less. Although that loss doesn't feel good, it's the reality of risk. Your investment can shrink in value!

If you think the stock market crash that occurred in the fall of 1987 was a hard, fast one (the market plunged 32 percent in a matter of weeks), consider these massive plunges in the Canadian and U.S. stock markets over the past several decades. Tables 2-1 and 2-2 list plunges that were all *worse* than the 1987 crash.

Table 2-1	Most Depressing Canadian Stock Market Declines*
Period	*Size of Fall*
1929–1932	80% (ouch!)
1937–1942	56%
2000–2002	50%
1980–1982	44%
1973–1974	38%
1987–1987	31%
1956–1957	30%
1969–1970	28%

*As measured by changes in the TSE composite index

Table 2-2	Most Depressing U.S. Stock Market Declines*
Period	*Size of Fall*
1929–1932	89% (argggh!!)
1937–1942	52%
1906–1907	49%
1890–1896	47%
1919–1921	47%
1901–1903	46%
1973–1974	45%
1916–1917	40%
2000– 2002	37%

As measured by changes in the Dow Jones Industrial Average

Real estate exhibits similar unruly, annoying tendencies. Although real estate (like stocks) has been a terrific long-term investment, various real estate markets get clobbered from time to time.

When the oil industry collapsed in Alberta in the early 1980s, real estate prices in the province dropped by 25 percent. And after a massive run-up in prices in the mid-1980s, house prices in the Toronto area plummeted by nearly 28 percent over the next few years.

U.S. housing prices took almost a 25 percent tumble from the late 1920s to the mid-1930s. When the oil industry collapsed in the southeast United States in the early 1980s, real estate prices took a beating in that area. Later in the 1980s and early 1990s, the northeastern United States became mired in a severe recession and in many areas real estate prices plummeted by 20 to 40 percent.

After peaking near 1990, many of the West Coast housing markets, especially those in California, experienced falling prices — dropping 20 percent or more in most areas by the mid-1990s.

The Japanese real estate market crash also began around the time of the California market fall. Property prices in Japan collapsed more than 60 percent since that market's peak.

After reading this section, you may want to keep all your money in the bank — after all, you know you won't lose your money, and you won't have to be a non-stop worrier. No one has ever lost 20, 40, 60, or 80 percent of his bank-held savings in a few years!

However, if you pass up the stock and real estate markets simply because of the potential market value risk, you miss out on a historic, time-tested method of building substantial wealth. Later in this chapter, we show you the generous returns that these investments historically provide. The following sections suggest some simple things you can do to lower your investing risk and help prevent your portfolio from suffering a huge fall.

Diversify for a gentler ride

Individual stock markets may crash. However, the various stock markets around the world have never all crashed at the same time. For example, when the Canadian and U.S. stock markets crashed in the fall of 1987, many foreign stock markets dropped far less or not at all. So if you had spread your money across the many different stock markets, your portfolio wouldn't have suffered nearly as much as if you had held all your stocks in the North American markets.

You can invest in the U.S. and overseas to reduce your investment risk if you worry about the health of the Canadian economy, the government, and the dollar. Most large Canadian companies do business overseas, so when you invest in larger Canadian company stocks, you get some international investment exposure. You can also invest in international company stocks, ideally via mutual funds (which we discuss in Chapter 8).

Of course, investing overseas can't totally protect you. You can't do much about a global economic catastrophe. If you worry about the risk of such a calamity, you should probably also worry about a huge meteor crashing into Earth. Maybe there's a way to colonize outer space. . . .

Diversifying your investments can involve more than just your stock portfolio, however. You can also hold some real estate investments to diversify your investment portfolio. Some real estate markets actually appreciated in the late 1980s and again in the early 2000s, while the Canadian and U.S. stock markets were in the doghouse during both periods.

Consider your time horizon

Investors who worry that the stock market may take a dive and take their money down with it should first consider the time period that they plan to invest. During a one-year period in the stock and bond markets, anything can happen (as shown in Figure 2-1). History shows that you lose money once in every three years that you invest in the stock and bond markets. However, stock market investors make money — sometimes substantial money — two-thirds of the time over a one-year period. (Bond investors make money about two-thirds of the time, too, although they make a good deal less.)

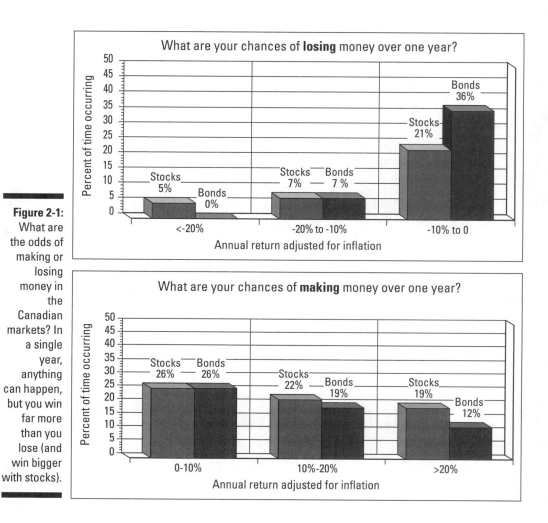

Figure 2-1:
What are the odds of making or losing money in the Canadian markets? In a single year, anything can happen, but you win far more than you lose (and win bigger with stocks).

Although the stock market is more volatile in the short term than the bond market, stock market investors earn far better long-term returns than do bond investors. (See the "Stock returns" section later in this chapter.) Remember, however, that bonds generally outperform a boring old bank account.

The risk of a stock or bond market fall becomes less of a concern the longer the time period that you plan to invest. As Figure 2-2 shows, as the holding period during which you own stocks increases from 1 year to 3 years to 5 years to 10 years, and then to 20 years, your likelihood of making a profit increases. In fact, over any 20-year time span, U.S. stock market investors have never lost money, even after you subtract for the effects of inflation.

We've used U.S. data in the chart below simply because there are several more decades of market data, which gives us a better view of the market's long-term behaviour. However, the same essential point holds true for Canada. Since 1957 only one five-year period has had a negative return. In other words, if you had invested in the broad market (meaning your returns were similar to the composite index) and held on for five years, in only one period would you have had less after five years than you started with. And if you had invested and stayed invested for *ten* years, you would always have come out ahead. In other words, starting in 1957, if you had invested in any year and held those investments for a minimum of ten years, you would have ended up with a profit, assuming your returns matched those of the index.

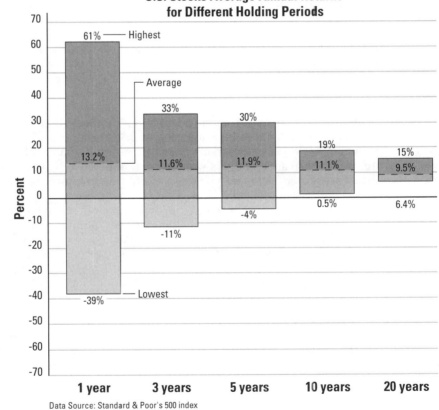

Figure 2-2:
The longer you hold stocks, the more likely you'll be to make money.

Most stock market investors we know are concerned about losing money. Figure 2-2 clearly shows that the key to minimizing this possibility is to hold stocks for the long term. As we detail in Part II of this book, stocks should be used as a long-term investment. Don't invest in stocks unless you plan to hold them for at least five years — and preferably a decade or longer.

Pare down holdings in bloated markets

Perhaps you've heard the expression "Buy low, sell high." Although we don't believe that you can time the markets (that is, predict the most profitable time to buy and sell), spotting a greatly overpriced market isn't too difficult. For example, in the previous edition of this book, published in 2000, we warned readers about the grossly inflated prices of many Internet and technology stocks. Throughout this book, we explain some simple yet powerful methods you can use to measure whether a particular investment market is of fair value, of good value, or overpriced.

 You should avoid overpriced investments for two important reasons. First, if and when they fall, they usually fall farther and faster than more fairly priced investments. Second, you can always find other investments that offer higher potential returns.

 Ideally, you want to avoid having a lot of your money in markets that appear overvalued (see Chapter 5 for how to spot pricey markets). Practically speaking, avoiding overvalued markets doesn't mean that you should try to sell all your holdings in such markets with the vain hope of buying them back at a much lower price. However, you may benefit from the following strategies:

✔ Focus investment of new money somewhere other than the overvalued market. As you save new investment money, put it into investments that offer you better values. Thus, without selling any of your seemingly expensive investments, they become a smaller portion of your total holdings. If you hold investments outside tax-sheltered retirement plans, focusing your money elsewhere also allows you to avoid incurring taxes from selling appreciated investments.

✔ If you need to raise money to live on, such as for retirement or for a major purchase, sell the expensive stuff. As long as the taxes aren't too troublesome, it's better to sell high and lock in your profits. Chapter 21 discusses issues to weigh when you contemplate selling an investment.

Individual investment risk

A downdraft can put an entire investment market on a roller-coaster ride, but healthy markets can also produce losers. From the early 1980s through the late 1990s, North American stock markets experienced one of the greatest appreciations in history. You'd never know it, though, if you look at these losers.

Consider a company now called Navistar, which has undergone enormous transformations in the past two decades. This company used to be called International Harvester and manufactured farm equipment, trucks, and construction and other industrial equipment. Today, Navistar makes mostly trucks.

As recently as late 1983, this company's stock traded at more than $140 (all dollar figures here are U.S.) per share. It then plunged more than 90 percent over the ensuing decade (as shown in Figure 2-3). Even with a rally in recent years, Navistar stock still trades at under $50 per share (after dipping below $10 per share). Lest you think that's a big drop, this company's stock traded as high as $455 per share in the early 1970s! If a worker retired from this company in the early 1970s with $200,000 invested in the company stock, the retiree's investment would be worth about $20,000 today! On the other hand, if the retiree had simply swapped his stock at retirement for a diversified portfolio of stocks, which we explain how to build in Part II, his $200,000 nest egg would've instead grown to more than $2,000,000!

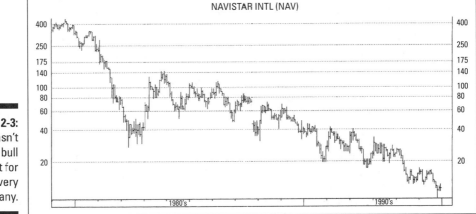

Figure 2-3:
It hasn't been a bull market for every company.

"Okay," you say, "I would have been smart enough to avoid sinking my money into a company that made farm equipment — heck, I knew we were in the industrial age and heading into the information and technology age! Any old idiot could've made money by following the right trends."

If that's what you think, then consider Data General, a company that plays in the lucrative software industry as well as the hardware part of the computer field. After trading as high as $76 in 1985 (again, all figures here are U.S. dollars), this stock fell off a cliff, plunging more than 95 percent to just $3 per share by 1990, and has languished mostly below $20 per share since.

Likewise, more than a few investors, large and small, rode the Digital Equipment roller coaster. The share value of Digital Equipment, once considered a premier company, has been clobbered in the years since 1987. From a high of nearly $200 per share, this stock dropped nearly 91 percent in the following seven years.

And while, like most other markets, the Canadian stock market paled by comparison with the U.S. juggernaut in the 1990s, we've had our share of stocks that have plummeted in value. How about Dylex, which through its many brand name outlets such as Suzy Shier at one time took in one out of every ten dollars consumers spent in retail clothing outlets. The stock, which began the 1990s at $24, ended the decade languishing beneath the $10 mark, dwindling lower and lower until the company eventually went under in 2001.

We've also had our share of high-tech stars that lost a lot of their lustre. Spar Aerospace, a world leader in, among other things, flight training units, traded as high as $30 in the 1980s. It came back to Earth in more recent years, with the stock stuck between $10 and $15 before being taken over in 2002.

And then, of course, there's Nortel. In the late 1990s, many of the investors Tony profiled in his *Globe and Mail* column happily recounted how well they'd done by buying Nortel, making two, three, even ten times or more on their original investment. Nortel, or so we were told, just couldn't keep up with the Internet-driven demand for its products. The stock peaked at over $120 in August of 2000. And then, in a matter of months, the company's cheerleaders were proven to be completely, hopelessly wrong. Nortel crumbled, and by October of 2002 it had literally turned into a penny stock, trading at under a buck. Tony soon found that many of the investors he profiled in his column were calling Nortel one of their "worst moves"!

Just as individual stock prices can plummet, so too can individual real estate property prices. In California, for example, earthquakes rocked the prices of properties built on landfill during the 1990s. These quakes highlighted the dangers of building on poor soil. In the early 1980s, real estate values in the communities of Times Beach, Missouri, and Love Canal, New York, plunged due to carcinogenic toxic waste contamination. (Ultimately, many property owners in these areas were compensated for their losses by the federal government, as well as by some real estate agencies that didn't disclose these known contaminants.)

Here are some simple steps you can take to lower the risk of individual investments that can upset your goals:

- ✔ **Do your homework.** When you purchase real estate, a whole host of inspections can save you from buying a money pit. With stocks, you can examine some measures of value and the company's financial condition and business strategy to reduce your chances of buying into an overpriced company or one on the verge of major problems. Parts II, III, and IV of this book give you more information on researching your investment.

- ✔ **Diversify.** Investors who seek growth invest in securities such as stocks. Placing significant amounts of your capital in one or a handful of securities is risky, particularly if the stocks are in the same type of industry. To reduce this risk, purchase stocks in a variety of industries and companies within each industry. (See Part II for details.)

- ✔ **Hire someone to invest for you.** The best mutual funds (see Chapter 9) offer low-cost, professional management and oversight as well as diversification. Stock mutual funds typically own 25 or more securities in a variety of companies in different industries. In Part III we explain how you can invest in real estate in a similar way (that is, by leaving the driving to someone else).

Liquidity

The term *liquidity* refers to how long and at what cost you can convert an investment into cash. The money in your wallet is considered perfectly liquid — it's already cash.

Suppose you invested money in a handful of stocks. Although you can't easily sell these stocks on a Saturday night, you can sell most stocks quickly through a broker for a nominal fee any day that the financial markets are open (normal working days). You pay a higher percentage to sell your stocks if you use a high-cost broker or if you have a small amount of stock to sell.

Real estate is generally much less liquid than stock. Preparing your property for sale takes time, and if you want to get fair market value for your property, finding a buyer may take weeks or months. Selling costs (agent commissions, fix-up expenses, and closing costs) can easily approach 10 percent of the home's value.

A privately run small business is among the least liquid of the better growth investments that you can make. Selling such a business typically takes longer than selling most real estate.

So that you're not forced to sell one of your investments that you intend to hold for long-term purposes, keep an emergency reserve of three to six months' worth of living expenses in a money market account or a high-interest savings account. Also consider investing some money in bonds (see Chapter 8), which pay higher than money market yields without the high risk or volatility that comes with the stock market.

Purchasing-power risk

Increases in the cost of living can erode the value of your retirement resources and what you can buy with that money — also known as its purchasing power. When Ethel retired at the age of 60, she was pleased with her retirement income. She was receiving an $800-per-month pension and $1,200 per month from money that she had invested in long-term bonds. Her monthly expenditures amounted to about $1,500, so she was able to save a little money for an occasional trip.

Fast-forward 15 years. Ethel still receives $800 per month from her pension, but now she gets only $900 per month of investment income, which comes from some GICs (*guaranteed investment certificates*). Ethel bailed out of bonds after she lost sleep over the sometimes roller-coaster-like price movements in the bond market. Her monthly expenditures now amount to approximately $2,400, and she uses some of her investment principal (original investment). She's terrified of outliving her money.

Ethel has reason to worry. She has 100 percent of her money invested without protection against increases in the cost of living. Although her income felt comfortable in the beginning of her retirement, it doesn't at age 75, and Ethel could easily live another 15 or more years.

The erosion of the purchasing power of your investment dollars can, over longer time periods, be as bad as or worse than the effect of a major market crash. Table 2-3 shows the effective loss in purchasing power of your money at various rates of inflation and over differing time periods.

Table 2-3	Inflation's Corrosive Effect on Your Money's Purchasing Power			
Inflation Rate	*10 Years*	*15 Years*	*25 Years*	*40 Years*
2%	−18%	−26%	−39%	−55%
4%	−32%	−44%	−62%	−81%
6%	−44%	−58%	−77%	−90%
8%	−54%	−68%	−85%	−95%
10%	−61%	−76%	−91%	−98%

We often see skittish investors who try to keep their money in bonds, GICs, and money market accounts, thinking they're playing it safe. The risk in this strategy is that your money won't grow enough over the years for you to accomplish your financial goals. In other words, the lower the return, the more you need to save to reach a particular financial goal. A 40-year-old wanting to accumulate $500,000 by age 65 would need to save $722 per month if she earns a 6 percent average annual return. If she earns a 10 percent average annual return, however, she'd need to save only $377 per month. Younger investors need to pay the most attention to the risk of generating low returns, but so too should younger senior citizens. At the age of 65, seniors need to recognize that a portion of their assets may not be used for a decade or more from the present.

Inflation ragin' outta control

You think 6, 8, or 10 percent annual inflation rates are bad? How would you like to live in a country that experienced that rate of inflation in a day?! As we discuss in Chapter 4, too much money in circulation chasing after too few goods causes high rates of inflation.

A government that runs amok with the nation's currency and money supply usually causes excessive rates of inflation — dubbed *hyperinflation.* Over the decades and centuries, hyperinflation has wreaked havoc in more than a few countries.

What happened in Germany in the late 1910s and early 1920s demonstrates how bad hyperinflation can get. Consider that during this time period, prices increased nearly one billion fold!!! What cost 1 reichsmark (the German currency in those days) at the beginning of this mess eventually cost nearly 1,000,000,000 reichsmarks. People had to cart around so much currency that at times they needed shopping-type carts to haul it! Ultimately, this inflationary burden was too much for the German society, creating a social climate that fuelled the rise of the Nazi party and Adolf Hitler.

In just the past decade, a number of countries, especially many of those that made up the former U.S.S.R. and others such as Brazil and Lithuania, have gotten themselves into a hyperinflationary mess with inflation rates of several hundred percent per year. In the mid-1980s, Bolivia's yearly inflation rate exceeded 10,000 percent.

Governments often try to slap on price controls to prevent runaway inflation (Pierre Trudeau did this in Canada in the 1970s, as did Richard Nixon in the U.S.), but the underground economy, known as the black market, usually prevails.

Career risk

Your ability to earn money is most likely your single biggest asset, or at least one of your biggest assets. Most people achieve what they do in the working world through education and hard work. By education, we're not simply talking about what one learns in formal schooling. Education is a lifelong process. We've learned far more about business from our own front-line experiences and those of others than we've learned in educational settings. We also read a lot. In Part V we recommend books and other resources that we've found most useful.

If you don't continually invest in your education, you risk losing your competitive edge. Your skills and perspectives can become dated and obsolete. Although that doesn't mean you should work 80 hours a week and never do anything fun, it does mean that part of your "work" time should always involve updating and building on your skills. The best organizations are those that recognize the need for continual knowledge and invest in their workforce through training and career development. Just remember to look at your own career objectives, which may not be the same as your company's.

Investment Returns and Components

When you make investments, you have the potential to make money in a variety of different ways. If you've ever had money in a bank account that pays *interest,* you know that the bank pays you a small amount of interest for your allowing them to keep your money. The bank then turns around and lends your money to some other person or organization at a much higher rate of interest. The rate of interest is also known as the *yield.* So if a bank tells you that its savings account pays 2 percent interest, the bank may also say that it is yielding 2 percent. Banks usually quote interest rates or yields on an annual basis.

If a bank pays monthly interest, for example, the bank also likely quotes a *compounded effective annual yield.* After the first month's interest is credited to your account, that *interest* starts earning interest as well. So the bank may say that the account pays 2 percent, which compounds to an effective annual yield of 2.04 percent.

When you lend your money directly to a company — which is what you do when you invest in a bond that a corporation issues — you also receive interest. Bonds, as well as stocks (which are shares of ownership in a company), fluctuate in value after they are issued.

When you invest in a company's stock, you hope that the stock increases (appreciates) in value. Of course, a stock can also decline, or depreciate, in value. This change in market value is part of your return from a stock or bond investment:

$$\frac{\text{Current investment value} - \text{Original investment}}{\text{Original investment}} = \text{Appreciation or depreciation}$$

For example, if one year ago you invested $10.000 in a stock (you bought 1,000 shares at $10 per share) and the investment is now worth $11,000 (each share is worth $11), your investment's appreciation is

$$\frac{\$11,000 - \$10,000}{\$10,000} = 10\%$$

But stocks can also pay dividends, which are a bit like the interest you earn from a bank account. Dividends are the company's sharing of some of its profits with you as a stockholder. Some companies, particularly those that are small or growing rapidly, choose to reinvest all their profits back into the company. (Of course, some companies don't turn a profit, so there's not much to pay out!) You need to factor these dividends into your return as well.

Suppose that in the previous example, in addition to your stock appreciating $1,000 to $11,000, it also paid you a dividend of $100 ($1 per share). Here's how you calculate your total return:

$$\frac{\text{Dividends} + \text{Current investment value} - \text{Original investment}}{\text{Original investment}} = \text{Total return}$$

Or, to apply it to the example

$$\frac{\$100 + \$11,000 - \$10.000}{\$10,000} = 11\%$$

Factoring in appreciation, dividends, interest, and so on helps an investor calculate what her *total return* is. The total return figure tells you the grand total of what you made (or lost) on your investment.

After-tax returns

Although you may be happy that your stock has given you an 11 percent return on your invested dollars, remember this: Unless you held your investment in a tax-sheltered retirement plan, you owe taxes on your return. Specifically, the dividends and investment appreciation that you realize upon selling are taxed.

Say you're in a moderate tax bracket, and taxes on your investment profits run in the neighbourhood of 17 percent. If your investment returned 11 percent before taxes, you're left with a return of 49.1 percent after taxes.

Except for those in the lowest marginal tax bracket (those earning approximately $32,000 or less), the tax rate on capital gains is lower than the tax rate on dividend and other income. In Chapter 3 we discuss the different tax rates that affect your investments and explain how to make tax-wise investment decisions that fit with your overall personal financial situation and goals.

Often, people make investing decisions without considering the tax consequences of their moves. This is a big mistake. What good is making money if the government takes a substantial portion of it away?

Psychological returns

Profits and tax avoidance can powerfully motivate your investment selections. However, as with other life decisions, you need to consider more than the bottom line. Some people want to have fun with their investments. Of course, they don't want to lose money or sacrifice a lot of potential returns — less expensive ways to have fun do exist!

Psychological rewards compel some investors to choose particular investment vehicles such as individual stocks, real estate, or a small business. Why? Because, compared with other investments, such as managed mutual funds, they see these investments as more tangible and, well, more fun.

Be honest with yourself about why you choose the investments that you do. Allowing your ego to get in the way can be dangerous. Do you invest in individual stocks because you really believe that you can do better than the best full-time professional money managers? Chances are high that you won't. (See Chapter 6 for the details.) Do you like investing in real estate more because of the gratification from driving by and showing off your properties to others than because of their investment rewards? Such questions are worth considering as you contemplate what investments you want to make.

Savings, high-interest, and money market account returns

You need to keep your extra cash that awaits investment (or an emergency) in a safe place, preferably one that doesn't get hammered by the sea of changes in the financial markets. No reason exists why you shouldn't earn a healthier rate of return on such savings than the paltry amount of interest that most bank accounts pay. Ideally, you should keep as little money as possible in your bank chequing account, for the simple reason that your bank likely pays you next to nothing (or actually nothing) in interest on this account.

By default and for convenience, many people keep their extra cash in a bank savings account. Although the bank offers some protection through the industry-run Canada Deposit Insurance Corporation (CDIC), it comes at a high price. Most banks pay a near microscopic interest rate on their savings accounts — in some cases a fraction of 1 percent.

A far better place to keep your liquid savings are the growing number of high-interest savings accounts offered by President's Choice Financial, ING Direct, and even some mutual fund companies. These accounts typically offer rates anywhere from four to forty — yes *forty* — times the rate on savings accounts.

Another good choice is a money market mutual fund. These are the safest types of mutual funds around and, for all intents and purposes, equal a bank savings account's safety. However, the best money market funds pay higher yields than most bank savings accounts. Unlike a bank, money market mutual funds tell you how much they skim off for the cost of managing your money. If you don't need immediate access to your money, consider using guaranteed investment certificates or Treasury bills, which are usually issued for terms ranging from three months to five years. Your money will surely earn more in one of these vehicles than in a bank savings account. The drawback to guaranteed investment certificates and Treasury bills is that you incur a penalty or fee if you get your investment back before the term expires. (See Chapter 8.)

Bond returns

When you buy a bond, you lend your money to the federal government or a corporation for a specific period of time, and you expect to earn a higher yield than you would with a money market or savings account. You're taking more risk, after all. Companies can and do go bankrupt, in which case you may lose some or all of your investment.

Generally, you can expect to earn a higher yield when you buy bonds that are:

- ✔ Issued for a longer term: because the bond issuer is tying up your money at a fixed rate for a longer period of time.
- ✔ Have lower credit quality: because the bond issuer may not be able to repay the principal.

Wharton School of Business professor Jeremy Siegel has tracked the performance of U.S. bonds and stocks all the way back to 1802. Although you may say that what happened in the nineteenth century has little relevance to the financial markets and economy of today, the period since the Great Depression, which is used to compile most investment return statistics, is a relatively small slice of time. Figure 2-4 presents the data, so if you'd like to give more credibility to the recent numbers, you may.

Note that although the rate of inflation has increased since the Great Depression, bond returns have not increased over the decades. Long-term bonds maintain slightly higher returns in recent years than short-term bonds. The bottom line: Bond investors typically earn about 4 to 5 percent per year.

Figure 2-4:
A historical view of U.S. bond performance: Inflation has eroded bond returns more in recent decades.

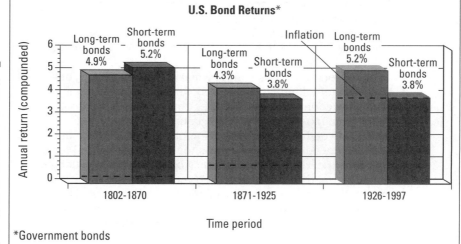

Stock returns

Let's face it: Most people are a little greedy. (Okay, some are a lot greedy.) People who invest in the stock market are prime examples of those who want to make the most of a potentially good thing. Investors expect, indeed they demand, what they consider a fair return on investment. And if one investment doesn't offer a high enough rate of return, investors can choose to move their money into other investments that they believe will perform better. Instead of buying a sound stock and holding on to it, some investors frequently buy and sell, hoping to cash in on the latest superstar investment. This tactic seldom works out best in the long run.

Unfortunately, some of these investors use a rear-view mirror when they purchase their stocks, chasing after investments that have recently performed strongly on the assumption (and the hope) that those investments will continue to earn strong returns. But chasing after the strongest performing investments can be dangerous if you catch the stock at its peak, ready to begin a downward spiral. You may have heard that the goal of investing is to buy low and sell high. Chasing high-flying investments can lead you to buy high, with the prospect of having to sell low if the stock has run out of steam. Even though stocks as a whole have proven to be a good long-term investment, picking individual stocks is a risky endeavour. See Chapters 5 and 6 for advice on making sound stock investment decisions.

A tremendous amount of data exists regarding stock market returns. In fact, in the U.S. markets, data going back nearly two full centuries documents the fact that stocks are a terrific long-term investment. The long-term returns that investors have enjoyed, and continue to enjoy, from stocks have been remarkably constant from one generation to the next.

Going all the way back to 1802, the U.S. stock market has produced an annual return of 8.4 percent while inflation has grown at 1.3 percent per year. Thus, after subtracting for inflation, stocks have appreciated about 7.1 percent faster annually than the rate of inflation.

The U.S. stock market returns have consistently and substantially beaten the rate of inflation over the years. (See Figure 2-5.)

Figure 2-5: History tells us that stocks are a consistent long-term winner.

Stocks don't exist only in Canada and the United States, of course. (See Figure 2-6.) More than a few investors seem to forget this fact, especially given the sizzling performance of the U.S. and Canadian stock markets during the late 1990s. As we discuss earlier in the chapter, one advantage of buying and holding overseas stocks is that they don't always fall when North American stocks drop. In other words, overseas stocks help diversify your portfolio.

Total Value of Stocks Worldwide

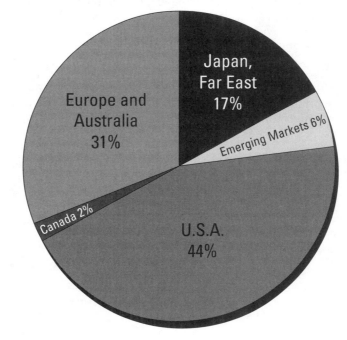

Figure 2-6:
Canada
represents
just a small
fraction of
the world's
total stock
market
value.

As well as enabling you to diversify, investing overseas has proven profitable. The investment banking firm Morgan Stanley tracks the performance of stocks in both economically established countries and so-called emerging economies. As the name suggests, countries with emerging economies are "behind" economically but show promise of healthy rates of growth and progress.

For example, between 1986 and 1995, Morgan Stanley's EAFE (which stands for Europe, Australasia, and Far East) index of foreign stocks appreciated at a rate of 17.9 percent per year. Emerging market stocks performed even better. This compares quite favourably with the Canadian stock markets, which averaged 11.6 percent per year during the same period, and the U.S. stock market, which averaged 13.9 percent. Over other periods (such as the latter 1990s), of course, overseas stock returns have lagged behind Canadian and U.S. stock returns.

Countries resemble companies in many ways. Smaller countries or companies can exhibit more explosive rates of growth. When a company or country reaches a large scale, lower rates of growth prevail because of its sheer size. Faster-growing countries tend to have fast-rising and more volatile stock prices.

Real estate returns

Over the years, real estate has proven to be about as lucrative as investing in the stock market. This makes sense because, ultimately, growth in the economy, in jobs, and in population fuels the demand for real estate.

Consider what has happened to the Canadian population over the past two centuries. In 1867 a mere 3.5 million people lived within our borders. In 1900 that figure grew to over 5 million, and by 1929 it had doubled to over 10 million. Today it's over 30 million. All these people need a place to live, and as long as jobs exist, the income from them largely fuels the demand for housing.

Businesses and people have an annoying tendency to cluster in major cities and suburban towns. Although some people commute, most people and businesses locate near airports and major highways. Thus, real estate prices in and near major metropolises and suburbs appreciate the most. Consider the areas of the world that have the most expensive real estate prices: Hong Kong, Tokyo, San Francisco, Los Angeles, New York, and Boston. Closer to home, our most expensive cities are Vancouver and Toronto. What all these areas have in common are lots of businesses and people and limited land.

Contrast these areas with the many rural parts of the country, such as those in the prairies, Atlantic Canada, and the North, where real estate is a veritable bargain because of the abundant supply of buildable land and relatively low demand for housing.

Small-business returns

As we discuss in Part IV of this book, you have several choices for tapping into the exciting potential of the small-business world. If you have the drive and determination, you can start your own small business. Or, perhaps you may have what it takes to buy an existing small business. If you obtain the necessary capital and skills to assess opportunities and risk, you can invest in someone else's small business.

What potential returns can you get from small business? Small-business owners like ourselves who do something they really enjoy will tell you that the non-financial returns can be huge! The financial rewards can be handsome as well.

Every year, *Forbes* magazine publishes a list of the world's wealthiest individuals. Perusing this list shows that most of these people built their wealth through a significant ownership stake in a small business that became large. These individuals achieved extraordinarily high effective returns (often in excess of hundreds of percent per year) on the amounts they invested to get their companies off the ground.

You may also achieve potentially high returns from buying and improving an existing small business. As we discuss in Part IV, such small business investment returns may be a good deal lower than the returns you may gain from starting a business from scratch.

Whereas plenty of historic rate-of-return data exists for the stock market, data on the success, or lack thereof, that investors have had with investing in small, private companies is harder to come by. Smart venture capitalist firms operate a fun and lucrative business: They identify and invest money in smaller start-up companies that they hope will grow rapidly and eventually go public. Venture capitalists allow outsiders to invest with them via limited partnerships. To gain entry, you generally need $1 million to invest. (We never said this was an equal opportunity investment club!)

Venture capitalists, also known as general partners, typically skim off 20 percent of the profits and also charge limited partnership investors a hefty 2 to 3 percent annual fee on the amount they've invested. The return left over for the limited partnership investors isn't stupendous. According to Venture Economics, a U.S. firm that tracks limited partners' returns, over the past 15 years venture funds have averaged annual returns of almost exactly what stock market investors have earned on average over this same period. The general partners that run venture capital funds make more than the limited partners do.

You can attempt to do what the general partners do in venture capital firms and invest directly in small, private companies. You're quite likely to be investing in much smaller and simpler companies. Earning venture capitalist returns isn't easy to do. If you think you're up to the challenge, we explain the best ways to invest in small business in Chapter 15.

How Much Do You Need or Want to Earn?

Asking you how much you need or want to earn may seem like an extraordinarily stupid question! Who *doesn't* want to earn a high return? However, although investing in stocks, real estate, or small business can produce high long-term returns, you invest in these vehicles with greater risk, especially over the short term.

Some people can't stomach the risk. Others are at a time in their lives when they can't afford to take great risk. If you're near or in retirement, your portfolio and nerves may not be able to wait a decade for your riskier investments to recover after a major stumble. Perhaps you have sufficient assets to accomplish your financial goals and are more concerned with preserving what you do have rather than risking it to grow more.

If you work for a living, odds are that you need and want to make your investments grow at a healthy clip. If your investments grow slowly, you may fall short of your goals of owning a home or retiring or changing careers. The next chapter helps you with the important issue of making investing decisions that fit with your financial goals and situation.

Are smaller company stock returns higher?

Stocks are generally classified by the size of the company. Small company stocks aren't stocks that physically small companies issue — they're simply stocks issued by companies that haven't reached the size of corporate behemoths like the big banks, Bombardier, and Barrick, or U.S. giants like IBM, AT&T, and Coca-Cola. (Here in Canada, the S&P/TSE SmallCap Index tracks the smallest companies that qualify for the TSE compound index, while the S&P/TSX Venture Composite Index measures the performance of the larger and more actively traded companies listed on the TSX Venture Exchange, where smaller/more speculative companies are listed. As for U.S. stocks, the Standard & Poor's 500 index tracks the performance of 500 large company stocks in the United States. The Russell 2000 index tracks the performance of 2,000 smaller company U.S. stocks.)

Small company stocks have outperformed larger company stocks during the past seven decades. Historically, small company stocks have produced slightly higher compounded annual returns than large company stocks. However, most of this extra performance is due to just one high-performance time period, from the mid-1970s to the early 1980s. If you eliminate this time period from the data, small stocks have actually underperformed larger company stocks.

Also, be aware that small company stocks can get hammered in down markets. For example, during the Great Depression, small company stocks plunged more than 85 percent between 1929 and 1932, while the S&P 500 fell only 64 percent. In 1937, small company stocks plummeted 58 percent; the S&P 500 fell 35 percent. And in 1969–1970, small company stocks fell 38 percent while the S&P 500 fell just 5 percent.

Chapter 3

Before You Invest

*W*e know you're eager to make some great, wealth-building investments. But if we told you to get your financial house in order first, you'd say "Forget it!" and likely close the book. The truth is that understanding and implementing some simple personal financial management concepts will pay off big for you in the decades ahead.

You want to know how to earn healthy returns on your investments without getting clobbered, right? Who doesn't? Although you generally must accept greater risk in exchange for potentially higher returns (see Chapter 2), in this chapter we tell you about some free lunches in the world of investing. You have a right to be sceptical about free lunches — but this chapter points out some easy-to-tap opportunities for managing your money that you've likely overlooked.

Establishing an Emergency Reserve

Because you never know what life will bring, it makes good financial sense to have a liquid reserve of cash to meet unexpected expenses. When talking about money, liquid doesn't mean you have it invested in fine wines. In the financial world, a liquid investment simply means it's easy to get your money — in the form of cash you can use for other purposes — out quickly and with few if any fees or penalties.

You likely don't have tens of thousands of dollars languishing in a low-interest bank account. If you have a sister who works on Bay Street as an investment banker, or a loaded and understanding parent, you can use them as your emergency reserve. (Ask them how they feel about that.)

But not everyone has such emergency reserves. Consider the case of Warren, who owned his home as well as an investment property that he rented. He felt — and appeared to be — financially successful. But then Warren lost his job (a not-uncommon occurrence given the corporate world's downsizing mood), accumulated sizable medical expenses, and had to sell his investment property to come up with cash to tide himself over.

Should you invest emergency money in stocks?

As interest rates drifted lower during the 1990s, keeping emergency money in money market accounts became less and less rewarding. When interest rates were 8 or 10 percent, fewer people questioned the wisdom of an emergency reserve. However, in the late 1990s, with money market interest rates of 5 percent or less and stock market returns of 15 to 25 percent per year, more investors balked at keeping a low-interest stash of cash.

Inevitably, articles began appearing that suggested you simply keep your emergency reserve in stocks. After all, you can easily sell stocks (especially those of larger companies) any day the financial markets are open. Why not treat yourself to the 20 percent annual returns that stock market investors enjoyed during the 1990s rather than earning a paltry 4 or 5 percent?

We aren't enthusiastic about investors keeping their emergency money invested in stocks and clearly stated so in the previous edition of this book, which was published in 2000. Here's what we said: "Stock market investors shouldn't expect to earn such generous returns as they did during the 1990s." That advice still stands. As we discuss in Chapter 2, stocks have historically returned about 9 to 10 percent per year. In some years — in fact, about one-third of the time — stocks decline in value, sometimes substantially.

Stocks can and have dropped 20, 30, or 50 percent or more over relatively short periods. Suppose such a drop coincides with an emergency — such as the loss of your job, major medical bills, and so on. Your situation may force you to sell at a loss, perhaps a substantial one.

Keeping emergency money in stocks is also not a good idea because if your stocks appreciate and you need to sell some of them for emergency cash, you get stuck paying taxes on your gains.

We suggest that you invest your emergency money in stocks (ideally through well-diversified mutual funds) only if you have a relative or some other resource to tap for money in an emergency. Having a back-up resource for money minimizes your need to sell your stock holdings on short notice. As we discuss in Chapter 5, stocks are intended as a longer-term investment, not an investment that you expect (or need) to sell in the near future.

If you don't have a financial safety net, you may be forced, as Warren was, into selling an investment that you've worked hard for. Selling some investments, such as real estate, costs big money (transaction costs, taxes, and so on). Warren wasn't able to purchase another investment property, and missed out on 300-plus percent appreciation over the subsequent two decades. And between the costs of selling and taxes, getting rid of the investment property cost Warren about 15 percent of its sales price. Ouch!

Make sure you have quick access to three to six months' worth of living expenses. Keep this emergency money in a high-yielding money market fund or high-interest savings account. (See Chapter 8.) You may also be able to borrow against your home equity. Warren didn't have enough equity in his home to borrow. He didn't have other sources — a wealthy banker sister, for example — to borrow from either, so was stuck selling his investment property.

Evaluating Your Debts

Yes, paying down debts is boring, but it makes your investment decisions less difficult. Rather than spending so much of your time investigating specific investments, paying off your debts (if you have them) may be your best high-return, low-risk investment. Consider the interest rate you pay and your investing alternatives to determine which debts you should pay off.

Conquering consumer debt

Many folks have credit card or other consumer debt, such as auto loans, that costs 8, 10, 12, or perhaps as much as 18-plus percent per year in interest. Paying off this debt with your savings is like putting your money in an investment with a guaranteed *tax-free* return equal to the rate that you pay on your debt.

For example, if you have outstanding credit card debt at 15 percent interest, paying off that debt is the same as putting your money to work in an investment with a guaranteed 15 percent tax-free annual return. Because the interest on consumer debt is not tax-deductible, you need to earn a good deal more than 15 percent investing your money elsewhere in order to net 15 percent *after* paying taxes. Earning such high investing returns is highly unlikely and, in order to have a chance, you'll be forced to take great risk.

Consumer debt is hazardous to your long-term financial health because it encourages you to borrow against your future earnings. We often hear people say such things as "I can't afford to buy most new cars for cash — look at how expensive they are!" That's true, new cars are expensive, so set your sights lower and buy a good used car that you can afford. You can then invest the money that you'd otherwise spend on your auto loan.

Borrowing via credit cards, auto loans, and the like is also one of the most expensive ways to borrow. Banks and other lenders charge higher interest rates for consumer debt than for debt for investments, such as real estate and business. The reason: Consumer loans are the riskiest type of loan for a lender.

However, using consumer debt may make sense if you're financing a business. If you don't have home equity, personal loans (through a credit card or auto loan) may actually be your lowest-cost source of small-business financing. (See Chapter 14 for more details.)

Mitigating your mortgage

Paying off your mortgage quicker may make sense for your financial situation. Making this financial move isn't as clear as paying off high-interest consumer debt because mortgage interest rates are generally lower. When used properly, debt can help you accomplish your goals — such as buying a home or starting a business — and make you money in the long run. Borrowing to buy a home generally makes sense. Over the long term, homes generally appreciate in value.

If your financial situation has changed or improved since you first needed to borrow mortgage money, you need to reconsider how much mortgage debt you need or want. Even if your income hasn't escalated or you haven't inherited vast wealth, your frugality may allow you to pay down some of your debt sooner than the lender requires. Whether paying down your debt sooner makes sense for you depends on a number of factors, including your other investment options and goals.

Considering your investment opportunities

Financially, your mortgage interest rate versus your investments' rates of return (which we define in Chapter 2) is what matters when you decide whether to pay down your mortgage faster. Suppose you have a fixed-rate mortgage with an interest rate of 7 percent. If you decide to make investments instead of paying down your mortgage more quickly, your investments need to produce an average annual rate of return, after taxes, of 7 percent to come out ahead financially.

Suppose you're in the middle tax bracket. The rate of tax you would pay on your profits from buying and selling units in an equity mutual fund, for example, would be about 22 percent. So in order to earn a better after-tax return than the 7 percent you'd earn by paying off some or all of your mortgage, you'd have to find an equity fund that paid around 9 percent. That's because after paying taxes of around 22 percent on your share of the fund's capital gains, you'd be left with a return of around the same 7 percent mark.

Many funds do provide investors with returns that high, but they typically aren't able to consistently sustain that kind of performance year after year. And you'll have to expose yourself to the possibility of your investment plunging in value if the stock markets take a dive, or if the manager of your fund just happens to lose his stock-picking smarts. Paying down your mortgage is a 100 percent guaranteed return.

Making your mortgage interest tax-deductible

If you have some extra money on hand and don't know whether you should pay down your mortgage or put it into an attractive investment, there is a way to do both at the same time. When you pay off some of your mortgage, you create more equity — the paid-off part of your home. You can usually use the difference between what you owe on your mortgage and 25 percent of your property's market value as the security for a loan. Say your home is worth $200,000, and you make a lump sum payment that reduces your mortgage to $100,000. You then have $50,000 of equity in your home that can be used as collateral for a line of credit. A line of credit is similar to a loan, except that you can borrow different amounts on it whenever you need the money. Because real assets back or secure the loan, the interest rate is usually at or close to the banks' prime rate — the rate they charge their best customers. Also, as long as you make the minimum monthly repayments required by your lender, you're usually free to pay back some or all of your borrowings at any time.

Interest on money you borrow in order to buy investments or earn business income is usually tax-deductible. Suppose you have $10,000 that you use to pay down your mortgage. If you then borrow the money back, with your home as security on the loan, your interest rate might be around 5 percent, for an annual cost of $500. The investment that you buy with your $10,000, though, earns you $1,000 — a 10 percent return. From the tax department's perspective, you've made a net profit of only $500, or 5 percent (10 percent – 5 percent). You'll have to pay capital gains tax on half of your profits. In other words, only $250 is taxed. If you're in a moderately high tax bracket, the end result is that you make $200, or 2 percent after tax on your investment, even after paying the cost of borrowing the money.

Besides the most common reason of lacking the funds to do so, other good reasons *not* to pay off your mortgage any quicker than necessary include the following:

- ✔ You contribute instead to your RRSP or other retirement plans. Paying off your mortgage faster has no tax benefit. By contrast, putting additional money into a retirement plan can immediately reduce your income tax. The more years you have until retirement, the greater the benefit you receive if you invest in your retirement plans. Thanks to the compounding of your RRSP investments without the drain of taxes, you can actually earn a lower rate of return on your investments than you pay on your mortgage and still come out ahead. (We discuss RRSPs in detail in the "Funding Your RRSP" section later in this chapter.)

✔ You're willing to invest in more growth-oriented, volatile investments, such as stocks and real estate. In order to have a reasonable chance of earning more on your investments than it costs you to borrow on your mortgage, you must be aggressive with your investments. As we discuss in Chapter 2, stocks and real estate have produced annual average rates of return of about 8 to 10 percent. You can earn even more with your own small business or investing in others' businesses. Some investors like to leverage (borrow money to have more to invest) their investments. Paying down a mortgage ties up more of your capital, reducing your ability to make other attractive investments. To more aggressive investors, paying off the house seems downright boring — the financial equivalent of watching paint dry.

✔ Remember that you have no guarantee of earning high returns from growth-type investments, which can easily drop 20 percent or more in value over a year or two.

✔ Paying down the mortgage depletes your emergency reserves. Psychologically, some people feel uncomfortable paying off debt more quickly if it diminishes their savings and investments. You probably don't want to pay down your debt if doing so depletes your financial safety cushion. Make sure you have access — through a money market fund or other sources (a family member, for example) — to at least three months' living expenses.

Finally, don't be tripped up by the misconception that somehow you'll be hurt worse financially if there's a real estate market crash and you've paid down your mortgage. Your home is worth what it's worth — its value has *nothing* to do with your debt load. Unless you're willing to walk away from your home and send the keys to the bank (also known as *default*), you suffer the full effect of a price decline, regardless of your mortgage size, if real estate prices collapse.

Establishing Financial Goals

Although you may save money only because Mom and Dad told you it was the right thing to do, or because it makes you feel good, odds are that you save money with some purpose in mind. Common financial goals include saving for retirement, purchasing a home, starting your own business, and so on.

You may want to invest money for different purposes simultaneously. For example, when you're in your 20s, you might put some money away toward retirement, but you might also save a stash so that you can hit the eject button from your job. You might know that you want to pursue an entrepreneurial path and that, in the early years of starting your own business, you won't be able to count on an income as stable or as large as what your job pays.

In this situation, you should invest your two "pots" of money — one for retirement, the other your small business cushion — quite differently. As we discuss in the section "Choosing the Right Investment Mix" later in this chapter, you can afford to take more risk with the money that you don't plan on using in the near term. So you could invest the bulk of your retirement nest egg in stock mutual funds.

With the money you've saved for the start-up of your small business, you should take an entirely different track. None of this money should go into risky stocks — what if the market plummeted just as you were ready to leave the security of your full-time job? Thus, you should keep this money safely invested in a money market fund or high-interest savings account that pays a healthy rate of interest but doesn't fluctuate in value.

Making sure that your savings stay on track

In order to accomplish your financial and some personal goals, you need to save money. However, many people haven't a clue what their savings rate is. Your *savings rate* is the percentage of your past year's income that you saved and didn't spend. You may already know that your rate of savings is low, non-existent, or negative, and that you need to save more.

Part of being a smart investor involves figuring out how much you need to save to reach your goals. Not knowing what you want to do a decade or more from now is perfectly normal — after all, your goals and needs evolve over the years. But that doesn't mean you should just throw your hands in the air and not make an effort to see where you stand today and think about where you want to be in the future.

An important benefit of knowing your savings rate is that you'll know better how much risk you need to take to accomplish your goals. Seeing the amount that you need to save to achieve your dreams may encourage you to take more risk with your investments.

If you consistently save about 10 percent of your income during your working years, you're probably saving enough to meet your goals, unless you want to retire at a relatively young age. On average, most people need about 75 percent of their pre-retirement income throughout retirement to maintain their standard of living.

If you're one of the many people who don't save enough, you need to do some homework. To save more, you need to reduce your spending, increase your income, or both.

For most people, reducing their spending is the more feasible method to save more. But where do you begin? First, figure out where your money goes. You may have some general idea, but you need to have facts. Get out your chequebook register, credit card bills, and any other documentation of your spending history and tally up how much you spend on dining out, operating your car(s), paying your taxes, and everything else. Then you can begin to prioritize and make the necessary trade-offs to reduce your spending and increase your savings rate.

Earning more income may help boost your savings rate as well. Perhaps you can get a higher-paying job or increase the number of hours that you work. But if you already work a lot, reining in your spending is usually better for your economic — and emotional — well-being.

If you don't know how to evaluate and reduce your spending or haven't thought about your retirement goals, looked into what you can expect from the Canada Pension Plan or Quebec Pension Plan, or calculated how much you should save for retirement, now's the time to do it. Pick up the latest edition of our first book, *Personal Finance For Canadians For Dummies* (published by John Wiley & Sons Canada, Ltd.), and find out all the necessary details for retirement planning and much more.

Determining your investment likes and dislikes

Many good investing choices exist — you can invest in real estate, the stock market, mutual funds, your own business or someone else's, or you can pay down mortgage debt more quickly. What makes sense for you depends on your goals as well as your personal preferences. If you detest taking risks and volatile investments, paying down your mortgage, as recommended earlier in this chapter, may make better sense than investing in the stock market.

How do you deal with an investment that plunges 20 percent, 40 percent, or more in a few years or less? Some of the more aggressive investments we discuss in this book can fall fast. (See Chapter 2 for examples.) You shouldn't go into the stock market, real estate, or a small-business investment arena if such a drop is likely to cause you to sell low or make you a miserable wreck. If you haven't tried riskier investments yet, you may want to experiment a bit to see how you feel with your money invested in them.

A simple way to "mask" the risk of volatile investments is to *diversify* your portfolio — that is, to put your money into different investments. (See Chapter 2.) Not watching prices closely helps, too — that's one of the reasons why real estate investors are less likely to bail out when the market declines. Stock market investors can (unfortunately, from our perspective) get daily and even minute-by-minute price updates. Add that fact to the quick phone call or click of the computer mouse that it takes to dump a stock in a flash, and you have all the ingredients for short-sighted investing — and financial disaster.

Investing as a couple

You've probably learned over the years how challenging it is just to navigate the investment maze and make sound investing decisions. With couples it's doubly hard, given the typically different money personalities and money emotions that come into play.

With most couples, usually one person takes primary responsibility for managing the household finances, including investments. As with most marital issues, the couples who do the best job with their investments are those who communicate well and compromise.

Here are a couple examples to illustrate our point. Martha and Alex scheduled meetings every three to six months with their financial adviser to discuss financial issues. Martha came prepared with a list of ideas about investments, and Alex would listen and explain what he liked or disliked about each option. Alex would tend toward more aggressive, growth-oriented investments, whereas Martha preferred conservative, less volatile ones. Inevitably, they would compromise and together develop a diversified portfolio that was moderately aggressive. Martha and Alex worked as a team, discussed options, compromised, and made decisions they were both comfortable with.

Henry and Melisa didn't do so well. The only times they managed to discuss investments were in heated arguments. Melisa often criticized what Henry was doing with their money. Henry got defensive and counter-criticized Melisa for issues he wasn't happy about with her. Much of their money lay dormant in a low-interest bank account, and they did little long-term planning and decision making. Melisa and Henry saw each other as adversaries, argued and criticized rather than discussed, and were plagued with inaction because they couldn't agree and compromise. They really needed some counselling or shift in behaviour toward one another to make progress with investing their money.

Funding Your RRSP and Other Retirement Plans

Saving money is difficult for most people. Don't make a tough job impossible by forsaking the terrific tax benefits that come from investing inside an RRSP.

Gaining those tax benefits

Registered retirement savings plans (RRSPs) should be called tax-reduction plans — if they were, people might be more jazzed about contributing to them. An RRSP is simply a special account into which you can contribute a portion of your income. Contributions to these plans are tax-deductible. If you contribute $5,000, for example, you can deduct that amount before calculating your taxable income for the year. Suppose you pay about 35 percent between federal and provincial income taxes on your last dollars of income. (To determine your tax bracket, see the "Determining your tax bracket" section later in this chapter.) With an RRSP, you'd save yourself about $350 in taxes for every $1,000 that you contribute in the year that you make your contribution. So, for that $5,000 contribution, you're looking at a saving of $1,750.

After your money is in an RRSP, any interest, dividends, and appreciation grow inside the account without being taxed. You can take the full amount of any earnings and reinvest it, year after year. With an RRSP, you defer taxes on all the accumulating gains and profits until you withdraw your money down the road. In the meantime, more of your money works for you over a long period of time.

Understanding RRSPs

Whether you're employed or work for yourself, you can contribute to an RRSP as long as you have what the government dubs *earned income*. For most people, their earned income is their salary, along with any bonuses or commissions. If you're self-employed or an active partner in a business, it includes any net income from your business. Earned income also includes any taxable alimony and maintenance payments as well as any research grants, royalties, and net rental income.

Any time you have earned income, you earn the right to contribute 18 percent of that amount to your RRSP in the following year. But no matter how much earned income you have, there is a maximum amount you'll be able to contribute for any one year. For the tax year 2003 the maximum was $14,500. The limit is scheduled to rise to $15,500 for the 2004 tax year, $16,500 for 2005, and $18,000 for 2006. After that the maximum will be indexed, meaning it will be increased at the rate of inflation.

In addition, the amount you may be allowed to contribute is reduced if you belong to a company pension plan. The government calculates the value of contributions made to your employer-sponsored pension plan, called a pension adjustment (PA), and deducts this from whichever is less — the absolute dollar maximum allowed for the year or 18 percent of your earned income — to arrive at your allowable contribution.

Note that when we talk about the maximum per year, we're referring to how much you can contribute _for_ each year. There's no limit on how much you can contribute _in_ any one year as long as you've built up that amount of allowable contributions.

If you don't put in the full amount you're allowed to in any given year, you can carry forward that amount — your _contribution room_ — and use it in the future. Think of it as having an ongoing allowable contribution account. Any time you have earned income, the next year you can add to your contribution room account the difference between the amount that year's earned income gave you the right to contribute and what you actually put into your RRSP.

Delaying increases your pain

The common mistake that investors make is neglecting to take advantage of RRSPs or other retirement plans because of their enthusiasm to spend or invest in "non-retirement" accounts. Not investing in tax-sheltered retirement plans can cost you hundreds, perhaps thousands, of dollars per year in lost tax savings. Add that loss up over the many years that you work and save, and not taking advantage of the tax benefits of RRSPs can easily cost you tens of thousands to hundreds of thousands of dollars in the long term. Ouch!

Although many people have made good money focusing on real estate and small-business investments — just ask Bill Gates or our own B.C.-based billionaire Jim Pattison if they have any regrets about focusing on their own businesses! — lesser mortals need to be careful that they don't put too many of their investing eggs in non-retirement-plan baskets. Of the money that you don't earmark for real estate or small-business investment, invest all that you can inside an RRSP. In fact, taking advantage of saving and investing in an RRSP should probably be your number one personal financial priority (unless you're still paying off high-interest consumer debt on credit cards or auto loans).

In order to take advantage of RRSPs and the tax savings that accompany them, you must first spend less than you earn. Only after you spend less than you earn can you afford to contribute to these retirement savings plans (unless you already happen to have a stash of cash from previous savings or inheritance).

The mistake that people of all income levels make is that they don't start saving in an RRSP at a younger age. The sooner you start to save, the less painful it is each year to save enough to reach your goals because your contributions have more years to compound.

Each decade you delay saving approximately doubles the percentage of your earnings that you need to save to meet your goals. For example, if saving 5 percent per year in your early 20s gets you to your retirement goal, waiting until your 30s to start may mean socking away 10 percent to reach that same goal; waiting until your 40s, 20 percent. Beyond that, the numbers get truly daunting.

If you enjoy spending money and living for today, find a way to motivate yourself to start saving sooner. The longer you wait to save, the more you ultimately need to save — and therefore, the less you can spend today!

Choosing investments within RRSPs and other tax-deferred plans

When you establish an RRSP or other tax-deferred plan, it's important to realize that it is simply a shell or shield that keeps the government from taxing your investment earnings each year. You still must choose what investments you want to hold inside your retirement plan shell.

You may invest your RRSP (or other retirement plan money such as a RRIF, or *Registered Retirement Savings Plan*) in stocks, bonds, mutual funds, and even small businesses. Mutual funds, which we cover in detail in Chapter 8, are an ideal choice because they offer diversification and professional management. After you decide which financial institution you want to invest through, simply obtain and complete the appropriate paperwork for establishing the specific type of plan you desire.

Taming Your Taxes

When you invest outside of an RRSP or other tax-sheltered retirement plan, the profits and distributions on your money are subject to taxation. So the type of investment that makes sense for you outside an RRSP or RRIF depends (at least partly) on your tax situation.

If you have money to invest, or if you're considering selling current investments that you hold, taxes are an important factor in your decision. But tax considerations alone shouldn't dictate how and where you invest your money. You should also weigh investment choices, your desire and the necessity to take risk, personal likes and dislikes, and the number of years you plan to hold the investment.

Consider how taxes affect investing in stocks and bonds. If you're in a high tax bracket, you should give preference to investments such as common stocks or preferred shares that pay dividends. Real estate and small business investments that you expect to appreciate are also tax-wise choices.

Determining your tax bracket

You may not know it, but the government charges you different tax rates for different parts of your annual income in any given year. You pay less tax on the *first* dollars of your earnings and more tax on the *last* dollars of your earnings. For example, say your taxable income totalled $65,000 during 2004. Thanks to a tax credit available to all taxpayers, the first $7,800 of income would be tax-free. After that, the approximate rates of tax would be 24 percent on the income between $7,800 and $32,000, 34 percent on the income from $32,000 to $64,000, and finally, 41 percent on the last $1,000.

Your *marginal tax rate* is the rate of tax that you pay on your *last* or so-called *highest* dollars of income in any given year. In the example of a single person with taxable income of $45,000, that person's marginal tax rate is around 34 percent. In other words, he or she effectively pays a 34 percent tax on his or her last dollars of income — those dollars earned between $32,000 and $45,000. (Don't forget to factor in the provincial income taxes that most provinces assess.) Since marginal tax rates start low and rise along with income, your average tax rate will be lower than your marginal tax rate.

Knowing your marginal tax rate allows you to quickly calculate the following:

- ✔ Any additional taxes that you would pay on additional income.
- ✔ The amount of taxes you save if you contribute more money into an RRSP or reduce your taxable income (for example, if you choose investments that produce tax-free income).

Table 3-1 shows the approximate 2004 tax rates. Note that the actual tax brackets and rates vary from province to province.

Table 3-1	2004 Income Tax Rates
Approximate Taxable Income	**Approximate Tax Rate**
$7,800 to $32,000	24%
$32,000 to $64,000	34%
$64,000 to $105,000	41%
$105,000 and higher	45%

Knowing what's taxed and when to worry

Interest that is paid on bank accounts, GICs, and bonds is generally taxable. That's fairly straightforward, but you may want to pop an Aspirin before we cover taxation on *capital gains* and *dividends*.

Capital gains are the *profits* (sales minus purchase price) on investments. If you make a profit on an investment, defined as selling it for more than your cost, you have to include half of your gain in your income, which is then taxed at your marginal tax rate. The result is that the current tax rate you effectively pay on capital gains — your effective tax rate — will be half of your marginal tax rate.

If you're in the lowest marginal tax bracket of 24 percent — remember that exact tax rates and marginal tax brackets vary from province to province — your effective capital gains tax rate will be 12 percent. If you are in the next tax bracket, where your salary is taxed at 34 percent, your effective tax rate on capital gains is 17 percent, while those in the 41 percent marginal tax bracket will have an effective capital gains tax rate of 20.5 percent. Finally, those in the top 45 percent marginal tax bracket will have capital gains taxed at 22.5 percent.

Table 3-2	2004 Income Tax Rates
Taxable Income	**Approximate Effective Tax Rate on Capital Gains**
$7,800 to $32,000	12%
$32,000 to $64,000	17%
$64,000 to $105,000	20.5%
$105,000 and higher	22.5%

Dividends from Canadian corporations are taxed at the lowest effective rate. (Dividends from foreign corporations are treated and taxed just like your regular income.) Dividends are the distribution of a company's after-tax profits, so you receive a special dividend tax credit to prevent the same profits being taxed twice. The result is that you have to use a somewhat strange formula to determine the tax on dividends.

First, the amount of the dividend actually received is increased by 25 percent — *grossed up* — in order to reflect what the corporation is assumed to have made pre-tax. This inflated number is what you actually show on your tax return as the amount of your dividend income. To offset this, you then get a tax credit, since it's assumed the corporation has already paid tax on the money at around 20 percent. The federal tax credit is two-thirds of the amount you increased your actual dividends by — the *gross-up*. You can also think of it as 13.33 percent of the total amount you list as your dividend income, including the gross-up. In addition, there is a corresponding provincial tax credit. (In Quebec, there is a separate dividend tax credit of 10.83 percent of the grossed-up dividend.) Table 3-3 shows the approximate rate that dividends are taxed at.

Table 3-3	2004 Income Tax Rates
Taxable Income	*Approximate Tax Rate on Dividends*
$7,800 to $32,000	7%
$32,000 to $64,000	19%
$64,000 to $105,000	26%
$105,000 and higher	31%

Use these strategies to reduce the taxes on investments exposed to taxation:

✔ **Invest in tax-friendly stocks funds.** Index funds are mutual funds that invest in a relatively fixed portfolio of securities, such as stocks and bonds. They don't attempt to beat the market. Rather, they invest in the securities to mirror or match the performance of an underlying index, such as the TSE composite index or the Standard & Poor's 500 (which we discuss in Chapter 5). Although index funds can't beat the market, they have several advantages over actively managed funds. Because index funds trade less, they tend to produce lower capital gains distributions. For mutual funds held outside tax-sheltered retirement plans, this reduced trading effectively increases an investor's total rate of return. See Chapter 8 to find out more about tax-friendly stock mutual funds.

✔ **Invest in tax-friendly stocks.** Companies that pay little in the way of dividends reinvest more of their profits back into the company. If you invest outside of a retirement plan, unless you need income to live on, minimize your exposure to stocks with dividends. Be aware that low-dividend stocks tend to be more volatile.

✔ **Invest in small business and real estate.** The growth in value of a business or real estate isn't taxed until you sell the asset. However, the current income that a small business and real estate produces is taxed as ordinary income. And if you sell the home you live in — your principal residence — for a profit, all your gains are tax-free.

BEWARE

Avoiding supposed "tax savings" investments

Brokers and financial planners who work on commission often try to sell you numerous investments that they claim offer big tax advantages. A limited partnership (LP) is a good example of a bad investment these salespeople may push. Limited partnerships invest in real estate and a variety of businesses, such as cable television, health care, and technology-related companies. Although some of the companies that LPs invest in are sound, the only sure thing about investing in LPs is that you won't earn the best possible returns for your money because of high sales commissions and ongoing management fees.

Commissions, which are immediately deducted from your investment, can run 10 percent or more. Annual management fees can also be steep, running up to 3 percent per year. The best no-load (commission-free) mutual funds, by comparison, charge 1 to 2 percent — and sometimes even less than 1 percent — per year for similar investments.

LPs also have poor liquidity — you must typically wait seven to ten years until the partnership investments are sold to access your investment dollars. If you need to sell before then, you may be able to sell through the informal secondary market, but you'll receive pennies on the dollar.

Another investment that many salespeople love to pitch is cash value life insurance. Life insurance that combines life insurance protection with an account that has a cash value is usually known as universal, whole, or variable life.

Life insurance with a cash value is, at best, a mediocre way to invest money and, at worst, a terrible mistake, especially if you haven't exhausted contributing money to an RRSP. Retirement plans give you an immediate tax deduction for your current contributions in addition to growth without taxation until withdrawal.

The only real advantage that cash value life insurance offers is that if you expect that your estate will face a hefty tax bill when you die, the proceeds paid to your beneficiaries can help reduce or eliminate the effect of taxes.

Choosing the Right Investment Mix

Diversifying your investments helps buffer your portfolio from being sunk by one or two poor performers. In this section, we explain how to mix up a great recipe of investments.

Considering your age

The younger you are and the more years you have until you plan to use your money, the more longer-term investment money should be in growth (ownership) vehicles, such as stocks, real estate, and small business. As we discuss in Chapter 2, the attraction of these types of investments is the potential to really grow your money. The risk: The value of your portfolio can plunge from time to time.

The younger you are, the more time your investments have to recover from a bad fall. In this respect, investments are a bit like people. If a 30-year-old and an 80-year-old fall on a concrete sidewalk, odds are higher that the younger person will fully recover. Such falls sometimes disable older people.

A long-held guiding principle says to subtract your age from 100 and invest the resulting number as a percentage of money to place in growth (ownership) investments. So if you're 35 years old:

100 – 35 = 65% of your investment money can be in growth investments.

If you want to be more aggressive, subtract your age from 120:

120 – 35 = 85% of your investment money can be in growth investments.

Note that even retired persons should often still have a healthy chunk of their investment dollars in growth vehicles like stocks. A 70-year-old person may want to totally avoid risk, but doing so is generally a mistake. Such a person can live another two or three decades. If you live longer than anticipated, you can run out of money if it doesn't continue to grow.

These tips are only general rules and apply to money that you invest for the long term (ideally for ten years or more). For money that you need to use in the shorter term, such as within the next several years, more-aggressive growth investments aren't appropriate. See Chapters 8 and 9 for more ideas.

Making the most of your investment options

No hard-and-fast rules exist that show you how to allocate the percentage that you've earmarked for growth investments among specific investments, like stocks and real estate. Part of how you decide to allocate your investments depends, for example, on the types of investments that you want to focus on. As we discuss in Chapter 5, diversifying in stocks worldwide can be prudent as well as profitable.

Here are some general guidelines to keep in mind:

- **Take advantage of your retirement plans.** Unless you need accessible money for shorter-term non-retirement goals, why pass up the free extra returns from the tax benefits of retirement plans?

- **Don't pile into investments that gain lots of attention.** Many investors make this mistake, especially those who lack a thought-out plan to buy stocks. In Chapter 5 we provide numerous illustrations of the perils of buying stocks garnering much attention.

- **Have the courage to be a contrarian.** No one likes to feel that he is jumping on board a sinking ship or supporting a losing cause. However, just like shopping for something at retail stores, the best time to buy something is when its price is reduced and on sale.

- **Diversify.** As we discuss in Chapter 2, the values of different investments don't move in tandem. So when you invest in growth investments, such as stocks or real estate, your portfolio's value will have a smoother ride if you diversify properly.

- **Invest more in what you know.** Over the years, we've met successful investors who have built substantial wealth without spending gobs of free time. Some investors, for example, concentrate more on real estate because that's what they best understand and feel comfortable with. Others put more money in stocks for the same reason. No one-size-fits-all dress code exists for successful investors. Just be careful that you don't put all your investing eggs in the same basket (for example, stocks in the same industry that you believe you know a lot about).

- **Don't invest in too many different things.** Diversification is good to a point. If you purchase so many investments that you can't perform a basic annual review of them (for example, reading the annual report from your mutual fund), then you may have too many different investments.

✔ **Be more aggressive inside retirement plans.** When you hit your retirement years, you'll probably begin to live off your non-retirement plan investments first. Why? For the simple reason that allowing your retirement plans — such as RRSPs and RRIFs — to continue growing will save you tax dollars. Therefore, you should be relatively less aggressive with investments outside of retirement plans because that money will be invested for a shorter time period.

Easing into risky investments with dollar cost averaging

Dollar cost averaging (DCA) is the practice of investing a regular amount of money at set time intervals, such as monthly or quarterly, into volatile investments, such as stocks and stock mutual funds. If you've ever deducted money from a pay cheque and pumped it into a retirement savings plan investment account that holds stocks and bonds, you've done DCA.

Most of us invest a portion of our employment compensation as we earn it, but if you have extra cash sitting around, you can choose to invest that money in one fell swoop or invest it gradually via DCA. The biggest appeal of gradually feeding money into the market via DCA is that you don't dump all your money into a potentially overheated investment just before a major drop. Thus, DCA helps shy investors psychologically ease into riskier investments.

DCA is made to order for skittish investors with a large sum of money sitting in safe investments like GICs or a savings account. For example, using DCA, an investor with $100,000 to invest in stock funds can feed her money into investments gradually — say, at the rate of $12,500 or so quarterly over two years — instead of investing her entire $100,000 in stocks at once and possibly buying all her shares at a market peak. Most larger investment companies, especially those that sell mutual funds, allow investors to establish automatic investment plans so that the DCA occurs without an investor's ongoing involvement.

Of course, like any risk-reducing investment strategy, DCA has drawbacks. If growth investments appreciate (as they're supposed to), a DCA investor misses out on earning higher returns on his money awaiting investment. Richard E. Williams and Peter W. Bacon, finance professors at Wright State University, found that approximately 64 percent of the time, a lump sum stock market investor earned higher first-year returns than an investor who fed the money in monthly over the first year. (They studied data from the U.S. market over the past seven decades.)

York University business professor Moshe Arye Milevsky found the same thing in his book *Money Logic*. According to his research, if you invested a $10,000 lump sum in a Canadian equity mutual fund, you would likely have $11,000 after a year's time had passed. In short, his research showed that two-thirds of the time your initial investment would be worth between $9,500 and $12,500. In contrast, if you invested the money in equal amounts over 12 months, by the end of that year your initial investment would likely be worth $10,748. More specifically, two-thirds of the time you could anticipate having somewhere between $9,898 and $11,598.

Knowing that you'll probably be ahead two-thirds of the time if you invest a lump sum into the stock market will be little solace if you happen to invest just before a major market plunge. In the fall of 1987, the Canadian stock market, as measured by the TSE index, plummeted 31 percent, and in 1973–74, the market shed 38 percent of its value.

So investors who fear that stocks are due for such a major correction should practise DCA, right? Well, not so fast. Apprehensive investors who shun lump sum investments and use DCA are more likely to stop the DCA investment process if prices plunge, thereby defeating the benefit of doing DCA during a declining market.

So what's an investor with a lump sum of money to do? First, weigh the significance of the lump sum to you. Although $100,000 is a big chunk of most people's net worth, it's only 10 percent if your net worth is $1,000,000 and not worth a millionaire's time to use DCA. If the cash you have to invest is less than a quarter of your net worth, you may not want to bother with DCA.

Second, consider how aggressively you invest (or invested) your money. For example, if you aggressively invested through an employer's retirement plan that you roll over, don't waste your time on DCA.

DCA makes sense for investors with a large chunk of their net worth in cash who want to minimize the risk of transferring that cash to riskier investments such as stocks. If you fancy yourself a market prognosticator, you can also assess the current valuation of stocks. Thinking that stocks are pricey increases the appeal of DCA.

Over how long a time period should you practise DCA? If you use it too quickly, you may not give the market sufficient time for a correction to unfold during and after which some of the DCA purchases may take place. If you use it over too long a period, you may miss a major upswing in stock prices. We suggest using DCA over one to two years to strike a balance.

As for timing, mutual fund investors should do their DCA early in each calendar quarter, because mutual funds that make taxable distributions tend to do so late in the quarter.

Your money that awaits investment should have a suitable parking place. Select a high-yielding money market fund or high-interest savings account. With rates on such funds just shy of those on more volatile bond funds, sitting on cash these days isn't so bad.

One last critical point: When you use DCA, establish an automatic investment plan so that you're less likely to chicken out. And for the more courageous, you may want to try an alternative strategy to DCA — value averaging — which gets you to invest more if prices are falling and less if prices are rising.

Suppose you want to use DCA and invest $500 per quarter into an aggressive stock mutual fund. After your first quarterly $500 investment, the fund drops 10 percent, reducing your account balance to $450. Dollar cost averaging has you invest $500 the next quarter plus another $50 to make up the shortfall. (Conversely, if the fund value increased to $550 after your first investment, you would invest only $450 in the second round.) Increasing the amount you invest requires confidence when prices fall, but doing so magnifies your returns when prices turn around.

Protecting Your Assets

You may be at risk of making a catastrophic investing mistake: not properly protecting your assets due to a lack of various insurance coverages. That's the error that Manny, a successful entrepreneur, made. Starting from scratch, he built up a successful million-dollar manufacturing operation. He invested a lot of his own personal money and sweat into building the business over 15 years.

One day, catastrophe struck: An explosion ripped through his building, and the ensuing fire destroyed virtually all the firm's equipment and inventory, none of which was insured. The explosion also seriously injured several workers, including Manny, who didn't carry disability insurance. Ultimately, Manny had to file bankruptcy.

Decisions regarding what amount of insurance you need to carry are somewhat a matter of your desire and ability to accept financial risk. Some risks aren't worth taking. Don't overestimate your ability to predict in advance what accidents and other bad luck may befall you. Here's what you need to protect yourself and your assets:

- ✔ **Adequate liability insurance on your home and car to guard your assets against lawsuits.** You should have at least enough liability insurance to protect your net worth (assets minus your liabilities/debts), or, ideally, twice your net worth. If you run your own business, get insurance for your business assets if they're substantial, such as in Manny's case. Also consider professional liability insurance to protect against a lawsuit. You may also want to consider incorporating your business (which we discuss more in Chapter 14).

- ✔ **Long-term disability insurance.** What would you (and your family) do to replace your income if a major disability prevents you from working? Even if you don't have dependants, odds are that you are dependent on you. Most larger employers offer group plans that have good benefits and are much less expensive than coverage you'd buy on your own. Also, check with your professional association for a competitive group plan.

- ✔ **Life insurance if others are dependent on your income.** If you're single or your loved ones can live without your income, skip life insurance. If you need coverage, buy term insurance that, like your auto and home insurance, is pure insurance protection. The amount of term insurance you need to buy largely depends on how much of your income you want to replace.

- ✔ **Estate planning.** At a minimum, most people need a simple will delineating to whom they would like to leave all their worldly possessions. If you hold significant assets outside retirement plans, you may also benefit from establishing a trust, which can keep your money from having to go through probate and saves you the associated fees. Living wills and medical powers of attorney are useful to have in case you're ever in a medically incapacitated situation. If you have substantial assets, doing more involved estate planning is wise to minimize taxes and ensure the orderly passing of your assets to your heirs.

In our experience, many people lack particular types of insurance while others possess unnecessary policies. Many people also keep very low deductibles. Remember to insure against potential losses that would be financially catastrophic for you — don't waste your money to protect against smaller losses. (See the latest edition of our book *Personal Finance For Canadians For Dummies* to discover the right and wrong ways to buy insurance, what to look for in policies, and where to get good policies.)

Treading Carefully When Investing for University

If you're like many folks, in addition to paying down your mortgage and keeping up RRSP contributions to save for your retirement, you're likely also trying to put some money away to pay for your children's post-secondary education.

One of the best approaches is often to simply pay attention to your first two goals and ignore the third. If you work hard and knock down your mortgage in size, there's a good chance that you'll be able to reduce or even eliminate your mortgage payments by the time the little ones are ready to go to university. If you've knocked a good deal off of your mortgage, you'll also be in the position to borrow against the equity you've built up in your home to pay for educational expenses.

By working hard to grow your RRSP, hopefully you'll accumulate a good-sized sum that has built up some compounding steam. If you're accustomed to "paying yourself first" — regularly diverting a portion of your income to your RRSP — you can turn your financial sights away from your old age and toward your children's educational bills while they're at school, and after they graduate, resume your RRSP contributions.

For some, education is so important that they don't feel comfortable unless they're putting away some dollars specifically earmarked for that purpose. Others may be in the enviable position of being able to set aside savings for future educational costs while also taking care of their mortgage and building up their RRSP. If you want to start an education savings program, you have two basic ways to do it, each with some distinct benefits and drawbacks you need to consider. The approach that works best for you will be determined by your family circumstances, your outlook, and your sense of where your children are heading.

Registered Education Savings Plans

You can contribute up to $4,000 a year into a *Registered Education Savings Plan (RESP)* for each of your children, with a lifetime maximum contribution ceiling of $42,000. RESPs differ from RRSPs in that if you put less than the maximum $4000 allowed into the plan in any one year, you can't carry that amount forward and use it in a future year. In other words, there is no catching up allowed.

Although you don't get a tax deduction for your contributions, you are not taxed on any gains inside the plan. Like an RRSP, the money is treated as income and taxed accordingly only when it's withdrawn. However, as long as it's used to pay for your child's education, the proceeds of the contributions are treated as if they are your child's income. In most cases, because your child will have little or no other income, the funds will be able to come out of the RESP tax-free.

One reason why RESPs are often a good choice is that the government now tops up contributions. Under the Canada Education Savings Grant (CESG), the federal government will put in another 20 percent of any contribution you make, to a maximum of $400 a year. If you put in $2,000 for a child, for example, the government automatically gives you an instant and tax-free return of $400 on your contribution.

If you don't make the most use of the CESG in any one year by contributing $2,000, don't worry. As noted above, you can't save up any unused allowable contribution if you don't put in the maximum of $4,000 a year. However, you don't lose the $400 annual grant you're eligible for. If you put in any less than the $2,000 that earns you the maximum grant, you can earn the untapped grant in future years. However, in any one single year, you're still limited to a maximum contribution of $4,000, so the most CESG you'll get in any one year is also capped, maxing out at $800.

Suppose this year you put $1,000 into an RESP. You could have put in up to $4,000, but once the year is over, the opportunity to make that extra allowable contribution of $3,000 is gone forever. As for the CESG, the $1,000 would earn your RESP a grant of $200. Given that the maximum grant each year is $400, you have a grant of $200 you can carry forward. In the next year, suppose you contribute $3,000. The first $2,000 earns you the regular annual maximum grant of $400. The other $1,000 also earns you a 20 percent grant — the $200 grant you had carried forward from the annual $400 potential grant.

RESPs also offer you a wide choice of investments. You can choose from the same shopping list that's available for purchase within an RRSP — including the many types of mutual funds and even individual stocks. (Be sure to opt for a self-directed plan, not one of the group plans that have higher fees and more restrictions.)

If your child does not pursue a further education that allows him or her to use the money inside the plan, you can take out the original contributions without any penalty. However, you'll have to return any grants you've received under the CESG. In addition, the money you've made on any grants as well as on your own contributions will be taxable. You can transfer up to $50,000 of profits to your own or your spouse's RRSP, as long as you have sufficient unused contribution room available. Any of the plan's profits that don't get sheltered in this way are taxed at your full marginal tax rate. In addition, you pay an extra 20 percent penalty. On top of your tax bill, that could mean giving up as much as 65 percent of the profits. Ouch!

Allocating university investments

If you keep up to 80 percent of your investment money in stocks (diversified worldwide) with the remainder in bonds when your child is young, you can maximize the money's growth potential without taking extraordinary risk. As your child makes his or her way through the later years of elementary school, you need to begin to make the mix more conservative — scale back the stock percentage to 50 or 60 percent. Finally, in the years just before your child enters university, you need to whittle the stock portion down to no more than 20 percent or so.

Diversified mutual funds (which invest in stocks in Canada and internationally) and bonds are an ideal vehicle to use when you invest for university. Be sure to choose funds that fit your tax situation if you invest in plans that don't have tax-deferred status. (See Chapter 8 for more information.)

INVESTIGATE

How to pay for university or college

If you keep stashing away money in an RRSP, it's reasonable for you to wonder how you'll actually pay for education expenses when the momentous occasion arises. In most cases, even if you have some liquid assets that can be directed to your child's university or college bill, you will, in all likelihood, need to borrow some money. Only the affluent can truly afford to pay for university or college with cash.

One good source of money is your home's equity. You can borrow against your home at a relatively low interest rate. Another place to look is the Canada Student Loans Program, which the federal government runs in conjunction with the various provinces. (Quebec and the Northwest Territories run their programs independently from Ottawa.) To apply, contact your provincial ministry of education. You can find out more online at www.canlearn.ca. While your child is at school the federal government pays the interest, but your child will have to start repaying the loan six months after he or she graduates.

In addition to loans, a number of grant programs are available through schools and the government, as well as through independent sources. A good starting point is your child's guidance counselling office. Most schools have lists of local government and private bursaries, grants and awards, and scholarships. You should also consider your family's various employers. A surprising number of companies have student

grants available for their employees, or children of employees. Contact the university or college your child is considering to see what other sources of funding are available. You can find easy links to their financial resources page by visiting www.canadian-universities. net/index.html and clicking on Financial Aid & Scholarships. You can then choose a province, and you'll get a page listing links to the financial aid page of each school.

Also, contact the Canada Millennium Scholarships Foundation. The federal government plans to distribute 100,000 scholarships to low- and middle-income students. The scholarships will average $3,000 a year, and may be awarded for four years. You can find out more at www.millenniumscholarships.ca.

Other lists of funding sources can be found online. Visit the sites of the universities or colleges your child is considering attending. You can find links to all the provincial and territorial student assistance offices at www.hrsdc. gc.ca. Another good source for grants and scholarships can be found at http://student awards.com/english/canlearn.

Your child can work and save money for university during high school. Besides giving your gangly teen a stake in his or her own future, this training encourages sound personal financial management down the road.

Part II
Stocks, Bonds, and Bay Street

In this part . . .

Stocks, bonds, and mutual funds are the core financial market instruments that investors play with these days. But what the heck *are* these devices, and how can you invest in them, make some decent money, and not lose your shirt? Here, you find out how and where to evaluate and buy these securities and how to comprehend the mind-numbing jargon the money pros use.

Chapter 4

Looking at How Stock and Bond Markets Work

. . . .

In This Chapter

▶ Going from a private to public company

▶ Looking at the workings of the stock and bond markets and the economy

▶ Deciphering interest rates, inflation, the Bank of Canada, and the Federal Reserve

. . . .

*L*iz, who had always wanted to run her own business, made necklaces and pins as a hobby. Her friends complimented her on the jewellery, so she began making some for them. Eventually, she started selling it to some local retail stores.

Put yourself in Liz's place. Suppose that a large retail department store chain like Sears was interested in buying thousands of your necklaces and pins and you had to contract for big-time manufacturing help. Newspapers and magazines begin featuring your work, and lots of retailers are lining up for your creations.

The money starts to roll in, and now you're in the big time. At some point, you may want to raise more money (known as *capital* in the financial world) to expand and afford your growing company's needs, such as hiring more employees, buying computer systems, and purchasing manufacturing equipment.

How Companies Raise Money Through the Financial Markets

Companies can choose between two major money-raising options when they go into the financial markets: issuing stocks or issuing bonds. A world of difference exists between these two major securities, from the perspective of the investor as well as from the issuing company, as the following explanations illustrate:

✔ Bonds are loans that a company must pay back. Rather than borrowing money from a bank, many companies elect to sell *bonds,* which are IOUs to investors. The primary disadvantage, from a company's perspective, is that the company must pay this money back with interest. On the other hand, the business doesn't have to relinquish ownership when it borrows money. Companies are also more likely to issue bonds if the stock market is depressed, meaning that companies can't fetch as much for their stock.

✔ Stocks are shares of ownership in a company. Some companies choose to issue stock to raise money. Unlike bonds, the money that the company raises through a stock issue isn't paid back, because it's not a loan. When the public (people like you and your sister-in-law) buys stock, outside investors continue to hold and trade it. (Although companies may occasionally choose to buy their own stock back, usually because they think it's a good investment, they are under no obligation to do so. If a company does a stock buyback, the price that the company pays is simply the price that the stock currently trades for.)

✔ Even though a company relinquishes some of its ownership when it issues stock, doing so allows its founders and owners to sell some of their relatively illiquid private stock and reap the rewards of their successful company. Many growing companies also favour stock issues because they don't want the cash drain that comes from paying loans (bonds) back.

✔ Although many company owners like to take their companies public to cash in on their stake of the company, not all owners want to go public, and not all who do go public are happy that they did. The numerous drawbacks of establishing your company as public include the burdensome financial reporting requirements, such as quarterly earnings statements and annual reports. These documents not only take lots of time and money to produce, but can also reveal competitive secrets. Some companies also harm their long-term planning ability because of the pressure and focus on short-term corporate performance that comes with being a public company.

Deciding whether to issue stocks or bonds

Companies that meet the requirements to sell stock on one of the exchanges try to do what's in their best interests. If the stock market is booming and new stock can sell at a premium price, companies opt to sell more stock. On the other hand, if investors don't believe that a company has good growth prospects and interest rates are relatively low, the company may lean toward selling bonds instead. Ultimately, companies seek to raise capital the lowest-cost way they can, so they'll elect to sell stocks or bonds based on what the finance folks tell them is the cheaper option.

From your perspective as a potential investor, you can usually make more money in stocks than bonds, but stocks are generally more volatile in the short term. (See Chapter 2 for more on stocks.)

Understanding IPOs

Suppose that Liz's Distinctive Jewellery wants to issue stock for the first time, which is called an *initial public offering (IPO)*. If Liz decides to go public, she works with *investment bankers* who, like real estate agents trying to sell homes, help companies decide when and at what price to sell stock. (Most investment bankers don't like being compared to real estate agents, but the successful ones in both professions make big bucks earning a percentage of every deal that they perform. Both investment bankers and real estate agents must determine their merchandise's asking price. Both sets of professionals also like to impress others by driving expensive cars and dressing slickly.)

Suppose further that the investment bankers believe that Liz's Distinctive Jewellery can raise $20 million issuing stock. When a company issues stock, the price per share that the stock is sold for is somewhat arbitrary. The amount that a prospective investor will pay for a particular portion of the company's stock should depend on the company's profits and future growth prospects. Companies that produce higher levels of profits and grow faster can generally command a higher sales price for a given portion of the company.

Consider the following ways that investment bankers can structure the IPO for Liz's Distinctive Jewellery:

Price of Stock	Number of Shares Issued
$5	4 million
$10	2 million
$20	1 million

In fact, Liz's Distinctive Jewellery can raise $20 million in an infinite number of ways, thanks to varying stock prices. If the company wants to issue the stock at a higher price, the company sells fewer shares.

A stock's price per share by itself is meaningless in evaluating whether to buy a stock. Ultimately, the amount that investors will pay for a company's outstanding stock should depend greatly on the company's financial condition. If Liz's Distinctive Jewellery produces annual earnings (profits) of $3 million and companies comparable to Liz's include stock outstanding that sells at ten times earnings, Liz's stock in the market is worth about $30 million.

$$\frac{\text{The value of a company's stock}}{\text{relative to (divided by) its earnings}} = \text{its } \textit{price-earnings ratio}$$

Here are the numbers for Liz's Distinctive Jewellery:

$$\frac{\$30 \text{ million}}{\$3 \text{ million}} = 10$$

In Chapter 5 we talk more about price earnings ratios and the factors that influence stock prices.

Understanding Financial Markets and Economics

We've made it to the moon, created powerful computer chips smaller than your fingernail, and cranked out $100 high-tops with air-inflatable insoles that allow slouching teenagers and wannabe athletes to aspire to the heights of their favourite NBA stars. But those advisers and money-savvy friends who are honest with you will admit that they still can't predict how the financial markets and the economy will perform in the years ahead.

Tens of thousands of books, millions of articles, and enough Ph.D. dissertations to supply a major landfill explore these topics. You can spend the rest of your life reading all this stuff and you still won't get through it. In this section, we explain what you need to know about the factors that make the financial markets and economy work so that you can make informed investing decisions.

Capitalism: The root of it all

In Canada, we live in a capitalistic (also known as free market) society. Have you ever stopped to think what that term means? Capitalism means that you have a tremendous (although not unlimited) amount of economic freedom.

If you want to start your own business, you can. However, that's not to say that you don't have to deal with obstacles, such as affording the start-up stages of your business and dealing with regulatory red tape. Most entrepreneurs will tell you that one of their greatest business frustrations is dealing with all the various government agencies. In addition to the long lists of licences that you need to obtain for certain businesses, you may have to deal with zoning and planning offices regarding the use of the location of your business. You may also have to work with other provincial and local agencies if you decide to incorporate, and with still more government folks to comply with the myriad tax laws of the land.

Whine, whine, whine. If you want to see really red tape and a lack of economic opportunity and mobility, go to a socialist country. Socialism, in contrast to capitalism, is an economic system that its nineteenth-century promoters, Karl Marx and Friedrich Engels, best sum up: "Abolish all private property."

What's good and not so good about capitalism

Both of us come from families that pulled themselves up by their own bootstraps. Our parents didn't enter the job market with university educations, yet they were able to own decent homes and retire comfortably in their 60s after many years of hard work, which included raising numerous children who went to college and university. And we all turned out all right, we think.

We are also both entrepreneurs. We feel fortunate because if we were living in a country like Cuba, we wouldn't be able to do the things that we like and have the enjoyment that our work and living in a free society brings us. That's the good side of capitalism — people who have some smarts and who roll up their sleeves and work hard can carve out a standard of living that many people around the world long for.

But, like any system, capitalism includes its warts. First, the free markets can be ruthless. People who lack particular skills (in some cases, through no fault of their own, but because of their lack of access to opportunities while growing up) get left behind or worse. Famous economist John Keynes, who is noted for clearly seeing some of the flaws of free markets, among other things, said, "The outstanding faults of the economic society in which we live are its failure to provide full employment and its arbitrary and inequitable distribution of wealth."

Another problem with capitalism is that, left to their own devices, some companies and their executives seek to maximize profits and ignore other important matters, such as ethics and the negative impact that their business practices may have on customers, the environment, and so on. In describing some of the less-savoury businessmen of his time, Abraham Lincoln said in 1837, "These capitalists generally act harmoniously and in concert to fleece the people."

Some companies do bad things in the pursuit of profits. Some opponents of any type of government regulation seem to forget about such companies. Some companies sell products that have been proven to harm users and other innocent bystanders. Tobacco, alcohol, and gun manufacturers come to mind. Even Malcolm Forbes, founder of one of the world's most pro-business, anti-big government magazines, said, "I'd say capitalism's worst excess is in the large number of crooks and tinhorns who get too much of the action."

But just because a company or person makes a great amount of money compared with others doesn't mean that they do less good than those who don't make as much money. We disagree with people such as Ayn Rand, author of *The Fountainhead*, who said, "Capitalism and altruism are incompatible; they are philosophical opposites; they cannot coexist in the same man or in the same society." Baloney. Our favourite examples of successful capitalists are those who succeed in business *and* accomplish a lot of good: You meet some of these people later in this book. We only wish there were more of them!

Vladimir Lenin transformed the socialist theory of Marx and Engels into a political system known as communism. In communism, the government largely controls and owns the organizations that provide what people need. Over time, various countries in Europe, the former Soviet Union (Russia), and China have tried to make communism work. However, as is old news by now, increasing parts of the world continue to become more capitalistic. (Please note that just as the labels Conservative and Liberal are somewhat meaningless, increasingly so too is the practice of labelling particular countries' economies as capitalistic or socialistic.) The low standard of living in communist countries, long waits in lines to purchase goods, and poor health care all contributed to the downfall of communist systems.

Profits drive stock prices

The goal of most companies is to make money, or *profits.* Profits result from the difference between what a company takes in, *revenue,* and what it expends, *costs.* We say *most* companies, because many organizations' primary purpose is not to maximize profits. Non-profit organizations, such as colleges and universities, are a good example. But even non-profits can't thrive and prosper without a steady flow of the green stuff.

Companies that trade publicly on the stock exchanges are supposed to maximize their profit — that's what their shareholders want. Higher profits generally make stock prices rise. Most private companies seek to maximize their profits as well, but they contain much more latitude to pursue other goals.

So what's the secret to maximizing profits? The key is to produce products and services for which the demand (ideally) greatly exceeds the supply. If you made the mistake of majoring in business or economics like we did, one of the few useful things that you learned about are supply and demand curves. These important conceptual devices explain why products are priced the way they are and why particular companies earn the profits they do.

The following are the major ways that successful companies increase profits:

✔ **Build a better mousetrap.** Some companies develop or promote an invention or innovation that better meets customer needs. Consider the personal computer. In the old days, if you wanted to write a business letter or report, you did it on a typewriter. Editing was a wearisome, time-consuming process. If you made a mistake, you started the page over or used white correction fluid. Personal computers revolutionized the way that people write and edit their work.

(Of course, computers aren't better in all ways — you can possibly lose an entire document because of a major computer glitch. Your home has to burn to the ground or your dog has to go on a paper-eating rampage for that to happen with your typed papers!)

✔ **Open new markets to your products.** Many successful Canadian companies, for example, have been stampeding into foreign countries to sell their products. Although some product adaptation is usually required to sell overseas, selling an already proven and developed product or service to new markets generally increases a company's chances for success.

✔ **Be in related businesses.** Being in a related business is what caused the Antitrust Division of the U.S. Justice Department to challenge Microsoft's business strategies. Microsoft develops the different Windows operating systems on which most personal computers run software. All the computer software, such as word-processing software, must run on and be compatible with the operating systems. Guess what — Microsoft is also in the business of developing and selling "compatible" software.

✔ **Build a brand name.** Coca-Cola, for example, and many types of well-known beers rate comparably in blind taste tests to many generic colas and beers that are far cheaper. Yet, consumers (perhaps you) fork over more of their hard-earned loot because of the name and packaging. Companies build brand names largely through advertising and other promotions. (...*For Dummies* is a brand name, but ...*For Dummies* books cost about the same as comparable size and quality books!)

✔ **Manage costs.** Smart companies control costs. Lowering the cost of manufacturing their products or of providing their services allows companies to offer their products and services more cheaply. Managing costs may help fatten the bottom line (profit). Sometimes, though, companies try to cut too many corners, and their cost-cutting ways come back to haunt them in the form of dissatisfied customers — or even lawsuits based on a faulty or dangerous product.

✔ **Watch the competition.** Successful companies don't follow the herd, but they do keep an eye on what their competition is up to. If lots of competitors target one part of the market, some companies target a less-pursued segment that, if they can capture it, may produce higher profits thanks to reduced competition.

Are markets efficient?

Companies generally seek to maximize profits and maintain a healthy financial condition. Ultimately, the financial markets judge the worth of a company's stock or bond. Trying to predict in advance what happens to the stock and bond markets and individual securities consumes many a market prognosticator.

In the late 1960s, somewhat to the chagrin of market soothsayers, academic scholars developed a theory called the *efficient market hypothesis.* This theory basically maintains the following logic: Lots of investors collect and analyze all sorts of information about companies and their securities. If investors think that a security, such as a stock, is overpriced, they sell it or don't buy it. Conversely, if the investors believe that a security is under-priced, they buy it or hold what they already own. Because of the competition among all these investors, the price that a security trades at generally reflects what many (supposedly informed) people think it's worth.

Therefore, the efficient market theory implies that trading in and out of securities and the overall market in an attempt to obtain the right stocks at the right time is a futile endeavour. Buying or selling a security because of "new" news is also fruitless because the current market value of a stock reflects the news. As Burton Malkiel so eloquently said in his classic book, *A Random Walk Down Wall Street,* this theory "taken to its logical extreme . . . means that a blindfolded monkey throwing darts at a newspaper's financial pages could select a portfolio that would do just as well as one carefully selected by the experts." Malkiel added that "financial analysts in pin-striped suits don't like being compared with bare-assed apes."

Some money managers have beaten the markets. In fact, beating the market over a year or three years isn't difficult, but few can beat the market over a decade or more. Efficient market supporters argue that some of those who beat the markets, even over a ten-year period, do so because of luck. Consider that if you flip a coin five times, on some occasions you get five consecutive heads. This coincidence actually happens, on average, once every 32 times you do five coin-flip sequences because of random luck, not skill. Consistently identifying in advance which sequence gives you five consecutive heads is not possible.

Strict believers in the efficient market hypothesis say that it's equally impossible to identify the best money managers in advance. Some money managers, such as those who manage mutual funds, possess publicly available track records. Inspecting those track records and doing other common-sense things, such as investing in funds that minimize your expenses, improve your odds of performing a bit better than the market.

Various investment markets differ in how efficient they are. Efficiency means that the current price of an investment accurately reflects its true value. Although the stock market is reasonably efficient, many consider the bond market even more efficient. The real estate market is less efficient because properties are unique and sometimes less competition and access to information exist. If you can locate a seller who really needs to sell, you may be able to buy property at a discount from what it's really worth. Small business is also less efficient. Entrepreneurs with innovative ideas and approaches can sometimes earn enormous returns.

One key to building wealth is to focus your time and investment strategies in a way that reflects the realities of the investment marketplaces that you invest in. If you desire to earn superior returns, you're better off trying to invest on your own in less-efficient markets like real estate and small business. On the other hand, trying to beat the market averages and the best professionals at picking stocks and bonds is a largely unproductive but entertaining and addictive endeavour for some people.

Market overreactions can create buying opportunities. Efficiency notwithstanding, the financial markets that reflect the collective forces of millions of buyers and sellers can sometimes go to extremes. In the mid-1970s, pessimism ran rampant. President Richard Nixon resigned in disgrace, inflation and unemployment spiralled upward, and the stock market fell out of bed. However, smart investors took advantage in this time period. Throughout this book, we show you how to evaluate different investment markets to identify if they've gone to extremes.

Moving the market: Interest rates, inflation, the Bank of Canada, and the U.S. Federal Reserve

For decades, economists, investment managers, and other (often self-anointed) gurus have attempted to understand the course of interest rates, inflation, and the monetary policies set forth by the U.S. Federal Reserve and, to a lesser degree, the Bank of Canada. Millions of investors follow these economic factors. Why? Because the interest rates, inflation rates, and monetary policies set out by the Fed and the Bank of Canada seem to move the financial markets and the economy.

High interest rates are generally bad

Many businesses borrow money to expand. People like you, who are affectionately referred to as consumers, also borrow money to buy things such as homes, cars, and educations.

Interest rate increases tend to slow the economy. Businesses scale back on expansion plans, and some debt-laden businesses can't afford high interest rates and go under. Most individuals possess limited budgets as well and have to scale back some purchases because of higher interest rates. For example, higher interest rates translate into higher mortgage payments for homebuyers.

If high interest rates choke business expansion and consumer spending, economic growth slows, or the economy shrinks in size, and the economy possibly ends up in a *recession.* The government-sanctioned definition of a recession is two consecutive quarters (six months) of declining total economic output.

The stock market usually develops a case of the queasies as corporate profits shrink. High interest rates usually depress many investors' appetites for stocks, as the yields increase on guaranteed investment certificates (GICs), Treasury bills, and other bonds.

Higher interest rates actually make some people happy. If you locked in a fixed-rate mortgage on your home or on a business loan, your loan looks much better than if you had a variable-rate mortgage. Some retirees and others who live off the interest income on their investments are happy with interest rate increases as well. Consider back in the early 1980s, for example, when a retiree received $10,000 per year in interest for each $100,000 that he or she invested in GICs that paid 10 percent.

Fast-forward to the late 1990s: A retiree purchasing the same GICs saw her income slashed by about 50 percent, because rates on the GICs then were just 5 percent. So for every $100,000 invested, only $5,000 in interest income was paid. By 2004, GIC rates had sagged even further, with even the better short-term GICs paying a mere 2 percent. So, for every $100,000 invested, only $2,000 interest income was earned.

If you try to live off the income that your investments produce, a 50 to 70 percent drop in that income is likely to cramp your lifestyle. So higher interest rates are better if you're living off your investment income, right? Not necessarily.

Discovering the inflation and interest-rate connection

Consider what happened to interest rates in the late 1970s and early 1980s. After Canada and the United States successfully emerged from a terrible recession in the mid-1970s, their economies seemed to be on the right track. But within just a few years, they were in turmoil again. The annual increase in the cost of living (known as the rate of inflation) burst through 10 percent on its way to 14 percent. The explosion in oil prices, which more than doubled in less than five years, was largely responsible for this increase. Interest rates, which are what bondholders receive when they lend their money to corporations and governments, followed inflation skyward.

Inflation and interest rates usually move in tandem. If you knew that, because of the ravages of inflation, your salary dollars for the next year would buy much less than they do in the present, wouldn't you too demand more interest? This is why interest rates soared along with inflation in the late 1970s and early 1980s, peaking at over 20 percent in 1981.

The primary driver of interest rates is the rate of inflation. Interest rates were much higher in the 1980s because Canada and the United States had double-digit inflation. If the cost of living increases at the rate of 10 percent per year, why would you, as an investor, lend your money (which is what you do when you purchase a bond or GIC) at 5 percent? Interest rates were so much higher in the early 1980s because you would never do such a thing.

In recent years, interest rates have been low because inflation has declined significantly since the early 1980s. Therefore, the rate of interest that investors could earn lending their money dropped accordingly. Although low interest rates reduce the interest income that comes in, the corresponding low rate of inflation doesn't devour the purchasing power of your principal balance. That's why lower interest rates aren't necessarily worse and higher interest rates aren't necessarily better as you try to live off your investment income.

So what's an investor to do, who's living off the income he receives from his investments but doesn't receive enough because of low interest rates? Some retirees have woken up to the risk of keeping all or too much of their money in short-term GIC and bond investments. Please review the sections in Chapter 3 dealing with asset allocation and investment mix. A simple but psychologically difficult solution is to use up some of your principal to supplement your interest and dividend income. Using up your principal to supplement your income is what effectively happens anyway when inflation is higher — the purchasing power of your principal erodes more quickly. You may also not have saved enough money to meet your desired standard of living — that's why you may want to run a retirement analysis (see Chapter 3).

The role of the Bank of Canada

What exactly is the "Bank of Canada," and what does it do? The Bank of Canada tries to influence *monetary policy*. Yes, we know that's jargon, but that's the term that you often hear thrown around. All this jargon means is that the Bank of Canada tries to affect the amount of money or currency in circulation, known as the *money supply*, and the level of interest rates.

Interest rates 101

Money is no different from lettuce, computers, or sneakers. All these products and goods cost you dollars to buy them. The cost of money is the interest rate that you must pay to borrow it. And the cost or interest rate of money is determined by many factors that ultimately influence the supply of and demand for money.

The Bank of Canada, from time to time and in different ways, attempts to influence the supply and demand for money and the cost of money: interest rates. The Bank raises or lowers the interest rates that they charge banks to borrow money in an attempt to influence the supply and demand for money. The Bank of Canada also buys or sells government bonds from time to time.

The senior officials at the Bank of Canada readily admit that the economy is quite complex and affected by many things, so it's difficult to predict where the economy is heading. If forecasting and influencing markets are so difficult, then why does the Bank of Canada exist? These officials believe that they can have a positive influence in creating a healthy overall economic environment; one in which inflation is low and growth proceeds at a modest pace. If the economy expands too rapidly, inflation can escalate. On the other hand, Bank of Canada officials believe that if the supply of money is too restricted and interest rates are too high, businesses won't be able to borrow and expand, and the economy will stagnate or, worse, actually shrink. So the Bank tries to keep everything just right!

If the Bank of Canada believes that prices are rising too strongly, it will boost the bank rate. In turn, consumers will likely face higher costs for mortgages, car loans, and so forth. As a result, they tend to spend less and save more. This reduces the demand for goods and services, and because people are saving more, decreases the amount of money in circulation. This leads to less demand, which cools off the economy and keeps a lid on price increases.

By contrast, if the Bank of Canada believes the economy is slowing too much, it can help boost spending by lowering the bank rate. This makes it cheaper for consumers to borrow for purchases, which increases demand. Companies hire more people to produce more goods and services, and also find it cheaper to borrow money to expand their operations, and the economy heats up.

The Bank of Canada has a stated goal of keeping the rate of inflation between 1 and 3 percent. Inflation is measured by a regular measurement of the change in the cost of a range of items. The resulting number is the *consumer price index*, or *CPI*.

The main tool the Bank of Canada uses to keep a lid on prices is the *bank rate*. This is the rate of interest it charges financial institutions on short-term loans. When the bank rate is changed, the big banks and trust companies usually change the rate of interest they charge their best customers, known as the *prime rate*.

Exploring the role of the U.S. Federal Reserve

The Fed is the U.S. equivalent of our Bank of Canada, only it's much, much, *much* more powerful and influential — not just in the U.S., but around the world. When U.S. Federal Reserve Board chairman Alan Greenspan speaks, an extraordinary number of people listen. Most financial market watchers and the media want to know what the Federal Reserve has decided to do about *monetary policy.* The 12 presidents from the respective Federal Reserve district banks and the 7 Federal Reserve governors conduct their Federal Open Market Committee meetings behind closed doors eight times a year.

Over the years, the Fed has come under attack for various reasons. Yale economist Edward Tufte's controversial book, *Political Control of the Economy,* argued that the Federal Reserve would, with a nudge of encouragement from the President, goose the economy. The Fed gooses the economy by loosening up on the money supply, which leads to an economic growth spurt and a booming stock market, just in time to make the U.S. Prez look good right before an election. Conveniently, the consequences of inflation take longer to show up — not until after the election. In recent years, others have questioned the Fed's ability to largely do what they want without accountability.

The Greenspan obsession

In the latter half of the 1990s the U.S. stock market continued to soar, and more and more investors jumped into the market. Unfortunately, encouraged in large part by hyped media coverage implying that Fed actions determine economic growth and future stock prices, some investors believed that they should move their money in and out of the market at particular times based on actions and statements that Federal Reserve officials made.

Perhaps you've read headlines that speculate about and document the Federal Reserve's moves to influence interest rates, inflation, and the economy. The stock market cable television channels are especially guilty of following every utterance that comes from Fed Chairman Alan Greenspan's mouth and trying to link the stock market's subsequent performance to what Greenspan said or didn't say.

If you've ever heard Fed officials speak, you know that they're always coy about tipping their hats, and they rarely give specifics, even when they testify before Congress. Alan Greenspan is widely considered a master of such verbal obfuscation. Most people can't understand half the (often run-on) sentences that this man speaks!

Here's a classic example of something that Greenspan said in a speech and that the media blew out of proportion (if you manage to get through it, we're sure you'll be grateful that Mr. Greenspan hasn't been retained to write *Fed Policy Explained For Dummies*!):

> Clearly, sustained low inflation implies less uncertainty about the future, and lower risk premiums imply higher prices of stocks and other earning assets. We can see that in the inverse relationship exhibited by price/ earnings ratios and the rate of inflation in the past. But how do we know when irrational exuberance has unduly escalated asset values, which then become subject to unexpected and prolonged contractions as they have in Japan over the past decade? And, how do we factor that assessment into monetary policy? We as central bankers need not be concerned if a collapsing financial asset bubble does not threaten to impair the real economy, its production, jobs and price stability.

Many in the media quickly focused on the sound bite "irrational exuberance" and linked it to the stock market. The morning after Greenspan's speech, stock prices dropped sharply, and the same media attributed the drop to — you guessed it — his "irrational exuberance" comments. Turns out that investors who sold when Greenspan made this speech in early December 1996 at the American Enterprise Institute for Public Policy kick themselves because stock prices subsequently soared.

Many, many factors influence the course of stock prices. Never, ever make a trade or investment based on what someone at the Federal Reserve (or the Bank of Canada) says or what someone in the media or some market pundit reads into the comments. Put simply, no one body has that much power or influence over the future. You need to make your investment plans based on your needs and goals, not what some much-followed banker — or broker — does or doesn't do.

Chapter 5

Building Wealth with Stocks

*T*he stock market seems mysterious — it operates amid lots of jargon and supposed experts. When you want to buy stocks, you generally need a broker, and you may have heard about how you can seem like shark bait to these commission-hungry folks. Brokers, the firms that employ them, and financial advisers possess many conflicts of interest. Many of them want to make the market seem complicated so that would-be investors come to them for help. If you understand the market and realize that the crystal balls these "experts" peer into have more than a few cracks in them, you can find better ways to invest your money in the stock market that don't involve their services.

Some people liken investing in the stock market to gambling — a giant craps game. A real casino structures its games — slot machines, poker, roulette, and so on — so that in aggregate, the casino owners siphon off a healthy quantity (40 percent) of the money that people bring with them. The vast majority of casino patrons lose money; in some cases, all of it. The few who leave with more money than they came with are usually people who are lucky and are smart enough to quit while they're ahead.

We can understand why some individual investors, perhaps you, feel that the stock market resembles legalized gambling. So why bother with the stock market if it's so confusing and filled with people who are eager to separate you from your money? In Chapter 2 we discuss the potential risks and rewards of different investments. Shares of stock, which represent portions of ownership in companies, offer a way for people of both modest and wealthy means, and everybody in between, to invest in companies and build wealth.

Fortunately, the stock market isn't a casino — far from it. A casino is a zero-sum game where for every dollar you win or lose, that dollar comes from the casino. History shows that nearly all long-term investors can win in the stock market because it appreciates over the years. We say *nearly* because even some people who remain active in the market over many years manage to lose some money because of easily avoidable mistakes, which we can help to keep you from making in the future.

R. Foster Winans, a former writer for *Newsweek* and *The Wall Street Journal,* said "The only reason to invest in the market is because you think you know something others don't." Mr. Winans (who, incidentally, was later convicted of insider trading) was wrong. You don't need any inside information to profit from stock investments. You simply need to understand this basic concept: The increasing profits that expanding companies produce ultimately propel stock prices higher. The trajectory path isn't a straight line up, but more like the path that a small bird takes when it fights to gain altitude in a fierce head wind. Although the bird sometimes hits an air pocket or spot of bad weather and loses some altitude, its aerodynamics win out.

The same theory applies to corporate profits. Corporate profits also tend to trend up, but sometimes the economy hits a bad patch and profits fall. As with the bird, economies don't usually get completely decimated. Yes, it's possible that if a huge meteor smashes into Earth or a horrible, contagious virus spreads like wildfire, society may be done for — people and companies may cease to exist and make a profit. In the meantime, why not share in the expansion of the economy and keep an optimistic view of life?

Defining "The Market"

So you invest in stocks to share in the spoils of capitalistic economies. When you invest in stocks, you do so through the stock market. What is the stock market? Everybody talks about "The Market" the same way they do a close personal friend:

> "The Market is down 137 points today."

> "With The Market hitting new highs, isn't now a bad time to invest in The Market?"

> "The Market seems ready for a fall."

When people talk about The Market, they're usually referring to the U.S. stock market. Even more specifically, they're speaking about the Dow Jones Industrial Average, created by Charles Dow and Eddie Jones. Dow and Jones, two reporters in their 30s, started publishing a paper that you may have heard of —

The Wall Street Journal — in 1889. Like its modern-day version, the nineteenth-century *Wall Street Journal* reported current financial news. Dow and Jones also compiled stock prices of larger, important companies and created and calculated indexes to track the performance of the U.S. stock market.

The Dow Jones Industrial Average (DJIA) market index tracks the performance of 30 large companies that are headquartered in the United States. The Dow 30 includes companies such as airplane manufacturer Boeing, soda maker Coca-Cola, oil giant Exxon Mobil, automaker General Motors, technology behemoths IBM, Intel, and Microsoft, fast food king McDonald's, and retailers Home Depot and Wal-Mart.

The 30 stocks that make up the Dow aren't the 30 largest or the 30 best companies in America. They just so happen to be the 30 companies that senior staff members at *The Wall Street Journal* think reflect the diversity of the economy in the United States. Some criticize the Dow index for encompassing so few companies and for a lack of diversity. The 30 stocks in the Dow change over time as companies merge, decline, and rise in importance.

In Canada, of course, we have a "Market" all our own — namely the Toronto Stock Exchange, where our largest and most well-known companies trade. When people talk about how "Toronto" performed, they're almost always referring to the S&P/TSE composite index. The index used to be called the TSE 300, but the 300-company requirement was dropped in 2002 when the indices were all revamped and Standard & Poor's became involved in administering the index. The number of companies included can now vary depending on how many meet the requirements. Recently, the number has been running in the low 200s.

Like the Dow Jones Industrial Average, the S&P/TSE composite tracks the performance of larger-company Canadian stocks. In general, the index is made up of the companies with the largest market capitalization — their stock price multiplied by the number of shares outstanding. Companies that are included in the index must meet a number of other criteria. The most important is liquidity. The number of shares traded, the number of transactions, and the total value are all looked at in deciding which companies make the index. There are also 14 sub-indexes of the TSE 300. These are used to assess the performance of many different industries. The subgroups are consumer discretionary, consumer staples, diversified metals and mining, energy, financials, gold, health care, industrial, information technology, materials, real estate, telecommunication services, utilities, and income trust.

Looking at major stock market indices

Just as Manhattan and Toronto (thankfully) aren't the only cities to visit or live in, the stocks in the Dow Jones Industrial Average and the TSE Composite are far from representative of all the different types of stocks that you can invest in. Here are some other important market indexes and the types of stocks that they track:

- **Standard & Poor's 500.** Like the Dow Jones Industrial Average, the S&P 500 tracks the performance of larger-company U.S. stocks. As the name suggests, this index tracks the prices of 500 stocks. These 500 big companies account for nearly 80 percent of the total market value of the tens of thousands of stocks traded in the United States. Thus, the S&P 500 is a much broader and more representative index of the larger company stocks in the United States than is the Dow Jones Industrial Average.

  Unlike the Dow index, which is largely calculated by adding the current share price of each of its component stocks, the S&P 500 index is calculated by adding the total market value (capitalization) of its component stocks. To impress your friends and colleagues, you can discuss with them the S&P 500's status as a capitalization weighted index.

- **S&P/TSE 60.** This index was introduced in 2000 to replace the TSE 35 and TSE 100 indexes. It was developed by the TSE in conjunction with Standard & Poor's Corp. of New York. To be considered for the index, a company must be part of the TSE 300 index, but those with poor liquidity or small market capitalization don't make the grade. An index committee then chooses 60 companies that offer a representation of the major industries. There's also a capped version of this index, which limits the weighting of any one stock to a maximum of 10 percent of the total market capitalization of all the stocks in the index. This was done to prevent situations where one company whose stock has soared (as Nortel's did in the late 1990s) dominates the index and gives an unbalanced reading of the market's overall performance.

- **S&P/TSX Venture Composite Index.** This index is a broad measure of the performance of the TSX Venture Exchange, home to Canada's smaller and often much more speculative companies. The index has a somewhat confusing past. When the Vancouver Stock Exchange and the Alberta Stock Exchange merged, the two exchanges were replaced by the new Canadian Venture Exchange, or *CDNX*, and a new index — the Canadian Venture Exchange Index — was created. But that index was short-lived, and was replaced by the new S&P/TSX Venture Composite Index in 2001. Unlike the new TSE Composite Index, this new index wasn't a continuation of the old Canadian Venture Exchange index but rather an entirely new index based on different rules and requirements. The Canadian Venture Exchange index was simply closed down, and the new index began on a different — and completely unconnected — level than its predecessor. The new index looks only at market capitalization when determining eligibility, and the number of companies it includes is typically in the low 500 range.

- ✔ **Russell 2000.** This index tracks the performance of 2,000 smaller U.S. company stocks of varying industries. While over the longer term small company stocks tend to move in tandem with larger company stocks, it's not unusual for one to rise or fall more than the other or for one index to fall while the other rises in a given year. For example, in 2001, the Russell 2000 actually rose 2.5 percent while the S&P 500 fell 11.9 percent. As we discuss in Chapter 2, be aware that smaller company stocks tend to be more volatile.

- ✔ **Wilshire 5000.** Despite its name, the Wilshire 5000 index actually tracks the prices of more than 6,500 stocks of U.S. companies of all sizes — small, medium, and large. Thus, many consider this index the broadest and most representative of the overall U.S. stock market.

- ✔ **Morgan Stanley EAFE.** Stocks don't exist only in Canada and the United States. Morgan Stanley's EAFE index (EAFE stands for Europe, Australasia, and Far East) tracks the prices of stocks in the other major developed countries of the world.

- ✔ **Morgan Stanley Emerging Markets.** This index follows the price movements of stocks in the less economically developed but "emerging" countries, which usually concentrate in Southeast Asia and Latin America. These stock markets tend to be more volatile than those in established economies. During good economic times emerging markets usually reward investors with higher returns, but stocks can plunge farther and faster than stocks in developed markets.

Conspicuously absent from this list of major stock market indexes is the NASDAQ index. With the boom in technology stock prices in the late 1990s, CNBC and other financial media started broadcasting movements in the technology-laden NASDAQ index, thereby increasing investor interest and the frenzy surrounding technology stocks. (See the section later in this chapter entitled "The Internet and technology bubble.") We're not fans of sector (industry) specific investing; it undermines diversification and places the everyday investor — you — in the role of a professional money manager in having to determine when and how much to invest in specific industry groups. We suggest treating the NASDAQ as an industry-concentrated index.

Recognizing bull and bear markets

If you read magazines or newspapers or listen to people talk about the stock market, you'll often hear references to bull markets and bear markets. You may know which term means a good market and which term means a bad market for investors, but even if you do, you may wonder where these silly terms came from.

It's hard to find agreement on their origin, but our favourite description comes from Robert Claiborne's *Loose Cannons and Red Herrings — A Book of Lost Metaphors*. The term *bear*, according to Claiborne, originates from a proverb that mocks a man who "sells the bearskin before catching the bear." This is the connection to the stock market: When dealers in the stock market thought it had become too pricey and speculative, they sold stock that they hadn't yet "caught" (bought). These dealers were labelled "bearskin jobbers" and, later, "bears."

The practice that these bearish dealers engaged in is short selling. They hoped that when they ultimately bought the stock that they had already sold, they could buy it back at a lower price. Their profit thus was the difference between the price they originally sold it for and what they later bought it for. Short selling is simply investing in reverse: You sell first and buy back later. The worst situation for a bear is if prices go up and he or she must buy back the stock at a high price. As Claiborne said, "He who sells what isn't his'n, must buy it back or go to prison."

The bulls, according to Claiborne, are those who work the "other side" of the street. Bulls buy stocks with the hope and expectation that they will rise in value. Ben Travato, a man whom Claiborne describes as one prone to inventing colourful but often inaccurate etymologies, said that bulls toss stocks up in the air with their horns.

Counting reasons to use indices

Indices (or the ungrammatical but sometimes easier to say *indexes*) serve several purposes. First, they can quickly give you an idea of how particular types of stocks perform in comparison with other types of stocks. In 1998, for example, the S&P 500 was up 28.6 percent whereas the small-company Russell 2000 index was down 2.5 percent. That same year, the Morgan Stanley foreign stock EAFE index rose 20.3 percent. In 2001, by contrast, the S&P 500 fell 11.9 percent and the EAFE foreign stock index had an even worse year — falling 21.4 percent.

Indexes also allow you to compare or benchmark the performance of your stock market investments. If you invest primarily in large Canadian company stocks, for example, you should compare the overall return of the stocks in your portfolio with a comparable index — in this case, the S&P/TSE 60. (As we discuss in Chapter 8, index mutual funds, which invest to match a major stock market index, offer a cost-effective, proven way to build wealth by investing in stocks.)

As we explain in the section "Looking at major stock market indices" earlier in this chapter, you may hear about other types of more narrowly focused indexes. These may track the performance of stocks in particular industries, such as banking, computers, mining, drugs, semiconductors, textiles, and utilities. As well, countries such as Japan, the United Kingdom, Germany, France, and Hong Kong have stock indices that track the performance of their own stock markets. But focusing your investments in the stocks of just one or two industries or in smaller countries is dangerous, given the lack of diversification and your lack of expertise in making the difficult decision about what to invest in and when to invest. Thus, we suggest that you ignore these narrower indexes. Many companies, largely out of desire for publicity, develop their own indices. If the news media report on these indexes, the index developer effectively obtains free advertising. (In Chapter 8 we discuss investing strategies, such as those that focus on value stocks or growth stocks, which also have market indices.)

Stock Buying Methods

When it comes to investing in stocks, many (perhaps too many) choices exist. Given the tens of thousands of stocks from which you can select, you can hire a mutual fund manager or stockbroker to pick for you. You can also choose your own stocks and even buy stock directly, in some cases, from the issuing company.

Buying stocks via mutual funds

If you're busy and suffer no delusions about your expertise, you'll love the best stock mutual funds. Investing in stocks through mutual funds can be as simple as dialling a toll-free phone number or logging on to a fund company's Web site, obtaining and completing some application forms, and mailing a cheque.

Mutual funds are sold by investment companies that invest money from people like you, your neighbour, and your Uncle Freddy into securities, such as stocks and bonds. Stock mutual funds, as the name suggests, invest primarily or exclusively in stocks (some "stock" funds sometimes invest a bit in other stuff, such as bonds).

Stock mutual funds include many advantages:

✔ **Diversification.** Buying individual stocks on your own is relatively costly, unless you buy reasonable chunks (100 shares or so) of each stock. But in order to buy 100 shares each in, say, a dozen companies' stocks to ensure diversification, you need about $60,000 if the stocks that you buy average $50 per share.

✔ **Professional management.** Even if you have big bucks to invest, mutual funds offer something that you can't deliver: professional, full-time management. Look at it this way: Mutual funds are a huge time-saver. It's Friday night — would you rather go to the local library and do some research on semiconductor and toilet paper manufacturers or enjoy dinner or a movie with family and friends? (We guess that the answer depends on who your family and friends are!)

Mutual fund managers peruse a company's financial statements and otherwise track and analyze a company's business strategy and market position. The best managers put in long hours and have lots of expertise and experience in the field. (If you've been misled into thinking that with minimal effort you can rack up market-beating returns by selecting your own stocks, please be sure to read the rest of this chapter.)

✔ **Low costs — if you pick 'em right.** Those with a vested interest, such as stock-picking newsletter pundits, may point to the high fees that some funds charge in order to convince you that mutual funds aren't a good way for you to invest. There's an element of truth here: Some funds are expensive, charging you a couple percent or more per year in operating expenses on top of hefty sales commissions.

But just as you wouldn't want to invest in a fund that a novice with no track record manages, why would you want to invest in a high-cost fund? Contrary to the "You get what you pay for" notion often trumpeted by those trying to sell you something at an inflated price, some of the best managers are the cheapest to hire. Through a no-load (commission-free) mutual fund, you can hire a professional, full-time money manager to invest your $10,000 for a mere $50 to $150 per year. And if you have far less than this to invest, they'll still invest your money at a low cost: $5 to $15 per year if you invest $1,000.

As with all investments, mutual funds have drawbacks. The issue of control is a problem for some investors. If you're a controlaholic, turning over your investment dollars to a seemingly black box process where others decide when and in what to invest your money may unnerve you. However, you need to be more concerned about the blunders you might make investing in individual stocks of your own choosing — or, even worse, stocks pitched to you by a broker. (You might also consider seeking a professional's perspective on why you're so control oriented.)

Taxes are another concern for investing in mutual funds outside retirement plans. Because the fund manager, and not you, decides when to sell specific stock holdings, some funds may produce somewhat high levels of taxable distributions. Fear not — simply select tax-friendly funds if taxes concern you.

In Chapter 8 we discuss investing in the best mutual funds that offer a time- and cost-efficient, high-quality way to invest in stocks worldwide.

Selecting individual stocks

More than a few investing books suggest and enthusiastically encourage people like you to do their own stock picking. However, the vast majority of people are better off *not* picking their own stocks.

Why do we make this statement? Not because we don't think highly of you and your capabilities; we do. We've long been an advocate of people educating themselves and taking responsibility for their own financial affairs. But taking responsibility for your own finances doesn't mean you should do *everything* yourself. Table 5-1 lists some things to consider about choosing your own stocks.

Table 5-1	The Pros and Cons of Buying Your Own Stocks
Good Reasons to Pick Your Own Stocks	*Bad Reasons to Pick Your Own Stocks*
You enjoy the challenge.	You think you can beat the best money managers. (If you can, you're likely in the wrong profession!)
You want to learn more about business.	You want more control over your investments, which you think may happen if you understand the companies that you invest in.
You have a substantial amount of money to invest.	You think mutual funds are for people who aren't smart enough to choose their own stocks.
You're a buy-and-hold investor.	You're attracted to the idea of trading your stocks any time you want.

Several popular investing books try to convince investors that they can do a *better* job than the professionals at picking their own stocks. Amateur investors, however, need to devote a lot of study to become proficient at stock selection. Many professional investors work 80 hours a week at investing, but it's unlikely that you're willing to spend that much time on it. Don't let the popularity of those "do-it-yourself" investing books lead you astray.

A U.S. investment club that claims to have beaten the market's returns by a wide margin wrote an investing book entitled *The Beardstown Ladies' Common-Sense Investment Guide.* This club's philosophy is to invest in companies whose businesses they're familiar with and can understand. (We discuss this book in Chapter 18.) However, such a simplistic investing approach can lead you to poor stock picks.

Although industry familiarity can, at times, supplement your choice of stocks, it's dangerous to base your investment decisions solely on your own knowledge and gut feelings. Allow us to introduce you to a company that attracted many people through this approach: Fresh Choice. The idea, as well as the restaurants based on it, is simple. You enter the restaurants, which originated in California, and walk down a self-serve line, which offers salads and other fresh and healthy choices. A pasta bar, soups, breads, and even a dessert bar greet hungry eyes. It's all you can eat for about seven bucks, and because it's self-serve, you don't tip.

Fresh Choice went public with the cute trading symbol SALD. In its early months it traded at around $23 per share (all figures here are U.S. dollars), which represented a multiple of nearly 60 times earnings (P/E) — a whopping figure.

With folks trying to eat healthier, how could you go wrong if you chose this stock? Brokerage analysts, many of whom worked for firms that sold shares in Fresh Choice's initial public offering (IPO), engaged in a love fest for owning the stock. Almost every Wall Street analyst who followed the stock recommended buying it in the years following the IPO, during which time its stock price bounced around between $25 and $30 per share while earnings steadily grew:

- ✔ Montgomery Securities said to "buy."

- ✔ Morgan Grenfell called it a "must own."

- ✔ Dain Bosworth said to "buy."

- ✔ Rauscher Pierce Refsnes rated it a "buy" and one of its "two favorite picks" in the restaurant business. The firm said that the company was "uniquely positioned" and had a "unique concept."

- ✔ Seidler said, "We are excited by the growth prospects for Fresh Choice, and we project a five-year earnings per share growth rate of 35 percent. . . . We believe the stock represents a good value. . . ."

- ✔ Lead underwriter Alex Brown rated it a "strong buy" and said of Fresh Choice, ". . . an excellent company and an exciting concept."

Less than two years after going public, some major problems became apparent. Fresh Choice's expansion plan was poorly managed. Some new restaurants opened too close to existing ones and cannibalized sales. Even new locations that weren't close seemed to cannibalize sales — it seemed that people who liked the idea had been driving a good distance to existing stores.

A warning sign that these analysts and investors should've heeded was Fresh Choice's refusal to release same-store sales data. This data would have allowed investors to distinguish between sales growth from existing stores and from new locations. It's easy for an expanding company to increase sales by simply opening new locations. Meanwhile, though, existing locations can suffer declining revenue that's masked in the company's aggregate revenue figures. This is what happened at Fresh Choice.

Also, outside the confines of California, the chain met with an audience that wasn't as attuned to the type of food that Fresh Choice specialized in. The all-you-can-eat format, not surprisingly, attracted bigger eaters. People looking for less food, as many health-conscious eaters do, stayed away. As people tired of the same menu, the stores had difficulty retaining repeat customers.

As the company's profits sank, so too did the stock price. From a high of $32^1/_2$, Fresh Choice's stock price plunged 84 percent in the next year, and by 2004 was trading at under $2 per share.

Although it may seem that we're trying to scare you away from buying individual stocks, we're not. But picking "good stocks," even those that seem easy to understand, isn't as easy as some people lead you to believe. Choosing a stock isn't as simple as visiting a restaurant chain, liking it, and then sitting back and getting rich watching your stock zoom to the moon. And, as Fresh Choice and scores of other company cases illustrate, analyst stock recommendations aren't generally worth the paper they're printed on.

In his *Globe and Mail* newspaper column "Me and My Money," Tony has detailed how many different individuals approach investing in stocks. In talking to hundreds of "non-professional" stock pickers, one of the most common characteristics he found was that those who were successful devote a lot — and in many cases an extraordinary amount — of time, energy, and resources to selecting and following their stocks. Another quality they shared was that they found researching companies, tracking financial ratios, and monitoring their portfolio both interesting and intrinsically rewarding. If you don't get some enjoyment out of picking stocks — beyond simply making more money — it's unlikely that you'll keep at it with the discipline and consistency required. And many people who devote a lot of time to picking their own stocks still don't manage to match the market averages, nor the long-term returns, of the best fund managers.

If you invest in stocks, we think you know by now that guarantees don't exist. But like many of life's endeavours, you can buy individual stocks in good and not-so-good ways. In Chapter 6 we explain how to research and trade individual stocks.

Purchasing stock "direct" from companies

Over the years, increasing numbers of companies have begun to sell their stock directly to the public. For example, suppose you've realized that near most medical office buildings, there's a lab run by MDS. After you research the company and make sure that owning its stock fits with your overall investment plan, you can buy shares of MDS direct from the company through its share purchase plan.

Proponents of these direct stock purchase plans say that you can invest in stocks without paying any commissions. This isn't quite true, and investing in such plans poses other challenges.

With MDS, for example, you need to first be a registered shareholder. You have to already have bought shares in the company, and then have them registered in your name. You're limited to spending a minimum of $50 and a maximum of $3,000 semi-annually. You can also choose to have any dividends reinvested to buy you more shares. In this case, MDS lets you buy shares at a 5 percent discount from the recent average stock price.

MDS doesn't charge any fees or transaction costs, but many plans do. Overall, these fees can easily add up to what you would pay to buy stock through a discount broker (see Chapter 21). In fact, in some cases these fees are higher. For example, you can reinvest dividends at no cost through many discount brokers.

Some direct stock purchase plans entail much more hassle — and cost — than the type we just discussed. With other plans, you must buy your initial shares through a broker and then transfer your shares to the issuing company in order to buy more! Also, some direct stock purchase plans can't be done within retirement accounts.

Every time you want to set up a stock purchase plan with a company, you must request and complete the company's application forms. If you go through the headache of doing so, say, a dozen times, you're rewarded with a dozen statements on a regular basis from each individual company. Frankly, based on this drawback alone we suggest you buy stock through a discount brokerage account that allows centralized purchasing and holding of various stocks as well as consolidated tax-reporting statements.

A small number of companies like MDS offer investors the ability to reinvest dividends and sometimes make additional stock purchases as well at a discount of 1 to 5 percent from the current market price of their stock. Buying stock at a discount gets us more excited, but the above-cited drawbacks still apply.

Skip direct stock purchase plans. If you want to buy good individual stocks, invest through your retirement plans and in tax-friendly stocks outside your retirement plans. In Chapter 6 we explain how to research for good companies. If you want to reinvest your dividends without cost, simply use one of the discount brokerage firms offering this service.

Spotting the Best Times to Buy and Sell

Now that you know about the different types of stock markets and ways to invest in stocks, you may wonder how you can build wealth with stocks and not lose your shirt. Nobody wants to buy stocks before the markets take a big drop (which we discuss in Chapter 2). Thousands of books have been written about how to get rich in the stock market by buying the best stocks cheaply and selling them when they become expensive.

As we discuss in Chapter 4, the stock market is reasonably efficient. A company's stock price normally reflects many smart people's assessments as to what is a fair price. Thus, it's not realistic for an investor to expect to discover a system for how to "buy low and sell high."

A few, rare professional investors may acquire the ability to spot good times to buy and sell particular stocks, but consistently doing so is enormously difficult. In fact, the investing public doesn't have a great track record with buying low and selling high. Smaller investors tend to sell heavily *after* major declines and step up buying *after* major price increases.

The simplest and best way to make money in the stock market is to consistently and regularly feed new money into building a diversified and larger portfolio. If the market drops, you can use your purchases to buy more shares. The danger of trying to time the market is that you may be "out" of the market when it appreciates greatly and "in" the market when it plummets.

Calculating price/earnings ratios

Suppose we tell you that Liz's Distinctive Jewellery's stock sells for $50 per share and another stock in the same industry, The Jazzy Jeweller, sells for $100. Which would you rather buy?

If you answer, "I don't have a clue because you didn't give me enough information," go to the head of the class! On its own, the price per share of stock is meaningless.

Although The Jazzy Jeweller sells for twice as much per share, its profits may also be twice as much per share — in which case The Jazzy Jeweller stock price may not be out of line given its profits. The level of a company's stock price relative to its earnings or profits per share helps you calibrate how expensively, cheaply, or fairly a stock price is valued.

$$\frac{\text{Stock Price Per Share}}{\text{Annual Earnings Per Share}} = \text{Price-earnings (P/E) ratio}$$

Over the long term, stock prices and corporate profits tend to move in sync, like good dance partners. The *price/earnings (P/E) ratio* (say "P E" — the slash isn't pronounced!) compares the level of stock prices with the level of corporate profits, giving you a good sense of the stock's value. Although over shorter periods of time investors' emotions as well as fundamentals move stocks, over longer terms fundamentals have a far greater influence on stock prices.

P/E ratios can be calculated for individual stocks as well as entire stock markets. Use this practical example to see how you can apply the use of P/E ratios.

A particular price level in and of itself is meaningless, like a given stock such as IBM that rises above a specific price such as $100 per share. The level of a stock's price, or a stock market index, is important and meaningful when you compare it with earnings for the company or companies in the stock market index.

Over the past 100-plus years, the P/E ratio of North American stocks has averaged around 15. During times of low inflation, the ratio has tended to be higher — in the high teens to low twenties. As we cautioned in the previous edition of this book, published in 2000, the P/E ratio for North American stocks got into the thirties, well above historic norms even for a period of low inflation. Thus, the down market that began in 2000 was no surprise to us, especially given the fall in corporate profits that put even more pressure on stock prices.

Just because stocks have historically averaged P/E ratios of about 15 doesn't mean that every individual stock will trade at such a P/E. Here's why: Suppose you have a choice between investing in two companies, Superb Software, which makes computer software, and Tortoise Technologies, which makes typewriters. If both companies' stocks sell at a P/E of 15 and Superb Software's business and profits grow 40 percent per year and Tortoise's business and profits remain flat, which would you buy?

Because both stocks trade at a P/E of 15, Superb Software appears to be the better buy. Even if Superb's stock continues to sell at 15 times the earnings, its stock price should increase 40 percent per year as its profits increase. Faster-growing companies usually command higher price/earnings ratios.

Just because a stock price or an entire stock market seems to be at a high price level doesn't necessarily mean that the stock or market is overpriced. Always compare the price of a stock with that company's profits per share, or the overall market's price level to overall corporate profits. The price/earnings ratio captures this comparison. Faster-growing and more profitable companies generally sell for a premium — higher P/E ratios. Also remember that future earnings, which are difficult to predict, influence stock prices more than current earnings, which are old news.

Sitting tight in times of speculative excess

Because the financial markets move as much on the financial realities of the economy as on people's expectations and emotions (particularly fear and greed), we don't believe that you should try to time the markets. Knowing when to buy and sell is much harder than you think.

Be careful that you don't get sucked into investing lots of your money in aggressive investments that seem to be in a hyped state. Many people go wrong when they begin to do this. In fact, many people don't become aware of an investment until it receives lots of attention. By the time everyone else talks about an investment, it's often nearing or at its peak. In the sections that follow, we walk you through some of the biggest speculative bubbles. Although some of these examples are from prior decades and even centuries, we chose them because we find that they best teach the warning signs and dangers of speculative fever times.

The Internet and technology bubble

Unless you've isolated yourself from what we call civilization, you've surely heard about the explosive growth in the Internet . . . and the Internet stock bubble. In the mid-1990s, a number of Internet-based companies launched initial public offerings of stock. (We discuss IPOs in Chapter 4.) Most of the early Internet company stock offerings failed to really catch fire. By the late 1990s, however, some of these stocks began meteoric rises.

The bigger-name Internet stocks included companies such as Internet service provider America Online, bookseller and online retailer Amazon.com, Internet auctioneer eBay, and Internet portal Yahoo!. As with the leading new consumer product manufacturers of the 1920s that we discuss in "The 1920s consumer spending binge" section later in this chapter, many of the leading Internet company stocks zoomed to the moon. Note that in the late 1990s the absolute stock price per share of these companies was meaningless — the P/E ratio is what mattered. Valuing Internet stocks based on earnings posed a challenge because many of these companies were losing money or just beginning to make money. Some Wall Street analysts, therefore, valued Internet stocks based on revenue and not profits.

Valuing a stock based on revenue and not profits can be highly dangerous. Revenues don't necessarily translate into high profits — or any profits at all.

In the case of Amazon.com, its stock price soared in early 1999 to $221 per share, which gave the company's stock a total market valuation in excess of $35 billion, or more than 12 times that of competing bookseller Barnes & Noble. B&N had prior-year sales of nearly $3 billion compared with Amazon.com's approximate $400 million sales as it was losing money! At its low in 2001, Amazon's market value had fallen nearly 95 percent to less than $2 billion, very nearly the same valuation that Barnes & Noble had at that time. (Since its low in 2001, Amazon's stock value has bounced back — but it was recently valued at $18 billion, which still represents almost a 50 percent decline since its 1999 peak.)

Now, Amazon.com, eBay, and other current leading Internet companies may go on to become some of the great companies and stocks of future decades. However, consider this perspective from veteran money manager David Dreman. "The Internet stocks are getting hundredfold more attention from investors than, say, a Ford Motor in chat rooms online and elsewhere. People are fascinated with the Internet — many individual investors have accounts on margin. Back in the early 1900s, there were hundreds of auto manufacturers, and it was hard to know who the long-term survivors would be. The current leaders won't probably be long-term winners."

Internet stocks weren't the only stocks being swept to excessive prices relative to their earnings at the dawn of the new millennium. Various traditional retailers announced the opening of Internet sites to sell their goods, and within days their stock prices doubled or tripled. Also, leading name-brand technology companies, such as Dell Computer, Cisco Systems, Lucent, and PeopleSoft, traded at P/E ratios in excess of 100. Companies in other industries, like investment brokerage firm Charles Schwab, which expanded to offer Internet services, saw their stock price balloon to push their P/E ratio over 100. As during the 1960s and 1920s, name-brand growth companies soared to high P/E valuations. For example, coffee purveyor Starbucks at times had a P/E near 100.

What we find troubling about the way investors piled into the leading name-brand stocks, especially in Internet and technology-related fields, is that many of these investors didn't even know what a price/earnings ratio is and why it's important. Before you invest in any individual stock, no matter how great a company you think it is, you need to understand the company's line of business, strategies, competitors, financial statements, and price/earnings ratio versus the competition, among many other issues. Selecting and monitoring good companies take lots of research, time, and discipline.

Also, remember that if a company taps into a product line or way of doing business that proves highly successful, that company's success invites lots of competition. So you need to understand the barriers to entry that a leading company has erected and how difficult or easy it is for competitors to join the fray. Also, be wary of analysts' predictions about earnings and stock prices. As more and more investment banking analysts initiated coverage of Internet companies and issued buy ratings on their stocks, investors bought more shares. Analysts, who are too optimistic (as shown in numerous independent studies), have a conflict of interest: The investment banks they work for seek to cultivate the business (new stock and bond issues) of the very companies they purport to rate and analyze. The analysts who say "Buy, buy, buy all the current market leaders" are the same analysts who generate much new business for their investment banks and get the lucrative job offers and multimillion-dollar annual salaries.

Simply buying today's rising and analyst-recommended stocks often leads to future investor disappointment. If the company's growth slows or the profits don't materialize as expected, the underlying stock price can nose-dive. This happened to investors who piled into the stock of computer disk-drive maker Iomega back in early 1996. After a spectacular rise to about $27^1/_2$ U.S. per share, the company fell on tough times. Iomega stock subsequently plunged to less than $3 per share. This stock probably won't recover to its early 1996 price levels for many more years.

Presstek, a company that uses computer technology for so-called direct imaging systems, rose from less than $10 U.S. per share in mid-1994 to nearly $100 per share just two years later — another example of supposed can't-lose technology that crashed and burned. As was the case with Iomega, herds of novice investors jumped on the Presstek bandwagon simply because they believed the stock price would keep rising. By 1999, less than three years after hitting nearly $100 per share, the stock plunged more than 90 percent to about $5 per share. It's been recently trading at around $10 per share.

ATC Communications, which was similar to Iomega and glowingly recommended by the Motley Fool Web site (see Chapter 19), plunged by more than 80 percent in a matter of months before the Fools recommended selling.

The Japanese stock market juggernaut

Lest you think the United States cornered the market on manias, overseas examples abound. A rather extraordinary mania happened just over a decade ago in the Japanese stock market.

After Japan's crushing defeat in World War II, its economy was in shambles. Two major cities — Hiroshima and Nagasaki — were destroyed, and more than 200,000 people died when the United States dropped atomic bombs to "win" the war.

Out of the rubble, Japan emerged a strengthened nation that became an economic powerhouse. Over 22 years, from 1967 to 1989, Japanese stock prices rose an amazing 30-fold (3,000 percent) as the economy boomed. From 1983 to 1989 alone, Japanese stocks soared more than 500 percent.

In terms of the U.S. dollar, the Japanese stock market rise was all the more stunning as the dollar lost value against Japan's currency, the yen. The dollar lost about 65 percent of its value during the big run-up in Japanese stocks. In dollar terms, the Japanese stock market rose an astonishing 8,300 percent from 1967 to 1989.

Many considered investing in Japanese stocks as close to a sure thing. Increasing numbers of people became full-time stock market investors in Japan. Many of these folks were actually speculators, since borrowed funds were used heavily. As the Japanese real estate market boomed in tandem with the stock market, real estate investors borrowed from their winnings to invest in stocks and vice versa.

Borrowing heavily was easy to do, as Japan's banks were awash in cash and it was cheap, cheap, cheap to borrow. Investors could borrow money for an interest rate of a mere few percent. "Established investors" could make property purchases with no money down. Cash abounded from real estate as the price of land in Tokyo, for example, soared 500 percent from 1985 to 1990. Despite the fact that Japan has only $1/25$ as much land as the United States, Japan's total land values at the close of the 1980s were four times that of all the land in the U.S.

Speculators also used futures and options (discussed in Chapter 1) to gamble on higher short-term Japanese stock market prices. Interestingly, Japan doesn't allow selling short. Likewise, given the strong Japanese currency, investors kept their money on their home turf, so they didn't lose out from devaluation of foreign currencies. Investing at home is one reason why many Japanese investors had little sense (from the perspective of other nation's stock markets) of what their investments were intrinsically worth.

Price/earnings ratios? Forget about it. To justify the high prices they paid for stocks, Japanese market speculators pointed out that the real estate many companies owned was soaring to the moon and making companies more valuable.

Price/earnings ratios on the Japanese market soared during the early 1980s and ballooned to more than 60 times earnings by 1987. As we point out elsewhere in this chapter, such lofty P/E ratios were sometimes awarded hot stocks in the United States. But the entire Japanese stock market, which included many mediocre and not-so-hot companies, possessed P/E ratios of 60-plus!

When Japan's version of AT&T, Nippon Telegraph and Telephone, went public in February 1987, it met such frenzied enthusiasm that its stock price was soon bid up to a stratospheric 300-plus price/earnings ratio. At the close of 1989, Japan's stock market, for the first time in history, unseated the U.S. stock market in total market value of all stocks. And this feat was accomplished despite the fact that the total output of the Japanese economy was less than half that of the U.S. economy.

Even some U.S. observers began to lose sight of the big picture and added to the rationalizations for the high levels of Japanese stocks. After all, it was reasoned, Japanese companies and executives were a tightly knit and "closed circle," investing heavily in the stocks of other companies they did business with. The supply of stock for outside buyers was thus limited as companies sat on their shares.

Corporate stock ownership went further, though, as stock prices were some-times manipulated. Speculators gobbled up the bulk of outstanding shares of small companies and traded shares back and forth with others they partnered with to drive up prices. Company pension plans began to place all (as in 100 percent) of their employees' retirement money into stocks with the expectation that stock prices would always keep going up. Surely someone else would always pay a higher price to buy stock.

The collapse of the Japanese stock market was swift. After peaking at the end of 1989, the Tokyo market plunged nearly 50 percent in the first nine months of 1990 alone. By the middle of 1992 the worst was over, with Japanese stocks down nearly 65 percent — a plunge that the U.S. market hasn't experienced since the Great Depression. Japanese investors who borrowed lost everything and sometimes more. The total loss in stock market value was about $2.5 trillion, about the size of the entire Japanese annual output.

Several factors finally led to the pricking of the Japanese stock market bubble. Japanese monetary authorities tightened credit as inflation started to creep upward and concern increased over real estate market speculation. As interest rates began to rise, investors soon realized that they could earn 15 times more interest from a safe bond than the paltry yield on stocks.

As interest rates rose and credit tightened, speculators were squeezed first. Real estate and stock market speculators began to sell their investments to pay off mounting debts. Higher interest rates, less available credit, and the already grossly inflated prices greatly limited the pool of potential stock buyers. The plunging stock and real estate markets fed off one another. Investor losses in one market triggered more selling and price drops in the other. The real estate price drop was equally severe — registering 50 to 60 percent or more in most parts of Japan since the late 1980s.

The 1960s weren't just about sex, drugs, and rock and roll

The U.S. stock market mirrored the climate of our country during this decade of change and upheaval. There were good years and bad years, but overall, the stock market gained. Unfortunately, most investors who were old enough to remember what happened to the stock market during the Great Depression were retired or had passed away. The majority of investors during the 1960s were born after the go-go years of the 1920s or were at that point still sucking on a pacifier.

During the 1960s, consumer product companies' stocks were quite popular and were bid up to stratospheric valuations. When we say "stratospheric valuations," we mean that some stock prices were high relative to the company's earnings — our old friend, the price/earnings (P/E) ratio. Investors had seen these stock prices rise for many years and thought the good times would never end.

Take the case of Avon Products, which sells cosmetics door-to-door, primarily with an army of women. During the late 1960s, Avon's stock regularly sold at a P/E of 50 to 70 times earnings. (Remember, the market average is about 14.) After trading as high as $140 per share in the early 1970s, Avon's stock took more than two decades to return to that price level. And during this period the overall U.S. stock market rose more than tenfold!

When a stock such as Avon's sells at such a high multiple of earnings, two factors can lead to a bloodletting. First, the company's profits may continue to grow, but investors may decide that the stock isn't such a great long-term investment after all and not worth, say, a P/E of 60. If investors decide it's worth a P/E of only 30 (still a hefty P/E), the stock price would drop 50 percent to cut the P/E in half.

The second shoe that can drop is the company's profits or earnings. If profits fall, say, 20 percent, as Avon's did during the 1974–75 recession, the stock price will fall 20 percent, even if it continued to sell for 60 times its earnings. But when earnings drop, investors' willingness to pay an inflated P/E plummets along with the earnings. So when Avon's profits finally did drop, the P/E that investors were willing to pay plunged to 9 — in less than two years, Avon's stock price thus dropped nearly 87 percent!

Avon wasn't the only stock whose price soared to a high multiple of its earnings in the 1960s and early 1970s. Well-known companies such as Black & Decker, Eastman Kodak, and Kmart (called S. S. Kresge in those days) sold for 60 to as much as 100 times earnings. All these companies sell today at about the same or lower price than they achieved decades ago. Many other well-known and smaller companies sold at similar and even more outrageous premiums to earnings.

The 1920s consumer spending binge

The Dow Jones Industrial Average soared nearly 500 percent in a mere eight years, from 1921 to 1929, one of the best bull market runs for the U.S. stock market. The country and investors had good reason for economic optimism. The "new" devices — telephones, cars, radios, and all sorts of electric appliances — were making their way into the mass market. The stock price of RCA, the radio manufacturer, for example, ballooned 5,700 percent during this great bull run.

Speculation in the stock market moved from Wall Street to Main Street. Investors during the 1920s were able to borrow lots of money to buy stock, through *margin borrowing*. You can still margin borrow today — for every dollar that you put up, you may borrow an additional dollar to buy stock. At times during the 1920s, investors were able to borrow up to nine dollars for every dollar they had in hand. The amount of margin loans outstanding swelled from $1 billion in the early 1920s to more than $8 billion in 1929. When the market plunged, margin calls forced margin borrowers to sell their stock, thus exacerbating the decline.

The steep run-up in stock prices was also due in part to market manipulation. Investment pools used to buy and sell stock among one another, thus generating high trading volume in a stock that made it appear as though interest in the stock was great. Also in cahoots with pool operators were writers who dispensed enthusiastic prognostications about said stock. (Reforms later passed by the U.S. Securities and Exchange Commission addressed these problems.)

Not only were members of the public largely enthusiastic, so too were the supposed experts. After a small decline in September 1929, economist Irving Fisher said in mid-October, "Stock prices have reached what looks like a permanently high plateau." High? Yes! Permanent plateau? Investors wish!

On October 25, 1929, just days before all heck began breaking loose, President Herbert Hoover said, "The fundamental business of the country . . . is on a sound and prosperous basis." Days later, multimillionaire oil tycoon John D. Rockefeller said, "Believing that fundamental conditions of the country are sound . . . my son and I have for some days been purchasing sound common stocks."

By December of that same year, the stock market dropped by more than 35 percent. General Electric President Owen D. Young said at that time, "Those who voluntarily sell stocks at current prices are extremely foolish."

Well, actually not. By the time the crash had run its course, the market had plunged 89 percent in value in less than three years.

The magnitude of this steep decline in stock prices couldn't have been predicted or expected in the late 1920s. The economy went into a tailspin. Unemployment soared to more than 25 percent of the labour force. Companies entered this period with excess inventories, which mushroomed further when people slashed their spending. High overseas tariffs stifled American exports. Thousands of banks failed, as early bank failures triggered "runs" on other banks. (No U.S. federal insurance existed in those days.)

Maniacal manias in prior centuries

We could fill an entire book with modern-day stock market manias. But bear with us as we roll back the clocks a couple of centuries to observe other market manias, the first being England's so-called South Sea bubble of 1719. The South Seas Company wasn't the kind that would've met today's socially responsible investor's needs. The company initially focused on the African slave trade, but too many enslaved people died in transit, so it wasn't a lucrative business.

If you think government corruption is a problem today, consider what politicians of those days did without the scrutiny of a widely read press. King George backed the South Seas Company and acted as its governor. Politicos in Parliament bought tons of stock in the company and even rammed through Parliament a provision that allowed investors to buy stock on borrowed money. The stock of the South Seas Company soared from about £120 to more than £1,000 in just the first six months in 1720.

After such an enormous run-up, insiders realized that the stock price was greatly inflated and quietly bailed. Citizens, meanwhile, fell all over themselves to get into this sure-fire money-maker. And when other seafaring companies pursued the South Seas trade business, greedy politicians passed a law stating that only government-approved companies could pursue trade. The stocks of these other companies tumbled, and investor losses led to a chain reaction that prompted the selling of the South Seas Company stock. By the fall of that same year the company's stock had plunged more than 80 percent.

Unfortunately, England wasn't the only European country that was swept up in an investment mania. Probably the most famous mania of them all was for the tulip bulb (yes, those flowers you can plant in your own home garden). A botany professor introduced tulips into Holland from Turkey in the late 1500s. Residents allowed a fascination with these bulbs to turn into an investment feeding frenzy.

At their speculative peak, the price of a single tulip bulb was the equivalent of more than $10,000 in today's dollars. Many people sold their land holdings to buy more. Documented cases show that people traded a bulb for a dozen acres of land! Labourers cut back on their work to invest. Eventually, tulip bulb prices came crashing back to earth. A trip to your local nursery shows you what a bulb sells for today — just a dollar or two.

Psychologically, it's easier for many people to buy stocks *after* they've had a huge increase in price. However, just as you shouldn't attempt to drive your car looking solely through your rear-view mirror, basing investments solely on past performance usually leads novice investors into overpriced investments. If you hear many people talk about the stunning rise in the market and you see new investors pile in based on the expectation of hefty profits, tread carefully.

We're not saying that you need to sell your current stock holdings if you see an investment market getting frothy and speculative. As long as you diversify your stocks worldwide and hold other investments, such as real estate and bonds, the stocks you hold in one market need to be only a fraction of your total holdings. Timing the markets is difficult: You can never know how high is high and when it's time to sell, and then how low is low and when it's time to buy. And if you sell non-retirement account investments at a profit, you end up sacrificing a lot of the profit to federal and provincial taxes.

Buy more when stocks are "on sale"

Along with speculative buying frenzies come valleys of pessimism, when stock prices fall sharply. Having the courage to buy when stock prices are "on sale" can pay bigger returns.

In the early 1970s, interest rates and inflation escalated. Oil prices shot up as the Arab oil embargo choked off supplies and North Americans had to wait in long lines for gas. Gold prices soared, and the U.S. dollar plunged in value on foreign currency markets.

If the economic problems weren't enough to make most everyone gloomy, the U.S. political system hit an all-time low during this period as well. Vice President Spiro Agnew resigned in disgrace under a cloud of tax evasion charges, and then Watergate led to President Nixon's August 1974 resignation, the first presidential resignation in U.S. history.

When all was sold and done, the Dow Jones Industrial Average plummeted more than 45 percent from early 1973 until late 1974. The TSE followed suit, dropping 38 percent. Among the stocks that fell the hardest and farthest included those that were most popular and selling at extreme multiples of earnings in the late 1960s and early 1970s. (See "The 1960s weren't just about sex, drugs, and rock and roll" section earlier in this chapter.)

Take a gander at Table 5-2 to see the drops in some well-known companies and how cheaply these stocks were valued relative to corporate profits (look at the P/E ratios) after the worst market drop since the Great Depression.

Table 5-2	Stock Bargains Galore in the Mid-1970s		
Company	**Industry**	**Stock Price Fall from Peak**	**1974 P/E**
Abbott Laboratories	Drugs	66%	8
AIG	Insurance	67%	10
H&R Block	Tax preparation	83%	6
Chemical Bank	Banking	64%	4
Coca-Cola	Beverages	70%	12
Dayton-Hudson	Department stores	86%	4
Disney	Entertainment	75%	11
Dun & Bradstreet	Business information	68%	9
General Dynamics	Military	81%	3
Hilton Hotels	Hotels	87%	4
Humana	Hospitals	91%	3
Intel	Semiconductors	76%	6
Kimberly-Clark	Consumer products	63%	4
McGraw-Hill	Publishing	90%	4
Mobil	Oil	60%	3
Pitney Bowes	Postage meters	84%	6
Potlatch	Lumber and paper	66%	3
PPG Industries	Glass	60%	4
Quaker Oats	Packaged food	76%	6
Rite Aid	Drug stores	95%	4
Sprint	Telephone	67%	7
Tandy	Consumer electronic retailer	70%	5
Textron	Aerospace	80%	4
U.S. Shoe	Shoes	82%	4
Woolworth	Discount stores	86%	3

Those who were too terrified to buy stocks in the mid-1970s actually had plenty of time to get on board and take advantage of the buying opportunities. The U.S. stock market did have a powerful rally; from its 1974 low it rose nearly 80 percent over the next two years. But over the next half-dozen years the market back-pedalled, losing much of its gains.

The mid to late 1970s was also a good time to take advantage of bargain prices on many Canadian stocks. From a low in late 1974 the TSE 300 climbed steadily to the end of the decade, rising 193 percent.

In the late 1970s and early 1980s inflation continued to escalate well into double digits. Corporate profits declined further and unemployment rose higher than in the 1974 recession. Although some stocks dropped, others simply treaded water and went sideways for years after major declines in the mid-1970s. As some companies' profits increased, P/E bargains abounded, as shown in Table 5-3.

Table 5-3   More Stock Bargains in the Late 1970s and Early 1980s

Company	Industry	Stock Price from Peak	P/E Late Fall 70s/Early 80s
Anheuser-Busch	Beer	75%	8
Campbell Soup	Canned foods	36%	6
Coca-Cola	Beverages	61%	8
Colgate-Palmolive	Personal care	69%	6
General Electric	Consumer/industrial products	44%	7
General Mills	Food	44%	6
Gillette	Shaving products	74%	5
McDonald's	Fast food	46%	9
MMM	Consumer/industrial products	50%	8
Pacific Gas & Electric	Utility	52%	6
J.C. Penney	Department stores	80%	6
Ralston Purina	Pet food	49%	6
Rubbermaid	Rubber products	60%	7
Sara Lee	Food	60%	5

(continued)

Table 5-3 *(continued)*

Company	Industry	Stock Price from Peak	P/E Late Fall 70s/Early 80s
Schering Plough	Drugs	71%	7
Seagram	Alcohol	60%	7
Tambrands	Feminine hygiene products	82%	7
Wells Fargo	Banking	50%	3
Whirlpool	Household appliances	63%	5
Xerox	Copiers	85%	5

When bad news and pessimism abound and the stock market has dropped, it's a much safer and better time to buy stocks by the truckload. You may even consider shifting some of your money out of your safer investments, such as bonds, and investing more aggressively in stocks. Investors feel during these times that prices can drop further, but if you buy and wait you'll be amply rewarded. Most of the stocks listed in the last several pages have appreciated 500 to 2,000-plus percent in the past couple of decades.

Avoiding Problematic Stock Buying Practices

You may be curious about other ways to buy individual stocks, but note that if we list those methods in this section, it's because we *don't* recommend using them. You can greatly increase your chances of success and earn higher returns if you avoid the commonly made stock investing mistakes that we present in this section.

Keep your eyes open if buying through commission-based brokers

Many investors invest in individual stocks through a broker who earns a living from commissions. The standard pitch of these firms and their brokers is that they maintain research departments that monitor and report on stocks. Their brokers, using this research, tell you when to buy, sell, or hold. Sounds good in theory, but this "research" and system have significant problems.

Many brokerage firms happen to be in another business that creates enormous conflicts of interest in producing objective company reviews. You see, these investment firms also solicit companies to help them sell new stock and bond issues. To gain this business, the brokerage firms need to demonstrate enthusiasm and optimism for the company's future prospects.

Brokerage analysts who, with the best of intentions, write negative reports about a company find their careers hindered in a variety of ways. Some firms fire such analysts. Companies that the analysts criticize exclude the analysts from meetings about the company. Analysts who know what's good for their career and their brokerage firm don't write disapproving reports.

Although investment insiders know that analysts are overly optimistic, little documented proof about this fact exists, and few people are willing to talk on the record about it. One firm got caught encouraging its analysts via a memo not to say negative things about companies. As uncovered by *Wall Street Journal* reporter Michael Siconolfi, Morgan Stanley's head of new stock issues stated in a memo that the firm's policy needed to include "no negative comments about our clients." The memo also stated that any analyst's changes in a stock's rating or investment opinion, "which might be viewed negatively" by the firm's clients, had to be cleared through the company's corporate finance department head!

Various studies of the brokerage firm's stock ratings have conclusively demonstrated that, from a predictive perspective, most of its research is barely worth the cost of the paper it's printed on. In Chapter 6 we recommend independent research reports that beat the brokerage industry track record hands down. In Chapter 9 we cover the important issues that you need to consider when you select a good broker.

Pass on initial public offerings

As we explain in Chapter 4, an initial public offering (IPO) occurs when a company offers new stock to the investing public. If you bought Microsoft's IPO back in the spring of 1986 and held on to it until today, you'd be a mighty happy camper, having made about a 300-times return on your money. If you invested $10,000 in Microsoft stock back then, it would have grown to approximately $3 million! Similar tales abound for investors who scooped up shares of McDonald's and other companies that have grown into behemoth, multibillion-dollar, worldwide enterprises.

So you'd like to buy shares of the next Microsoft and McDonald's? Who wouldn't? Investors and brokers who tell you they bought IPOs that became big successes have a lot in common with some people who go fishing and tell you about the days that the fish were really biting and they landed some big catches. But you hear less — or nothing at all — about the hours and days in which they caught nothing or only small fry.

Even factoring in the Microsofts and the McDonald's restaurants of the world, IPOs as a group are poor investments. You read that right! Two university professors, Jay Ritter and Timothy Loughran, went to the trouble of documenting the performance of the thousands of IPOs that have happened since 1970. Here's what they found:

Average annual return on the IPO stocks	5 percent per year
Average annual return on comparable stocks	12 percent per year

If you buy IPOs, you miss out on a lot of personal investing profits.

Don't invest in IPOs. Instead of IPO standing for *initial public offering,* it's more apt to mean "It's probably overpriced." It's easy to see a decade later which companies dominate their industries and whose stock prices rocket skyward. However, picking these companies in advance is a difficult task. Investing in IPOs has proven to be a losing stock market investment strategy. Not surprisingly, most IPOs come to market when the market is high (as happened in the late 1990s) so that companies can maximize their take. Just don't buy IPOs — and run from them as fast as you can in an overheated market. If you can get in on the ground floor of an IPO (buy at the offering price) it's generally a sign that the stock is a turkey or a small, risky offering.

Don't day trade or short-term trade

Unfortunately (for themselves), some investors track their stock investments closely and believe that they need to sell after short holding periods — in months, weeks, or even days. With the growth of Internet and computerized trading, such short-sightedness has taken a turn for the worse as more investors now engage in a foolish process known as *day trading,* where you buy and sell a stock within the same day!

If you hold a stock for only a few hours or a few months, you're not investing; you're gambling. Specifically, the numerous drawbacks that we see in short-term trading include the following:

✔ **Higher commissions.** Although the commission that you pay to trade stocks has declined greatly in recent years, especially through online trading (which we discuss in Chapter 9), the more you trade, the more of your investment dollars go into a broker's wallet. Commissions are like taxes — once collected, your dollars are forever gone, and your return is reduced.

- ✔ **More taxes (and tax headaches).** When you invest outside of tax-sheltered retirement plans, you must report the results of the sale of any stocks on your annual income tax return. If you make a profit, you must part with a portion of it through the capital gains tax you owe on the sale of your stock. Remember: The return you keep (after taxes) is more important than the return you make (before taxes).

- ✔ **Lower returns.** If stocks increase in value over time, long-term buy-and-hold investors will enjoy the fruits of the stock's appreciation. However, when you jump in and then out of stocks, your money spends a good deal of time *not* invested in stocks. The overall level of stock prices in general and individual stocks in particular sometimes rises sharply during short periods of time. Thus, day traders and other short-term traders inevitably miss stock run-ups. The best professional investors we know don't engage in short-term trading for this reason (as well as the increased transaction costs and taxes that such trading inevitably generates).

- ✔ **Lost opportunities.** Most of the short-term traders we've met over the years spend inordinate amounts of time researching and monitoring their investments. During the late 1990s we began to hear of more and more people who quit their jobs so they could manage their investment portfolio full time! Some of the firms selling day trading seminars claim that you can make a living trading stocks. Your time is clearly worth something. Put it into building your own business instead of wasting all those extra hours each day and week watching your investments like a hawk, which hampers rather than enhances your returns.

- ✔ **Poorer relationships.** Time is our most precious commodity. In addition to the financial opportunities you lose when you indulge in unproductive trading, you need to consider the personal consequences. Like drinking and smoking, short-term trading is an addictive, gambling-like behaviour. Spouses of day traders and other short-term traders report unhappiness over how much time and attention their mates give to their investments rather than themselves. And what about the lack of attention they give friends and other relatives? (See the sidebar "Recognizing an investment gambling problem in yourself or someone you love" in this chapter to help determine whether you or a loved one has a gambling addiction.)

How a given stock performs in the next few hours, days, weeks, or even months may have little to do with the underlying financial health and vitality of the company's business. In addition to short-term swings in investor emotions, unpredictable events (the emergence of a new technology or competitor, analyst predictions, changes in government regulation, and so on) often push stocks one way or another for short periods of time.

As we say throughout this part of the book, stocks are intended as long-term holdings. You shouldn't buy into stocks if you don't plan on holding them for at least five, and preferably seven to ten, years or more. When stocks suffer a setback, it may take months or even years for them to come back.

Recognizing an investment gambling problem in yourself or someone you love

Some gamblers spend their time at the racetrack, and you can find others in casinos. Increasingly though, you can find gamblers at their personal computers, tracking and trading stocks.

More investors than ever are myopically focused on stocks' short-term price movements. Several factors contribute to this troubling activity: the strong stock market performance in the late 1990s, increased media coverage (including cable stock market channels), the slide in stock prices that began in 2000, and the ensuing market volatility. Also, companies touting themselves as educational institutions suck legions of novice investors into dangerous practices. Masquerading under such pompous names as institutes or academies, these firms purport to teach you how to get rich by day-trading stocks. Perhaps you've heard their ads for "seminars" or other "training" methods on the radio or seen them on stock market cable television channels or on the Internet. All you have to do is part with several thousand dollars for the training, but the only people getting rich are the owners of such seminar companies.

The non-profit organization Gamblers Anonymous developed the following 20 questions to help you identify if you or someone you know is a compulsive gambler who needs help:

1. Did you ever lose time from work or school due to gambling?
2. Has gambling ever made your home life unhappy?
3. Did gambling affect your reputation?
4. Have you ever felt remorse after gambling?
5. Did you ever gamble to get money with which to pay debts or otherwise solve financial difficulties?

6. Did gambling cause a decrease in your ambition or efficiency?
7. After losing, did you feel you must return as soon as possible and win back your losses?
8. After a win, did you have a strong urge to return and win more?
9. Did you often gamble until your last dollar was gone?
10. Did you ever borrow money to finance your gambling?
11. Have you ever sold anything to finance gambling?
12. Were you reluctant to use "gambling money" for normal expenditures?
13. Did gambling make you careless of the welfare of your family?
14. Did you ever gamble longer than you had planned?
15. Have you ever gambled to escape worry or trouble?
16. Have you ever committed, or considered committing, an illegal act to finance gambling?
17. Did gambling cause you to have difficulty in sleeping?
18. Do arguments, disappointments, or frustrations create within you an uge to gamble?
19. Did you ever have an urge to celebrate any good fortune by a few hours of gambling?
20. Have you ever considered self-destruction as a result of your gambling?

According to Gamblers Anonymous, compulsive gamblers typically answer yes to seven or more of these questions.

Don't buy penny stocks

One of the worst mistakes many investors make — particularly when they first start out — is purchasing stocks through a broker who specializes in penny stocks. As we explain in Chapter 4, tens of thousands of smaller-company stocks trade on the over-the-counter market. Some of these companies are quite small and sport low prices per share that range from pennies to several dollars, hence the name *penny stocks*.

Here's how penny stockbrokers typically work. Many of these firms purchase prospect lists of people who have demonstrated a propensity for buying other lousy investments by phone. Brokers are taught to first introduce themselves by phone and then call back shortly thereafter with a tremendous sense of urgency about a great opportunity to get in on the "ground floor" of a small but soon-to-be stellar company. Not all these companies and stocks have terrible prospects, but many do.

The biggest problem with buying penny stocks through such brokers is that they're grossly overpriced. Just as you don't make good investment returns by purchasing jewellery that's marked up 100 percent, you don't have a fighting chance to make decent money on penny stocks that the broker may flog with similar mark-ups. The individual broker who cons you into "investing" in such cheap stocks gains a big commission, which is why he continues to call you with "opportunities" until you send him a cheque. Many brokers in this business who have records of securities' violations also possess an ability to sell, so they have no problem gaining employment with other penny stock peddlers.

A number of penny stock brokerage firms are known for engaging in manipulation of stock prices, driving up prices of selected shares to suck in gullible investors and then leaving the public holding the bag. These firms may also encourage companies to issue new overpriced stock that their brokers can then flog to people like you.

If you remember or know of a fellow by the name of Robert Brennan, then you know that he's the granddaddy of this reptilian business. We won't bore you with all the details, except to say that after more than a decade of financial shenanigans, Brennan was ordered by a judge to pay investors more than $70 million for all the bad stuff that he did. Pending suits may lead to hundreds of millions of dollars in additional judgments against Brennan's companies.

We remember when Brennan ran his infamous "Come Grow With Us" television ads in which he hopped out of a helicopter. He was always nicely dressed and maintained a polished image. And it's interesting to note that, as well as being in the penny stock trade, he owned a racetrack and wanted to get into the casino business. All Brennan's businesses share the same characteristics — they don't involve investments and they stack the deck against the gullible members of the public they hoodwink.

Don't buy broker-sold limited partnerships

At their peak, brokers and brokers who masquerade as financial planners sold more than $10 billion U.S. per year of limited partnerships (LPs). Prudential Securities sold more of these terrible investments than any other organization and has consequently suffered the most pain, having to cough up hundreds of millions of dollars as a result of lawsuits. We explain in Chapter 3 the fundamental problems (mainly outrageous commissions and fees) that drain your LP investment returns.

The Keys to Stock Market Success

Anybody, no matter what their educational background, IQ, occupation, income, or assets, can make good money through stock investments. Over long periods of time, you can expect to earn an average of 9 to 10 percent per year total return by investing in stocks.

To maximize your chances of stock market investment success, we suggest you do the following:

- **Don't try to time the markets.** Anticipating where the stock market and specific stocks are heading is next to impossible, especially over the short term. Economic factors, which are influenced by thousands of elements, and human emotions determine stock market prices. Be a regular buyer of stocks with new savings. As we discuss earlier in this chapter, buy more stocks when they're on sale and market pessimism is running high.

- **Diversify.** Invest in the stocks of different-size companies in varying industries around the world. When you assess the performance of your investments, look at your whole portfolio at least once a year and calculate your total return after expenses and trading fees.

- **Keep trading costs, management fees, and commissions to a minimum.** These represent a big drain on your returns. If you invest through a broker or "financial adviser" who earns a living on commissions, odds are high that you're paying far more than you need to be — and you may also be receiving biased advice.

- **Pay attention to taxes.** Like commissions and fees, taxes are another major investment "expense" you can minimize. Contribute most of your money to your tax-advantaged retirement plans. You can invest your money outside of retirement plans, but keep an eye on taxes (see Chapter 3). Calculate your annual returns on an *after*-tax basis.

✔ **Don't overestimate your ability to pick the big winning stocks.** One of the best ways to invest in stocks is through mutual funds (see Chapter 8), where you can hire an experienced, full-time money manager at a low cost to perform all the investing grunt work for you. If you want to invest in individual stocks, stay clear of initial public offerings, particularly trendy popular ones and ones that are issued during an overheated stock market.

Chapter 6

Investigating Individual Stocks

· ·

In This Chapter

▶ Looking at the best individual stock research resources

▶ Figuring out what those annual reports really mean

▶ Deciphering quarterly and annual reports, 10-Ks, 10-Qs, information circulars, and proxies

▶ Placing stock trades

· ·

*I*n the earlier chapters in this part, we cover how the financial markets work and what drives stock prices. We also explain the different ways that you can buy stocks, such as through stock mutual funds or by picking your own. This chapter provides a crash course in researching individual companies and their stocks. Be sure to consider your reasons for taking this approach before you head down the path of picking and choosing your own stocks. If you haven't already done so, read Chapter 5 now to help you better understand the process of purchasing stocks without the help of a broker or mutual fund.

If you decide to tackle the task of researching your own stocks, don't worry about finding enough information to peruse — your biggest challenge will be information overload. You can literally spend hundreds of hours researching and reading information on one company alone. Therefore, unless you're financially independent and you want to spend nearly all your productive time investing, you need to focus on where you can get the best bang for your buck and time.

Leveraging Others' Research

If you were going to build a house, we bet that you wouldn't literally try to do it on your own. You may likely see whether you can obtain some sort of kit or plans drawn up by others who have built many houses. You can do the same when it comes to picking individual stocks. In this section, we highlight useful resources that allow you to hit the ground running when trying to pick the best stocks.

Checking out the Canadian Shareowners Association

A terrific starting point for investigating Canadian and U.S. stocks is the Canadian Shareowners Association. As a non-profit organization, the Association's goal is to help educate individual investors. Their philosophy is straightforward: Individual investors are best off putting their money into the highest quality stocks, and investing in those stocks regularly over the long term.

The association has a simple, easily understood method. To find what it dubs "Great Stocks," it suggests looking for two key criteria: steadily growing revenues and ever-increasing earnings per share (EPS).

To help investors assess how companies are doing on these two fronts, the Association offers several tools for charting the numbers. First is the aptly named *The Picture Book of Great & Grief Stocks*. It contains easy-to-read charts displaying the revenue and earnings-per-share growth of over 2,000 popular Canadian and U.S. stocks. The book retails for $129, and is updated every two months.

You can also collect your own data and do the charting yourself using the Association's one-page Stock Selection Guide. Once a stock has passed this first test, you can use the Guide's other sections to investigate its price, price/earnings ratio, and dividend yield to see if the stock is, in the Association's words, "overpriced" or "on sale." In this way, the Guide also offers an easy way to estimate a stock's buy and sell zones.

Another option is the software version of the Stock Selection Guide (also $129), which allows you to enter historical data and have the program run the calculations for you. You can also go all-electronic. The Association has a database of over 6,000 Canadian and U.S. companies available on CD. The $199 yearly price includes bi-monthly updates (you can also choose to buy data for specific companies for around $1.00 each).

Membership in the Canadian Shareowners Association is $99 a year (800-268-6881, or www.shareowner.com). As a member, you get a subscription to *Canada Shareowner*, a bi-monthly magazine that offers quick updates on many stocks, in-depth assessments of two companies per issue, and updated revenue and EPS growth charts for about 100 of the companies the Association follows. You also receive the basic education manual *Buy Only the Great Stocks*, which walks you through the association's methodology for how to distinguish between good and bad stock investments. Being a member gets you use of the CSA's Low Cost Investing Program (see the sidebar below). You can also be an account holder without becoming a member.

How to minimize commissions with the Canadian Shareowners Association Buying Plan

One of our themes throughout this book is keeping investment fees and other costs to a minimum. Any money that's wasted on transaction costs directly eats into your returns. We also recommend staying diversified, so that if one of your investments collapses, the other healthy securities you hold will limit the overall damage.

Thanks to the Canadian Shareowners share-buying plan, you aren't limited to mutual funds to accomplish these two goals. The Association offers a pooled-buying service to help individual investors make small purchases of stocks and keep commissions low. You can choose from about 100 of the largest Canadian and U.S. stocks. When you enter your order it's pooled with other orders for the stock from individual investors, and the money saved on trading costs is passed on in lower commissions. This is a great way for smaller investors to cost-effectively buy stocks they feel are good long-term investments.

There is a one-time $8 set-up fee for each company you want to invest in, but if you do this online, there's no charge. You can then buy or sell stock in that company through the CSA, which groups your orders with those of others wanting to buy the same stock(s) and processes them at regular times each month. The commission on single purchases of a stock is $14 plus a few cents a share. If you invested $1,500 to buy 30 shares of a stock trading at $50, for example, the commission would be $14 plus $0.06 a share, or $1.80, for a total commission of $15.80. This is about half the commission you'd be charged for the same trade with a discount broker. And if you arrange for pre-authorized purchases of a stock every one, two, or three months through the Silver Service, the commission is just $8.00 per trade, plus a few cents per share.

The commissions really drop to bargain-basement levels with the Gold Service. With this plan, you can arrange to invest in any number of stocks — right up to the full 100 companies available through the program — on a regular basis for a single flat transaction fee of just $29. You can choose to invest every month, every two months, or every three months. For example, you could choose to invest in 30 different stocks in different amounts every two months. Your commission would then be $29 every second month, the month you make your purchase. You can buy as much or as little of each stock as you desire — there's no minimum purchase. The only major limitation is that your overall investment can't be more than $20,000 a month.

Discovering the Value Line Investment Survey

Value Line's securities analysts have tracked and researched stocks since the Great Depression. Their analysis and recommendation track record is quite good, and the analysts are beholden to no one. Many professional money managers use *Value Line* as a reference because of its comprehensiveness.

The beauty of *Value Line*'s service is that it condenses the key information and statistics about a stock (and the company behind the stock) to a single page. Suppose you're interested in investing in Starbucks, the retail coffee-house operator. You've seen their stores go up in trendy shopping areas around your neck of the woods, and you figure that if you're going to shell out more than $3 for a cup of their flavoured hot water, you may as well share in the company's profits and growth. You look up the current stock price (we explain how to do that later in this chapter if you don't know how) and are happy to see that it's a mere $21 per share.

Take a look at the important elements of a *Value Line* page for Starbucks, shown in Figure 6-1.

1. **Business.** This section describes the business(es) that Starbucks participates in. You can see that Starbucks is the largest retailer of specialty coffee in the world. Although 85 percent of the company's sales come from retail, note that 15 percent come from other avenues, including mail order and supermarket sales. You find details about such joint ventures as the partnership of Starbucks and Pepsi to develop and sell a bottled coffee drink. You might also note that the senior executives and directors of the company own a decent share (5.5 percent) of the stock — it's good to see these folks have a financial stake in the success of the company and stock.

2. **Analyst assessment.** A securities analyst (in this case, Justin Hellman) follows each *Value Line* stock. An analyst focuses on specific industries and follows a few dozen stocks. This section provides the analyst's summary and commentary of the company's current situation and future plans. Hellman notes that on a critical measure of success for chains — namely, same-store sales — Starbucks has been making impressive gains. What's more, those gains were the result of better processes as well the growing popularity of the Starbucks Card, a loyalty reward program. In an earlier report Hellman noted that the company was also seeking growth from specialty businesses, and he now says that strategy is paying off, allowing it to boost sales even in markets where it's already well-established. He points out the importance of this feat, given that investors worried that Starbucks had little room left to grow domestically. In fact, he forecasts further domestic growth, in part due to Starbucks' newer drive-throughs. While he foresees higher prices for coffee and dairy supplies, he predicts this will be at least partially offset by supply-chain efficiencies boosting profit margins. Hellman warns of ongoing weak sales in Japan and the U.K. The long-term international outlook is, however, very positive, owing to growing economies of scale as well as the sharing of Starbucks' investment costs with its joint partners. Summing up, Hellman says that despite the relatively high price the shares are trading at, he sees them appreciating well into 2009.

STARBUCKS CORP. NDQ-SBUX

RECENT PRICE	37.81	P/E RATIO	43.0 (Trailing: 51.1 / Median: 47.0)	RELATIVE P/E RATIO	2.21	DIVID YLD	Nil	VALUE LINE

| | | High: | 3.5 | 4.1 | 5.9 | 10.1 | 11.2 | 15.0 | 20.5 | 25.4 | 25.7 | 25.7 | 33.4 | 39.7 |
| TIMELINESS | **2** Lowered 6/13/03 | Low: | 2.0 | 2.4 | 2.8 | 3.6 | 6.5 | 7.2 | 9.9 | 11.6 | 13.5 | 18.4 | 19.6 | 32.9 |

SAFETY **3** New 5/23/97
TECHNICAL **2** Raised 3/5/04
BETA .75 (1.00 = Market)

2007-09 PROJECTIONS

	Price	Gain	Ann'l Total Return
High	70	(+85%)	17%
Low	45	(+20%)	5%

LEGEND
— 17.0 x Cash Flow p sh
.... Relative Price Strength
2-for-1 split 8/93
2-for-1 split 2/95
2-for-1 split 8/99
2-for-1 split 4/01
Options: Yes
Shaded areas indicate recession

Insider Decisions

	A	M	J	J	A	S	O	N	D
to Buy	0	0	1	0	0	0	0	0	0
Options	0	1	0	2	3	6	5	0	2
to Sell	0	1	0	4	3	6	5	0	1

Institutional Decisions

	1Q2003	2Q2003	3Q2003
to Buy	220	214	185
to Sell	161	169	192
Hld's(000)	257945	254648	268046

Percent shares traded: 60 40 20

Target Price Range 2007 2008 2009

% TOT. RETURN 2/04

	THIS STOCK	VL ARITH. INDEX
1 yr.	59.5	65.3
3 yr.	57.1	37.3
5 yr.	180.6	83.6

© VALUE LINE PUB., INC. 07-09

1988	1989	1990	1991	1992	1993	1994	1995	1996	1997	1998	1999	2000	2001	2002	2003	2004	2005		07-09
--	--	--	--	.44	.75	1.23	1.64	2.24	3.06	3.65	4.58	5.76	6.97	8.47	10.35	**12.80**	**14.70**	Sales per sh A	25.00
--	--	--	--	.03	.07	.12	.18	.24	.35	.43	.54	.71	.91	1.09	1.29	**1.60**	**1.95**	Cash Flow per sh	3.35
--	--	--	--	.02	.04	.05	.09	.12	.18	.22	.27	.36	.46	.55	.67	**.88**	**1.05**	Earnings per sh B	1.90
--	--	--	--	--	--	--	--	--	--	--	--	--	--	--	--	**Nil**	**Nil**	Div'ds Decl'd per sh	Nil
--	--	--	--	.36	.40	.47	1.10	1.46	1.68	2.22	2.62	3.05	3.62	4.45	5.29	**6.15**	**7.15**	Book Value per sh	11.80
--	--	--	--	209.60	268.68	231.75	283.83	310.34	316.24	353.53	366.56	376.32	380.04	388.23	393.69	**399.00**	**405.00**	Common Shs Outst'g C	420.00
--	--	--	--	NMF	NMF	NMF	41.5	NMF	49.3	16.4	NMF	46.5	45.0	38.6	35.9	*Bold figures are*	*Value Line*	Avg Ann'l P/E Ratio	30.0
--	--	--	--	NMF	NMF	NMF	2.78	NMF	2.84	2.41	NMF	3.02	2.31	2.11	2.04	*estimates*		Relative P/E Ratio	2.00
--	--	--	--	--	--	--	--	--	--	--	--	--	--	--	--			Avg Ann'l Div'd Yield	Nil

CAPITAL STRUCTURE as of 12/28/03
Total Debt $4.9 mill. Due in 5 Yrs $3.5 mill
LT Debt $4.2 mill. LT Interest $.2 mill.
(less than 1% of Cap'l)

Leases, Uncapitalized Annual rentals $293.9 mill.

No Defined Benefit Pension Plan

Pfd Stock None.

Common Stock 396,140,031 shs.
as of 2/2/04

MARKET CAP: $15.0 billion (Large Cap)

	284.9	465.2	696.5	966.9	1308.7	1680.1	2169.2	2649.0	3288.9	4075.5	**5100**	**5950**	Sales ($mill) A	10500
	20.1%	20.1%	19.2%	20.4%	21.0%	20.5%	20.3%	21.4%	21.0%	20.4%	**21.0%**	**21.0%**	Gross Margin D	21.5%
	13.1%	14.0%	13.8%	14.5%	15.1%	15.1%	15.3%	15.7%	14.9%	15.3%	**16.0%**	**16.0%**	Operating Margin	16.5%
	425	676	1006	1270	688	2135	2519	3266	3880	4546	**5200**	**5950**	Number of Stores E	8500
	12.9	26.1	36.4	57.4	31.4	101.7	136.9	181.2	218.0	268.3	**355**	**435**	Net Profit ($mill)	815
	40.4%	39.5%	38.5%	38.5%	38.3%	38.0%	37.6%	37.3%	37.0%	38.5%	**38.0%**	**38.0%**	Income Tax Rate	38.0%
	4.5%	5.6%	5.2%	5.9%	6.2%	6.1%	6.3%	6.8%	6.6%	6.6%	**7.0%**	**7.3%**	Net Profit Margin	7.8%
	44.2	134.6	238.4	177.6	157.8	134.9	146.5	148.6	310.0	315.3	**425**	**450**	Working Capital ($mill)	600
	80.5	81.4	166.8	167.0	--	7.0	6.5	5.8	5.1	4.4	**5.0**	**5.0**	Long-Term Debt ($mill)	5.0
	109.9	312.2	451.7	531.8	794.0	961.0	1148.4	1375.9	1726.6	2082.4	**2450**	**2895**	Shr. Equity ($mill)	4950
	7.8%	7.1%	6.6%	8.7%	10.3%	10.6%	11.9%	13.1%	12.6%	12.9%	**14.5%**	**15.0%**	Return on Total Cap'l	16.5%
	11.7%	8.4%	8.1%	10.8%	19.2%	10.6%	11.9%	13.2%	12.6%	12.9%	**14.5%**	**15.0%**	Return on Shr. Equity	16.5%
	11.7%	8.4%	8.1%	10.8%	19.2%	10.6%	11.9%	13.2%	12.6%	12.9%	**14.5%**	**15.0%**	Retained to Com Eq	16.5%
	--	--	--	--	--	--	--	--	--	--	**Nil**	**Nil**	All Div'ds to Net Prof	Nil

CURRENT POSITION ($MILL.)

	2002	2003	12/28/03
Cash Assets	402.2	350.0	665.0
Receivables	97.6	114.4	122.8
Inventory (FIFO)	263.2	342.9	305.5
Other	84.5	116.7	131.4
Current Assets	847.5	924.0	1224.7
Accts Payable	136.0	169.0	144.7
Other	401.5	439.7	645.3
Current Liab.	537.5	608.7	790.0

ANNUAL RATES of change (per sh)

	Past 10 Yrs.	Past 5 Yrs.	Est'd '01-'03 to '07-'09
Sales	30.5%	23.5%	19.5%
"Cash Flow"	36.5%	26.5%	20.5%
Earnings	34.5%	26.5%	22.5%
Dividends	--	--	Nil
Book Value	28.0%	20.0%	17.5%

Fiscal Year Ends	QUARTERLY SALES ($ mill.) A				Full Fiscal Year
	Dec.31	Mar.31	Jun.30	Sep.30	
2001	667.4	629.3	662.8	689.5	2649.0
2002	805.3	783.2	835.2	865.2	3288.9
2003	1003.5	954.2	1036.8	1081.0	4075.5
2004	1281.2	1168.8	1260	1390	5100
2005	1500	1370	1480	1600	5950

Fiscal Year Ends	EARNINGS PER SHARE A B				Full Fiscal Year
	Dec.31	Mar.31	Jun.30	Sep.30	
2001	.12	.08	.12	.14	.46
2002	.15	.11	.14	.15	.55
2003	.20	.13	.17	.17	.67
2004	.27	.16	.21	.24	.88
2005	.32	.19	.25	.29	1.05

Calendar	QUARTERLY DIVIDENDS PAID				Full Year
	Mar.31	Jun.30	Sep.30	Dec.31	
2000					
2001	NO CASH DIVIDENDS				
2002	BEING PAID				
2003					
2004					

BUSINESS: Starbucks Corp. is the leading retailer, roaster, and brand of specialty coffee in the world. Sells whole bean coffees through its specialty sales group, mail-order business, supermarkets, and online. Has 3,879 company-owned stores in the U.S. and 804 in international markets. Also has 2,884 licensed stores worldwide. Retail sales: 85% of '03 total; Specialty sales, 15%. Has joint ventures with Pepsi-Cola and Dreyer's to develop bottled coffee drinks and ice creams, respectively; partnership with Kraft Foods to distribute coffee in grocery stores. Has 74,000 emp.; 12,137 sh'hldrs. Off./Dirs. own 5.5% of common (1/04 proxy). CEO: Orin Smith. Inc.: WA. Addr.: 2401 Utah Ave. So., Seattle, WA 98134. Tel.: 206-447-1575. Internet: www.starbucks.com.

Starbucks remains in a league of its own. The Seattle-based coffeehouse chain posted same-store sales growth of 10% in the first quarter of fiscal 2004 (ends October 3rd), on top of a hefty 9% comp gain a year earlier. The impressive advance, easily the best of any large restaurant operator in the U.S., was fueled by speed-of-service improvements and increased penetration of the Starbucks Card (there were a record number of card activations during the December period), which now accounts for about 20% of all retail transactions. Also, new noncaffeinated beverages and an enhanced food program enabled the company to grow its customer base, even in its more mature domestic markets. This suggests that, contrary to investor fears, Starbucks is still far from reaching the saturation point at home. Indeed, we think that the company, equipped with a cash-rich balance sheet, has plenty of healthy expansion years in the U.S. ahead of it. The firm's new drive-through store format holds especially good promise, in our view, as these units offer a higher return on investment than the traditional locations. **The near-term outlook seems bright.**

Despite the lapping of some very difficult year-over-year comparisons, we expect comp growth to track in the mid-single digits in the coming quarters. This should allow Starbucks to effectively leverage its fixed occupancy expenses and to offset an expected uptick in coffee and dairy costs. Meanwhile, we look for greater supply chain efficiencies to give margins an additional boost, and for the company's overseas operations to be profitable in fiscal 2004, notwithstanding ongoing weakness in Japan and the U.K. **The international business, which has long been a drag on earnings, is finally realizing significant economies of scale.** And we expect it to be a major bottom-line contributor over the next 3 to 5 years. In fact, the overseas units should eventually own 5.5% of common than the domestic ones, because the company's joint partners abroad typically carry most of the investment burden. **Starbucks shares are timely for the year ahead.** What's more, despite the rich valuation, they appear to have worthwhile appreciation potential to 2007-2009.
Justin Hellman March 12, 2004

(A) Fiscal year ends the Sunday closest to September 30th.
(B) Based on primary earnings through '96; diluted thereafter. Excludes nonrecurring gains
(C) In millions, adjusted for stock splits.
(losses): '94, $0.03; '96, $0.04; '98, $0.04; '07-'07) '00, ($0.11); '02, ($0.01). Next earnings report due in late April.
(D) Excludes occupancy costs prior to '94.
(E) Includes company-operated stores only.

Company's Financial Strength	B++
Stock's Price Stability	55
Price Growth Persistence	100
Earnings Predictability	100

To subscribe call 1-800-833-0046.

Figure 6-1:
Value Line's report on Starbucks.

3. *Value Line*'s **rating.** *Value Line* provides a numerical ranking for each stock's timeliness (expected performance) over the next year. One is highest and five is lowest, with only about 5 percent of all stocks receiving these extreme ratings. A two rating is above average and a four rating below average, with about one-sixth of the ranked stocks receiving each of these ratings. All remaining stocks, a little more than half the total ranked, get the average three rating.

The safety rank works the same way as the timeliness rating, with one representing the best and least-volatile stocks and the most financially stable companies. Five is the worst safety ranking and is given to the most volatile stocks and least financially stable companies.

We've never been fans of predictions and short-term thinking. (One year is a very short period of time for the stock market.) But according to the *Hulbert Financial Digest,* which tracks the actual performance of investment newsletter recommendations, *Value Line*'s system holds one of the best overall track records. This doesn't mean you should run out and buy Starbucks because of its ranking. Just keep in mind that higher-ranked stocks within *Value Line* have historically outperformed those without such ratings.

4. **Stock price performance.** The graph shows you the stock price's performance over the past decade or so. The highest and lowest points of the line on the graph indicate the high and low stock price for each month. At the top of the graph you see the year's high and low prices. Starbucks stock has steadily risen since it was first issued in 1992. (The small box in the lower right-hand corner of the graph shows you the total return that an investor in this stock earned over the previous one, three, and five years and how those returns compare with the average stock. This graph shows you that Starbucks has risen sharply and has beaten the average stock's return in recent years.)

The graph also shows how the price of the stock moves with changes in the company's cash flow. Cash flow is an important measure of a company's financial success and health — and it's different from the "net profits" that the company reports for tax purposes. For example, the tax laws allow companies to take a tax deduction each year for the depreciation (devaluation) of the company's equipment and other assets. Although depreciation is good because it helps lower a company's tax bill, subtracting it from the company's revenue gives an untrue picture of the company's cash flow (money coming in minus money going out). Thus, in calculating a company's cash flow, depreciation is not subtracted from revenue.

5. **Historic financials.** This section shows you 12 to 18 years of financial information on the company (in the case of Starbucks, you get information going back to just 1992 because that's when the company went public).

Book value per share indicates the value of the company's assets, including equipment, manufacturing plants, and real estate, minus any liabilities. Book value gives you somewhat of a handle on what the company would sell for if it had a "going out of business sale." We say *somewhat* because the value of some assets on a company's books isn't correct. For example, the book value of a bank can mislead you if the bank makes loans that won't be paid back and the bank's financial statements don't document this fact. Or some companies may have bought real estate long ago that's worth far more than the company's current financial statements indicate. Conversely, some manufacturers find that if they had to dump some equipment in a hurry, they'd likely need to sell it at a discount to entice a buyer.

All these complications with book value are why full-time, professional money managers exist. (If you want to delve more into a company's book value, you need to look at its other financial statements, such as the annual report — which we discuss in the "Understanding Annual Reports" section later in this chapter.)

For some companies (not Starbucks), *Value Line* also provides another useful number in this section — the *market share,* which indicates the portions of the industry that the company has captured in a given year. A sustained slide in a company's market share may indicate its customers are leaving for other companies that presumably offer better products at lower prices. But that doesn't mean you should avoid investing in a company that possesses such problems. You can produce big returns if you can identify companies that reposition and strengthen their product offerings to reverse a market share slide.

6. **P/E ratio.** This tells you that Starbucks sells at a P/E of 43 because of its recent stock price and earnings. This P/E is quite high relative to the overall market. (You can see that Starbucks' P/E is 2.21 times that of the overall market.) To understand the importance of P/E in evaluating a stock, see Chapter 5.

7. **Capital structure.** This section summarizes the amount of outstanding stocks and bonds the company possesses. Remember that when a company issues these securities, it receives capital (money). What is most useful to examine in this section is the company's debt. If a company accumulates a lot of debt (as many governments have), the burden of interest payments can create a real drag on profits. If profits stay down for too long, debt can even push some companies into bankruptcy.

Figure 6-1 shows you that Starbucks has outstanding debt of $4.9 million. This section distinguishes between short- and long-term debt. *Short-term debt* is due within one year; *long-term debt* has to be paid back in more than a year. So how do you know if this is a lot, a little, or just the right amount of debt? You can calculate "Long-term interest earned," which compares a company's annual profits to the yearly interest payments on its long-term debt. For example, if a company has long-term interest earned of 4.5x, that means that the company's most recent yearly profits can cover the interest payments on its long-term debt for about $4^1/_2$ years. Starbucks' has little debt — the company's most recent annual profits of $268.3 million dwarf its long-term interest payments of $0.2 million.

Possessing a larger cushion to cover debt is more important when the company's business is volatile. *Total interest coverage* represents a similar comparison of profits to interest owed for all the debt that a company owes, not just long-term debt. This number tells you the number of years that the company's most recent annual profits can cover interest on all the company's debt. Warning signs for total interest coverage numbers include a steep decline in this number over time and profits that cover less than one year's worth of interest.

8. **Current position.** This section provides a quick look at how the company's *current assets* (*current* meaning an asset that can be sold and converted into cash within a year relatively easily) compared with its *current liabilities* (debts due within the year). Trouble may be brewing if a company's current liabilities exceed or are approaching its current assets.

Some financial analysts calculate the quick ratio. The quick ratio ignores inventory when comparing current assets with current liabilities. A company may have to dump inventory at a relatively low price if it needs to raise cash quickly. Thus, some analysts argue, you need to ignore inventory as an asset.

9. **Annual rates.** This nifty section can save wear and tear on your calculator. The good folks at *Value Line* calculate rates of growth (or shrinkage) on important financial indicators, such as sales (revenues) and earnings (profits) over the past five and ten years. *Value Line* also lists their projections for the next five years.

Projections can prove highly unreliable, even from a research firm as good as *Value Line*. In most cases, the projections assume that the company will continue as it has in the most recent couple years.

10. **Quarterly financials.** For the most recent years, *Value Line* shows you an even more detailed quarterly breakout of sales and profits that may disclose changes that annual totals mask. You can also see the seasonality of some businesses. Starbucks, for example, tends to have its slowest quarter in the winter (quarter ending March 31). This makes sense if you figure that many of the customers who frequent Starbucks coffee shops do so as they walk around town, which people tend to do less of on a blustery winter day.

The information in *Value Line* reports is in no way inside information. Look at these reports the same way that you review a history book — they're useful background information that can keep you from repeating common mistakes.

Getting your hands on *Value Line* reports

The least costly way to obtain *Value Line* pages on stocks that interest you is to visit your local library. A number of libraries that include decent business sections subscribe to it.

If you want a copy of *Value Line* to read in the comfort of your home, *Value Line* (800-634-3583) offers a 13-week trial subscription to its *Value Line Investment Survey* for $75 U.S. An annual subscription costs $598 U.S. At the start of your subscription, you receive a rather large binder, divided into 13 sections, that includes the most recent reports on the 1,700 large- and medium-size company stocks that this publication tracks. Every week you receive a new packet of reports that replaces one of the 13 sections.

Thus, at the end of 13 weeks, you have new reports on all the stocks.

The trial subscription is a great place to start your research because you receive all the current reports plus the next ten weeks' worth of updates for a reasonable fee. You can also see how much use you get out of the reports. The trial offer is available to each household only once every three years.

Value Line also offers a "Small and Mid-Cap Edition" that contains reports on 1,800 additional smaller companies. Unlike traditional *Value Line* pages, these pages include no analyst commentary or projections. A one-year subscription to this publication costs $249 U.S.

Introducing CorporateInformation.com

In addition to providing access to Wright Investors' Services' (CorporateInformation.com's corporate parent) detailed company summaries (similar in some respect to *Value Line*'s reports), this site is a treasure trove of links to other investing information and research. You can also easily access news on specific companies as well as links to other Web sites with information on that company.

From the home page www.corporateinformation.com, begin by selecting the country of the stock(s) you're interested in. The site is chock-a-block with links for researching U.S. companies, but there are also a number of useful links for researching Canadian and other countries' stocks.. Among this site's major categories of information(which include brief reviews of the linked Web sites) you may find the following:

- ✔ **General Information.** This category includes such sites as SEDAR (the System for Electronic Document Analysis and Retrieval), which contains information that publicly traded companies in Canada are required to file with regulators. (See Chapter 19 for more details.) On the U.S. site is a link to the Securities and Exchange Commission (SEC) Edgar site, which contains information that publicly traded companies in the United States are required to file with the SEC. You'll also find links to sites such as the "10-K Wizard," which allows for efficient text searches of company filings, and "Wall Street Research Network," which provides tons of corporate financial and other data.

✔ **Earnings Estimates and Analysts Reports.** These sites track the earnings estimates and reports produced by various analysts who follow companies. Representative sites include "Zack's Company Report," which compiles analysts' earnings estimates as well as current stock recommendations (strong buy, buy, hold, sell, and so on), and "INVESTools," which sells analysts' research reports.

✔ **Ownership Information.** A variety of Web sites provide information on the major owners of stock in various companies as well as data on the buying and selling of company stock by insiders (for example, corporate senior management).

✔ **Delayed Quotes and Graphs.** Here's where you can find current stock price data as well as historic data, which in some cases goes back more than a decade.

✔ **Historical Data.** While there are numerous sites that let you chart a stock's history and carry out technical analysis, it can be informative to peruse the actual numbers involved. The sites listed here allow you to do just that for both stocks and market indices.

✔ **Comparisons to Other Firms.** When researching specific companies and their stocks, you should do comparisons among similar companies. Sites in this section allow you to do just that.

✔ **Screening.** Some Web sites allow you to do searches (screens) for stocks and companies that meet specific criteria — for example, companies that have increased their revenue an average of more than 15 percent over the past five years and that have stock selling at a P/E ratio of no more than 25.

✔ **Other Information.** Are you interested for some perverse reason in researching class action lawsuits against companies for alleged securities law violations? How about wanting to know the makeup of select stock price indexes like the S&P 500? You can access that information here as well.

Examining successful money managers' stock picks

To make money in stocks, you certainly don't need an original idea. In fact, it makes sense to examine what the best money managers are buying for their portfolios. Don't worry; we're not suggesting that you invade their privacy or ask rude questions!

The best mutual fund managers are required to disclose at least twice a year what stocks they hold in their portfolio. You can call the fund companies and ask them to send their most recent semi-annual reports that detail their stock holdings. (See Chapter 8 for more information on the best stock mutual funds.)

Through software and via its Web site, Morningstar (www.morningstar.com and www.morningstar.ca) allows you to see which mutual funds hold large portions of a given stock that you may be researching.

Finally, you can follow what investment legend Warren Buffett is buying through his holding company, Berkshire Hathaway. Check out its corporate filings on the Securities and Exchange Commission Web site at www.sec.gov.

Reviewing financial publications

Many publications cover the world of stocks. Be careful. Just because a columnist or publication advocates particular stocks or investing strategies doesn't mean that you'll achieve success by following them.

The following publications offer useful columns and commentary, sometimes written by professional money managers, on individual stocks: *Investor's Digest, Canadian Business, Report on Business Magazine, Barron's, Business Week, Forbes, Kiplinger's,* and *The Wall Street Journal.*

Understanding Annual Reports

After you review the *Value Line* page on a company and you want to dig further into its financial documents, the next step is to ask yourself "Why?" That is, why do you want to torture yourself so?

We've taken more than our fair share of accounting and finance courses. And over the years we've gotten to know investment managers and financial analysts who research companies. Although some financial documents aren't that difficult to read (we show you how in this section), interpreting what they mean with respect to a company's future isn't easy. You've surely heard of the accounting scandals at companies such as Enron. These companies manipulated their financial books, with the blessing of supposedly blue-chip corporate auditors, to mislead investors into believing they were more profitable than they actually were. Identifying trouble *before* other investors do is a skill that many professional investors haven't mastered — if you can identify trouble early, go manage other people's money!

All publicly traded companies must annually file certain financial documents. Consider reviewing these documents to enhance your understanding of a company's businesses and strategies rather than for the predictive value you might hope they provide.

The first of such documents is the *annual report*. It provides standardized financial statements as well as management's discussion about how the company has performed and how it plans to improve its performance in the future. If you're a bit of the sceptical sort like we are, you may think, "Aren't the company's officials going to make everything sound wonderful?"

To a certain extent yes, but not as badly as you may think, especially at companies that adhere to sound accounting principles and good old-fashioned ethics. First, a large portion of annual reports include the company's financial statements, which an accounting firm must audit. Audits don't mean that companies and their accounting firms can't (often legally) structure the books to make them look rosier than they really are, however. There's far more room for creative and artistic flair in the accounting world than you may have realized. And some companies have pulled the wool over the eyes of their auditors, who then became unwitting accomplices in producing false financial figures.

Also keep in mind that more than a few companies have been sued for misleading shareholders with inflated forecasts or lack of disclosure of problems. Responsible companies try to present a balanced and, of course, hopeful perspective in their annual reports. Most companies' annual reports are written by non–techno geeks, so you have a decent chance of understanding them.

Financial and business highlights

The first section of most annual reports presents a description of a company's recent financial highlights and business strategies. You can use this information to find out about the businesses that the company is in and where the company is heading. For example, in Figure 6-1, *Value Line* mentions that Starbucks is also in the specialty sales business. The annual report can provide more detail about Starbucks' specialty business.

Okay, enough about the coffee business — we want to expose you to another industry. Sears is one of Canada's best-known retailers. As its annual report points out, "Over 93 percent of Canadians live within a 10-minute drive of a Sears full-line store, Sears Home store, Dealer store, Outlet store, Floor Covering Centre, or Catalogue agent. As well . . . we are Canada's most popular general merchandise retail website."

Balance sheet

You can find a company's hard-core financials in the back portion of most annual reports. You can find many of these same numbers in many research reports and from numerous financial Web sites, except you get more specific details in the company's annual report. (You'll find annual reports for publicly traded companies as well a other regulatory filings at www.sedar.com.)

All annual reports contain a *balance sheet*. This is a snapshot summary of all the company's assets and liabilities from the beginning of the year to the last day of the company's year-end, which is typically December 31. Some companies use a fiscal year that ends at other times of the year.

A company's balance sheet resembles a personal balance sheet. The entries, of course, look a little different because you likely don't own things like manufacturing equipment. (And if you read our *Personal Finance For Canadians For Dummies* book, you know that we're against listing personal property, such as furniture and cars, as assets. After all, do you plan to sell these things to raise money for retirement, home buying, and so on?) Figure 6-3 shows a typical corporate balance sheet.

60   SEARS CANADA INC.

CONSOLIDATED STATEMENTS OF FINANCIAL POSITION

(in millions)	As at January 3, 2004	As at December 28, 2002
ASSETS		
Current Assets		
Cash and short-term investments	$ 82.6	$ 142.8
Accounts receivable (Notes 2 and 3)	1,249.1	1,322.5
Income taxes recoverable	11.8	4.1
Inventories	801.3	754.0
Prepaid expenses and other assets	110.6	109.4
Current portion of future income tax assets (Note 4)	149.7	183.1
	2,405.1	2,515.9
Investments and other assets (Note 5)	76.8	59.7
Capital assets (Note 6)	1,042.8	1,036.9
Long term deferred receivables	229.9	61.7
Deferred charges (Note 7)	293.6	309.3
Future income tax assets (Note 4)	17.5	77.8
	$ 4,065.7	$ 4,061.3
LIABILITIES		
Current liabilities		
Accounts payable	$ 728.2	$ 799.0
Accrued liabilities	486.4	517.3
Income and other taxes payable	95.9	99.1
Principal payments on long-term obligations due within one year (Note 9)	7.3	6.2
Current portion of deferred credit (Note 4)	–	30.0
	1,317.8	1,451.6
Long-term obligations (Note 9)	763.1	770.2
Deferred credit	–	24.2
Accrued benefit liability (Note 8)	173.9	168.4
	2,254.8	2,414.4
SHAREHOLDERS' EQUITY		
Capital stock (Note 10)	458.8	458.1
Retained earnings	1,352.1	1,188.8
	1,810.9	1,646.9
	$ 4,065.7	$ 4,061.3

Figure 6-3: The balance sheet from Sears annual report.

Assets

The assets section lists the following items that the company holds or owns that are of significant value:

- ✔ **Cash.** We think you know what cash is. Lest you think there are stacks of blue, purple, green, red, and brown bills just sitting around in corporate vaults, rest assured that companies invest this money to earn interest.

- ✔ **Accounts receivable.** This is money that is owed to the company. Just as your employer pays you at the month's end for your work during the entire month, the company is paid for services previously provided. If you're paid $4,000 monthly at month's end and you prepare your own personal balance midmonth, you can list a salary of $2,000 as an asset because it's money due you that you haven't yet received.

  As companies grow, their accounts receivable usually do, too. Watch out for cases where the receivables grow faster than the sales (revenue). This growth may indicate that the company is having problems with its products' quality or pricing. Unhappy customers pay more slowly or demand bigger price discounts.

- ✔ **Inventories.** Manufacturing and retail companies (such as Sears) also track and report *inventory* (the products that haven't yet been sold) as an asset. Generally speaking, as a business grows, so too does its inventory. If inventory grows more quickly than revenue, such growth may be a warning sign. This growth can indicate that customers are scaling back purchases and that the company miscalculated and overproduced. It can also be a leading indicator of an obsolete or inferior product offering.

- ✔ **Prepaid expenses.** This refers to payments the company has already made for products or services that will be used in the future. Insurance premiums, rent, heating, and telephone services are typical expenses that are paid for in advance.

- ✔ **Investments.** In addition to cash, some companies may invest in other securities, such as bonds and stocks. Just as with your own personal situation, companies usually invest money that they don't expect to use in the near future. Many items are explained in more detail in notes that follow these financial statements. Sears, for example, details in an explanatory note how its investments are divvied up, with different amounts invested in unsecured debentures, subordinated loans, and so on.

- ✔ **Property and equipment.** (Sometimes referred to as *fixed assets* or, as Sears does, *capital assets*.) All companies need equipment to run their business. This equipment can include office furniture, computers, real estate they own, and manufacturing machinery that companies use to make their products. Equipment becomes less valuable over time, so companies consider this depreciation as a cost of doing business each year. Therefore, if a company ceases buying new equipment, this entry on the balance sheet gradually decreases because the depreciation is subtracted from the value of the equipment.

✔ **Goodwill and other assets.** One of the assets that doesn't show up on most companies' balance sheets is their *goodwill.* Companies work hard through advertising, product development, and service to attract and retain customers. *Name-brand recognition* is a term that you sometimes hear thrown around. Companies can't put a value on the goodwill that they've generated, but when they purchase (acquire) another firm, some of the purchase price is considered goodwill. Specifically, if a company is acquired for $100 million but has a net worth (assets minus liabilities) of just $50 million, the extra $50 million goes to goodwill. The goodwill then becomes an asset which, like equipment, is depreciated or amortized over the years ahead.

"Other assets" is a catchall category that may include some stuff that'll make your eyes glaze over. For example, companies keep a different set of books for tax purposes (yes, this is legal). Not surprisingly, companies do this because the tax authorities allow, in some cases, more deductions than what the company is required to show from an accounting standpoint on its financial statements. (If you were a company, wouldn't you want your shareholders, but not the tax collectors, to see gobs of profits?) Companies treat tax deferment as an asset until the tax department receives more of its share down the road.

Liabilities

This section summarizes all the money that the company owes to others.

✔ **Accounts payable.** When companies make requests to purchase things for their business, they sometimes have time to pay the bills. As with inventory and accounts receivable, accounts payable generally increases with a company's increasing revenue.

If accounts payable increases faster than revenue, it can indicate a problem. On the other hand, that increase can also be a sign of good financial management. The longer you take to pay your bills, the longer you have the money in your pocket working for you.

✔ **Accrued liabilities.** This line tallies money that the company must someday pay to its employees. For example, many larger firms maintain pension plans. These plans promise workers who retire with at least five years of service a monthly income cheque in retirement. The company must reserve the money it owes and list it as a liability or debt that it will someday have to pay. This is sometimes called *accrued compensation.*

✔ **Income taxes payable.** Companies are in business to make a profit, and as they earn those profits, they need to reserve a portion to pay income taxes. As we explain earlier, some of the taxes that the company owes can be caused by accounting differences between the company's financial statements and those filed with the tax authorities.

✔ **Dividends payable.** Not all companies pay dividends (see Chapter 4) to their shareholders. But those companies that do pay dividends typically declare the dividend several weeks in advance of when it's actually owed. During this interim period the company lists the dividends that are promised but not yet paid as a liability.

Shareholders' equity

The difference between a company's assets and liabilities is known as *shareholders' equity*. Shareholders' equity is what makes balance sheets always balance. When companies issue stock, for example, they receive cash, which they then list as an asset, for the stock sold.

Companies divide stock proceeds between *par value* and *capital in excess of par value*. Par values are arcane — and largely meaningless.

Income statement

The other big financial statement in an annual report is the income statement (see Figure 6-4).

Revenue

Revenue is simply the money that the company receives from its customers as compensation for its products or services. Just as you can earn income from your job(s) as well as investments and other sources, a company can also make money from a variety of sources. Sears, of course, makes its money from retail sales, along with other ventures, including its travel division and its credit card operations.

Ideally, you want to see a steady or accelerating rate of growth in a company's revenues. If a company's revenue grows more slowly, you need to inquire why. Is it because of poor service or product performance, better competitor offerings, ineffective marketing, or all the above?

For companies with multiple divisions or product lines, the annual report may detail the revenue of each product line in a later section. Sears breaks its numbers out into three segments: merchandising, credit operations, and real estate.

If a company doesn't break out revenues in this way, look at some of the other financial statements that the next section, "Exploring Other Useful Corporate Reports," recommends. Examine what spurs or holds back the company's overall growth, and what different businesses the company operates in. Businesses that were acquired but that don't really fit with the company's other business units are a red flag. Large companies that have experienced stalled revenue growth sometimes try to "enter" new businesses through acquisition but then don't manage them well because they don't understand the keys to their success.

2003 ANNUAL REPORT **61**

CONSOLIDATED STATEMENTS OF EARNINGS

For the 53 and 52 week periods ended January 3, 2004 (fiscal 2003) and December 28, 2002, respectively

(in millions, except per share amounts)	2003	2002
Total Revenues	$ 6,222.7	$ 6,535.9
Cost of merchandise sold, operating, administrative and selling expenses	5,775.9	6,107.9
Depreciation and amortization	146.6	148.7
Interest expense, net	59.5	59.8
Unusual items — expense (Note 12)	5.0	189.1
Earnings before income taxes	235.7	30.4
Income taxes (Note 4)		
Current	7.5	49.3
Future	93.5	(71.1)
	101.0	(21.8)
Net earnings	$ 134.7	$ 52.2
Earnings per share (Note 19)	$ 1.26	$ 0.49
Diluted earnings per share (Note 19)	$ 1.26	$ 0.49

CONSOLIDATED STATEMENTS OF RETAINED EARNINGS

For the 53 and 52 week periods ended January 3, 2004 (fiscal 2003) and December 28, 2002, respectively

(in millions)	2003	2002
Opening Balance	$ 1,188.8	$ 1,162.2
Adoption of new accounting policy for Business Combinations (Note 1)	54.2	–
Net earnings	134.7	52.2
Dividends declared	(25.6)	(25.6)
Closing Balance	$ 1,352.1	$ 1,188.8

Figure 6-4:
Sears income statement.

When researching retail stores like Sears (or restaurant chains like McDonald's or clothing stores like The Gap), examine the revenue changes that come from opening new locations versus the changes at existing locations, sometimes referred to as *same stores*. Be concerned if you find that a company's revenue growth largely comes from opening new locations rather than growth at existing locations.

Expenses

If only you got to keep all the income that you make. Just as personal income taxes, housing, food, and clothing expenses gobble up much of your personal income, company expenses use up much and sometimes all of a company's revenue.

Even healthy, growing businesses can get into trouble if their expenses balloon faster than their revenue. Well-managed companies stay on top of their expenses during good and bad times. Unfortunately, it's easy for companies to get sloppy during good times.

It's particularly useful to examine each category of expenses relative to (in other words, as a percentage of) the company's revenue to see which grow or shrink. As a well-managed and financially healthy company grows, expenses as a percentage of revenue should decrease. As this happens, profits as a percentage of revenue increase. When you examine how a company's profits change relative to total revenue received, focus on operating income. Sometimes companies experience one-time events that can change profits temporarily. Companies usually list these one-time events in the section under expenses.

Last, but not least, and of great importance to shareholders, is the calculation of the earnings per share. Higher profits per share generally help fuel a higher stock price, and declining profits feed falling stock prices. Remember, though, that smart financial market participants are looking ahead, so if you run out to buy stock in a company that's reporting higher profits, it's old news and likely already priced into the company's current market value.

Exploring Other Useful Corporate Reports

In addition to annual reports, companies produce other financial statements that you may want to peruse. You can generally obtain these from the company for free or from the SEDAR site (www.sedar.com) for Canadians companies, and from the Securities and Exchange Commission site (www.sec.gov) for U.S. companies. (See Chapter 19 for more on these sites.)

10-Ks

*10-K*s are expanded versions of an annual report filed by U.S.-based companies. Most investment professionals read the 10-K instead of the annual report because the 10-K contains additional data and information, especially for a company's various divisions and product lines. Also, 10-Ks contain little of the verbal hype that you sometimes find in annual reports. The 10-K is probably one of the most objective reports that a company publishes. If you're not intimidated by annual reports, or you want more company meat, go for it!

Quarterly Reports

Quarterly Reports (called *10-Q*s in the U.S.) provide information on a quarterly basis. These reports are worthwhile if you like to read a reasonably detailed discussion by management of the latest business and financial developments at the company. However, we recommend leaving the research to folks like *Value Line*'s analysts.

The financial data in these reports is unaudited and not of great use for the long-term investor. If you want to watch your investments like a hawk and try to be among the first to detect indications of financial problems (easier said than done), these reports are required reading.

REMEMBER Many companies go back to restate their quarterly financials. Remember that the accountants haven't approved these numbers. Sometimes companies take their financial lump in one quarter to get problems behind them, so one bad quarter doesn't necessarily indicate a harmful long-term trend.

Proxy forms and information circulars

The final corporate documents that you may want to review are the annual *proxy form* and *information circular* (the two are collectively referred to as a *proxy statement* in the U.S.), which are sent out in advance of a company's annual meeting.

A proxy is a power of attorney that transfers the right of a shareholder to vote at a shareholders' meeting to someone else, typically the company's management. The information circular tells you who serves on the board of directors as well as how much they and the executives of the company are paid. It also must contain information on any important matters that will be under discussion, and the interest of management in these issues.

The circular contains information on other corporate matters, such as the election of the board of directors. Directors, who are usually corporate executives, lawyers, accountants, and other knowledgeable luminaries, serve as a sounding board, counsellor, and sometimes overseer to the management team of a company.

The proxy form and information circular become much more important when a company faces a takeover or some other controversial corporate matter, such as the election of an alternative board of directors.

At annual meetings, where the board of directors discusses proxy statements, shareholders sometimes get angry and ask why the executives are paid so much when the company's stock price and business underperform the competition.

Fundamental versus technical analysis

Throughout this chapter and the previous one, we talk a lot about companies' financial statements — balance sheets, revenues, expenses, earnings, price/earnings ratios, and so on. Analyzing financial statements and making investing decisions based on them is known as *fundamental analysis.*

But another school of stock market analysis, known as *technical analysis,* exists. Folks who employ technical analysis like to examine chart patterns, volume, and all sorts of indicators that have little, if anything, to do with the underlying stock.

Technicians say things like "Stock XYZ has a major support area at $20 per share" or "Stock ABC has broken out above $30 per share." Although it may be a bit extreme to say that all the technicians that have ever existed have never produced anything of value, you can

safely ignore this school of thinking. In fact, ignoring the technicians will likely increase your stock market profits. Why? Because technical analysis thinking encourages a trader's, not an investor's, mindset.

Not surprisingly, most technicians come from one of two camps. Many technical analysts work for brokerage firms and write daily, weekly, or monthly assessments of the entire stock market and some individual stocks. Recommendations and advice change over time, and the result is that you trade more. Curiously, these brokerage firms make more money the more you trade!

Investment newsletter writers are the other big advocates of this Ouija-board approach to investment management. Again, it's a great system for the newsletter writers that hook you on a $200-per-year monthly newsletter.

Getting Ready to Invest in Stocks

Especially during the late 1990s, amidst the chorus of self-anointed gurus saying that you could make fat profits if you pick your own stocks, we sometimes thought we were a lone voice urging caution and sensible thinking. Unless you're extraordinarily lucky or unusually gifted at analyzing company and investor behaviour, you won't earn above-average returns if you select your own stocks.

Keep to a minimum — ideally no more than 20 percent of your invested dollars — the amount you dedicate to individual stock investments. We encourage you to do such investing for the educational value and enjoyment that you derive from it, not because you think you're smarter than the best professional money managers. (If you want to find out more about analyzing companies, read the chapters in Part IV on small business as well as investing resource chapters in Part V.)

Understanding stock prices

Most major newspapers print a listing of the prior day's stock prices (unless you live in an area with a late-afternoon paper that publishes that day's activity). Major daily business papers such as *The Globe and Mail*, the *National Post*, *The Wall Street Journal*, and *Investor's Business Daily* publish stock prices daily. Likewise, just about every major financial site on the Internet offers stock prices (usually for free as a lure to get you to visit their site). To view a stock price quote online, all you need is the security's trading symbol (which you obtain by looking up the company's name, if you don't already know it).

For a thrill, you can stop by a local brokerage office and see the current stock quotes whizzing by on a long, narrow screen on a wall. Stock market channels on cable television often have this ticker-tape banner running on the bottom of your television screen. Many brokerage firms also maintain publicly accessible terminals (which look a lot like a personal computer) on which you can obtain current quotes for free.

The following table is a typical example of the kinds of information that you can find in daily price quotes in papers and online.

Stock	*Canadian National Railway (CNR)*
52-wk High	$55.74
52-wk Low	$42.63
Last Traded	16:44
Last Trade	$51.70
Net Change	$-0.49
% Change	-0.94
Open	52.26
Day High	52.40
Day Low	51.43
Volume	683,500
P/E	15.30
Mkt Cap	15,093,524,653
Div/Shr	0.78
Yield	1.40

This listing examines the stock price information for one of Canada's best-known companies, transportation giant Canadian National Railway (also known as CNR). After the name of the company, you see the trading symbol, CNR, which is the code that you and brokers use to look up the price on computer-based quotation systems.

The next two lines indicate the high ($55.74) and low ($42.63) trading prices for CNR during the past 52 weeks.

Last Trade indicates the most recent price that the stock traded at, and Last Traded at the time. The % Change indicates how that price differs from the previous day's close. In this case, you can see that the stock was down $0.49 points (0.94 percent) from the prior day's close.

Day's Open, High, and Low show, respectively, the price the stock first traded at when the market opened in the morning, and the highest and lowest price that the stock traded at during the day.

Volume indicates the number of shares that traded through this point in the trading day. (To conserve space, many newspapers indicate the volume in hundreds of shares — in other words, you must add two zeros to the end of the number to arrive at the actual number of shares.)

The P/E ratio, as we explain in Chapters 4 and 5, measures the price of CNR's stock relative to the company's earnings or profits.

Market Capitalization calculates the current market value of all of CNR's stock, which in this case is $15 billion. It is arrived at by multiplying the current price per share by the total number of shares outstanding. (See Chapter 8 for an explanation of so-called market caps as they apply to stocks and stock funds.)

Dividends/Share shows you the current dividend, which in this case is $0.78 per share, which the company pays yearly to shareholders. Most companies actually pay out one-quarter of their total annual dividend every three months.

Yield indicates the effective percentage yield that the stock's dividend produces. To calculate the effective yield, divide the dividend by the current stock price. CNR shareholders can expect to receive a dividend worth about 1.40 percent of the current stock value.

Now you know how to read stock quotes!

Placing your trade through a broker

After you decide to buy some stock, you generally need a broker. (In Chapter 5 we explain an alternative, the somewhat administratively hassled way to buy direct from some companies.) As we explain in Chapter 9, discount brokers are generally the best way to go — they take your orders and charge far less than do conventional brokers who pay their brokers on commission.

After you decide which discount broker you want to use, request (by phone or via the Internet) an account application package for the type of account that you desire (regular, RRSP, RRIF, RESP, and so on). Complete the forms (call the firm's toll-free number or visit a branch office if you get stuck) and mail or bring them back to the discounter.

When it comes time to place your order, simply call the discount broker and explain what you want to do (or use your touch-tone phone or computer to place your order). One approach is to place what's known as a *market order*. Such an order instructs your broker to buy you the amount of stock that you desire, 100 shares for example, at the current and best (lowest) price that another investor is willing to sell her shares at.

Alternatively, you can try to buy a desired stock at a specific price — for example, you can place a purchase order at $32 per share when the stock's last trade was $33 per share. This type of order is known as a *limit order* and is good for as long as you want it to be . . . today, four months from now, or until you cancel it. This generally means you're hoping to get the stock for less than the current market price, and so you're gambling that the stock drops a little before it rises.

One final word of advice: Try to buy stock in reasonable-size chunks, such as 100 shares. Otherwise, commissions gobble a large percentage of the small dollar amount that you invest. If you don't have enough money to build a diversified portfolio all at once, don't sweat it. Diversify over time. Purchase a chunk of one stock after you have enough money accumulated and then wait to buy the next stock until you've saved up another chunk to invest.

Chapter 7

Bonds and Other Lending Investments

. . . .

. . . .

*I*n Chapters 1 and 2 we discuss the major types of investments and their potential risks and returns. *Lending investments* are those in which you lend your money to an organization, such as a company or government, which typically pays you a set or fixed rate of interest. (Ownership investments, by contrast, provide partial ownership of a company or some other asset, such as real estate, that has the ability to generate revenue and potential profits.)

If you really want to make your money grow, lending investments aren't for you. However, even the most aggressive investors have a legitimate purpose for putting some of their money into lending investments. Table 7-1 shows some of the logic behind lending investments and when such investments do and don't make sense.

Lending investments are available everywhere — at your local bank and through brokerage firms, insurance companies, and mutual fund companies. Lending investments that you may have heard of include bank accounts (savings and certificates of deposit), Treasury bills and other bonds, bond mutual funds, mortgages, and guaranteed-investment certificates (GICs).

In this chapter we walk you through these investments and explain what's good and bad about each of them and when you should and shouldn't use them. We also tell you what to look for and look out for when comparing them.

Table 7-1	Lending and Ownership Investments Compared
Consider Lending Investments if . . .	*Consider Ownership Investments when . . .*
You need current income.	You don't need or want much current income.
You expect to sell within five years.	You're investing for the long term (seven to ten-plus years).
Investment volatility makes you a wreck or you just want to cushion some of the volatility of your other investments.	You don't mind/can ignore significant ups and downs.
You don't need to make your money grow after inflation and taxes.	You need more growth to reach your goals.

Banks: The Cost of Feeling Secure

Putting your money in a bank may make you feel safe for a variety of reasons. If you're like most people, your first investing experience was at your neighbourhood bank where you established a savings account. Depending on your situation, this event may have happened as early as elementary or high school or as late as university or after university.

Part of the comfort of keeping money in the bank stems from the fact that the bank is where many of our parents first steered us financially. Also, relatively large branches, often within walking distance of your home or office, have vaults, security monitoring cameras, and barriers in front of the tellers. These accoutrements shouldn't make you feel safer about leaving your money with the bank — they're needed because of bank robberies and the preponderance of guns in our society.

Large bank branches with all the trimmings cost a lot of money to operate. Guess where that money comes from? From you, of course! That's one of the reasons why the interest rates that banks pay often pale in comparison with secure alternatives.

The realities of bank insurance

Some people are consoled by the Canada Deposit Insurance Corporation (CDIC) insurance that comes with most bank accounts. It's true that if your bank fails, your deposits with any particular member of the CDIC are insured up to $60,000. (If you have deposits in joint accounts, RRSPs, RRIFs, or held in trust, each type of deposit is also covered up to $60,000 with each member of the CDIC.) So what, we say. Treasury bills are issued and backed by the federal government. Plenty of other equally safe lending investments yield higher returns.

Just because the CDIC — a federal Crown corporation — stands behind the CDIC insurance system doesn't mean that in the event of a bank failure a 100 percent certainty exists that you'll be paid back in full or paid back with dollars worth anywhere near what a dollar is worth today. Although you're insured for $60,000 in a bank, if the bank fails, you'll likely wait quite a while to get your money back — and you may well get less interest than you thought you would.

Any investment that involves lending your money to someone else or to some organization carries risk. That includes putting your money into a bank or buying a Treasury bill that the federal government issues. Although we're not doomsayers, any student of history knows that governments and civilizations fail. It's often not a matter of *whether* they'll fail; it's a question of *when*.

The overused guaranteed investment certificate (GIC)

Other than savings accounts, banks also sell *guaranteed investment certificates* (GICs). GICs are without a doubt the most overused bank investment around. The attraction is that you get a higher rate of return on a GIC than on a bank savings or money market account. And unlike a bond, which we soon discuss, a GIC's principal value does not fluctuate. Of course, GICs also give you the peace of mind afforded by the CDIC insurance program.

GICs pay higher interest rates than savings accounts because you typically commit to tie up your money for a period of time, such as 6, 12, or 24 months. The bank pays you 2 to 3 percent and then turns around and lends your money to people through credit cards, auto loans, and the like and charges the borrower an interest rate of 10-plus percent. Not a bad business, eh?

When you tie up your money in a GIC, you make a sacrifice. If you want it back before the GIC matures (unless you have a cashable GIC which comes with an even lower interest rate), a hefty penalty is shaved from your return. With other lending investments, such as bonds and bond mutual funds, discussed in the section "Bonds: Jargon for IOU" later in this chapter, you can access your money without penalty and generally at little or no cost.

In addition to penalties for early withdrawal, GICs yield less than a high-quality bond with a comparable maturity (for example, two, three, or five years). Often, the yield difference is 1 percent or more, especially if you don't shop around and simply buy GICs from your local bank where you keep your chequing account without asking for a better rate.

You can earn higher returns and have better access to your money in bonds than in GICs. GICs make the most sense when you know, for example, that you can invest your money for one year, after which you need the money for some purchase that you expect to make. Just make sure that you shop around to get the best interest rate. Begin by simply asking for a better rate than the posted rate at your bank or trust company. If you do a reasonable amount of other business with your financial institution, or are simply a good bargainer, you may be able to get an increase of half a percent or even more. To get a sense of what the competition is offering, you'll find sample GIC rates in the financial section of many newspapers. A number of sites offer extensive lists of up-to-date GIC rates, including www.moneysense.ca and online deposit broker www.gicdirect.com. If having the CDIC insurance gives you peace of mind, take a look at Government of Canada bonds, which we discuss later in this chapter. These bonds usually pay more interest than the vast majority of GICs available.

The money market fund alternative to savings accounts

You likely have a chequing account at a local bank that you use to pay household bills and to access cash through bank machines. But beyond keeping enough money in your chequing account to pay the bills, it doesn't pay to keep extra savings in the bank. Because most bank accounts generally pay pretty crummy interest rates, you need to think long and hard about keeping spare cash in the bank.

Keep your chequing account at your local bank but not your extra savings. Money market funds, which are a type of mutual fund (other common funds focus on bonds or stocks), are a great place to keep your extra savings. Money market funds offer a higher yielding alternative to bank savings and bank money market deposit accounts.

Money market funds, which are offered by mutual fund companies (see Chapter 8), are unique among mutual funds because they don't fluctuate in value and maintain a fixed $10 per share price. As with a bank savings account, your principal investment in a money market fund does not change in value. If you invest your money in a money fund, it earns dividends (which is just another name for the interest you would receive in a bank account).

Money market fund advantages

The best money market mutual funds offer several significant benefits over bank savings accounts. The biggest advantage is higher yields. Money market mutual funds pay higher yields because they don't have the high overhead that banks do. The most efficient mutual fund companies (we discuss them in Chapter 8) don't have scads of branch offices on every street corner. Another reason why banks can get away with paying lower yields is that many depositors, perhaps including you, think the CDIC insurance that comes with a bank savings account makes it safer than a money market mutual fund. In fact, the CDIC insurance is an expense that banks ultimately pass on to their customers.

Money market funds are a good place to keep your emergency cash reserve of at least three to six months' living expenses. They're also a great place to keep money awaiting investment elsewhere in the near future. If you're saving money for a home that you expect to purchase soon (in the next year or so), a money fund can be a safe place to accumulate and grow the down payment. You don't want to risk placing such money in the stock market because the market can plunge in a relatively short period of time.

Just as you can use a money market fund for your personal purposes, you can open a money market fund for your business. You can use this account to deposit cheques that you receive from customers, to hold excess funds, and sometimes even to pay bills.

Money funds lack insurance

So what's the catch? Good money market funds really don't have any, but you need to know about an important difference between bank accounts and money market mutual funds. Money funds are not insured. As we discuss earlier in this chapter, bank accounts come with CDIC insurance that protects your deposited money up to $60,000. So, if a bank fails because it lends too much money to people and companies that go bankrupt or abscond with the funds, you should get your money back from the CDIC.

The lack of CDIC insurance on a money fund shouldn't trouble you. Mutual fund companies can't fail because they have a dollar invested in securities for every dollar that you deposit in their money fund. By contrast, banks are required to have available just a fraction of every dollar that you hand over to them.

A money market fund's *investments* can decline slightly in value, which can cause the money fund's share price to fall below a dollar. A few cases have occurred where money market funds bought some bad investments. However, in every case except one, the parent company running the money fund infused cash into the affected fund, thus enabling it to maintain the $1-per-share price.

One U.S. money market fund did "break the buck." It didn't take money in from people like you or us, but was run by a bunch of small banks for themselves. This money market fund made some bone-headed investments. The share price of the fund declined by 6 percent, and the fund owners decided to disband the fund; they didn't bail it out, because they would be repaying themselves.

Stick with bigger mutual fund companies if you're worried about the lack of CDIC insurance. They have the financial wherewithal and the largest incentive to save a floundering money fund. You can find more details about money market funds in Chapter 8.

High-interest savings accounts

Money market funds are still a good temporary parking place for your money, particularly if you're contributing to an RRSP but aren't sure what specific investment to purchase. While you're making up your mind, or finding the time to do a little research, put it in a money market fund. Regardless of who your RRSP is with, be it a financial institution, discount brokerage, or full-service brokerage, they will likely have an in-house money market fund with little if any restrictions or fees, as well as offering money market funds of other companies.

In many cases, however, you may be looking for a place where you can simply keep some money on stash. Perhaps you know you'll need to tap into it in the short term. Or maybe you want a place to put your emergency funds that will ensure your capital is protected but still earn you a decent return. High-interest savings accounts offer a great and in some ways superior alternative to money market funds.

High-interest savings accounts are typically made available by institutions that don't have — and don't have plans to build — a nation-wide string of bricks-and-mortar branches. This saves them substantially on staffing and other overhead. As a result, they're able to offer interest rates that equal and even surpass those offered by money market funds. They generally have no minimum balance requirements, and offer other benefits not available with money market mutual funds. This can include the convenience of telephone and online transactions, as well as access to your money through bank machines, often with no fees attached.

While the idea of dealing at arm's length with a company without a branch on your local street corner may seem a little unsettling, you need not worry. These accounts are not fly-by-night operations. President's Choice Financial, for example, is a co-venture between Loblaw Ltd. and Canadian Imperial Bank of Commerce, while ING Direct Bank is a division of International Nederlanden Groep, a Dutch bank. They also come with CDIC insurance, which protects you up to $60,000.

To open an account, you'll need to fill out an application and send in a cheque. You can then set up your account so that money can be electronically moved back and forth between your regular bank or trust account and your high-interest account. You arrange deposits and withdrawals over the telephone or on the Internet. The transaction in most cases is completed by midnight of the next business day after you place your order. You can even arrange to have your pay cheque deposited directly.

ING Direct

The first into the field was ING Direct, with its 'Canadian Dollar Income Savings Account." In early 2004 ING's investment savings account was paying 2.5 percent interest. While that's an admittedly small return, it was far in excess of the banks' rates on savings accounts, which were generally a fraction of a percentage. ING has no minimum balance requirement, and there are no fees. The only restriction is that you have to wait five days after making a deposit before you can withdraw those funds. Interest is earned daily and compounded monthly. You get a bank card with your account, which can be used to make withdrawals. While the card can be used at any bank machine that's part of the Interac system, you'll pay a fee for each transaction.

In addition to its savings account ING has introduced many other financial products. It offers GICs, no-haggle (at least on the interest rate) mortgages, and lines of credit.

President's Choice Financial

President's Choice Financial has taken a somewhat different approach. Its "Interest First" savings account is similar to ING's savings account. However, it's a stripped-down affair that doesn't come with a bank card or bank machine access. President's Choice also offers a chequing account. This account has no fees, and you also get free chequing privileges. You can access the money at no charge by using your President's Choice Financial bank card at any CIBC bank machine or PC machines at grocery stores. You can use the bank card at any machine on the Interac system, but you'll pay the extra Interac fee. The chequing account can also be used to pay bills, and can be set up for automatic bill payments, again with no fees. President's Choice Financial's savings account was paying around 2.15 percent in the summer of 2004. The attraction of President's Choice Financial is that the company offers an appealing package that brings together convenience, high interest rates, few restrictions, and no fees.

President's Choice Financial has recently expanded its range of services and now offers competitively priced mortgages and lines of credit. It's also trying to add more value to its products through a system that gives you points for your various banking business as well as on your grocery shopping at Loblaws stores.

Bonds: Jargon for IOU

In the 1920s Andrew Mellon remarked, "Gentlemen prefer bonds." We've never figured out why, and we're convinced that Mr. Mellon wasn't serious or sober when he said this. Our observation is that *conservative investors* prefer bonds. That is, conservative when it comes to taking risk, not when professing their political preference.) Otherwise aggressive investors who seek diversification or investments for shorter-term financial goals also prefer bonds. The reason: Bonds offer higher yields than bank accounts without as much volatility as the stock market.

Bonds are similar to GICs (discussed in the section "The overused guaranteed investment certificate (GIC)" earlier in this chapter). For example, you can purchase a bond, scheduled to mature five years from now, that a company such as Bombardier issues. A Bombardier five-year bond may pay you 6 percent interest. As long as Bombardier doesn't have a financial catastrophe and after five years of receiving interest payments on the bond, Bombardier returns your original investment to you. So, in effect, you're loaning your money to Bombardier (instead of the bank when you deposit money in a bank account).

The worst that can happen to your bond investment is that Bombardier's business goes into a tailspin and the company ends up in financial ruin — also known as bankruptcy. If that happens, you may lose all your original investment and miss out on some of the expected interest.

But bonds that high-quality companies such as Bombardier issue are quite safe — they rarely default. Heck, many companies have been around longer than you've been alive. Besides, even if every now and then a big company goes under, you don't have to invest all your money in just one or two bonds. If you own bonds in many companies (which you can easily do through a good bond mutual fund) and one bond unexpectedly takes a hit, it affects only a small portion of your portfolio. And, unlike a GIC, which usually comes with stiff early withdrawal penalties, you can generally sell your bonds any time you desire at minimal cost. Selling (and buying) most bond mutual funds costs nothing, as we explain in Chapter 8.

Bond investors accept the risk of default because bonds pay higher interest rates than the bank. If you take extra risk and forsake the CDIC insurance, you should receive a higher rate of interest investing in bonds. Remember that when you invest in bank savings accounts and GICs, you're paid less interest in part because of the overhead of the bank branches as well as the cost of the CDIC insurance.

The uses for bonds

Investing in bonds is a time-honoured way to earn a better rate of return on money that you don't plan to use within the next couple years or more. As with stocks, bonds can generally be sold any day that the financial markets are open. Because their value fluctuates, though, you're more likely to lose money if you're forced to sell your bonds sooner rather than later. In the short term, if the bond market happens to fall and then you need to sell, you could lose money. In the longer term, as is the case with stocks, you're far less likely to lose money.

Bonds generally pay you more than bank savings and money market mutual funds, but with a catch. As we discuss later in this chapter, bonds are riskier than money market funds and savings accounts because their value can fall if interest rates rise. However, bonds tend to be more stable in value than stocks. (We cover the risk and return of bonds and stocks in Chapter 2.)

Don't put your emergency cash reserve into bonds — that's what a money market fund or high-interest savings account is for. But don't put too much of your longer-term investment money in bonds, either. As we show in Chapter 2, bonds are generally inferior investments for making your money grow. Growth-oriented investments, such as stocks, real estate, and your own business, hold the potential to build real wealth.

The following list provides some common financial goals and reasons why investing money in bonds can make sense:

- ✔ **A major purchase** that won't happen for at least two years, such as the purchase of a home or some other major expenditure. Shorter-term bonds may work for you as a higher-yielding and slightly riskier alternative to money market funds.

- ✔ **Diversification.** Bonds don't move in tandem with the performance of other types of investments, such as stocks. In fact, in a terrible economic environment (such as occurred during the Great Depression), bonds may appreciate in value while riskier investments such as stocks plunge.

✔ **Retirement investments.** You may invest some of your money in bonds as part of a longer-term investment strategy, such as for retirement. You should have an overall plan for how you want to invest your money, sometimes referred to as an *asset allocation strategy* (see Chapter 8). Aggressive, younger investors should keep less of their retirement money in bonds than older folks who are nearing retirement.

✔ **Income-producing investments.** If you're retired or not working, bonds can be useful because they're better at producing current income than many other investments.

The differences among bonds

Bonds aren't as complicated and unique as people, but they're certainly more complex than a bank savings account. And, thanks to shady marketing practices by some investing companies and salespeople who sell bonds, you have your work cut out for you trying to get a handle on what many bonds really are and how they differ from their peers.

Bonds differ from one another according to the type of organization that issues them — in other words, what kind of organization you lend your money to. The following sections present the major options and when each option may make sense for you.

Treasury bills

Treasury bills, or T-bills, are short-term government bonds issued by the federal government as well as some provinces. They are issued in large denominations, but many financial institutions repackage them and make them available to the public in amounts as small as $1,000. T-bills are available for terms of three, six, and twelve months. T-bills don't pay any actual interest. Instead, you purchase them at a discount to their face value. Your return is the difference between your purchase price and the face value, which you receive at maturity. You'll usually see this return displayed as an interest rate by most financial institutions. This is done simply as a way to help you assess the return you'll make.

Government of Canada bonds

In addition to Treasury bills, the federal government — Canada's biggest debtor of them all — issues marketable bonds. These can be bought in denominations as low as $1,000. There is no commission on buying or selling these securities. Instead, brokers make their money by building a commission into the price of the bond. Government of Canada marketable bonds — like most bonds — are usually quoted as a price per $100 of the value at maturity of the bond. Interest on Government of Canada bonds is paid twice a year.

The best use of T-bills and Government of Canada Bonds is in place of bank GICs. If you feel secure with the insurance that a bank GIC provides, check out a T-bill or federal marketable bond. Government of Canada bonds almost always pay the same or better interest rate as a GIC that matures in the same length of time. If you hunt around, you may stumble upon a bank that pays a slightly higher interest rate than a comparable marketable bond. Unless you really shop around for a GIC, you'll likely earn a lower return on a GIC than on a marketable bond.

Canada Savings Bonds

Unlike other bonds, Canada Savings Bonds (CSBs) are registered in your name. You can't sell them to others, including your broker, or on the bond market. CSBs go on sale every fall, when they're made available for several weeks up to several months, depending on anticipated demand. They can be bought from almost all financial institutions, including banks, trust companies, and credit unions. You can also buy them from most investment dealers and discount brokers.

One major attraction of CSBs is that they can be easily cashed in at any time. When you cash them in you get back your original investment, known as the face amount, as well as the interest that has been earned up to the end of the previous month. So if you cash in your CSBs before they mature, try to do it at the beginning rather than the end of a month to maximize your interest. If you cash them in within three months of the issue date, you get only your original investment back.

The interest rate on CSBs is guaranteed for at least one year. When interest rates are climbing, the government sometimes also guarantees minimum rates for a set period. Because they can be cashed in at any time, CSBs offer another useful feature: If interest rates rise, the government often resets their rates to keep them attractive and prevent large-scale redemptions.

You have to pay tax each year on the interest earned on CSBs issued from 1990 onwards. This applies even if you choose the compound-interest option. For compound interest CSBs purchased before 1990, you can choose to declare earned interest once every three years.

There are two basic types of Canada Savings Bonds. *Regular interest bonds* pay interest annually until they mature on the anniversary of the issue date or when you redeem them. You can have the interest sent to you by cheque or deposited directly into your bank account. Regular interest bonds come in denominations of $300, $500, $1,000, $5,000, and $10,000.

The second type of CSBs are *compound interest bonds*. Instead of receiving the interest payments as they come become payable, the interest is automatically reinvested and added to your original principal until your bonds mature or you cash them in. Compound interest bonds can be bought in denominations of $100, $300, $1,000, $5,000, and $10,000. Many companies set up purchase plans so that you can buy them through automatic deductions from your pay cheque. Compound interest CSBs issued since 1990 require that you pay tax on the interest earned each year, even though you don't actually receive the money.

Compound interest bonds, unlike regular interest bonds, also give you the option of holding them inside a self-directed RRSP or RRIF. If you don't have a self-directed RRSP, you can designate that you want to hold your CSBs in an RRSP when you make your purchase. The government will create what's called *The Canada RSP* — a no-fee plan in which you can hold your CSBs and benefit from tax-free growth. You can also contribute other CSBs you may have into this account.

A new type of CSB was introduced in 1998 called the *Canada Premium Bond*, or *CPB*. You can buy a CPB for as little as $100. Unlike regular CSBs, Canada premium bonds can only be redeemed for a short period each year — on the anniversary of the issue date and for the following 30 days. In return for this lack of liquidity compared with regular CSBs, Canada premium bonds come with a slightly higher rate of interest. If you hold CSBs inside a *Canada RRIF* — a Registered Retirement Income Fund set up with the government to hold your CSBs — you can cash them in order to meet your minimum mandatory RRIF withdrawals without paying a penalty. Canada premium bonds are available as both regular interest bonds and compound interest bonds.

CSBs are a good choice for a short-term investment when you want to earn a decent return on your money while having the option to cash out at any time. One alternative to CSBs is high-interest savings accounts, which we discuss earlier on in this section.

Municipal bonds

Municipal bonds are city and regional government bonds that pay interest. The rate is typically better than what you'd receive from other bonds with a similar maturity. They also usually offer a better rate than that paid by GICs with a comparable term. Unlike a GIC, though, you're not locked in, and you can sell them when you want.

Corporate bonds

Companies such as the big banks, utilities like Bell Canada and TransCanada, and businesses such as Bombardier and Canadian Pacific all issue corporate bonds. In the "Understanding individual bond prices" section later in this chapter we show you how to read the newspaper listings for such bonds. If you buy corporate bonds through a well-managed mutual fund, an approach we advocate, you don't need to read the newspaper listings.

Mortgage bonds

Remember that mortgage you took out when you purchased your home? Well, you can actually purchase a bond to invest in the mortgages of people just like you! Many banks actually sell their mortgages as bonds in the financial markets to allow other investors to invest in them. The mortgages are bundled together and sold as *mortgage-backed securities*, or *MBSs*. The Canada Mortgage and Housing Corporation, a government agency, usually guarantees repayment of principal on MBSs at the bond's maturity. MBSs are sometimes referred to as Cannie Maes, a play on Ginnie Maes, the nickname for the U.S. mortgage-backed securities called Government National Mortgage Associations certificates.

Convertible bonds

Convertible bonds are hybrid securities — they're bonds that you can convert under specified circumstance into a preset number of shares of stock in the company that issued the bond. Although these bonds do pay interest, their yield is lower than nonconvertible bonds because convertibles offer you the upside potential of being able to make more money if the underlying stock rises.

International bonds

You can buy bonds outside the country that you call home. If you live in Canada, for example, you can buy most of the bonds that we describe in this chapter from foreign issuers as well. International bonds are riskier to you because their interest payments can be offset by currency price changes.

The prices of foreign bonds tend not to move in tandem with Canadian bonds. Foreign bond values benefit from and thus protect against a declining Canadian dollar and therefore offer some diversification value. That said, foreign bonds are not a vital holding for a diversified portfolio. They're generally more expensive to purchase and hold than comparable domestic bonds.

Likelihood of default

In addition to being issued by different organizations, bonds differ from one another in the creditworthiness of the issuer. Every year, billions of dollars' worth of bonds default. To minimize investing in bonds that default, purchase high-credit quality bonds. The two main Canadian credit rating agencies, Dominion Bond Rating Service and Canadian Bond Rating Service, rate bonds' credit quality and the likelihood of default.

The credit rating of a bond depends on the issuer's (company or government) ability to pay back its debt. Bond credit ratings are usually done on some sort of a letter-grade scale, where AAA is the highest rating, descending through AA and A, followed by BBB, BB, B, CCC, CC, C, and so on. AAA- and AA-rated bonds are considered "high-grade" or "high-credit quality." Such bonds possess little chance — a fraction of 1 percent — of default.

Bonds rated A and BBB are considered "general" grade or quality. Junk bonds (known more by their marketed name, *high yield*) are rated BB or lower. Junk bonds are more likely to default — perhaps as many as a couple of percent per year actually default.

You may ask yourself why any right-minded investor would buy a bond with a low credit rating. Companies pay a higher interest rate on lower-quality bonds to attract investors. The lower a bond's credit rating and quality, the higher the yield you can and should expect from such a bond. Poorer quality bonds, though, are not for the faint of heart because they're generally more volatile in value.

In addition to paying attention to the credit quality of the bonds that you buy, make sure that you diversify. Don't put all your money earmarked for corporate bonds into just one or two corporate bonds. Bond mutual funds are a great way to invest in bonds because they typically invest in dozens of bonds. We don't recommend buying individual junk bonds — consider investing in these only through a junk bond fund.

Maturity matters: When bonds pay back

Maturity simply means the time at which the bond pays you back — next year, in 5 years, in 30 years, and so on. You need to care how long it takes a bond to mature. Why? Because a bond's maturity gives you a good (although far from perfect) sense of how volatile a bond may be if interest rates change.

Suppose you're considering investing in two bonds that are issued by the same organization and have the same yield of 7 percent. The bonds differ only in when they will mature: One is a 2-year bond and the other a 20-year bond. If interest rates were to rise just 1 percent (from 7 to 8 percent), the 2-year bond might decline about 2 percent in value whereas the 20-year bond could fall approximately five times as much — 10 percent.

If you hold a bond until it matures, you get your principal back unless the issuer defaults. In the meantime, however, if interest rates fall, bond prices rise. The reason is simple: If the bond you hold is issued at, say, 7 percent and interest rates on similar bonds rise to 8 percent, no one (unless they don't know any better) wants to purchase your 7 percent bond. The value of your bond has to decrease enough so that it effectively yields 8 percent.

Bonds are generally classified by the length of time until maturity:

- ✔ **Short-term bonds** mature in the next few years.

- ✔ **Intermediate-term bonds** come due within three to ten years.

- ✔ **Long-term bonds** mature in more than 10 years and generally up to 30 years. Although rare, a number of companies issue 100-year bonds! Several railroads did, as well as Disney and Coca-Cola in recent years. Such bonds are quite dangerous to purchase, especially if they're issued during a period of relatively low interest rates. As we explain earlier in this section, longer-term bonds drop more in price when the overall level of interest rates rise.

Most of the time, longer-term bonds pay higher yields than short-term bonds. You can look at a chart of the current yield of similar bonds plotted against when they mature — such a chart is known as a *yield curve*. At most times, this curve slopes upward. Investors generally demand a higher rate of interest for taking the risk of holding longer-term bonds. Most financial newspapers, magazines, and Web sites carry a current chart of the yield curve.

The simplicity of strip bonds

You can also buy marketable bonds that don't pay any interest. These bonds have had their interest coupons removed, or stripped off, thus the name *stripped bonds*, or *strips*. Stripped bonds are sold at a discount to the face value. The difference between the price you pay to buy a stripped bond and its value when it matures is expressed as an annual yield.

One benefit of strips is that they save you from having to reinvest the twice-yearly interest payments if you aren't using the bond as a source of regular income. This same feature makes their market price respond much more dramatically to changes in general interest rate levels. If interest rates rise, for example, someone who is receiving semi-annual interest payments has a chance to put that income back to work at the higher available rates. An investor who holds a stripped bond, however, has all her money locked in at the lower rates that were available when she purchased the bond.

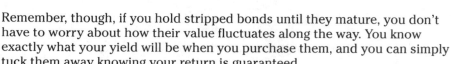

Similarly, if interest rates fall, the value of the stripped bond will rise higher than that of regular bonds. With a regular bond, some of the interest is being paid out which, if reinvested, will earn a lower rate of return than the original rate at which the stripped bond was sold. As a result, strip bonds are highly sensitive to interest rate changes, which is why we don't recommend them unless you plan on holding them until they mature.

Remember, though, if you hold stripped bonds until they mature, you don't have to worry about how their value fluctuates along the way. You know exactly what your yield will be when you purchase them, and you can simply tuck them away knowing your return is guaranteed.

One drawback to stripped bonds is that you have to declare the accrued interest each year as income, even though you don't actually receive any ongoing payments. As a result, they generally should be purchased only inside an RRSP or Registered Retirement Income Fund, where you don't have to pay any tax on the accrued interest. Shopping around is important when buying strips.

Inflation effects: Protected bonds

Marketable government bonds are also available with an interest rate that fluctuates with the rate of inflation, called Government of Canada Real Return Bonds. Unlike the standard *fixed-coupon* marketable bonds that pay out a fixed amount of interest, the interest paid on Real Return Bonds is adjusted according to the cost of living, measured by the consumer price index.

Compared with traditional Government of Canada bonds, the inflation-indexed bonds carry a lower interest rate. The reason is that the other portion of your return with these inflation-indexed bonds comes from the inflation adjustment to the principal you invest. The inflation portion of the return gets added back into principal. For example, if inflation were 3 percent the first year you hold your inflation-indexed bond into which you invested $10,000, your principal would increase to $10,300 at the end of the first year.

What's appealing about these bonds is that no matter what happens with the rate of inflation, investors who buy inflation-indexed bonds will always earn a decent return (the yield or interest rate paid) above and beyond the rate of inflation. Thus, holders of inflation-indexed Government of Canada bonds won't have the purchasing power of their principal or interest eroded by high inflation.

Because inflation-indexed bonds protect the investor from the ravages of inflation, they represent a less risky security. As we discuss in Chapter 2, lower risk usually translates into lower returns. You should also know that these bonds are less attractive for investors seeking more income to live on because a portion of the return, which is for increases in the cost of living, is added to the bond's principal.

Individual bonds or bond mutual funds?

You can invest in bonds in one of two major ways: You can purchase individual bonds, or you can invest in a professionally selected and managed portfolio of bonds via a bond mutual fund.

Unless the bonds you're considering purchasing are easy to analyze and homogeneous (such as Government of Canada bonds), you're generally better off investing in bonds through a mutual fund. The first reason is diversification. You shouldn't put your money into a small number of bonds that companies in the same industry issue or that mature at the same time. It's difficult to cost-effectively build a diversified bond portfolio with individual issues unless you have several hundred thousand dollars that you want to invest in bonds.

If you purchase individual bonds through a broker, you're going to pay a commission. In most cases the commission cost is hidden — the broker quotes you a price for the bond that includes the commission. Even if you use a discount broker, though, these fees take a healthy bite out of your investment. The smaller the amount you invest, the bigger the bite. On a $1,000 bond, the commission fee can equal up to 5 percent. Commissions take a smaller bite out of larger bonds — perhaps less than 0.5 percent if you use discount brokers.

The best reason to invest in bond funds instead of individual bonds is that you've got better things to do with your time. Do you really want to research bonds and go bond shopping? Bonds are boring! And bonds and the companies that stand behind them aren't that simple to understand. For example, did you know that some bonds can be "called" before their maturity date? Companies often call bonds (repay the principal before maturity) to save money if interest rates drop significantly. After you purchase a bond, you need to do the same things that a good bond mutual fund portfolio manager needs to do, such as track the issuer's creditworthiness and monitor other important financial developments.

A final reason to invest in bonds through a mutual fund is that it's cost-effective. Great bond funds are yours for less than 1 percent per year in operating expenses. Selecting good bond funds isn't hard, as we explain in Chapter 8.

The major drawback to bond funds is how much of your return typically goes toward paying management and administrative costs. Over three-quarters of Canadian bond funds have an operating expense ratio of 1.0 percent or higher, for example. This annual cost is usually referred to as the fund's *MER*, short for *management expense ratio*. It's calculated on the total assets the fund manages, and is deducted before your return is arrived at. If a fund makes a 6 percent return and a 1.5 percent MER, for example, your actual gain is 4.5 percent.

While the MERs of a number of bond funds are comparable to those of many equity funds, equities have historically offered higher returns. If a bond fund is unable to rack up big capital gains, its return will be close to the yield on its bonds, less the MER. If a bond fund's securities yield around 6 percent and the MER is 2 percent, you're giving up a full third of your return to have someone else purchase your bonds for you. (Like other funds, the quoted returns for bond funds are the returns they made after management fees are deducted.)

As a result, if you buy your bonds through a bond mutual fund, finding funds that are cost-effective is important. An alternative is to seek out actively managed bond funds that have a track record of consistently beating the averages by managing their portfolio. Selecting good bond funds isn't hard, as we explain in Chapter 9.

Buying individual bonds

The problem with buying individual bonds is that you must do it in a murky marketplace that's anything but consumer-friendly. When trying to buy (or sell) a bond at a competitive price you'll face two major difficulties.

First, unlike stocks, bonds aren't traded on an open exchange where you can see what the going price is. Bonds are traded between dealers in an over-the-counter market. It's very difficult for individual investors to find out the current prices and yields. While you can find bond listings in most financial papers, the prices and yields you'll see are those available to dealers making large, million-dollar purchases.

Second, the commission you'll pay to buy or sell a bond is buried in the price. Given that yields are hard to understand in the first place, it's not surprising that some dealers build in commissions of 1 percent or higher. Your yield may end up being cut by commissions as high as 2 percent.

To get the best price on individual bonds, you have to be willing to do some ground work. Start by asking your broker or discount broker what their commission policy is on fixed income securities. Next, do some comparison shopping and check out a discount broker to see what the current price and yield quotes are for the bonds you're interested in buying. The information you glean puts you in a much better position to assess just how good or bad is the price you're being quoted .

Purchasing other types of individual bonds, such as corporate and mortgage bonds, is even more treacherous and time-consuming than buying Government of Canada bonds. Here's our advice for doing it right and minimizing the chance of a catastrophic mistake:

✔ **Don't buy through salespeople.** Brokerage firms that employ representatives on commission are in the sales business. Many of the worst bond investing disasters have befallen customers of such brokerage firms. Your best bet is to purchase individual bonds through discount brokers (see Chapter 9).

✔ **Don't be suckered into high yields — buy quality.** Yes, junk bonds pay higher yields, but they also have a much higher chance of default. Nothing personal, but you're not going to do as good a job as a professional money manager at spotting problems and red flags with a bond's issuing company. Thus, you're more likely to be left holding the bag when some of your junk bond purchases end up in the junkyard. Stick with highly rated bonds so that you don't have to worry about and suffer through these unfortunate consequences.

✔ **Understand callability.** Many bonds, especially corporate bonds, can legally be called before maturity. This means that the bond issuer pays you back early because it doesn't need to borrow as much money or because interest rates have fallen and it wants to reissue new bonds at a lower interest rate. Be especially careful about purchasing bonds that were issued at higher interest rates than those that currently prevail. Borrowers pay off such bonds first.

✔ **Diversify.** Invest and hold bonds from a variety of companies in different industries to buffer changes in the economy that adversely affect one industry or a few industries more than others. Of the money that you want to invest in bonds, don't put more than 5 percent into any one bond. That means you need to hold at least 20 bonds. Diversification requires a good chunk of change to invest given the size of most bonds and because high fees erode your investment balance if you invest too little.

✔ **Shop around.** Just like when you buy a car, you need to shop around for good prices on the bonds you have in mind. The hard part is doing an apples-to-apples comparison, as different brokers may not be able to offer the same exact bond as other brokers. Remember that the two biggest determinants of what a bond should yield are its maturity date and its credit rating.

Unless you invest in boring, simple-to-understand bonds such as Government of Canada bonds, you're better off investing in bonds via mutual funds. One exception is if you absolutely, positively must receive your principal back on a certain date. Because bond funds don't mature, individual bonds with the correct maturity for you may best suit your needs. Consider Government of Canada bonds because they carry such low default risk. Otherwise, you need a lot of time, money, and patience to invest well in individual bonds.

Understanding individual bond prices

Most daily newspapers don't publish the prices of individual bonds. Newspapers don't have a lot of interest in devoting what space they have to bonds. More business-focused publications, however, such as *The Globe and Mail* and *The Financial Post*, do provide daily bond pricing. You may also call a broker or browse online to obtain bond prices. The following steps walk you through the bond listing for Bell Canada:

Figure 7-1:
Sample
bond listing

CORPORATES						
407 Intl	6.050	2009-Jul-27		106.32	4.63	+0.031
Aliant Telec	6.450	2004-Oct-15		101.13	2.16	+0.016
Aliant Telec	6.700	2005-Nov-24		104.94	3.00	-0.016
Aliant Telec	5.350	2007-Jan-15		103.84	3.74	-0.006
BCE Inc.	7.350	2009-Oct-30	111.30 111.83	4.90	4.80	+0.006
BMO	7.000	2010-Jan-28		111.42	4.64	+0.021
BMO	5.750	2008-Feb-04		105.30	4.14	+0.010
BMO Cap Tr	6.685	2011-Dec-31	107.85 108.35	5.39	5.32	+0.019
Bell CDA	6.500	2005-May-09		103.28	2.50	-0.018

1. **Bond name.** This tells you who issued the bond. In this case, the issuer is Bell Canada.

2. **Coupon.** The number here — 6.500 — refers to the original interest rate that this bond paid when it was issued. This interest rate is known as the *coupon rate*.

3. **Maturity.** The date here refers to when the bond matures; in this case, May 9, 2005.

4. **Bid Price/Ask Price.** Shows the last prices that investors were willing to pay and to sell the bonds for.

5. **Bid Yield/Ask Yield.** The rate of interest the bond will yield, given the current bid (or ask) price, until it matures.

6. **Yield Change.** Indicates how the bond's yield, given the previous day's closing price, differs from the yield given by the closing price on the day before.

   Some bonds don't trade all that often. Notice that on some days, some bonds are up and others down. The demand of new buyers and the supply of interested sellers influence the price movement of a given bond.

   In addition to the direction of overall interest rates, changes in the financial health of the company that stands behind the bond most affect the price of an individual bond.

Assessing individual bonds that you already own

If you already own individual bonds and they fit your financial objectives and tax situation, you can hold them until maturity because you've already incurred a commission when they were purchased; selling them now would just create an additional fee. When the bonds mature, the broker who sold them to you will probably be more than happy to sell you some more. That's the time to check out good bond mutual funds (see Chapter 8).

Don't mistakenly think that your current individual bonds pay the yield that they had when they were originally issued. (That yield is the number listed in the name of the bond on your brokerage account statement.) As the market level of interest rates changes, the effective yield (the interest payment divided by the bond's price) on your bonds fluctuates as well, rising and falling with the market level of rates. So if rates have fallen since you bought your bonds, the value of those bonds has increased — which in turn reduces the effective yield that you currently earn.

Other Lending Investments

Bonds, money market funds, and bank savings vehicles are hardly the only lending investments that exist. A variety of other companies are more than willing to have you lend them your money and pay you a relatively fixed rate of interest. In most cases, you're better off staying away from the following investments.

Too many investors get sucked into lending investments that offer higher yields. Remember, remember, remember: Risk and return go hand in hand. Higher yields mean greater risk and vice versa.

In the "Mortgage bonds" section earlier in this chapter we discuss investing in mortgages that resemble the one you take out to purchase a home. To directly invest in mortgages, you can loan your money to people who need money to buy or refinance real estate. Such loans are known as *mortgages* or *second mortgages*.

Why companies offer GICs in their retirement plans

In their retirement plans, more than a few companies offer guaranteed investment certificates (GICs) as an investment option. You may rightfully ask why because, as we discuss in this chapter, GICs are investments that leave much to be desired. We see GICs most often in companies where an insurer is already entrenched as the provider of the company's retirement plan investment options. Insurers love GICs because they're so profitable — for them, that is.

Historically, companies were attracted to GICs as a defensive measure. GICs seemed so safe and conservative. Therefore, GICs made company officials who selected their retirement plan investment options feel safe. (More than a few benefits administrators and other corporate personnel who establish and maintain these plans aren't exactly investing geniuses.)

Over the years, as more people and companies have discovered attractive alternative investment options, such as mutual funds that offer higher returns and low expenses, the popularity of GICs has waned. If your company's retirement plan doesn't offer good investment choices and has too many GIC-like investments, talk to your benefits department. You can also anonymously leave the employees there a copy of this book so they can better educate themselves!

Private mortgage investments appeal to investors who don't like the volatility of the stock and bond markets and aren't satisfied with the seemingly paltry returns on bonds or other common lending investments. Private mortgages seem to offer the best of both worlds — stock-market-like 10-plus percent returns without volatility.

Mortgage and real estate brokers often arrange mortgage investments, so you must tread carefully because these people have a vested interest in seeing the deal done. Otherwise, the mortgage broker doesn't get paid for closing the loan and the real estate broker doesn't get a commission for selling a property.

One broker who also happens to write about real estate wrote a newspaper column describing mortgages as the "perfect real estate investment," adding that mortgages are a "high-yield, low-risk investment." If that wasn't enough to get you to whip out your chequebook, the writer/broker further gushed that mortgages are great investments because you have "little or no management, no physical labour. . . ."

You know by now that a low-risk, high-yield investment does not exist. Earning a relatively high interest rate goes hand in hand with accepting relatively high risk. The risk is that the borrower can default — which leaves you holding the bag. More specifically, you can get stuck with a property that you may need to foreclose on, and if you don't hold the first mortgage, you're not first in line with a claim on the property.

The fact that private mortgages are high risk should be obvious when you consider why the borrower elects to obtain needed funds privately rather than through a bank. Put yourself in the borrower's shoes. As a property buyer or owner, if you can obtain a mortgage through a conventional lender, such as a bank, wouldn't you do so because banks generally give better interest rates? If a mortgage broker offers you a deal where you can borrow money at 9 percent when the going bank rate is 5 to 6 percent, the deal must carry a fair amount of risk.

We would avoid this type of investment. If you want to invest in such mortgages, you must do some time-consuming homework on the borrower's financial situation. A banker doesn't lend someone money without examining a borrower's assets, liabilities, and monthly expenses, and you shouldn't either. Be careful to check the borrower's credit and get a large down payment (at least 20 percent). The best case to be a lender is if and when you sell some of your own real estate and you're willing to act as the bank and provide the financing to the buyer in the form of a first mortgage.

Also recognize that your mortgage investment carries interest rate risk: If you need to "sell" it early, you'd have to discount it, perhaps substantially if interest rates have increased since you purchased it. Try not to lend so much money on one mortgage that it represents more than 5 percent of your total investments.

If you're willing to lend your money to borrowers who carry a relatively high risk of defaulting, consider investing in high-yield (junk) bond mutual funds instead. With these funds, you can at least diversify your money across many borrowers, and you benefit from the professional review and due diligence of the fund management team. You can also consider lending money to family members.

Out of sight: Fluctuations of mortgages, GICs, and T-bills

One of the allures of non-bond investments, such as private mortgages, GICs, and T-bills, is that they don't fluctuate in value — at least not that you can see. Such investments appear safer and less volatile. You can't watch your principal fluctuate in value because you can't look up the value daily the way you can with bonds and stocks.

But the principal values of your mortgage, GIC, and T-bill investments really do fluctuate; you just don't see the fluctuations! As we explain in the section "Maturity matters: When bonds pay back" earlier in this chapter, just as the market value of a bond drops when interest rates rise,

so too does the market value of these investments, and for the same reasons. At higher interest rates, investors expect a discounted price on your fixed-interest rate investment because they always have the alternative of purchasing a new mortgage, GIC, or T-bill at the higher prevailing rates. Some of these investments are actually bought and sold (and behave just like bonds) among investors on what's known as a secondary market.

If the normal volatility of a bond's principal value makes you queasy, try not to follow your investments so closely!

Chapter 8

Mutual Funds: Stock, Bond, and Money Market Funds

. . . .

In This Chapter

▶ Looking at reasons to invest in mutual funds

▶ Uncovering the secrets of successful fund investing

▶ Deciding how to allocate your assets

▶ The best stock, bond, and money market funds

. . . .

*I*n the earlier chapters of this part, we explain all about stocks, bonds, and other common securities. If you understand these securities, you can understand mutual funds. A *mutual fund* is simply a big pool of money from lots of investors, like you and your cousin Sally, that a mutual fund manager uses to buy a bunch of stocks, bonds, and/or other assets that meet the fund's investment criteria. The better funds enable you to easily and cost-effectively diversify your investments — that is, invest in many different industries and companies.

When you invest in a fund, you buy shares and become a shareholder of the fund. Good mutual funds enable you to have some of the best money managers in the country direct the investment of your money. Because efficient funds take most of the hassle and cost out of figuring out which companies to invest in, they're one of the finest investment vehicles available today. Different types of mutual funds can help you meet various financial goals — that's one reason why by 2004 Canadian investors had some $464 billion invested in funds! You can use money market funds for something most everybody needs: an emergency savings stash of three to six months' living expenses. Or, perhaps you're thinking about saving for a home purchase, retirement, or future educational costs. If so, you can consider some stock and bond mutual funds.

Too many people plunge into mutual funds without looking at their overall financial situation and, in their haste, often end up paying more taxes and overlooking other valuable financial strategies. If you haven't taken a comprehensive look at your personal finances, you're not alone. Read Chapter 3 to begin this important process.

Discovering the Benefits of the Best Funds

The best mutual funds are superior investment vehicles for people of all economic means and for accomplishing many financial objectives. Following are the main reasons why investing in mutual funds rather than individual securities best serves you.

Professional management

The mutual fund investment company hires a portfolio manager and researchers whose full-time jobs are to research and purchase suitable investments for the fund. These people screen the universe of investments for those that meet the fund's stated objectives.

Typically, fund managers are graduates of the top business and finance schools, where they learned portfolio management and securities valuation and selection. Many have additional investing credentials, such as the Chartered Financial Analyst's (CFA) designation. In addition to their educational training, the best fund managers typically possess ten or more years of experience in analyzing and selecting investments.

For most fund managers and researchers, finding the best investments is more than a full-time job. Fund managers do tons of analysis that you probably lack the time or expertise to do. For example, fund managers assess company financial statements; interview a company's managers to get a sense of the company's business strategies and vision; examine competitor strategies; speak with company customers, suppliers, and industry consultants; and attend trade shows and read industry periodicals.

In short, a mutual fund management team does more research, number crunching, and due diligence than you could ever have the energy or expertise to do in what little free time you have. Investing in mutual funds frees up time for friendships, family relationships, and maybe even your sex life — don't miss the terrific time-saving benefits of fund investing!

Cost efficiency

Mutual funds are a cheaper, more communal way of getting your investment work done. When you invest your money in an efficiently managed mutual fund, it likely costs you less than trading individual securities on your own. Fund managers can buy and sell securities for a fraction of the cost that you would pay to buy and sell them yourself.

Funds also spread the cost of research over thousands of investors. The most efficiently managed mutual funds cost less than 2 percent per year in fees. (Bonds and money market funds cost much less.) Some funds that track indices charge fees of under 1 percent, and as low as 0.31 percent — that's an annual charge of just $3.10 per $1,000 you invest. Not a bad deal!

Diversification

Diversification is a big attraction for many investors who choose mutual funds. Most funds own stocks or bonds from dozens of companies, thus diversifying against the risk of bad news from any single company or sector. Achieving such diversification on your own is difficult and expensive unless you have a few hundred thousand dollars and a great deal of time to invest.

Mutual funds typically invest in 25 to 100 securities, or more. Proper diversification increases the chances of the fund earning higher returns with less risk.

Although most mutual funds are diversified, some aren't. For example, some stock funds invest exclusively in stocks of a single industry (science and technology, for example) or country (such as Japan). We're not a fan of these funds because of the narrowness of their investments and their typically higher operating fees.

Reasonable investment minimums

Most funds have low minimum investment requirements. Many funds have minimums of $500 or $1,000 or less. Retirement plan investors can often invest with even less. Some funds even offer monthly investment plans, so you can start with as little as $50 per month.

Even if you have lots of money to invest, you also should consider mutual funds. Join the increasing number of companies with millions to invest that use the low-cost, high-quality money management services that you can get from a mutual fund.

Different funds for different folks

Many people, including some financial writers, think that mutual funds = stock market investing = risky. That's wrong. In fact, the majority of money in mutual funds is *not* in the stock market. You may select the funds that take on the kinds of risks that you're comfortable with and that meet your financial goals. Here's a list of the three major types of mutual funds:

- ✔ **Stock funds.** If you want your money to grow over a long period of time (and you can handle down as well as up years), choose funds that invest more heavily in stocks.

- ✔ **Bond funds.** If you need current income and don't want investments that fluctuate as widely in value as stocks do, consider some bond funds.

- ✔ **Money market funds.** If you want to be sure that your invested principal does not decline in value because you may need to use your money in the short term, select a money market fund.

Most investors choose a combination of these three types of funds to diversify and help accomplish different financial goals.

High financial safety

Thousands of banks and insurance companies have failed in North America in recent decades. Banks and insurers can fail because their *liabilities* (the money customers give them to invest, which they can be called upon to return on short notice) can exceed their *assets* (the money they've invested or lent). For example, when a big chunk of a bank's loans goes sour at the same time that its depositors want their money, the bank fails because banks typically have only a fraction on deposit for every dollar that people like you and us place with them. Likewise, if an insurance company makes several poor investments or underestimates the number of insurance policyholder claims, it too can fail.

Such failures can't happen with a mutual fund because the value of the fund's shares fluctuates as the securities in the fund fluctuate in value. For every dollar of securities they hold for their customers, mutual funds have a dollar's worth of securities. The worst that can happen with a fund is that if you want your money, you may get less cash than you originally put into the fund because the value of the investments the fund holds have declined. You won't lose all your investment unless every security the fund manager has purchased suddenly becomes worthless.

For added security, the specific stocks, bonds, and other securities that a mutual fund buys are held at a *custodian,* a separate organization independent of the mutual fund company. A custodian ensures that the fund management company can't embezzle your funds or use assets from a better-performing fund to subsidize a poor performer.

Accessibility

What's really terrific about dealing with mutual funds is that they're set up for people who value their time and don't like going to a local branch office and standing in long lines. With funds, you can fill out a simple form and write a cheque in the comfort of your living room to make your initial investment. You can then typically make subsequent investments by mailing in a cheque or authorizing money transfers from your other accounts, such as bank savings or chequing accounts.

Additionally, most money market funds offer cheque-writing privileges. Many mutual fund companies also allow you to wire money back and forth from your local bank account; you can access your money almost as quickly through a money market fund as you can through your local bank.

Selling shares of your mutual fund is usually simple. Generally, all you need to do is call the fund company's toll-free number or visit its Web site. Some companies have representatives available around the clock, all year round. Most fund companies also offer online account access and trading capabilities (although, as we discuss in Chapter 19, some people are prone to overtrading online).

The Keys to Successful Fund Investing

This chapter helps explain why funds are a good investment vehicle to use, but not all funds are worthy of your investment dollars. Would you, for example, invest in a mutual fund run by an inexperienced and unproven 18-year-old? How about a fund that charges high fees and produces inferior returns compared with other similar funds? These are common-sense questions, aren't they? You don't have to be an investing wizard to know the correct answers.

When you select a fund, you can use a number of simple, common-sense criteria to greatly increase your chances of investment success.

Minimize costs

For a particular type of mutual fund (Canadian stock funds, for example), dozens to sometimes hundreds of choices are available. The charges you pay to buy or sell a fund, as well as the ongoing fund operating expenses, have a big impact on the rate of return you earn on your investments.

Fund costs are an important factor in the return you earn from a mutual fund. Why? Fees are deducted from your investment returns and can attack a fund from many angles. All other things being equal, high fees and other charges depress your returns.

Understand load and no-load funds

The first such fee you'll often encounter with mutual funds are *sales loads*, which are commissions paid to brokers and "financial planners" who work on commission and sell mutual funds.

It's not where you buy your funds but the fund company itself that determines whether you'll pay a commission to make an investment. No-load fund companies allow you to buy their funds without paying a sales fee. Typically you can buy directly from the fund company as well as through brokers and planners. All the major financial institutions, and a number of other solid companies, offer their own line of no-load mutual funds. These include Altamira, Bissett & Associates, and Vancouver-based Phillips, Hager & North.

Load funds are usually not available directly from the fund company itself. Instead, they must be purchased from a third party, who is compensated with the commissions the fund company allows them to charge you. Some discount brokers, however, allow you to purchase load funds without paying a commission.

There are two distinct types of fund commissions. Some funds charge you a commission when you make your purchase. These funds are called *front-end load* funds. The bulk of load funds that Canadians buy, though, are *back-end load* funds — you pay a commission if and when you sell your units. Typically, most back-end load funds have a sliding scale. For instance, if you want to take your money out after one year, you may get hit by a 4.5 percent commission. Wait five years, and the exit fee may drop to 2.5 percent.

With many load funds, you can choose whether to pay your admission fee when you're going in or on your way out the door. The attraction of back-end loads is that you get all your money working for you right away. And if you leave your money in the fund for several years, you avoid paying the commission altogether. However, these funds have two major strikes against them.

Hiding loads

Unfortunately, fund companies have come up with craftier ways of hiding sales loads. Increasing numbers of brokers and "financial planners" sell funds that they call no-loads but that actually aren't.

In back-end or deferred sales load funds, the commission is hidden. Salespeople tell you that as long as you stay in a fund for five to seven years, you need not pay the back-end sales charge that applies when you sell the investment. This claim may be true, but it's also true that these funds pay investment salespeople a hefty commission.

The salespeople can receive their commissions because the fund company charges you exorbitant continuing operating expenses (which are usually 1 percent more per year than the best funds). So, one way or another, they get their commissions from your investment dollars.

On funds that offer you the choice of paying your commission either when you make your purchase or when you sell your units, the back-end load version usually has a higher management fee than the front-end load option. More importantly, back-end loads are an unfair arrangement that's tilted in the fund company's favour. You offer to lock up your money with a fund for a set number of years in return for them decreasing or eliminating the commission. The problem is that the fund can change the rules of the game, but you still aren't allowed to get out of the contract. The manager may leave or be fired, the fund may change its investing focus, or the results may simply turn out to be much worse than the fund's history suggested. Regardless of what happens to the fund, you can't get your money out unless you pay the exit fee.

While no-load funds are at first blush the cheapest and best choice, there are many situations in which it may make sense to pay a commission. There may simply not be a comparable no-load fund with the past performance and investment mandate you're interested in. Or you may already have many of your funds with a fund family, and don't want the hassle and added paperwork of opening an account with another fund company. And in some situations no-loads may be almost as costly to buy and sell as load funds. Some discounters still charge a commission on some fund transactions that can work out to be 2 percent or higher.

Get what you pay for

For many people, the biggest reason for choosing load funds is to compensate an adviser who's providing them with help in assembling a fund portfolio. At the very minimum, if you're a new customer, request a written financial plan that examines your wider financial circumstances, not just your investment needs. Remember, too, that the commissions in mutual fund prospectuses and so forth are simply the maximum allowed by the fund company. You can and should negotiate those fees down.

There's also no reason why an adviser who's compensated through sales commissions shouldn't include some no-load funds in your portfolio. What's important to remember is that financial advisers, whether they charge fees or commissions, are making a living at what they do. Just make sure that whichever route you choose you get what you pay for.

A good adviser should act as a sober, second opinion that comes between you and your desire to trade, buy, or sell. Discount brokers, instant access to information, and the ease of executing trades over the phone or on the Internet all make it very easy and hassle-free to buy and sell mutual funds and other investments. Many people have a tough time fighting the desire to trade in and out of investments in a never-ending search for a better return. For some investors, an adviser can more than earn back his keep by serving as a hand-holder when the markets take a tumble or an investment doesn't immediately pan out like you hoped it would.

A good adviser will be open and forthcoming about commissions. Beware those who only sing the praises of buying a load fund, warn against the pitfalls of no-loads, or even try to obscure the load altogether. For example, brokers may tell you that the commission doesn't cost you because the mutual fund company pays it. But the commission always comes out of your investment dollars, regardless of how cleverly some load funds and brokers disguise it. Some brokers and planners may even encourage you to regularly switch out of some funds and into other funds in order to earn themselves more money.

Some brokers also may say that load funds perform better than no-load funds. One reason put forward is that load funds supposedly hire better fund managers. Absolutely no relationship exists between paying a sales charge to buy a fund and gaining access to better investment managers. Remember that the sales commission goes to the selling broker, *not* to the management of the fund.

Another problem with commission-driven load fund sellers is the power of self-interest. This issue is rarely talked about, but it's even more important than the extra costs that you pay with load funds. For example, you may be better off paying down your debts or investing in something entirely different from a mutual fund. Some salespeople almost never advise you to pay off your credit cards or your mortgage — or to invest through your company's retirement plan — instead of buying an investment through them.

Beware of high operating expenses

In addition to loads, the other costs of owning funds are the ongoing *operating expenses.* All mutual funds charge fees as long as you keep your money in the fund. The fees pay for the costs of running a fund, such as employees' salaries, marketing, toll-free phone lines, printing and mailing prospectuses (legal disclosure of the fund's operations and fees), and so on.

A mutual fund's operating expenses are essentially invisible to you because they're deducted from the fund's share price. Companies charge operating expenses on a daily basis, so you don't need to worry about trying to get out of a fund at a particular time of the year before the company deducts these fees.

Although expenses are invisible to you, their impact on your returns is very real. Expenses are critical on money market mutual funds and bond funds because these funds buy securities that are so similar and so efficiently priced in the financial markets that most fund managers in a given type of money market or bond fund earn quite similar returns before expenses.

With stock funds, expenses may play less of an important role in your fund decision. However, don't forget that over time stocks have averaged returns of about 10 percent per year. So if one stock fund charges 1.5 percent more in operating expenses than another, you give up an extra 15 percent of your expected annual returns.

All types of funds with higher operating expenses tend to produce lower rates of return, on average. Conversely, funds with lower operating costs can more easily produce higher returns for you than a comparable type of fund with high costs. This effect makes sense because companies deduct operating expenses from the returns that your fund generates. Higher expenses mean a lower return to you.

Fund companies quote a fund's operating expenses as a percentage of your investment. The percentage represents an annual fee or charge, and is typically called the *management expense ratio*, or *MER*. The fund's prospectus includes this number in the fund expenses section, usually in a line that says something like "Total Fund Operating Expenses." Or you can call the mutual fund's toll-free phone number and ask a representative, or try to find the information at the fund company's Web site. Make sure that a fund doesn't appear to have low expenses simply because it's temporarily waiving them. (You can ask the fund or look in its prospectus at its fees to find out this information.)

Stick with funds that maintain low total operating expenses and that don't charge sales loads (commissions). Both types of fees come out of your pocket and reduce your rate of return. Plenty of excellent funds are available at reasonable annual operating expense ratios (less than 2.0 percent for stock funds; less than 1.5 percent for bond funds). See our recommendations later in this chapter in the sections on the best stock mutual funds, bond funds, and money market funds.

Consider performance and risk

A fund's historical rate of return or performance is another important factor to weigh when you select a mutual fund. However, keep in mind that, as all mutual fund materials must tell you, past performance is no guarantee of future results. In fact, many former high-return funds achieved their results only by taking on high risk. Funds that assume higher risk should produce higher rates of return. But high-risk funds usually decline in price faster during major market declines. Thus, a good fund should consistently deliver a favourable rate of return given the level of risk it takes.

A big mistake that many investors make when they choose a mutual fund is overemphasizing the importance of past performance numbers. The shorter the time period, the greater the danger of misusing high performance as an indicator of a good future fund.

Although past performance *can* be a good sign, high returns for a fund, relative to its peers, are largely possible only if a fund takes more risk. The danger of taking more risk is that it doesn't always work the way you'd like. The odds are high that you won't be able to pick the next star before it vaults to prominence in the investing sky. You have a far greater chance of boarding that star when it's ready to plummet back to Earth.

In fact, one study of U.S. funds showed that if you had invested in the annual number one top-performing stock and bond funds over the last 15 years, 80 percent of those top performers subsequently performed worse, over the next 3 to 10 years, than the average fund in their peer group! Two of these former number one funds actually became the worst-performing funds in their particular category.

One clever way that mutual funds make themselves look better than other similar funds is to compare themselves to funds that aren't really comparable. The most common ploy is for a fund to invest in riskier types of securities and then compare their performance with funds that invest in less risky securities. Examine the types of securities that a fund invests in and make sure that the comparison funds or indexes invest in similar securities.

Stick with experience

A great deal of emphasis is put on who manages a specific mutual fund. Although the individual fund manager is important, a manager isn't an island unto himself or herself. The resources and capabilities of the parent company are equally, if not more, important. Managers come and go, but fund companies don't.

Different companies maintain different capabilities and levels of expertise with different types of funds. Phillips, Hager & North, for example, is terrific at money market, bond, and conservative Canadian stock funds, thanks in part to their low operating expenses. Fidelity and Templeton have significant experience with investing in international stocks.

A fund company gains more or less experience than others, not only from the direct management of certain fund types but also through hiring out. For example, some fund families contract with private money management firms that have significant experience. In other cases, private money management firms with long histories in private money management, such as Mawer Investment Management and Sceptre Investment Counsel, offer mutual funds.

Buy index funds

Unlike other mutual funds, in which the portfolio manager and a team of analysts scour the market for the best securities, an index fund manager simply invests to match the performance of an index such as the TSE composite index of big Canadian companies or the Standard & Poor's 500 index of 500 large U.S. company stocks. Index funds are funds that are mostly managed by a computer.

Index funds deliver relatively good returns by keeping expenses low, staying invested, and not trying to jump around. Over ten years or more, index funds typically outperform about three-quarters of their peers! Most other so-called actively managed funds cannot overcome the handicap of high operating expenses that pulls down their funds' rates of return. Index funds can run with far lower operating expenses because significant ongoing research doesn't need to be conducted to identify companies to invest in.

The average Canadian stock mutual fund, for example, has an operating expense ratio of around 2.80 percent per year. (Some funds charge expenses as high as 3.5 percent or more per year.) That being the case, a Canadian stock index fund with an expense ratio of just 1.0 percent per year has an advantage of 1.80 percent per year over the average fund. A 1.80 percent difference may not seem like much, but in fact it is a significant difference. Because stocks tend to return about 10 percent per year, you end up throwing away about 18 percent of your expected stock fund returns with an "average fund" in terms of expenses. (If you factor in the taxes that you pay on your fund profits, these higher expenses gobble up perhaps a quarter of your after-tax profits.)

With actively managed stock funds, a fund manager can make costly mistakes, such as not being invested when the market goes up, being too aggressive when the market plummets, or just being in the wrong stocks. An actively managed fund can easily underperform the overall market index that it's competing against.

Don't overestimate your ability to pick *in advance* the few elite money managers who manage to beat the market averages by a few percentage points per year in the long run. Also, don't overestimate the pros' ability to consistently pick the right stocks. Index funds make sense for a portion of your investments, especially when you invest in bonds and larger, more conservative stocks, where beating the market is difficult for portfolio managers.

In addition to lower operating expenses, which help boost your returns, index mutual funds are tax friendlier to invest in when you invest outside retirement plans. Mutual fund managers of actively managed portfolios, in their attempts to increase returns, buy and sell securities more frequently. However, this trading increases a fund's taxable capital gains distributions and reduces a fund's after-tax return.

Creating Your Fund Portfolio

When you invest money for the longer term, such as for retirement, you can choose among the various types of funds that we discuss in this chapter. Most people get a big headache when they try to decide how to spread their money across the choices. (We discuss recommended funds for shorter-term goals later in this chapter as well.) The specific amount that you decide to invest in any of the major types of securities is known as *asset allocation*. Asset allocation simply means that you decide what percentage of your investments you place — or *allocate* — into bonds versus stocks and into international versus Canadian stocks.

Many working folks have time on their side, and they need to use that time to make their money grow. You may have two or more decades before you need to draw on some portion of your retirement plan assets. If some of your investments drop a bit over a year or two — or even over five years — the value of your investments has plenty of time to recover before you spend the money in retirement.

Your current age and the number of years until you retire should be the biggest factors in your allocation decision. The younger you are and the more years you have before retirement, the more comfortable you should be with growth-oriented (and more volatile) investments such as stock funds. (See Chapter 2 for the risks and historic returns of different investments.)

Table 8-1 lists guidelines for allocating money that you've earmarked for long-term purposes, such as retirement. You don't need an M.B.A. or Ph.D. to decide your asset allocation — all you need to know is how old you are and the level of risk you want!

Table 8-1	Asset Allocation for the Long Haul	
Your Investment Attitude	*Bond Allocation (%)*	*Stock Allocation (%)*
Play it safe	= Age	= 100 – age
Middle of the road	= Age – 10	= 110 – age
Aggressive	= Age – 20	= 120 – age

What's it all mean, you ask? Consider this example: If you're a conservative sort who doesn't like a lot of risk but you recognize the value of striving for some growth to make your money work harder, you're a middle-of-the-road type. Using Table 8-1, if you're 35 years old you may consider putting 25 percent (35 – 10) into bonds and 75 percent (110 – 35) into stocks.

Now divvy up your stock investment money between Canadian and international funds. Here's what portion of your "stock allocation" we recommend investing in overseas stocks:

✔ 20 percent (for play it safe)

✔ 35 percent (for middle of the road)

✔ 50 percent (for aggressive)

If, for example, in Table 8-1, the 35-year-old, middle-of-the-road type invests 75 percent in stocks, he or she can then invest about 35 percent of the stock fund investments (which works out to be around 25 percent of the total) in international stock funds.

So here's what the 35-year-old, middle-of-the-road investor's portfolio asset allocation looks like so far:

Bonds	25%
Canadian stocks	50%
International stocks	25%

Now let's take things a step further. Suppose your investment allocation decisions make you want to invest 50 percent in Canadian stock funds. Which ones do you choose? As we explain in the "Exploring the different types of stock funds" section later in this chapter, stock funds differ from one another on a number of levels. There are growth-oriented stocks and funds and those that focus on value stocks. Small-, medium-, and large-company stocks and funds also invest in such stocks. We explain these types of stocks and funds later in the chapter. You also need to decide what portion you want to invest in index funds (which we discuss in the preceding "Buy index funds" section) versus actively managed funds that try to beat the market.

Generally, it's a good idea to diversify into different types of funds. You can diversify in one of two ways. Your first option is to purchase several individual funds, each of which focuses on a different style. For example, you can invest in a large-company value stock fund and in a small-company growth fund. We find this approach somewhat tedious. Granted, it does allow a fund manager to specialize and gain greater knowledge about a particular type of stock. But many of the best managers invest in more than one narrow range of security. A second approach is to invest in a handful of funds (five to ten), each of which covers several bases, and that together cover them all. Remember, the investment delineations are somewhat arbitrary, and most funds do more than just one type of investment. For example, a fund may focus on small-company value stocks but also invest in medium-size company stocks, as well as in some that are more growth oriented.

Slash your expenses with Exchange Traded Funds (ETFs)

The benefit of using index funds is that they're a low-cost way to make above-average returns. Since they're designed to simply mirror the performance of various stock market indices, managing them can largely be handled by computers. There's no need for researching companies, deciding when to buy and sell stocks, or how much weighting to give to particular companies or sectors. As for performance, you're basically assured of above-average returns, simply because the majority of actively managed funds fail to match the indices.

Another way to get the returns of index funds, and pay even less in fees — sometimes a good deal less — is to use *exchange-traded funds* (*ETFs*). As the name suggests, these are funds that you can buy and sell like regular stocks on the stock exchange. Most ETFs, like index funds themselves, mirror the performance of a particular stock market index. In fact, a better name for them would be *exchange-traded index funds*.

The great feature of ETFs is they come with rock-bottom expense ratios. The MERs of iUnits (the ETFs run by Barclays Global Investors in Canada, the biggest provider of ETFs in Canada) run from 0.17 percent to 0.55 percent. This is about 2 percent lower than the MER charged by the average Canadian stock mutual fund. Looked at another away, the management expenses charged by ETFs are a tenth of what most equity mutual funds charge.

With mutual funds, you have to enter your buy or sell order through the mutual fund company itself or through your broker or discount broker. Even then, the price at which you can buy or sell is set once a day, after the stock market closes.

Since ETFs are bought and sold in the same way stocks are traded, there aren't any fees to pay (*loads*) when you buy or sell. Remember that you can sometimes get hit with redemption fees — a charge when you sell your funds — even on no-load funds.

Another attraction of ETFs is that they tend to be much more tax-efficient. ETFs do very little trading, buying or selling shares only in response to the composition of the index they track. By buying and holding stocks, they put off the capital gains taxes that other actively managed funds ring up from their regular selling. The more a fund manager trades, the higher the taxable gains the funds realizes, and you have to pay your share of the tax bill.

There are a few things to be aware of, however. When you buy or sell ETFs, there's a commission, just as there is when you buy or sell stocks. Also, investors who are prone to overtrading can easily find themselves spending too much on commissions, as well as buying high and selling low with ETFs. And, like index funds, ETFs will be just as volatile as the overall market, since no manager is continually pruning and reshaping the basket of investments.

Barclays is the major provider of ETFs in Canada. You can reach them at 877-464-8648 or through their Web site, www.iunits.com. In addition to Canadian stock and bond ETFs, Barclays offers two ETFs that, while they invest in foreign stocks, qualify as Canadian content in your RRSP. The iUnits S&P 500 Index RRSP Fund tracks the performance of 500 large U.S. companies as measured by the S&P 500. The iUnits MSCI International Equity Index RSP Fund mirrors the return of the MSCI index, which represents the performance of 21 individual country indices outside of North America, including Europe, Australasia, and the Far East. TD Bank also offers a few ETFs.

In the U.S., there are a number of longstanding ETFs, all with quirky names. *Spiders* (a play on SPDR, short for *Standard & Poor's depositary receipts*) mirror the return of the S&P 500. The symbol for the ETF is SPY, and it has an MER of 0.12 per cent. *Diamonds* — the symbol is DIA — buys the 30 stocks in the Dow Jones industrial average. The DIA expense ratio is 0.18 percent. For tracking the NASDAQ there's QQQ, with an expense ratio of 0.20 percent.

Barclays also offers a range of U.S. ETFs called iShares. As well, the giant U.S. index fund — and low-fee — fund company Vanguard has entered the business, offering 14 ETFs that are mirrors of its index funds, except with even lower expense ratios, ranging from 0.12 to 0.28 percent. Vanguard's ETFs are called *VIPERS*, short for *Vanguard Index Participation Equity Receipts*.

As for how much you should use actively managed funds versus index funds and exchange-traded funds, it's really a matter of personal taste. If you're happy knowing that you'll get the market rate of return and that you can't underperform the market, there's no reason why you can't index your entire portfolio. On the other hand, if you enjoy the challenge of trying to pick the better managers and want the potential to earn better than the market level of returns, don't use index funds at all. A happy medium is to do both. (You may be interested in knowing that John Bogle, founder of the U.S. company Vanguard and pioneer of index investment funds, has about half his money invested in index funds.)

If you haven't experienced the sometimes significant plummets in stock prices that occur, you may feel queasy when it next happens and you've got a chunk of your nest egg in stocks. Be sure to read Chapters 2 and 5 to understand the risk in stocks and what you can and can't do to reduce the volatility of your stock holdings.

The Best Stock Mutual Funds

Earlier in this book we made the case for investing in stocks (also known as equities) to make your money grow. However, stock market investing carries risk because stocks sometimes plummet or otherwise remain depressed for a few years. Thus, stock mutual funds (also known as equity funds), which as their name suggests invest in stocks, are not a place for money that you know you may need to protect in the next few years.

Unless you have a lot of money to invest, you're likely to buy only a handful of stocks. If you end up with a lemon in your portfolio it can devastate your other good choices. If such a stock represents 20 percent of your holdings, the rest of your stock selections need to increase about 25 percent in value just to get you back to even. Stock mutual funds reduce your risk because they invest in dozens of stocks. For example, if a fund holds 50 stocks and one goes to zero, you lose only 2 percent of the fund value if the stock was an average holding. Similarly, if the fund holds 100 stocks, you lose just 1 percent. Remember that a good fund manager is more likely than you are to sidestep disasters.

Another way that stock funds reduce risk (and thus volatility) is to invest in different types of stocks, such as growth stocks, or in the stocks of larger, established companies. Some funds also invest in U.S. and international stocks. Different types of stocks (which are explained in the upcoming section entitled "Exploring the different types of stock funds") don't move in tandem. So if smaller-company stocks get beat up, larger-company stocks may fare better. If Canadian stocks are in the tank, international stocks may be faring better.

Making money with stock funds

When you invest in stock mutual funds, you can make money in three ways. First, most stocks pay dividends. Companies hopefully make some profits during the year. Some high-growth companies reinvest most or all their profits right back into the business. Many companies, however, pay out some of their profits to shareholders in the form of dividends. As a mutual fund investor, you can choose to receive these dividends as cash or reinvest them by purchasing more shares in the fund.

Unless you need the income to live on (if, for example, you're already retired), reinvest your dividends into buying more shares in the fund. If you do this outside a retirement account, keep a record of those reinvestments because you need to factor those additional purchases into the tax calculations you make when you sell your shares.

The second way you can make money with a stock fund is through capital gains distributions. When a fund manager sells stocks for more than he or she paid, the resulting profits, known as *capital gains,* must be netted against losses and paid out to the fund's shareholders. Just as with dividends, you can reinvest your capital gains distributions in the fund.

The final way that you can make money with stock funds is via appreciation. The fund manager isn't going to sell all the stocks that have gone up in value. Thus, the price per share of the fund increases to reflect the gains in its stock holdings. For you, these profits are on paper until you sell the fund and lock them in. Of course, if a fund's stocks decline in value, the share price depreciates.

If you add together dividends, capital gains distributions, and appreciation, you arrive at the *total return* of a fund. Stocks, and the funds that invest in them, differ in the dimensions of these three possible returns, particularly with respect to dividends. Utility companies, for example, tend to pay out more of their profits as dividends. But don't buy utility stocks thinking that you'll make more money because of the heftier dividends. Utilities and other companies paying high dividends tend not to appreciate as much over time because they don't reinvest as much in their businesses, and they're not growing.

Bond funds can make you money in all three ways that a stock fund can. However, most of the time, the bulk of your return in a bond fund comes from dividends. With money market funds, all your return comes from dividends.

Exploring the different types of stock funds

Stock funds and the stocks they invest in are usually put into different categories based on the types of stocks they focus on. Categorizing stock funds is often tidier in theory than in practice though, because some funds invest in an eclectic mix of stocks. Don't get bogged down in the names of funds — funds sometimes have misleading names and don't necessarily do what their names imply. The investment strategies of the fund and the fund's typical investments are what matter.

The first dimension in which a stock fund's stock selection differs is the size of the company — small, medium, or large — in which the fund invests. The size of a company is determined by its total market value, referred to as its *market capitalization*. This is simply the current stock price multiplied by the number of shares outstanding.

In Canada, small-company stocks, for example, are usually defined as stocks of companies that have a total market capitalization of less than $500 million. Medium-capitalization stocks have market values between $500 million and $1 billion or so. Large-capitalization stocks (also known as large caps) are those of companies with market values greater than $1 billion. Not surprisingly, the numbers used in the U.S. to define different sized companies are a lot bigger. South of the border, companies are considered small-cap until their market capitalization exceeds $2 billion. Medium-capitalization U.S. stocks have market values between $2 billion and $10 billion, and large-capitalization U.S. stocks have market values greater than $10 billion. These dollar amounts are arbitrary, and as stock prices increase over time, investment market analysts have moved up their cutoffs.

Why care about the size of the companies that a fund holds? Historically, smaller companies pay lower dividends but appreciate more. They have more-volatile share prices but tend to produce slightly higher total returns. Larger companies' stocks tend to pay greater dividends and on average are less volatile and produce slightly lower total returns than small company stocks. Medium-size, as you may suspect, falls between the two. Investors looking for income as well as appreciation from their stock market investments can focus more on larger-company stocks. And, because smaller-company stocks don't move in lockstep with larger-company stocks, investing in both reduces a portfolio's volatility.

Stock fund managers and their funds are further categorized by whether they invest in growth or value stocks. *Growth stocks* are companies that experience rapidly expanding revenues and profits. These companies tend to reinvest most of their earnings in the company to fuel future expansion; thus, these stocks pay low dividends.

Value stocks are priced cheaply in relation to the company's assets, profits, and potential profits. It's possible that such a company is a growth company, but that's unlikely because growth companies' stock prices tend to sell at a bigger premium compared with what the company's assets are worth.

Mutual fund companies sometimes use other terms to describe other types of stock funds. Aggressive growth funds tend to invest in the most growth-oriented companies and may undertake riskier investment practices, such as frequent trading. Growth and income funds tend to invest in stocks that pay decent dividends, thus offering the investor the potential for growth and income. Income funds tend to invest more in higher-yielding stocks. Bonds usually make up the other portion of income funds.

Stocks and the companies that issue them are also divvied up based on the location of their main operations and headquarters. Funds that specialize in U.S. stocks are, not surprisingly, called U.S. stock funds; those focusing on stocks worldwide except for Canada are called *international* funds, while those that can put their money into stock anywhere around the globe — including Canada — are referred to as *global* funds.

Putting together two or three of these major classifications, you can start to comprehend all those silly and lengthy names that mutual funds give their stock funds. You can have funds that focus on large-company value stocks or small-company growth stocks. You can add in U.S., international, and global funds to further subdivide these categories into more fund types. For example, you can have international stock funds that focus on small-company growth stocks.

You can purchase several stock funds, each focusing on a different type of stock, to diversify into different types of stocks. Two potential advantages result from doing so. First, not all your money rides in one stock fund and with one fund manager. Second, each of the different fund managers can look at and track particular stock investment possibilities.

The following sections describe the best stock funds that are worthy of your consideration, using the selection criteria we outline in "The Keys to Successful Fund Investing" section earlier in this chapter. The funds differ from one another primarily in the types of stocks they invest in. Keep in mind as you read through these funds that they also differ in their tax friendliness (see Chapter 3). If you invest inside a retirement plan, you don't need to worry about tax friendliness.

All-in-one funds

Balanced and asset allocation mutual funds, also known as *hybrid funds,* invest in a mixture of different types of securities. Most commonly, they invest in both bonds and stocks. These funds are usually less risky and less volatile than funds that invest exclusively in stocks; in an economic downturn, bonds usually hold value better than stocks.

Hybrid funds make it easier for investors who are skittish about investing in stocks to hold stocks because they reduce the volatility that normally comes with pure stock funds. Because of their extensive diversification, hybrid funds are excellent choices for an investor who doesn't have much money to start with.

Balanced funds generally try to maintain a fairly constant percentage of investment in stocks and bonds. Asset allocation funds, in contrast, normally adjust the mix of different investments according to the portfolio manager's expectations. Some asset allocation funds, however, tend to keep more of a fixed mix of stocks and bonds, whereas some balanced funds shift the mix around quite frequently. (Although the concept of a manager being in the right place at the right time and beating the market averages sounds good in theory, most funds that shift assets fail to outperform a buy-and-hold approach.)

Here's our recommended short list of great balanced-type mutual funds.

> Bissett Canadian Balanced
>
> CIBC Monthly Income
>
> Mawer Canadian Balanced RSP
>
> McLean Budden Balanced Growth
>
> RBC Monthly Income
>
> Saxon Balanced
>
> TD Balanced Income

Canadian stock funds

Of all the different types of funds offered, Canadian stock funds are the largest category. To see the forest amid the trees, refer to the classifications that we cover earlier in this section. Stock funds differ mainly in the size of the companies they invest in and whether the funds focus on growth or value companies. Some funds do all these things, and some funds may even invest a bit overseas.

The only way to know for sure where a fund currently invests (or where the fund may invest in the future) is to ask. You can call the mutual fund company you're interested in or visit its Web site. You can also read the fund's annual report. Don't waste your time looking for this information in the fund's prospectus, because it doesn't give you anything beyond general parameters that guide the range of investments. The prospectus doesn't tell you what the fund currently invests in or has invested in.

For mutual funds you hold outside of retirement plans, you gotta pay current income tax on distributed dividends and capital gains. (This is another reason why most investors, during their working years, are best off sheltering more money into retirement plans.) If your circumstances allow you to invest money in stock funds outside retirement accounts, then by all means do it. But pay close attention to the dividend and capital gains distributions that funds make. In the following list we indicate which funds are tax friendly.

Here's our short list of Canadian stock funds:

> Bissett Canadian Equity
>
> Chou RRSP
>
> Fidelity Canadian Growth
>
> GBC Canadian Growth

Mac Cundill Canadian Security

Mawer Canadian Equity

Phillips, Hager & North Canadian Equity

RBC O'Shaughnessy Canadian Equity

Resolute Growth

Saxon Stock

Sceptre Equity Growth

Trimark Canadian

Canadian dividend funds

Dividend funds invest in preferred shares that pay fixed dividends, as well as common shares of large, blue chip companies that pay high yields, such as the big banks. The goal of these funds is to maximize the amount of dividend income.

Dividends used to have the honour of being the least-taxed pay-out from investing compared with capital gains and interest. However, that's no longer true, due to falling rates for capital gains. The actual tax rate depends on your tax bracket. If you earn $32,000 or less, your effective dividend tax rate is approximately 7 percent compared with an effective tax on capital gains of around 12 percent. If you make between $32,000 and $64,000, the effective tax rate on dividends is approximately 19 percent, and on capital gains, 17 percent. If your income is between $64,000 and $105,000, the dividend rate is 26 percent and the capital gains rate 20.5 percent. Finally, those who make $105,000 or more will be taxed at around 31 percent on dividends and 22.5 percent on capital gains.

If you're looking for a steady flow of income on your investments with a moderate tax level, consider these dividend funds:

Bissett Dividend Income

Empire Dividend Growth

National Bank Dividend

Phillips, Hager & North Dividend Income

RBC Dividend

Signature Dividend Income

TD Dividend Income

U.S. stock funds

The U.S. accounts for almost half of the world's stock market capitalization, so it makes sense to allocate a portion of your portfolio to American investments. While investors were richly rewarded for holding U.S stocks in the late 1990s, don't forget that it was one of the biggest and best bull markets in history. Don't expect that kind of return, and remember that other markets — including Canada's — will likely outpace the U.S. market from time to time.

Here's our short list of U.S. stock funds:

Chou Associates

Fidelity Growth America

McLean Budden American Equity

RBC O'Shaughnessy U.S. Value (and U.S. Growth)

TD U.S. Mid-Cap Growth

Trimark Fund

International stock funds

For diversification and growth potential, you should include stock funds that invest overseas as part of your portfolio. Normally, you can tell that you're looking at a fund that focuses its investments overseas if its name contains words such as *international* (foreign only) or *global* (foreign and Canadian).

As a general rule, avoid foreign funds that invest in just one country, regardless of whether that country is Australia, Zimbabwe, or anywhere in between. (The obvious exception to this rule, of course, is the U.S.) As with investing in a sector fund that specializes in a particular industry, this lack of diversification defeats the whole purpose of investing in funds. Funds that focus on specific regions, such as Southeast Asia, are better but still generally problematic because of poor diversification and higher expenses than other, more-diversified international funds.

In addition to the risks normally inherent in stock fund investing, changes in the value of foreign currencies relative to the Canadian dollar can subject international securities and funds to buffeting. A decline in the value of the Canadian dollar helps the value of foreign stock funds. Some foreign stock funds hedge against currency changes. Although this hedging helps reduce volatility a bit, it does cost money.

Here are our picks for diversified international funds that may meet your needs:

AGF International Stock Class

Bissett International

CI International Value

Mawer World Investment

McLean Budden International

Templeton International Stock

The following global equity funds have good long-term track records:

AGF International Value

Fidelity International Portfolio

Mackenzie Cundill Recovery

Mackenzie Cundill Value

Saxon World Growth

Templeton Growth

Trimark Fund

Sector funds

Sector funds invest in securities in specific industries. In most cases, you should avoid sector funds. Investing in stocks of a single industry defeats a major purpose of investing in mutual funds — you give up the benefits of diversification. Also, just because the fund may from time to time be dedicated to a "hot" sector (different examples of these sector funds are often at the top of short-term performance charts), you can't assume that the fund will pick the right securities within that sector.

Another reason to avoid sector funds is that they tend to carry much higher fees than other mutual funds. Many sector funds also have high rates of trading or turnover of their investment holdings. Investors who use these funds outside of retirement accounts have to face the tax folks for the likely greater capital gains distributions that this trading produces.

The only types of specialty funds that may make sense for a small portion (10 percent or less) of your investment portfolio are funds that invest in real estate or precious metals. These funds can help diversify your portfolio because they can perform better during times of higher inflation — which often depresses bond and stock prices. You can comfortably skip these funds because diversified stock funds tend to hold some of the same stocks as these specialty funds.

Real estate investment trusts (REITs) are stocks of companies that invest in real estate. REITs typically invest in properties such as apartment buildings, shopping centres, and other rental properties. REITs allow you to invest in real estate without the hassle of being a landlord. REITs usually pay decent dividends. As it can be a hassle to evaluate REIT stocks, you can always invest in a mutual fund of REITs. Some good funds to choose from are CIBC Canadian Real Estate, Dynamic Focus Plus Real Estate, Dynamic Global Real Estate, and Sentry Select REIT.

If you expect high inflation, consider a gold fund. But know that these funds swing wildly in value and are not for the faint of heart. Also, know that over the long term such funds provide lousy returns — on about par with increases in the cost of living. A good precious metals fund is the Royal. Don't buy the bullion itself; storage costs and the concerns over whether you're dealing with a reputable company make buying gold bars a pain. Also avoid futures and options, which are gambles on short-term price movements. Good gold funds to choose from are AGF Precious Metals, CIBC Precious Metals, Dynamic Precious Metals, RBC Precious Metals, and Sprott Gold and Precious Minerals.

The Best Bond Funds

When selecting bond funds to invest in, investors are often led astray as to how much they can expect to make. The first mistake is to look at recent performance and assume you'll get that return in the future. Investing in bond funds based only on recent performance is tempting right after a period where interest rates have declined, because declines in interest rates pump up bond prices and, therefore, bond fund total returns. But remember that an equal and opposite force waits to counteract pumped-up bond returns — bond prices fall when interest rates rise.

Don't get us wrong: Past performance is an important issue to consider. In order for performance numbers to be meaningful and useful, you must compare bond funds that are similar (such as intermediate-term funds that invest exclusively in high-grade corporate bonds).

Recognizing the importance and dangers of yield

Bond mutual funds calculate their yield after subtracting their operating expenses. When you contact a mutual fund company seeking a fund's current yield, make sure you understand what time period the yield covers.

Unfortunately, if you select bond funds based on advertised yield, you're almost guaranteed to purchase the wrong bond funds. Bond funds and the mutual fund companies that sell them can play more than a few games to fatten a fund's yield. Such sleights of hand make a fund's marketing and advertising departments happy because higher yields make it easier for salespeople and funds to hawk their bond funds. But remember that yield-enhancing shenanigans can leave you poorer. Here's what you need to watch out for:

- ✔ **Lower quality.** In comparing one short-term bond fund with another, you may discover that one pays 0.5 percent more and decide that it therefore looks better. However, it turns out that the higher-yielding fund invests 20 percent of its money in junk bonds, whereas the other fund fully invests in high-quality bonds.

- ✔ **Longer maturities.** Bond funds can usually increase their yield just by increasing their maturity a bit. If one long-term bond fund invests in bonds that mature in an average of 17 years and another fund has an average maturity of 12 years, comparing the two is a classic case of comparing apples to oranges.

- ✔ **Giving your money back without your knowing it.** Some funds return a portion of your principal in the form of dividends. This move artificially pumps up a fund's yield but depresses its total return. When you compare bond funds with each other, make sure to compare their total return over time (in addition to making sure that the funds have comparable portfolios of bonds).

You can earn a higher yield from investing in a bond fund that holds longer-term bonds, holds lower-quality bonds, or that has lower operating expenses. After you settle on the type of bonds you want, a bond fund's costs — its sales commissions and annual operating fees — are a huge consideration. Stick with no-load funds that maintain lower annual operating expenses.

Although hundreds of bond funds exist (an overwhelming number of choices), not that many remain after you eliminate high-cost funds (those with loads and high ongoing fees), low-performance funds (which are often the high-cost funds), and funds managed by fund companies and fund managers with minimal experience investing in bonds.

Although telling a good bond fund from a bad one isn't difficult, make sure you're in the right category. Bond fund objectives and names usually fit one of two maturity categories — short and long term.

The riskier the bonds that a fund holds, the higher the yield that fund should have. Generally speaking, the longer their maturity and the lower their issuer's credit rating, the riskier the bond. A higher yield is the bond market's way of compensating you for taking greater risk.

Invest in bond funds only if you have sufficient money in an emergency reserve. If you invest money for longer-term purposes, particularly retirement, you need to come up with an overall plan for allocating your money among a variety of different funds, including bond funds. (See our asset allocation discussion in the "Creating Your Fund Portfolio" section earlier in this chapter.)

Treading carefully with actively managed bond funds

Some bond funds are aggressively managed funds. Managers of these funds have a fair degree of latitude to purchase and trade bonds that they think will perform best in the future. For example, if a fund manager thinks interest rates will rise, he or she usually buys shorter-term bonds and keeps more of a fund's assets in cash. The fund manager may invest more in lower-credit-quality bonds if he or she thinks the economy is improving and that more companies will prosper and improve their credit standing.

Aggressively managed funds are a gamble. If interest rates fall instead of rise, the fund manager who moved into shorter-term bonds and cash suffers worse performance. If interest rates fall because the economy sinks into recession, the lower-credit-quality bonds will likely suffer from a higher default rate and depress the fund's performance even further.

Some people think it isn't difficult for the "experts" to predict which way interest rates or the economy is heading. The truth is that economic predictions are difficult, and the experts are often wrong. Few bond fund managers have been able to beat a buy-and-hold approach.

Trying to beat the market can lead to getting beaten! In recent years an increasing number of bond funds have fallen on their face after risky investing strategies backfire. Interestingly, the bond funds that charge sales commissions (loads) and higher ongoing operating fees are the bonds that are more likely to blow up, perhaps because these fund managers are under more pressure to pump up returns to make up for higher operating fees.

It's fine to invest some of your bond fund money in funds that try to hold the best position for changes in the economy and interest rates, but remember that if these fund managers are wrong, you can lose more money. Over the long term, you'll probably do best with efficiently managed funds that stick with an investment objective and that don't try to time and predict the bond market. Index funds that invest in a relatively fixed basket of bonds so as to track a market index of bond prices are a good example of this passive approach.

Short-term bond funds

Of all bond funds, short-term bond funds are the least sensitive to interest rate fluctuations. The stability of these funds makes them appropriate investments if you're seeking a better rate of return than what a money market fund can produce. But with short-term bond funds you also have to tolerate the risk of losing a percentage or two in principal value if interest rates rise.

Short-term bonds work well for money that you earmark for use in a few years, such as the purchase of a home or a car, or for money that you plan to withdraw from your retirement account in the near future.

A few good choices include the following:

CIBC Canadian Short Term-Bond Index

Fidelity Canadian Short Term Bond

iUnits GOC 5 Year Bond

Phillips, Hager & North Short-Term Bond and Mortgage

TD Short Term Bond

Long-term bond funds

Long-term bond funds are more volatile than short-term bond funds. If interest rates on long-term bonds increase substantially, you can easily see the principal value of your investment decline 10 percent or more. (See the discussion in Chapter 7 of how interest rate changes impact bond prices.)

Long-term bond funds are generally used for retirement investing in one of two situations:

✔ Investors don't expect to tap their investment money for a decade or more.

✔ Investors want to maximize current dividend income and are willing to tolerate volatility.

Don't use these funds to invest money that you plan to use within the next five years, because a bond market drop can leave your portfolio short of your monetary goal.

We recommend looking at the following bond funds:

Altamira Bond

Beutel Goodman Income

Bissett Bond

iUnits Government of Canada 10 year Bond

McLean Budden Fixed Income

Mulvihill Canadian Bond

Phillips, Hager & North Bond

TD Canadian Bond

The Best Money Market Funds

As we explain in Chapter 7, money market funds are a safe, higher yielding alternative to bank accounts. Money market funds can invest only in the highest credit-rated securities, and their investments must have an average maturity of less than 180 days. The short-term nature of these securities effectively eliminates the risk of money market funds being sensitive to changes in interest rates.

The securities that money market funds use are extremely safe. General-purpose money market funds invest in Treasury bills, guaranteed investment certificates, and short-term corporate debt that the largest and most creditworthy companies issue.

The main motivation for investing in a money market fund instead of a bank savings account is that you earn a greater rate of return, or yield. In addition to higher yields, good money market funds offer such useful services as telephone exchange and redemptions and automated, electronic exchange services with your bank account.

Within a given category of money market funds (the two main categories in Canada are general or Treasury bill), money market fund managers invest in the same basic securities. The market for these securities is pretty darn efficient, so "superstar" money market fund managers may eke out an extra 0.1 percent per year in yield, but not much more.

Select a money market fund that does a good job controlling its expenses. The operating expenses that the fund deducts before payment of dividends are the single biggest determinant of yield. All other things being equal (which they usually are with different money market funds), lower operating expenses translate into higher yields for you.

You have no need or reason to tolerate annual operating expenses of greater than 1.0 percent. Some top-quality funds charge a quarter of 0.75 percent or less annually. Remember, lower expenses don't mean that a fund company cuts corners or provides poor service. Lower expenses are possible in most cases because a fund company is successful in attracting much money to invest.

Expenses are important, but so too are the consequences of taxes. What you actually get to keep of your investment returns (on non-retirement account investments) is what's left over after the government takes its cut of your investment income.

Another factor that may be important to you in determining which money fund to use is what other investing you plan to do at the fund company where you establish a money market fund. For example, suppose you decide to make mutual fund investments in stocks and bonds at TD Bank. Keeping a money market fund at a different firm that offers a slightly higher yield may not be worth the time and administrative hassle, especially if you don't plan on keeping much cash in your money market fund.

Most mutual fund companies don't have many local branch offices. Generally, this helps fund companies keep their expenses low and pay you greater money market fund yields. As we discussed earlier, you may open and maintain your mutual fund account via the fund's toll-free phone lines, the mail, and the company's Web site. You don't really get much benefit, except psychological, if you select a fund company with an office in your area. (But we don't want to diminish the importance of your emotional comfort level.)

Using the criteria that we just discussed, we recommend in this section the best money market funds: those that offer competitive yields, access to other excellent mutual funds, and other commonly needed money market services.

General money market funds

Here are the best money market funds to consider:

> Beutel Goodman Money Market
>
> Capstone Cash Management
>
> Empire Money Market
>
> Ferique Short Term Income
>
> Franklin Templeton Money Market
>
> Legg Mason T-Plus
>
> McLean Budden Money Market
>
> Mulvihill Canadian Money Market

Canadian Treasury bill money market funds

Consider Canadian Treasury bill money market funds if you prefer a money market fund that invests solely or primarily in T-bills, which maintain the safety of government backing.

We recommend these funds that invest primarily in Canadian Treasury bills:

Altamira T-Bill

Franklin Templeton Treasury Bill

RBC Canadian T-Bill

TD Canadian T-Bill

How to contact fund providers

Here are the phone numbers and Web sites you can use to contact the mutual fund companies and discount brokers that sell the mutual funds we discuss in this chapter.

AIM Trimark Investments: (800) 874-6275; www.aimtrimark.com

Altamira Investment Services: 800-263-4769; www.altamira.com

Barclays Global Investors: 800-474-2737; www.ishares.com

Beutel Goodman & Company: 800-461-4551; www.beutel-can.com

Bissett Funds: 800-387-0830; www.bissett.com

Capstone Consultants: 800-207-0067; www.capstonefunds.com

Chou Associates Management: 416-214-0675; www.choufunds.com

CI Mutual Funds: 800-563-5181; www.cifunds.com

CIBC Funds: 800-465-2422; www.cibc.com/ca/mutual-funds/

Empire Financial Group: 800-561-1268; www.empire.ca

Fidelity Investments Canada: 800-263-4077; www.fidelity.ca

First Associates (Resolute funds): 866-775-7704; www.firstassociates.com

Franklin Templeton Investments: 800-387-0830; www.templeton.ca

GBC Asset Management: 800-668-7383; www.gbc.ca

Legg Mason Canada: 888-437-3333; www.leggmasoncanada.com

Mackenzie Financial: 800-387-0614; www.mackenziefinancial.com

Mawer Investment Management: 800-889-6248; www.mawer.com

McLean Budden Funds: 800-884-0436; www.mclean budden.com

Mulvihill Capital Management: 800-725-7172; www.mulvihill.com

National Bank: 888-270-3941; www.bnc.ca

Phillips, Hager & North Investment Management: 800-661-6141; www.phn.com

RBC Funds: 800-769-2599; www.rbcfunds.com

RBC O'Shaughnessy Funds: 800-769-2599; www.rbcfunds.com

Saxon Mutual Funds: 888-287-2966; www.saxonfunds.com

Sceptre Investment Counsel: (800) 265-1888; www.sceptre.ca

TD Funds: 866-567-8888; www.tdassetmanagement.com

Chapter 9

Choosing a Brokerage Firm

. . . .

In This Chapter

▶ Understanding the different types of brokerage firms

▶ Shopping for a discount broker

▶ Assessing a full-service broker

. . . .

*Y*ou can invest in most securities investments — such as the stocks and bonds that we discuss in Chapters 4 to 7 — on your own, without using a broker. But someday you may need brokerage services. Brokers execute your trades to buy or sell stocks, bonds, and other securities.

Consider setting up a brokerage account for one or both of the following reasons:

✔ If you hold or invest in individual stocks and bonds

✔ If you seek to invest in and hold mutual funds from a variety of fund companies through a single account

In this chapter we explain the ins and outs of discount brokers and full-service brokers to help you find the right broker for your investment needs.

Getting Your Money's Worth: Discount Brokers

When you hear the word "discount," you probably think of adjectives like cheap, inferior quality, and such. However, when it comes to the securities brokerage field, the brokers who place your trades at substantial discounts can offer you even better value and service than high-cost brokers.

Birth of the discount broker

Prior to 1975, all securities' brokerage firms charged the same fee, known as a *commission,* to trade stocks and bonds. In the U.S., the Securities and Exchange Commission (SEC), the federal government agency responsible for overseeing investment firms and their services, regulated commissions.

Beginning May 1, 1975 — known in the brokerage business as "May Day" — U.S. brokerage firms were free to compete with one another on price, like companies in almost all other industries. Most of the firms in existence at that time, such as Prudential, Merrill Lynch, E.F. Hutton, and Smith Barney, largely continued with business as usual, charging relatively high commissions. Canadians finally got the benefits of deregulated commissions in 1983, when the Toronto and Montreal stock exchanges deregulated the retail brokerage industry here.

These moves led to the birth of a new type of brokerage firm, the *discount broker.* Discount brokerage firms charge substantially lower commissions — typically 50 to 75 percent lower — than the other firms. Today, discount brokers, which include many online brokers, abound and continue to capture the lion's share of new business.

The following list offers some of the reasons why discount brokers give you more bang for your buck:

- ✔ Discount brokers can place your trades at a substantially lower price because they have much lower overhead.

- ✔ Discount brokers tend not to rent the most posh, downtown office space they can find — complete with mahogany-panelled conference rooms — in order to impress customers.

- ✔ Discounters also don't waste tons of money employing economists and research analysts to produce forecasts and predictive reports.

In addition to lower commissions, a major benefit of using discount brokers is that they generally work on salary. Working on salary removes a significant conflict of interest that continues to get commission-paid brokers and firms such as Prudential, Salomon Smith Barney, Merrill Lynch, and Morgan Stanley Dean Witter into trouble. Although many of these firms today claim to offer financial planning, the reality is that commission-paid brokers aren't any different from other salespeople, whether the product is cars, copy machines, or computers. People who sell on commission to make a living aren't inherently evil, but don't expect to receive holistic, in-your-best-interest investing counsel.

Ignoring the naysayers

One of the many sales tactics of high-commission brokerage firms is to try to disparage discounters by saying things such as "You'll receive poor service from discounters." High-commission firms used to argue that discount brokerage customers received worse trade prices when they bought and sold. This assertion is a bogus argument, because all brokerage firms use a computer-based trading system for smaller retail trades. Trades are processed in seconds. High-commission brokers also say that discounters are only "for people who know exactly what they're doing and don't need any help." This statement is also false.

Our own experience, as well as that of others, suggests that in many cases, discounters actually offer *better* service. Many of the larger discounters with convenient branch offices offer help that includes access to independent research reports. And, as we discuss in Chapter 8, you can buy no-load (commission-free) mutual funds run by management teams that make investment decisions for you. Such funds can be bought from mutual fund companies as well as through many discount brokerage firms.

Choosing a discount broker

Which discount broker is best for you depends on what your needs and wants are. If you seek to invest in some mutual funds as well, the discount brokerage firms we list below also offer access to good funds. In addition, these firms offer money market funds into which you can deposit money awaiting investment or proceeds from a sale.

Here are our top picks for discount brokers, as well as the pros and cons of each:

✔ **TD Waterhouse** (800-465-5463; www.tdwaterhouse.ca). TD Waterhouse has a solid range of competitive services. There's an annual RRSP fee, but it's only $25 and is waived once your account reaches $25,000. You can choose from TD's solid in-house funds as well as a wide selection of other funds. Under its FundSmart plan, there are no buy or sell commissions. TD Waterhouse also offers several funds that boast bargain-basement-level management expenses — the *MER* or *management expense ratio* — if you buy them online. In addition, TD Waterhouse offers a strong array of stock research tools and online bond investing.

✔ **CIBC Investor Edge** (800-567-3343; www.investorservicesinc.cibc.com). CIBC's FundPlus RRSP lets you invest in funds and fixed income securities for an annual fee of $25, which disappears once your account tops $15,000. There is no commission when you buy either no-load or load funds, but there is a fee when you sell. There are good stock-screening tools and access to loads of CIBC World Markets equity research. CIBC has recently added online bond trading.

✔ **BMO InvestorLine** (800-387-7800; www.bmoinvestorline.com). BMO InvestorLine's Web site is well thought-out and easy to navigate. There's no commission for buying and selling mutual funds, and you can also trade bonds and GICs online. The site has some strong tools, including good asset allocation and financial planning features that let you approach your finances from a life-goal perspective. One drawback is that, unlike the discount brokerages run by other banks, InvestorLine doesn't give you access to equity research from BMO's full service brokerage. There's also a $5,000 minimum on RRSPs, and a $100 annual fee' that no longer applies once the value of your account reaches $15,000.

✔ **E*Trade Canada** (888-872-3368; www.etrade.ca). E*Trade targets active investors. Its regular commission rate of $27 for most trades is mid-range. However, the rates fall as the number of trades you do increases. E*Trade's Web site has some good stock screening tools, including the ability to do technical analysis, and you can trade bonds online. It also offers real-time portfolio updating that allows you to see your investments' book and market value. That, along with its lower commissions in reward for more trades, may contribute to unprofitable overtrading. To guard against this, take advantage of another feature — the ability to track your percentage gains . . . or losses.

One final recommendation: If you want a really cut-rate discounter for stock and other securities trading, consider Interactive Brokers Canada (800-822-2021; www.interactivebrokers.ca). The company charges a mere 1 to 2 cents a share, with a minimum per trade of just $2.00. When you buy U.S. stocks, the commission is even less — 1 cent (U.S.) a share with a minimum of just $1.00 on the first 500 shares. If you buy more than that number, the commission on any further shares is just half a cent. However, the prices are high for telephone orders — $40 — and there's a $10 minimum a month in commissions and market data fees. This is a stripped-down, no-frills way to trade. There are no research or planning tools.

Considering Online Brokers and Online Trading

Anyone familiar with the economics of running a brokerage firm can tell you that technology, properly applied, reduces a broker's labour costs. Some brokerages — thanks to technology — can now perform market orders (which means they will execute your trade at the best current available price) for a mere five bucks. Hence the attraction of online trading.

Before you jump at the chance to save a few dollars by trading online, read the following sections for other considerations that should factor into your choice of an online broker — or your decision to trade online at all.

Examining your motivations for trading online

If trading online attracts you, first examine why you're motivated to do so. Tracking prices daily — or even worse, hourly — and frequently checking your account balances lead to addictive trading. Saving a few dollars per trade makes little difference if you trade a lot and rack up significant total commissions, and you pay more in capital gains taxes. Don't forget that, as with trading through a regular brokerage firm, you also lose the "spread" (the difference between the bid and ask prices when you trade), in addition to the explicit commission rates that online brokers charge. Likewise, more online brokers share in the spread on NASDAQ stocks, which is how they can offer some trades for "free."

Investment Web sites also push the surging interest in online trading with the pitch that you can beat the market averages and professionals at their own game if you do your own research and trade online. Beating the market and professionals is highly unlikely. You can save some money trading online, but probably not as much as the hype will have you believe.

Considering other costs

Online brokerage customers often shop for low costs. However, simply talking with enough people who have traded online and reviewing online message boards where customers speak their minds clearly show that shopping merely for low-cost trading prices often leads investors to overlook other important issues.

For starters, there's more to your costs of trading online than simply the commission on a trade. Unless you use your employer's computer or work for or attend a university, you must pay fees for Internet access (including relevant local phone charges) as well as connect-time fees in some cases. Some discounters don't provide toll-free phone numbers, so bear this in mind if you need to call with questions and service problems.

When you buy or sell an investment, you may have cash sitting around in your brokerage account. Not surprisingly, the online brokers pitching their cheap online trading rates in three-inch-high numbers don't reveal their money market rates in such large type (if at all). Some don't pay interest on the first $1,000 or so of your cash balance, and even then, some companies pay half to a full percent less or so than their best competitors. In the worst cases, some online brokers have paid up to 3 percent less during periods when interest rates were a little higher. Under those terms, you'd earn up to $150 less in interest per year if you average a $5,000 cash balance during the year.

Finally, some brokers whack you $20 here and $50 there for services such as wiring money or simply closing your account. Also beware of "inactivity fees" that some brokers levy on accounts that have infrequent trading. So before you sign up with any broker, make sure to examine its entire fee schedule.

Examining service quality

Common complaints among customers of online brokers include slow responses to e-mail queries, lengthy waits to speak with a live person to answer questions or resolve problems, delays in opening accounts and receiving literature, unclear statements, incorrect processing of trading requests, and slow Web response during periods of heavy traffic. We sometimes experienced phone waits of up to ten minutes with a number of the firms we called, and were often transferred several times to retrieve answers to simple questions, such as whether the firm carried a specific family of mutual funds.

When you shop for an online broker, check your prospects thoroughly. Call for literature and see how long reaching a live human being takes. Ask some questions and see how knowledgeable and helpful the representatives are. For non-retirement accounts, if the quality of the firm's year-end account statements concern you, ask prospective brokerages to send you a sample. Try sending some questions to the broker's Web site and see how accurate and timely the response is. If you're a mutual fund investor, check out the quality of the funds the company offers — and don't allow the sheer number of funds to impress you. Also, inquire about the interest rates the company pays on cash balances, as well as the rates the company charges on margin loans, if you want such borrowing services.

Consider checking online message boards to see what current and past customers are saying about the firms you're considering. Most online brokers that have been around for more than six months lay claim to a number one rating with some survey or ranking of online brokers. Place little value on such claims.

Abuses and uses of online brokerage accounts

Frankly, trading online is an unfortunately easy way for people to act impulsively and emotionally when making important investment decisions. Use the Internet rather than the telephone to check account information and gather factual information. Also, know that most of the best investment firms allow you to trade via touch-tone phone. In most cases, touch-tone phone trading is discounted when you compare it with trading through a live broker, although it's admittedly less glitzy than trading through a Web site.

Why you should keep your securities in a brokerage account

When most investors purchase stocks or bonds today, they don't receive the actual paper certificate demonstrating ownership. Broke-rage accounts often hold the certificate for your stocks and bonds on your behalf. Holding your securities through a brokerage account is beneficial because most brokers charge an extra fee to issue certificates.

Sometimes people hold stock and bond certificates themselves — a practice that was more common among your parents' and grandparents' generations. The reason: During the Great Depression, many brokerage firms failed and took people's assets down with their sinking ships. Since then, various reforms have greatly strengthened the safety of money and the securities you hold in a brokerage account.

Just as the CDIC insurance system backs up money in bank accounts, the CIPF (Canadian Investor Protection Fund) provides insurance to customers of investment brokerage firms that are members of the Fund. The base level of insurance is $1,000,000 per account held with each financial institution.

What constitutes an "account"? If you have a basic investment account, it's lumped in with your other accounts at that institution that aren't deemed to be "*separate*" accounts. This is called your *regular* account, and each regular account is insured up to $1,000,000 with each institution. It includes other related accounts, including an interest in a private holding company or an account you hold jointly with others. Many different types of accounts are treated as separate accounts, including RRSPs, RRIFs, RESPs, and trusts. If you have three different RRSPs with the same financial institution, they're pooled and the entire *separate* account is insured up to the $1,000,0000

maximum. However, many firms purchase additional protection — some as high as $100 million total!

Brokerage firms don't often fail these days but, unlike during the Depression, the CIPF protects you if they do. However, the CIPF coverage doesn't protect you against a falling stock market. If you invest your money in stocks, bonds, or whatever that plunge in value, it's your own problem!

Another good reason to hold securities with a broker is so you don't lose them — literally! Surprising numbers of people — the exact number is unknown — have lost their stock and bond certificates. Those who realize their loss can contact the issuing firms to replace them, but doing so takes a good deal of time. However, just like future goals and plans, some certificates are simply lost, and owners never realize it. This financial fiasco sometimes happens when people die and their heirs don't know where to look for the certificates or the securities their loved ones held.

A further advantage of holding your securities in a brokerage account is that doing so cuts down on processing all those dividend cheques. If you own a dozen stocks that each pay you a quarterly dividend, you must receive, endorse, and otherwise deal with 48 separate cheques. Some people enjoy this practice — for them it's part of the "fun" of owning securities. Our advice: Stick all your securities into one brokerage account that holds your paid dividends. With brokerage accounts you can move these payments into a reasonably good-yielding money market fund. Some of the better discount brokers even allow you to reinvest stock dividends into the purchase of more shares of that stock at no charge.

Some brokers offer account information and trading capabilities via personal digital assistants, which, of course, add to your costs. Digital assistants can also promote addictive investment behaviours.

No matter how you trade, keep track of your overall annual returns, minus trading costs, and see how your performance compares with the market averages. Unless you invest purely for thrill and education, consider tossing in your modem for some well-managed mutual funds that won't glue you to your computer screen.

Considering Full-Service Brokers

Despite the growing interest in discount brokers, many Canadians still work with full-service brokers, whom they continue to regard as the traditional "stockbrokers." That is, in return for access to his or her company's research, advice on structuring your portfolio, and other services, you compensate your broker through commissions when you buy and sell. These commissions have declined somewhat with the advent of discount brokerages, but it will still cost you a lot to do transactions through a full-service broker compared with what you'd pay a discount broker.

There are numerous reasons why people stick with full-service brokers. They may feel they benefit from the research they receive. They may look to them for advice on larger financial planning issues. Or maybe it's just t what their parents did, and setting up an account with Dad's — or Mom's — broker was a rite of passage. Some people simply like to be able to say "My broker says . . ." just like they enjoy being able to talk about their lawyer, their accountant, and so on.

Full-service brokers have one major strike against them: The more you buy and sell, the more money they make, plain and simple. That's not to say there aren't good, competent, trustworthy full-service brokers out there — there are. But if you're going to deal with one, you need to take a few basic steps in order to get your money's worth.

Your first step should be to educate yourself before you go any further with your full-service broker — or open up an account with one. Knowing what products and approach will best suit your circumstances will go a long way toward helping ensure your interests come first. Next, have a frank discussion about the commissions you'll pay. Most brokers know that discount brokerages are a big competitive force, and are usually willing to reduce their commissions to keep your business. For instance, you could propose that when an investment comes from your own research and homework, you pay the commission that you'd otherwise pay a discount broker. In this way you can keep your investments in one place and keep costs down while still drawing on your broker's knowledge and advice.

Another strike against full-service brokers is that they often won't recommend no-load funds because they won't make a commission. Consider proposing a flat fee — say, 1 percent — to your broker to buy into these funds. In many cases, that will be close to what you may end up paying with some discounters, once you count in the many buried fees that often exist.

The biggest benefit of using a full-service broker — and one not to be underestimated — is that they can serve as a sober second opinion. Too many individual investors fail to even match the market indices because they're too quick to sell when prices fall and too slow to buy when prices rise. If a full-service broker saves you from selling at discount prices when the market corrects, they may more than earn their keep.

Part III
Real Estate

The 5th Wave · By Rich Tennant

"Here's to the new owners of our house — may you have better luck with the plumbing, electricity, and foundation than we did!"

In this part . . .

Owning a home and investing in real estate are time-proven methods for building wealth. However, if you're not careful, you can easily fall prey to a number of pitfalls. In this part, you discover the right and wrong ways to purchase real estate and how to build your real estate empire. Even if you don't want to be a real estate tycoon, you also see how simply owning your own home can help build your net worth and accomplish future financial goals.

Chapter 10

Investing in a Home

● ●

● ●

We hesitate somewhat to call the home in which you live an investment. Homes suck up money the same way politicians do. And most people don't view their homes as a ticket to important financial goals, such as retirement.

Calling a home an investment may be problematic for another reason. Perhaps you've owned a home or seen others who own homes that have declined in value. Remember that all investments go through up and down periods. Those who stick with homeownership profit over the long term, where there's a lot more up than down in home values. Over the decades, the rate of home investment return has been comparable to the rates of return that stock market investments achieve (see Chapter 2).

For most people, buying a home in which to live is their first, best, and only real estate investment. Homes may require a lot of financial feeding, but over the course of your life, owning a home (instead of renting) can make and save you money. And although the pile of mortgage debt seems daunting in the years just after your purchase, someday your home may well be among your biggest assets.

Even though your home consumes a lot of dough (mortgage payments, property taxes, insurance, maintenance, and so on) while you own it, it can help you accomplish important financial goals, such as:

✔ **Retiring.** By the time you hit your 50s and 60s, the size of your monthly mortgage payment should start to look small or nonexistent. Relatively low housing costs can help you afford to retire or cut back from full-time work. Some people are choosing to sell their homes and buy less costly ones or rent and use some or all the cash to live on in retirement. Other homeowners enhance their retirement income by taking out a reverse mortgage to tap the *equity* (market value of your home minus the outstanding mortgage debt) they've built up in their properties.

✔ **Pursuing your small-business dreams.** Running your own business can be a source of great satisfaction. Financial barriers, however, prevent many people from pulling the plug on a regular job and taking the entrepreneurial plunge. You may be able to borrow against the equity you've built up in your home to get the cash to start up your own business. Depending on what type of business you have in mind, you may even be able to run your enterprise from your home.

✔ **Financing university.** While it may seem like only yesterday that your kids were born, soon enough they're ready for an expensive four-year undertaking: university. Borrowing against the equity in your home is a viable way to help pay for your kids' educational costs.

Perhaps you won't use your home's equity for retirement, a small business, educational expenses, or other important financial goals. But even if you decide to pass your home on to your children, charity, or a long-lost relative, it's still a valuable asset and a worthwhile investment. This chapter explains how to make the most of it.

The Buying Decision

Because buying a home is probably the largest financial transaction of a lifetime, most people approach property ownership with trepidation. Who wants stress? Why not keep renting and be happy? Actually, some people may be better off doing just that. More than a few couples have landed in divorce court thanks to squabbles over homeownership. Remodelling debates and arguments can drain your savings and your psyche.

We're not trying to scare you off from buying a home — we believe most people should buy and own a home. But homeownership isn't for everybody, and certainly not at all times in your adult life.

The decision about if and when to buy a home may be complex. Money matters, but so do personal and emotional issues. Buying a home is a big deal — you're settling down. Can you really see yourself coming home to this same place day after day, year after year? Of course, you can always move, but now you've got a financial obligation to deal with.

Financially speaking, we advise that you wait to buy a home until you can see yourself staying put for a minimum of three years. Ideally, we'd like you to think you've got a solid chance of staying with the home for five or more years. Why? Buying and selling a home cost big bucks, including these expenses:

- ✔ **Inspection fees.** You shouldn't buy a property without checking it out, so you'll have inspection expenses. Good inspectors can help you identify problems with the plumbing, heating, and electrical systems as well as the foundation, roof, termites, and so on.

- ✔ **Appraisal fee.** Your lender may require you to get your home appraised so that they can have an independent assessment of its value. An appraisal typically costs between $100 and $250 or more.

- ✔ **Survey fee.** Unless the sellers have recently had a survey done of the property, you'll need to have a new one prepared. Done by a registered land surveyor, a survey is simply a drawing of your property that lets you and your lender ensure that the buildings you're buying are indeed on your property, that your neighbours' homes aren't on your land, and that any buildings meet zoning regulations. An up-to-date survey is generally needed before you can legally be awarded title. A survey will typically cost around $400 to $500.

- ✔ **Legal fees.** While you can prepare an offer to purchase yourself and tend to the closing costs, using a lawyer to at least search the title is usually advisable. A title search is carried out to determine that the vendor actually owns the home and has the right to sell it to you, and that the property doesn't have any claims against it. While you can save some money by using a paralegal, it's generally best to use a lawyer. Except in British Columbia and Quebec, they're the only folks legally allowed to complete the purchase. Using a lawyer also gives you valuable insurance. If the lawyer certifies that the seller has the right to sell you the property and that it doesn't have any claims against it — known as *free and marketable title* — and this later proves to be wrong, you can pursue a claim against the lawyer. When you buy a home, you and your lender need to protect yourselves against the chance — albeit small — that the property seller doesn't actually legally own the home you're buying.

- ✔ **Moving costs.** You can transport all that furniture, clothing, and other personal belongings yourself, but your time is worth something and your moving skills are likely limited. Besides, do you want to end up in a hospital emergency room after you're pinned by a runaway couch at the bottom of a stairwell?

- ✔ **Real estate agents' commissions.** A commission of 5 to 7 percent of the purchase price of most homes goes into the pockets of real estate salespeople and the companies they work for.

On top of all these "transaction costs" of buying and then selling a home, you also have maintenance expenses — for example, fixing leaky pipes and painting. To cover all the transaction and maintenance costs of homeownership, the value of your home needs to appreciate about 15 percent over the years you own it just for you to be as well off financially as if you had continued renting. Fifteen percent! If you need or want to move elsewhere in a few years, relying on that kind of appreciation in those few years is risky. If you happen to buy just before a sharp upturn in housing prices, you may get this much appreciation in a short time. But you can't count on this upswing — you'll probably lose money on such a short-term deal.

Some people invest in real estate even when they don't expect to live in the home for long and may consider turning their home into a rental if they move within a few years. Doing so can work well financially in the long haul, but don't underestimate the responsibilities that come with rental property, which we discuss in Chapter 11.

Weighing the pros and cons of homeownership

To hear some people talk — particularly enthusiastic salespeople in the real estate business — it would seem that everybody should own a home. You may hear them say things like

> "Buy a home for the tax breaks."

> "Renting is like throwing your money away."

As we discuss later in this chapter, it's true that the profit you make on your home is tax-free. However, many people end up living in their home for many, many years — perhaps for the rest of their lives — while others use all the profits from one home along with extra savings in order to buy a larger property as their family grows. Tax-free profits are great, but they often don't get redirected to your investment account. Don't buy a home just because of the tax break.

Renting is not necessarily throwing your money away. In some communities, you can get more for your money by renting, thus enabling you to keep your housing expenses lower than if you buy. Happy and successful renters that we've seen include people who pay low rent, perhaps because they've made housing sacrifices. If you're able to sock away 10 percent or more of your earnings while renting, you're probably well on your way to accomplishing your future financial goals.

Another benefit of renting is that you can save money and hopefully invest in financial assets, such as stocks, bonds, and mutual funds, which are quite accessible and possibly helpful in retirement. Most homeowners, by contrast, have a substantial portion of their wealth tied up in their homes. (Accessibility is a double-edged sword, because it may tempt you as a cash-rich renter to blow the money in the short term.)

Renting has potential emotional and psychological rewards, too. First is the not-so-inconsequential fact that you have more flexibility to pack up and move on. You may have a lease to fulfill, but you can renegotiate it if you need to move on. As a homeowner, you have a large monthly payment to take care of — and to some people, this feels like a financial ball and chain. And if you want to move you have no guarantee that you can sell your home in a timely fashion or at the price you want.

Although renting has its benefits, it has at least one big drawback: exposure to inflation. As the cost of living increases, your landlord can (unless you live in a rent-controlled unit) keep jacking up your rent. If you're a homeowner, however, the big monthly expense of the mortgage payment doesn't increase, assuming you buy your home with a fixed-rate mortgage. (Your property taxes, homeowners insurance, and maintenance expenses *are* exposed to inflation, although these expenses are usually much smaller than your monthly mortgage payment or rent.)

Here's a quick example of how inflation can work against you as a long-term renter. Suppose you're comparing the costs of owning a home that costs $180,000 with renting a similar property for $900 a month. Buying at $180,000 sounds a lot more expensive than renting, doesn't it? But this isn't a fair apples-to-apples comparison. You must compare the monthly cost of owning to the monthly cost of renting. Figure 10-1 does just that for a 25-year example.

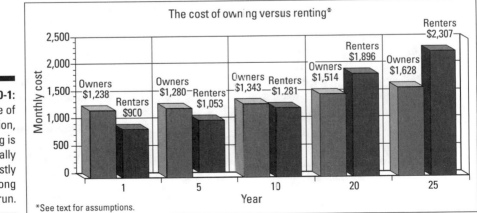

Figure 10-1: Because of inflation, renting is generally more costly in the long run.

As you can see in Figure 10-1, although it costs more in the early years to own, owning should be less expensive in the long run. Renting is higher in the long term because all your rental expenses increase with inflation. (*Note:* we haven't factored in the potential change in the value of your home over time. Over long periods home prices tend to appreciate, which makes owning even more attractive. And any profit you make when you sell the home you've been living in — your *principal residence* — is tax-free).

The example in Figure 10-1 assumes that you make a 25 percent down payment, and that your mortgage is at 7.5 percent. We also assume that the rate of inflation of your homeowners insurance, property taxes, maintenance, and rent is 4 percent per year. If inflation is lower, renting doesn't necessarily become cheaper in the long term. In the absence of inflation, your rent should escalate less, but your homeownership expenses, which are subject to inflation (property taxes, maintenance, and insurance), should increase less too. And with low inflation, you can probably renew your mortgage at a lower interest rate, which reduces your monthly mortgage payments. With low or no inflation, owning can still cost less, but the savings versus renting aren't as dramatic as when inflation is greater.

Knowing when to buy

If you're considering buying a home, you may be concerned whether home prices are poised to rise or fall. No one wants to purchase a home that then plummets in value. And who wouldn't like to buy just before prices go on an upward trajectory?

It's not easy to predict what's going to happen with real estate prices in a particular city, province, or country over the next one, two, or three or more years. Ultimately, the economic health and vitality of an area drive the demand and prices its homes. An increase in jobs, particularly ones that pay well, increases the demand for housing. And when demand goes up, so do prices.

If you first buy a home when you're in your 20s, 30s, or even your 40s, you may end up as a homeowner for several or more decades. Over such a long time, you'll experience lots of ups and downs, but most likely more ups than downs, so we wouldn't be too concerned about trying to predict what's going to happen to the

real estate market in the near term. We know some long-term renters who avoided buying homes years ago because they thought prices were high and have missed out on tremendous appreciation in real estate values.

That said, you may be, at particular times in your life, ambivalent about buying a home. Perhaps you're not sure you'll stay put for more than three to five years. Therefore, part of your home-buying decision may hinge on whether current home prices in your local area offer you a good value. The level of real estate prices as compared with rent, the state of the job market, and the number of home listings for sale are useful indicators of the housing market's health. Trying to time your purchase has more importance if you think you may move in less than five years. In that case, avoid buying in a high market. If you expect to move so soon, renting generally makes more sense because of the high transaction costs of buying and selling real estate.

Deciding how much to spend

Buying a home is a long-term financial commitment. You'll probably spread the repayment of the money you borrow to purchase your home — the *amortization* of your mortgage — over 25 years, and the home you buy will need all sorts of maintenance over the years. So before you make a decision to buy, take stock of your overall financial health.

If you have good credit and a reliable source of employment, lenders will eagerly offer to loan you money. They'll tell you how much you may borrow from them — the maximum you're qualified to borrow. But that doesn't mean you should borrow the maximum. What about your other financial options and goals?

If you buy without factoring in your other monthly expenditures and long-term goals, you may end up with a home that dictates much of your future spending. Have you considered, for example, how much you need to save monthly to reach your retirement goals? How about the amount you want to spend on recreation and entertainment?

If you want to continue your current lifestyle, you have to be honest with yourself about how much you can really afford to spend as a homeowner. First-time homebuyers in particular run into financial trouble when they don't understand their current spending. Buying a home can be a wise decision, but it can also be a huge burden. And, there are all sorts of nifty things to buy for a home. Some people prop up their spending habits with credit cards — a dangerous practice.

Don't let your home control your financial future. Before you buy property or agree to a particular mortgage, make sure you can afford to do so — and be especially careful not to ignore your retirement planning (if you hope to someday retire). Start by reading Chapter 3.

Looking through a lender's eyes

All mortgage lenders want to know that you can repay the money you borrow, so you have to pass a few tests. Mortgage lenders calculate the maximum amount you can borrow to buy a piece of real estate.

For a home you'll live in, lenders total up your monthly housing expense. They define your housing costs as:

Mortgage payment + Property taxes (and sometimes heating) + Condominium maintenance fees (for condominium buyers)

A lender does not consider the maintenance and upkeep expenses of owning a home. (You shouldn't ignore this important issue in your budget, however.) Lenders typically loan you *up to* an amount so that no more than 30 to 32 percent of your monthly gross (pre-tax) income goes toward housing expense. The percentage of your income that your housing costs will eat up is called the *gross debt service ratio*. (If you're self-employed, determining what a lender will allow you to borrow is much less formulaic. Lenders will typically want to see your financial statements and income tax returns for the last few years. Just how much you'll be able to borrow is often worked out on an individual basis.) Lending ratios vary slightly from lender to lender.

Consumer debt is bad news even without considering that it hurts your qualification for a mortgage. Consumer debt is costly and encourages you to live beyond your means. Get rid of it — curtail your spending and adjust to living within your means. If you can't live within your means as a renter, doing so is going to be even harder as a homeowner.

Homeownership tax savings

Any profit you make when you sell your home is generally tax-free. In addition to a house, this includes condos, townhouses, as well as a share in a co-operative housing corporation.

To qualify, the property you're selling has to be what's called your *principal residence* — you or your spouse or child must have "ordinarily inhabited" the property. This doesn't mean you have to live there the majority of the year. Just staying there a day or two in the year is sufficient.

You are, however, limited to designating a single property as your principal residence in any given year. If you have a home and a cottage, for example, you could choose to designate the home as your principal residence for some years and the cottage for others. When you sell a property, just how much of your gain will be tax-free is determined by a formula that looks at how many years you owned it, how many years it was your principal residence, and the overall increase in value.

Determining your down payment

Another factor to consider when you decide how much you should borrow is that you're required to purchase *mortgage insurance* if your down payment is less than 25 percent of your home's purchase price. Mortgage insurance protects the lender from getting stuck with a property that may be worth less than the mortgage you owe, in the event that you default on your loan. On a moderate-size loan, mortgage insurance can add hundreds of dollars per year to your payments.

What if you have so much money that you can afford to put down more than a 25 percent down payment? How much should you put down then? (This problem doesn't usually arise — most buyers, especially first-time buyers, struggle to get a 25 percent down payment together.) The answer depends on what else you can or want to do with the money. If you're considering other investment opportunities, determine whether you can expect to earn a higher rate of return on those investments than the interest rate you'll pay on the mortgage.

During the 20th century, stock market and real estate investors have enjoyed average annual returns of around 10 percent per year. So if you borrow mortgage money at around 6 to 7 percent, in the long term you should come out ahead if you put the money that would have gone toward a larger down payment into such growth investments. In other words, you'd make more from these investments than you would save in interest from paying down your mortgage, after tax. One way to better your chances is to invest inside an RRSP so that your profits can grow tax-free. It's not guaranteed, of course, that your other investments can earn 10 percent yearly. (Remember that past returns don't guarantee the future.) And don't forget that all investments come with risk. The advantage of putting more money down for a home and borrowing less is that it's essentially a risk-free investment (as long as you have adequate insurance on your property).

If you prefer to put down just 25 percent and invest more money elsewhere, that's fine. Just don't keep the extra money (beyond an emergency reserve) under the mattress, in a savings account, or in bonds that pay less in interest than your mortgage costs you in interest. Invest in stocks, real estate, or a small business. Otherwise, you don't have a chance to earn a higher return than the cost of your mortgage, and you're therefore better off paying down your mortgage.

Selecting Your Property Type

If you're ready to buy a home, you must make some decisions about what and where to buy. If you grew up in the suburbs, your image of a home may include the traditional single-family house with a lawn, a couple of kids, and the family pets. But single-family homes, of course, aren't the only or even the main types of residential housing in many areas, especially in some higher-cost, urban neighbourhoods. Other common types of higher-density housing include the following:

- ✔ **Condominiums.** These are generally apartment-style units that are stacked on top of and adjacent to one another. Many condo buildings were originally apartments that were converted — through the sale of ownership of separate units — into condos. When you buy a condominium, you buy a specific unit as well as a share of the common areas (for example, the pool, grass and other plantings, entry and hallways, laundry room, and so on).

- ✔ **Townhouses.** Townhouses are just a fancy way of saying attached or row houses. Think of townhouses as a cross between a condominium and a single-family house. They're condo-like because they're attached (generally sharing walls and a roof), and are homelike because they're often two-storey buildings that come with a small yard.

- ✔ **Co-operatives.** Co-operatives resemble apartment and condominium buildings. When you buy a share in a co-operative, you own a share of the entire building, including some living space. Unlike a condo, you generally need to get approval from the co-operative association if you want to remodel or rent your unit to a tenant. In some co-ops, you must even gain approval from the association for the sale of your unit to a proposed buyer. Co-ops are generally much harder to obtain loans for and to sell, so we don't recommend you buy one unless you get a deal and can easily obtain a loan.

All types of shared housing (the types of housing in the preceding list) offer two potential advantages. First, this type of housing generally gives you more living space for your dollars. That's because with a single-family home, a good chunk of the property cost is for the land the house sits on. Land is good for decks, recreation, and playing children, but you don't live "in" it the way you do your home. Shared housing maximizes living space for your housing dollars.

Another benefit of shared housing is that in many situations, you're not personally responsible for general maintenance. Instead, the homeowners association (which you pay into) takes care of it. If you don't have the time, energy, or desire to keep up a property, shared housing can make sense. Shared housing units may also provide you with better safety than a stand-alone house and may give you access to shared recreation facilities, such as a pool, tennis courts, and exercise equipment.

So why doesn't everyone buy shared housing? As an investment, single-family houses generally perform better in the long run. In a good real estate market, these and other types of housing appreciate, but single-family homes tend to outperform other housing types. Shared housing is easier to build (and to overbuild) — the greater supply tends to keep its prices depressed. Single-family homes tend to attract more potential buyers — most people, when they can afford it, prefer a stand-alone house, especially for the increased privacy.

If you can afford a smaller single-family home instead of a larger shared-housing unit, buy the single-family home. Shared housing makes more sense for people who don't want to deal with building maintenance and who value the security of living in a larger building with other people. Also know that shared-housing prices tend to hold up better in developed urban environments. If possible, avoid shared housing units in suburban areas where the availability of developable land makes building many more units possible, thus increasing the supply of housing and slowing growth in values.

If shared housing interests you, make sure you have the property well inspected. Also, examine the trend in maintenance fees over time to ensure that these costs are under control. (See Chapter 11 for more specifics on how to check out property.)

Finding the Right Property and Location

Some people know where they want to live, so they look at a handful of properties and then buy. Most people take much more time — finding the right house in a desired area at a fair price can be a lengthy process. Buying a home can also entail much compromise when you buy with other family members (particularly spouses).

Be realistic about how long it may take you to get up to speed about different areas and to find a home that meets your many needs and concerns. If you're a normal person with a full-time job and you're confined to occasional weekends and evenings to look for a house, three to six months is a short amount of time to settle on an area and actually find and successfully negotiate on a property. Six months to a year is not unusual or slow. Remember that you're talking about an enormous purchase that you'll come home to every day until you move or sell it.

Real estate agents can be a big barrier to taking your time with this monumental decision. Some agents are pushy and want to make a sale and get their commission. Don't work with such agents as a buyer — they can make you miserable, unhappy, and broke. If necessary, begin your search without an agent to avoid this outside pressure.

Keep an open mind

Before you start your search, you may have an idea about the type of property and location that interests you or that you think you can afford. You may think, for example, that you can afford only a condominium in the neighbourhood that you want. But if you take the time to check out other communities, you may find another area that meets most of your needs and has affordable single-family homes. You'd never know that, though, if you narrowed your search too quickly.

Even if you've lived in an area for a while and think you know it well, look at different types of properties in a variety of locations before you start to narrow your search. Be open-minded and make sure you know which of your many criteria for a home you *really* care about. You may have to be flexible with some of your preferences.

After you focus on a particular area or neighbourhood, make sure you see the full range of properties available. If you want to spend $200,000 on a home, look at properties that are more expensive. Most real estate sells for less than its listing price, and you may feel comfortable spending a little bit more if you see what you can purchase if you stretch your budget a little bit. Also, if you work with an agent, don't overlook homes that are for sale by their owners (that is, not listed with real estate agents). Otherwise, you may miss out on some good properties.

Research, research, research

Assuming what an area is like from anecdotes or from a small number of personal experiences is a mistake. You may have read or heard that someone was mugged in a particular area. That doesn't make that area dangerous or more dangerous than others. *Get the facts!* Anecdotes and people's perceptions are often not accurate reflections of the reality. Check out the following key items:

- **Amenities.** Hopefully you don't spend all your time at work, slaving away to make your monthly mortgage payment. We hope you've got the time to use parks, sports and recreation facilities, and so on. Drive around the neighbourhood to get a sense of these attractions — most real estate agents just love to show off their favourite neighbourhoods. Cities and towns can also mail you information booklets that detail what their town has to offer and where you can find it.

- **Schools.** If you have kids, you care about this issue a lot. Unfortunately, many people make snap judgments about school quality without doing their homework. Visit the schools and don't blindly rely on test scores. Talk to parents and teachers and discover what goes on at the school.

If you don't have (or want!) school-age children, you may be tempted to say, "What the heck do I care about the quality of the schools?" You need to care about the schools because even if you don't have kids, the quality of the local schools has direct bearing on the value of your property. Consider these issues even if they're not important to you, because they can affect the resale value of your property.

✔ **Property taxes.** What will your property taxes be? Property tax rates vary from community to community. Check with the town's assessment office or with a good real estate agent.

✔ **Crime.** Call the local police department or visit your public library to get the facts on crime. Cities and towns keep all sorts of crime statistics for neighbourhoods — use them!

✔ **Future development.** Check with the planning department in towns that you're considering living in to find out what types of new development and major renovations are in the works. Planning people may also be aware of problems in particular areas.

✔ **Catastrophic risks.** Are the neighbourhoods you're considering buying a home in susceptible to major risks, such as floods, tornadoes, mudslides, fires, or earthquakes? Although proper homeowners insurance can protect you financially, consider how you may deal with such catastrophes emotionally — since insurance eases only the financial pain of a home loss. All areas have some risk, and a home in the safest of areas can burn to the ground. Although you can't eliminate all risks, you can at least educate yourself about the potential catastrophic risks in various areas.

If you're new to an area or don't have a handle on its risks, try a number of different sources. Knowledgeable and honest real estate agents may help, but you can also dig for primary information. Contact Environment Canada as well as the Public Safety and Emergency Preparedness Canada office (www.ocipep.gc.ca/index.html) to find out about potential flooding and earthquake risks in the area you're considering. Insurance companies and agencies can also tell you what they know of risks in particular areas.

Understand market value

Over many months, you'll look at lots of properties for sale, perhaps dozens or even hundreds. Use these viewings as an opportunity to find out what places are worth. The listing price isn't what a house is worth — it may be, but odds are it's not. Property that's priced to sell usually does just that — sell. Properties left on the market are often overpriced. The listing price on such properties may reflect what an otherwise greedy or uninformed seller and his or her agent hope some fool will pay.

Keep track of the prices that the properties you see end up selling for. (Good agents can help you obtain this information.) Properties usually sell for less than the listed price. Keeping track of selling prices gives you a good handle on what properties are really worth — and a better sense of what you can afford.

Pound the pavement

After you set your sights on that special home, thoroughly check out the surroundings — you should know what you're getting yourself into.

Go back to the neighbourhood in which the property is located at different times of the day and on different days of the week. Knock on a few doors and meet your potential neighbours. Ask questions. Talk to property owners as well as renters. Because they don't have a financial stake in the area, renters are often more forthcoming with negative information about an area.

After you decide where and what to buy, you're ready to try to put a deal together. We cover issues common to both home and investment property purchases — such as mortgages, negotiations, inspections, and so on — in Chapter 12.

Chapter 11

Investing in Real Estate

● ●

In This Chapter

▶ Looking at the attractions and drawbacks of real estate investing

▶ Figuring out what it takes to become a successful real estate investor

▶ Discovering simple and profitable ways to invest in real estate

▶ Exploring some hands-on real estate investments

▶ Avoiding bad real estate investments

▶ Evaluating properties

● ●

*I*f you've already bought your own home (and even if you haven't), using real estate as an investment may interest you. Over the years, decades, and centuries, real estate investing, like the stock market and small-business investments, has generated vast wealth for participants. As we discuss in Chapters 2 and 10, the rate of return from good real estate investments is comparable to that available from investing in the stock market.

Real estate is like other types of ownership investments, such as stocks, where you have an ownership stake in an asset. Although you have the potential for significant profits, don't forget that you also accept greater risk. Real estate is not a gravy train or a simple way to get wealthy. Like stocks, real estate goes through good and bad performance periods. Most people who make money investing in real estate buy and hold property over many years. The vast majority of people who *don't* make money in real estate make easily avoidable mistakes. In this chapter we discuss how to make the best real estate investments and avoid the rest.

Real Estate Investment Attractions

As we discuss in Chapter 1, many types of people build their wealth by investing in real estate. Some people focus exclusively on real estate investments, but many others first build their wealth through companies they start or through other avenues and then diversify into real estate investments. What do these wealthy folks know, and why do they choose to invest in real estate? Here are some of real estate's attractions:

✔ **Limited land.** Short of using landfill to build buildings over water, the supply of land on planet Earth is fixed. And because people are prone to reproduce (we both must confess to being party to this as well), demand for land and housing continues to grow. Land and what you can do with it are what make real estate valuable. Cities and islands such as Hawaii, Tokyo, Vancouver, San Francisco, Los Angeles, Toronto, and New York City have the highest housing costs around because land is limited.

✔ **Leverage.** Real estate is different from most other investments in that you can borrow up to 75 to 90 percent or more of the value of the property. Thus, you can use your small down payment of 10 to 25 percent of the purchase price to buy, own, and control a much larger investment. Of course, you hope that the value of your real estate goes up — if it does, you make money on your investment as well as on the money you borrowed.

Here's a quick example to illustrate. Suppose you purchase a rental property for $100,000 and make a $20,000 down payment. Over the next three years, imagine that the property appreciates to $120,000. You've made a profit (on paper at least) of $20,000 on an investment of just $20,000. In other words, you've made a 100 percent return on your investment. (Note that in this scenario we ignore whether your expenses from the property exceed the rental income you collect.)

Leverage is good if property prices appreciate, but leverage can also work against you. If your $100,000 property decreases in value to $80,000, even though it has dropped only 20 percent in value you actually lose (on paper) 100 percent of your original $20,000 investment. If you have an outstanding mortgage of $80,000 on this property and you need to sell, you must actually pay money into the sale to cover selling costs in addition to losing your entire original investment. Ouch!

✔ **Growth and income.** Another reason why real estate is a popular investment is that you can make money from it in two major ways. First, you hope and expect over the years that your real estate investments appreciate in value. The appreciation of your properties compounds tax deferred during your years of ownership. You don't pay tax on this profit until you sell.

You can also make money from the ongoing business you run — renting the property. You rent out investment property to make a profit based on the property's rental income that (hopefully) exceeds your expenses (mortgage, property taxes, insurance, maintenance, and so on). Unless you make a large down payment, your monthly operating profit is usually small or nonexistent in the early years of rental property ownership. Over time, your operating profit, which is subject to ordinary income tax, should rise as you increase your rental prices faster than your expenses. During soft periods in the local economy, however, rents may rise more slowly than your expenses do (or rents may even fall).

✔ **Diversification.** An advantage of holding some investment real estate is that its value doesn't necessarily move in tandem with other investments, such as stocks or small-business investments.

✔ **Ability to "add value."** You may have some good ideas about how to improve a property and make it more valuable. Perhaps you can fix it up or develop it further and raise the rental income accordingly. Perhaps through legwork, persistence, and good negotiating skills you can purchase a property below its fair market value.

Relative to investing in the stock market, persistent and savvy real estate investors can more easily buy property below its fair market value. You can do the same in the stock market, but the scores of professional, full-time money managers who analyze stocks make finding bargains more difficult.

✔ **Ego gratification.** Face it, investing in real estate appeals to some investors because it's one of the few investments that's tangible. Although few admit it, some real estate investors get an ego rush from a tangible display of their wealth. You can drive past an investment in real estate and show it off to others. In "What My Ego Wants, My Ego Gets" (a piece appropriately written for The New York Times), Donald Trump publicly admitted what most everyone else knew long ago: He holds his real estate investments partly for his ego. As Trump confessed of his purchase of the famed Plaza Hotel in the Big Apple, "I realized it was 100 percent true — ego did play a large role in the Plaza purchase and is, in fact, a significant factor in all of my deals."

✔ **Less emotionally based decisions.** One problem with investing in the securities markets, such as the stock market, is that prices are constantly changing. Newspapers, television news programs, and Web sites dutifully report the latest price quotes. Based on our observations and discussions with individual investors, the constant changes in the financial markets and the constant reports on those changes cause some to lose sight of the long-term and the big picture. In the worst cases, large short-term drops lead them to panic and sell at what end up being bargain prices. Or, headlines about big increases pull them, lemming-like, into an over-heated and peaking market. In short, since all they need to do is click their computer mouse or dial a toll-free phone number to place a sell or buy order, some stock market investors fall prey to snap, irrational judgments.

Like the stock market, the real estate market is constantly changing. However, to a real estate investor, short-term, day-to-day, and week-to-week changes are invisible. Publications don't report the value of your real estate holdings daily, weekly, or even monthly, which is good because you can focus more on the longer term. If prices do decline over the months and years, you're much less likely to sell in a panic with real estate. Preparing a property for sale and eventually getting it sold takes a good deal of time, and this barrier to quickly selling helps keep your vision in focus.

BEWARE

Real estate investing isn't as wonderful as they say

If you've attempted to read or have read some of the many real estate investment books that have been published over the years, you may need to slightly deprogram yourself. Too often, authors attempt to make real estate investments sound like the only sure way to become a multimillionaire with little effort. Consider the following statements made by real estate book authors. Our rebuttals to their claims follow:

"Rather than yielding only a small interest payment or dividend, real estate in prime locations can appreciate 20 percent a year or more."

Bank accounts, bonds, and stocks pay interest or dividends that typically amount to 1 to 6 percent per year. However, bank accounts and bonds aren't comparable investments — they're far more conservative and liquid and therefore don't offer the potential for double-digit returns. Stock market investing is comparable to investing in real estate, but you shouldn't go into real estate investments expecting annual returns of 20 percent or more. True, those who purchased good real estate in Toronto or Vancouver in the 1950s and held on to it for the next three decades earned handsome returns as the populations of the two cities boomed. But deciding where to buy and knowing how long to hold on to investments in these areas is easier said than done. With real estate investments, you can expect to earn 8 to 12 percent per year, but not 20 percent or more.

"A good piece of property can't do anything but go up!"

Any city, town, or community has good pieces of real estate. But that doesn't mean communities can't and won't have slow or depressed years. Real estate in some parts of the Maritimes and the prairies, for example, has appreciated quite slowly — at or just above the rate of inflation — for periods as long as a generation or more.

"Real estate is the best way of preserving and enhancing wealth. . . . [It] stands head and shoulders above any other form of investment."

Investing in stocks or in a small business is every bit as profitable as investing in real estate. In fact, more great fortunes have been built in small business than in any other form of investment. Over the long term, stock market investors have enjoyed (with far less hassle) average annual rates of return comparable to real estate investors' returns.

Real estate, like all investments, has its pros and cons. Investing in real estate is time intensive, carries investment risks, and, as you can see later in this chapter, comes with other risks. Invest in real estate because you enjoy the challenge of the business and because you want to diversify your portfolio, not because you seek a get-rich-quick outlet.

Who Should Avoid Real Estate Investing?

Real estate investing isn't for everyone; not even close. Most people do better financially when they invest their ownership holdings in a diversified portfolio of stocks, such as through stock mutual funds. Shy away from real estate investments that involve managing property if you fall into any of the following categories:

- ✔ **You're time starved and anxious.** Buying and owning investment real estate and being a landlord takes a lot of time. If you fail to do your homework before purchasing property, you can end up overpaying or buying a heap of trouble. As for managing a property, you can hire a property manager to help with screening and finding good tenants and troubleshooting problems with the building, but this step costs money and still requires some time involvement. Also, remember that most tenants don't care for a property the same way property owners do. If every little scratch or carpet stain sends your blood pressure skyward, avoid distressing yourself as a landlord.

- ✔ **You're not funding your RRSP, and you don't like to pay unnecessary taxes.** Use up all your allowable RRSP contributions (or other contributions to retirement savings plan) before you seriously invest in real estate. Funding an RRSP gives you an immediate tax deduction for your contribution. And after the money is inside an RRSP, all the growth and income from your investments compound without taxation. However, you derive no tax benefits while you accumulate your down payment for an investment real estate purchase. Furthermore, the operating profit or income from your real estate investment is subject to taxes as you earn it.

- ✔ **You're not interested in real estate.** Some people simply don't feel comfortable and informed when it comes to investing in real estate. If you've had experience and success with stock market investing, that's a good reason to stick with it and avoid real estate. Over long periods of time, both stocks and real estate provide comparable returns.

Part III: Real Estate

Simple, Profitable Real Estate Investments

Investing in rental real estate that you're responsible for can be a lot of work. With rental properties you have all the headaches of maintaining a property, including finding and dealing with tenants, without the benefits of living in and enjoying the property.

Unless you're extraordinarily interested in and motivated to own investment real estate, start with and perhaps limit your real estate investing to a couple of much simpler yet still profitable methods that we discuss in this section.

A place to call home

During your adult life, you need to provide a roof over your head. However, you may be able to sponge off your folks or some other relative for a number of years. If you're content with this arrangement, you can minimize your housing costs and can save more for a down payment and possibly toward other goals. Go for it, if your relatives will!

What about converting your current home into a rental when you move?

If you move into another home, turning your current home into a rental property may make sense. After all, it saves you the time and cost of finding a separate rental property.

Unfortunately, many people make the mistake of holding on to their current home for the wrong reasons when they buy another. This often happens when homeowners must sell in a depressed market. Nobody likes to lose money and sell their home for less than they paid for it. Thus, some owners hold on to their homes until prices recover.

If you plan to move and want to keep your current home as a long-term investment property, you can. But turning your home into a short-term rental is usually a bad move for a couple of reasons. First, you may not want the responsibilities of a landlord, but when you rent you force yourself into that very role. Second, if the home eventually does rebound in value while you're renting it out, you owe tax on the profit for the time when it wasn't your principal residence.

But what if neither you nor your relatives are up for the challenge? For the long term, because you need a place to live, why not own real estate instead of renting it? Real estate is the only investment you can live in or rent to produce income. You can't live in a stock, bond, or mutual fund! Unless you expect to move within the next few years, buying a place probably makes good long-term financial sense. That's because, in the long term, owning usually costs less than renting and allows you to build equity in an asset. Read Chapter 10 to find out more about buying and profiting from home ownership.

Real estate investment trusts

Real estate investment trusts (REITs) are entities that generally invest in different types of property, such as shopping centres, apartments, and other rental buildings. For a fee, REIT managers identify and negotiate the purchase of properties that they believe are good investments and manage these properties, including all tenant relations. REITs are a good way to invest in real estate for people who don't want the hassles and headaches that come with directly owning and managing rental property.

Surprisingly, most books that focus on real estate investing neglect REITs. Why? We've come to the conclusion that they do so for three major reasons. First, if you invest in real estate through REITs, you don't need to read a long, complicated book on real estate investment. Second, real estate brokers write many of these books. Not surprisingly, the real estate investment strategies touted in these books advocate the use of such brokers. You can buy REITs without real estate brokers. Finally, a certain snobbishness prevails among people who consider themselves "serious" real estate investors. One real estate writer/investor went so far as to say that REITs aren't "real" real estate investments.

Please. No, you can't drive your friends by a REIT and show it off. But those who put their egos aside when making real estate investments are happy that they considered REITs and have enjoyed handsome annual gains over the decades.

You can research and purchase units in individual REITs, which trade as securities on the major stock exchanges (see Chapter 8 for more information). An even better approach is to buy a mutual fund that invests in a diversified mixture of REITs (see Chapter 8).

In addition to providing you with a diversified, low-hassle real estate investment, REITs offer an advantage that traditional rental real estate does not. You can easily invest in REITs with your RRSP or RRIF. As with traditional real estate investments, you can even buy REITs and mutual fund REITs with borrowed money. You can often buy with 50 — or sometimes 30 — percent down when you purchase such investments through a brokerage account. (You can buy with a certain percentage down, called *buying on margin*, only if the money is not in an RRSP, RRIF, or other registered retirement plan.)

Advanced (Direct) Real Estate Investments

Every year several publications put out lists of the wealthiest people. (They generally leave out mobsters and drug kingpins — the money must be made through seemingly legitimate and legal channels.) Numerous people get on these lists primarily because of their real estate investments. For others, real estate was an important secondary factor that contributed to their wealth.

Consider Marcel Adams. Born in Romania, Mr. Adams was forced into a labour camp during the Second World War, escaped his native country, and landed in Canada in the 1950s. After working as a hide tanner and trader in Quebec City, he got into real estate and began building strip malls and shopping centres. Once he'd built up his cash flow and minimized his debts, he moved into the lending business with Les Placements Jeton Bleu Inc. (Blue Chip Investments). The company specialized in lending money at high rates to high-risk commercial real estate ventures. In the early 1990s real estate prices plummeted, dozens of owners defaulted on their over-leveraged properties, and Mr. Adams's company took them back. The company expanded to own many buildings and malls, including some of Quebec's most well-known shopping centres. Recently, Mr. Adams's worth was estimated to be over $900 million.

Orey Fidani began building homes when still in his teens, and he achieved his early goal of making $100,000 his first year. He expanded into a string of business parks in the Greater Toronto Area and managed to avoid becoming over-leveraged in the late 1980s, a mistake that spelled the end for many other developers. Today, his company, Orlando Corp., where his two sons work, owns millions of square feet of offices, industrial buildings, and malls. Mr. Fidani's net worth had been estimated at around $750 million before he died of lung cancer in 2000. (An ex-smoker, Mr. Fidani had quit smoking 20 years earlier. Aware how harmful it was, he offered $1,000 to any of his employees who quit smoking for a year.)

If you think you're cut out to be a landlord and are ready for the responsibility of buying, owning, and managing rental real estate, you have literally millions of direct real estate investment options from which to choose.

Before you begin this potentially treacherous journey, we strongly recommend that you read Chapter 10. Many concepts you need to know to be a successful real estate investor are similar to those you need when you buy a home. However, the rest of this chapter focuses on issues that are more unique to real estate investing.

Evaluating your options

As we discuss in Chapter 10, purchasing real estate if you don't intend to hold it over a number of years — preferably at least five — doesn't make a whole lot of sense. Even if you're lucky enough to buy your property right before big price increases, you're not likely to make an immediate profit. All the costs associated with buying and then selling a property can easily gobble up your profit, and can sometimes cause you to lose money. You'll also lose money if prices hold steady or decline during your short period of ownership. Ideally, you should plan to make real estate investments that you hold until, and perhaps through, your retirement years.

But what should you buy? The following is our take on various real estate investments.

Residential housing

Your best bet for real estate investing is to purchase residential property. People always need a place to live. Residential housing is easier to understand, purchase, and manage than most other types of property, such as office and retail property. And if you're a homeowner, you already have experience locating, purchasing, and maintaining residential property.

The most common residential housing options are single-family homes, condominiums, and townhouses. You can also purchase multi-unit buildings. In addition to the considerations that we address in Chapter 10, from an investment and rental perspective, consider the following issues when you decide what type of property to buy:

✔ Tenants. Single-family homes with just one tenant are simpler to deal with than a multi-unit apartment building that requires the management and maintenance of multiple renters and units.

✔ Maintenance. Condominiums are generally the lowest-maintenance properties because most condominium associations deal with issues such as roofing, gardening, and so on for the entire building. Note that, as the owner, you're still responsible for maintenance needed inside your unit, such as servicing appliances, interior painting, and so on. Beware, though, that some condo complexes don't allow you to rent your unit. With a single-family home or apartment building, you're responsible for all the maintenance. Of course, you can hire someone to do the work, but you still have to find the contractors and coordinate and oversee the work.

✔ **Appreciation potential.** Look for property where simple cosmetic and other fixes may allow you to increase rents. Such improvements can increase the market value of the property. Although condos may be somewhat easier to keep up, they tend to appreciate less than homes or apartment buildings, unless the condos are located in a desirable urban area. One way to add value to some larger properties is to "condo-ize" them. In some areas, if zoning allows, you can convert a single-family home or multiunit apartment building into condominiums. Keep in mind, however, that this metamorphosis requires significant research, both on the zoning front as well as with estimating remodelling and construction costs.

✔ **Cash flow.** As we discuss in the "Cash flow" section later in the chapter, your rental property brings in rental income that you hope covers and exceeds your expenses. The difference between the rental income that you collect and the expenses that you pay out is known as your cash flow.

Unless you can afford a large down payment (25 percent or more), the early years of rental property ownership may financially challenge you. Making a profit in the early years from the monthly cash flow with a single-family home is hard because such properties usually sell at a premium price relative to the rent they can command. Remember, you pay extra for the land, which you can't rent. Also, the downside to having just one tenant is that when you have a vacancy, you have no rental income.

Apartment buildings, particularly those with more units, can generally produce a small positive cash flow, even in the early years of rental ownership. With all properties, as time goes on, generating a positive cash flow gets easier as you pay down your mortgage debt and hopefully increase your rents.

Unless you really want to minimize maintenance responsibilities, we would avoid condominium investments. Single-family home investments are generally more straightforward for most people. Just make sure that you run the numbers (we show you how in the "Cash flow" section later in this chapter) on your rental income and expenses to see whether you can afford the negative cash flow that often occurs in the early years of ownership. Apartment building investments are best left to sophisticated investors who like a challenge and can manage more complex properties. And as we discuss in Chapter 12, do thorough inspections before you buy any rental property.

Land

If tenants are a hassle and maintaining a building is a never-ending pain, why not invest in land? You can simply buy land in an area that will soon experience a building boom, hold on to it until prices soar, and then cash in. Such an investment idea sounds good in theory. In practice, however, making the big bucks through land investments isn't easy. Although land doesn't require upkeep and tenants, it does require financial feeding.

Investing in land is a cash drain, and because it costs money to purchase land, you also have a mortgage payment to make. Mortgage lenders charge higher interest rates on loans to buy land because they see it as a more speculative investment. You don't get depreciation tax write-offs because land isn't depreciable. You also usually have property tax payments to meet, as well as other expenses. However, with land investments, you don't receive income from the property to offset these expenses.

If you decide to develop the property, that will also cost you a hefty chunk of money. Obtaining a loan for development is challenging and more expensive (because it's riskier for the lender) than obtaining a loan for a developed property. You'll also have to invest time and money into getting the needed permits and any zoning changes required.

Identifying many years in advance which communities will experience rapid population and job growth is not easy. Land prices in areas that people believe will be the next hot spot already sell at a premium price. If property growth doesn't meet expectations, appreciation will be low or nonexistent.

If you decide to invest in land, be sure that you:

- ✔ Can afford it. Tally up the annual carrying costs so that you can see what your cash drain may be. What are the financial consequences of this cash outflow? For example, will you be able to fully fund your tax-advantaged RRSP? If you can't, count the lost tax benefits as another cost of owning land.

- ✔ Understand what further improvements the land needs. Running utility lines, building roads, landscaping, and so on all cost money. If you plan to develop and build on the land you purchase, research what these things may cost. Make sure you don't make these estimates with your rose-tinted sunglasses on — improvements almost always cost more than you expect.

- ✔ Know its zoning status. The value of land is heavily dependent on what you can develop on it. Never, ever purchase land without thoroughly understanding its zoning status and what you can and can't build on it. Also research the disposition of the planning department and nearby communities. Areas that are anti-growth and anti-development are less likely to be good places to invest in land, especially if you need permission to do the type of project you have in mind. Beware that zoning can change for the worse — sometimes a zoning alteration can reduce what you can develop on a property and, consequently, the property's value.

- ✔ Are familiar with the local economic and housing situations. In the best of all worlds, you want to buy land in an area that's home to rapidly expanding companies and that has a shortage of housing and developable land. We discuss how to research these issues in the upcoming section, "Deciding where and what to buy."

Commercial real estate

Ever thought about owning and renting out a small office building or strip mall? If you're really motivated and willing to roll up your sleeves, you may want to consider commercial real estate investments. Generally, you're better off not investing in such real estate because it's much more complicated than investing in residential real estate. It's also riskier from an investment and tenant-turnover perspective. When tenants move out, new tenants sometimes require extensive and costly improvements, which you'll likely need to provide to compete with other building owners.

If you're a knowledgeable real estate investor and you like a challenge, there are two good reasons to invest in commercial real estate:

✔ If your analysis of the local market suggests that it's a good time to buy.

✔ If you can use some of the space to run your own small business.

Just as owning your home is generally more cost-effective than renting over the years, so it is with commercial real estate, if — and this is a big if — you buy at a reasonably good time and hold the property for many years.

So how do you evaluate the state of your local commercial real estate market? Examine the supply and demand statistics over recent years. How much space is available for rent, and how has that changed over time? What is the vacancy rate, and how has that changed in recent years? Also, investigate the rental rates, usually quoted as a price per square foot. See the "Deciding where and what to buy" section later in this chapter to find out how to gather this kind of information.

Watch out for those areas where the supply of available space has increased faster than demand, leading to falling rental rates and higher vacancies. A slowing local economy and a higher unemployment rate also spell trouble for commercial real estate prices. Each market is different, so be sure to check out the details of your area. In the next section we explain where you can find such information.

Deciding where and what to buy

If you're going to invest in real estate, you can do tons of research to decide where and what to buy. Keep in mind, though, that you can spend the rest of your life looking for the perfect real estate investment, never find it, never invest, and miss out on lots of opportunities, profit, and even fun. In the following sections we explain what to look for in an area you seek to invest in.

Considering economic issues

People need a place to live, but an area doesn't generally attract home buyers if no jobs exist. Ideally, look to invest in real estate in communities that maintain diverse job bases. If the local economy is heavily reliant on jobs in a small number of industries, that dependence increases the risk of your real estate investment. Also, check out the unemployment situation and examine how the jobless rate has changed in recent years. Good signs to look for are declining unemployment and increasing job growth. Statistics Canada tracks this data — you'll find their number in the blue pages of your local telephone book, or visit www.statcan.ca.

Also, consider which industries are more heavily represented in the local economy. If most of the jobs come from slow-growing or shrinking employment sectors, such as farming, small retail, and shoe and apparel manufacturing, real estate prices are unlikely to rise quickly in the years ahead. On the other hand, areas with a greater preponderance of high-growth industries stand a better chance of faster price appreciation.

We're not suggesting that you need to conduct a nation-wide search for the best areas. In fact, investing in real estate closer to home is best, because you're probably more familiar with the local area and should have an easier time researching and managing local property. If you live in or near a major metropolitan area, you can find some areas that easily fit the bill.

Evaluating the real estate market

The price of real estate, like the price of anything else, is driven by supply and demand. The smaller the supply and the greater the demand, the higher prices climb. Some real estate investors find this out the hard way. One such investor (John Reed, who also writes about real estate) lost all the money he'd made in 15 years of apartment investing as a result of owning apartments in Texas when the overbuilding occurred in the mid-1980s.

Ouch! Imagine investing for 15 years and then losing it all! Credit was loose in some areas during the 1980s, which led to a building boom. But in many parts of Texas, as in other parts of North America, a ton of buildable land existed. This abundance of land and available credit inevitably led to overbuilding. When the supply of anything expands at a much faster rate than demand, prices usually fall.

Upward pressure on real estate prices tends to be greatest in areas with little buildable land. This was one of the things that attracted Eric to real estate in the San Francisco Bay Area when he moved there in the mid-1980s. If you look at a map of this area, you can see that the city of San Francisco and the communities to the south are on a peninsula. Ocean, bay inlets, and mountains bound the rest of the Bay Area. More than 80 percent of the land in the greater Bay Area isn't available for development — either state and federal government parks, preserves, and other areas protect it from development or it's impossible to develop. And of the land that was available, about 98 percent of it in San Francisco and two-thirds of it in nearby counties had already been developed.

In the long term, the lack of buildable land in an area can prove a problem. Real estate prices that are too high may cause employers and employees to relocate to less expensive areas. If you want to invest in real estate in an area with little buildable land and sky-high prices, run the numbers to see whether the deal makes economic sense. (We explain how to do this later in this chapter.)

In addition to buildable land, consider these other important real estate market indicators to get a sense of the health, or lack thereof, of a particular market:

- **Building permits.** The trend in the number of building permits tells you how the supply of real estate properties may soon change. A long and sustained rise in permits over several years can indicate that the supply of new property may dampen future price appreciation. Many areas experienced enormous increases in new building during the late 1980s, right before prices peaked due to excess inventory. Conversely, back in the late 1970s and early 1980s new building dried up in many areas as onerous interest rates strangled builders and developers.

- **Vacancy rates.** If few rentals are vacant, that means more competition and demand for existing units, which bodes well for future real estate price appreciation. Conversely, high vacancy rates indicate an excess supply of real estate, which may put downward pressure on rental rates as many landlords compete to attract tenants.

- **Listings of property for sale and number of sales.** Just as the building of many new buildings is bad for future real estate price appreciation, increasing numbers of property listings are also an indication of potential future trouble. As property prices reach high levels, some investors decide that they can make more money by cashing in and investing elsewhere. When the market is flooded with listings, prospective buyers can be choosier, exerting downward pressure on prices. At high prices (relative to the cost of renting), more prospective buyers elect to rent, and the number of sales relative to listings drops.

  A sign of a healthy real estate market is a decreasing and low level of property listings, indicating that the demand from buyers meets or exceeds the supply of property for sale from sellers. When the cost of buying is relatively low compared with the cost of renting, more renters can afford and choose to purchase, thus increasing the number of sales.

- **Rents.** The trend in rental rates that renters are willing and able to pay over the years gives a good indication of the demand for housing. When the demand keeps up with the supply and the local economy continues to grow, rents generally increase. This increase is a positive sign for continued real estate price appreciation. Beware of buying rental property subject to rent control — the property's expenses may rise faster than you can raise the rents.

Refuting the wisdom of buying in the "best" areas

Some people, particularly those in the real estate business, say, "Buy real estate close to a good school" or "Buy the least expensive home in the best neighbourhood." Conventional wisdom is often wrong, and these examples are yet another case.

Remember that as a real estate investor, you hope to profit from selling your properties, many years in the future, for a much higher price than you purchased them. If you buy into the "best," there may not be as much room for growth.

Take schools, for example. Conventional wisdom says that you should look at the test scores of different schools and buy real estate in the catchment area for the best (that is, highest

score) schools. But odds are that real estate in those areas is probably already priced at a premium level. If things deteriorate, such an area may experience more decline than an area where property buyers haven't bid prices up into the stratosphere.

The biggest appreciation often comes from those areas and properties that benefit the most from improvement. Identifying these in advance isn't easy, but look for communities where the trend in recent years has been positive. Even some "average" areas perform better in terms of property value appreciation than today's "best" areas.

Examining property valuation and financial projections

How do you know what a property is really worth? Some say it's worth what a ready, willing, and financially able buyer is willing to pay. But some buyers pay more than what a property is truly worth. And sometimes buyers who are patient, do their homework, and bargain hard are able to buy property for less than its fair market value.

Crunching some numbers to figure out what revenue and expenses a rental property may bring is one of the most important exercises you can go through when you determine the property's worth and decide whether you should buy it. In the sections that follow, we walk you through these important calculations.

Determining cash flow

Cash flow is the difference between the money that a property brings in and what goes out for its expenses. If you pay so much for a property that its expenses (including the mortgage payment and property taxes) consistently exceed its income, you have a money drain on your hands. Maybe you have the financial reserves to withstand the temporary drain for the first few years, but you need to know upfront what you're getting yourself into.

One of the biggest mistakes that novice rental property investors make is not realizing all the costs associated with investment property. In the worst cases, some investors end up in personal bankruptcy from the drain of *negative cash flow* (expenses exceeding income). In other cases, we've seen negative cash flow hamper people's ability to accomplish important financial goals.

The second biggest mistake rental property investors make is believing the financial statements that sellers and their real estate agents prepare. Just as an employer views a résumé, you should always view such financial statements as advertisements rather than sources of objective information. In some cases, sellers and agents lie. In most cases, these statements contain lots of projections and best-case scenarios.

For property that you're considering purchasing, ask for a copy of the Canada Revenue Agency Form T776 (Statement of Real Estate Rentals) from the property seller's federal income tax return. When most people complete their tax returns, they try to minimize their revenue and maximize their expenses — the opposite of what they and their agents normally do on the statements they sometimes compile to hype the property sale. Confidentiality and privacy aren't an issue when you ask for Form T776 because you're asking only for this one schedule and not the person's entire income tax return. (If the seller owns more than one rental property for which financial data is compiled, he can simply black out this other information if he doesn't want you to see it.)

You should prepare financial statements based on facts and a realistic assessment of a property (see Table 11-1). There's a time and a place for unbridled optimism and positive thinking (such as when you're lost in a major snowstorm — if you think pessimistically, you may not make it out alive!). But deciding whether to buy a rental property is not a life-or-death situation. Take your time and do it with your eyes and ears open and with a healthy degree of scepticism.

The monthly rental property financial statement that you prepare in Table 11-1 is for the present. Over time, you hope and expect that your rental income will increase faster than the property's expenses, thus increasing the cash flow. If you want, you can use Table 11-1 for future years' projections as well.

Table 11-1	Monthly Rental Property Financial Statement

(Note: If you're purchasing a simple residential rental property, such as a single-family home, some of the following does not apply.)

$ per month

Rents: Ask for copies of current rental or lease agreements and also check comparable unit rental rates in the local market. Ask if the owner made any concessions (such as a month or two of free rent), which may make rental rates appear inflated. Make your offer contingent on the accuracy of the rental rates. $_____

Garage rentals: Some properties come with parking spaces that the tenants rent. As with unit rental income, make sure you know what the spaces really rent for.   + $_____

Laundry income: Dirty laundry isn't just on the evening news — it can make you wealthier! Don't underestimate or neglect to include the cost of laundry machine maintenance when you figure the expenses of your rental building.   + $_____

Other income: $_____

Vacancy allowance: Keeping any rental occupied all the time is difficult, and finding a good tenant who's looking for the type of unit(s) you have to offer may take some time. You can do occasional maintenance and refurbishing work in between tenants. Allow for a vacancy rate of 5 to 10 percent (multiply 5 to 10 percent by the rent figured in the first line). Subtract this amount.   – $_____

Total income: = $_____

Mortgage: Enter your expected mortgage payment. $_____

Property taxes: Ask a real estate person, mortgage lender, or your local assessor's office what your annual property tax bill would be for a rental property of comparable value to the one you're considering buying. Divide this annual amount by 12 to arrive at your monthly property tax bill.   + $_____

Utilities: Get copies of utility bills from the current owner. Get bills over the previous 12-month period — a few months won't cut it because utility usage may vary greatly during different times of the year. (In a multi-unit building, it's a plus for each unit to have a separate utility meter so that you can bill each tenant for what he/she uses.)   + $_____

(continued)

Table 11-1 *(continued)*

	$ per month
Insurance: Ask for a copy of the current insurance coverage and billing statement from the current owner. If you're considering buying a building in an area that has floods, earthquakes, and so on, make sure the cost of the policy includes these coverages. Although you can insure against most catastrophes, we would avoid buying property in a flood-prone area. Flood insurance normally does not cover lost rental income.	+ $_____
Water: Again, ask the current owner for statements that document water costs over the past 12 months.	+ $_____
Garbage: Get the bills for the last 12 months from the owner.	+ $_____
Repairs/maintenance/cleaning: You can ask the current owner what to expect and check the tax return, but even doing this may provide an inaccurate answer. Some building owners defer maintenance. (A good property inspector can help ferret out problem areas before you commit to buying a property.) Estimate that you'll spend at least 1 to 2 percent of the purchase price per year on maintenance, repairs, and cleaning. Remember to divide your annual estimate by 12!	+ $_____
Rental advertising/management expenses: Finding good tenants takes time and promotion. If you list your rental through rental brokers, they normally take one month's rent as their cut. Owners of larger buildings sometimes have an on-site manager to show vacant units and deal with maintenance and repairs. Put the monthly pay for that person on this line or the preceding line. If you provide a below-market rental rate for an on-site manager, make sure you factor this into the rental income section.	+ $_____
Extermination/pest control: Once a year or every few years, you likely need to take care of pest control. Spraying and/or inspections generally start at $200 to $300 for small buildings.	+ $_____
Legal, accounting, and other professional services: Especially with larger rental properties, you'll likely need to consult with lawyers and tax advisers from time to time.	+ $_____
Total expenses	= $_____
Total income (from preceding page)	= $_____
Total expenses (from above)	– $_____
Pretax profit or loss	= $_____

(continued)

	$ per month
Table 11-1 (continued)	

Depreciation: The tax law allows you to claim a yearly tax deduction for depreciation, but remember that you can't depreciate land. Break down the purchase of your rental property between the building and land. You can make this allocation based on the assessed value for the land and the building or on a real estate appraisal. Residential property is depreciated at 4 or 5 percent per year of the remaining unde-preciated value, depending on the type of building and when it was purchased. (You're generally limited to half that rate in the year you make your purchase.) For example, say you buy a residential rental property for $300,000 and $200,000 of that is allocated to the building, which can be depreciated at 4 percent. In the first year, you can take $4,000 as a depreciation tax deduction ($200,000 X 1/2 of 0.004%.) The next year you can claim 4 percent of the remaining undepreciated value of $196,000, or $7,840, as your depreciation expense. — $_____

Net income = $_____

Important note: Although depreciation is a deduction that helps you reduce your profit for tax purposes, it doesn't actually cost you money. Your cash flow from a rental property is the revenue minus your out-of-pocket expenses.

Valuing property

Examining and estimating a property's cash flow is an important first step toward deciding a property's value. But on its own, a building's cash flow doesn't provide enough information to intelligently decide whether to buy a particular real estate investment. Just because a property has a positive cash flow doesn't mean that you should buy it. Real estate generally sells for less — and therefore has better cash flow — in areas where investors expect to earn lower rates of appreciation.

In the stock market, you have more clues about a specific security's worth. Most companies' stocks trade on a daily basis, so you at least have a recent sales price to start with. Of course, just because a stock recently traded at $20 per share doesn't mean that it's *worth* $20 per share. Investors may be overly optimistic or pessimistic.

Just as you should compare a stock to other comparable stocks, so too should you compare the asking price of a property with other comparable real estate. But what if all real estate is overvalued? Such a comparison doesn't necessarily reveal the state of inflated prices. In addition to comparing a real estate investment property to comparable properties, you need to perform some global evaluations of whether prices from a historic perspective appear too high, too low, or just right. To answer this last question, see Chapter 10.

To value a piece of property, you can try one of three approaches. You can hire an appraiser, enlist the help of a real estate agent, or crunch the numbers yourself. These approaches aren't mutually exclusive — you probably want to at least review the numbers and analysis that an appraiser or real estate agent puts together. Here are the pros and cons of the different approaches you can use to value property:

✔ **Appraisers.** The biggest advantage of hiring an appraiser is that he or she values property for a living. An appraisal also gives you some hard numbers to use for negotiating with a seller. Hire an appraiser who works at it full time and has experience valuing the type of property you're considering. Ask for examples of a dozen similar properties that he or she has appraised in the past three months in the area.

The drawback of appraisers is that they cost money. A small home may cost several hundred dollars to appraise, and a larger multi-unit building may cost $1,000 or more. The danger is that you can spend money on an appraisal for a building you don't end up buying.

✔ **Real estate agents.** If you work with a good real estate agent (we discuss how to find one in Chapter 12), ask him or her to draw up a list of comparable properties and to help you estimate the value of the property you're considering buying. The advantage of having your agent help with this analysis is that you don't pay extra for the service.

The drawback of asking an agent what to pay for a property is that his or her commission depends on your buying it and the amount you pay for it. The more you're willing to pay, the more likely the deal flies, and the more the agent makes on commission.

✔ **Do-it-yourself.** If you're comfortable with numbers and analysis you can try to estimate the value of a property yourself. The hard part is identifying comparable properties. It's usually impossible to find identical properties, so you need to find similar properties and then make adjustments to their selling price so that you can do an apples-to-apples comparison.

Among the factors that should influence your analysis of comparable properties are the date the properties sold; the quality of their location; lot size; building age and condition; the number of units; the number of rooms, bedrooms, and bathrooms; garages; fireplaces; and yard. A real estate agent can provide this information, or you can track it down for properties you've seen or that you know have recently sold.

For example, if a similar property sold six months ago for $250,000 but prices overall have declined 5 percent in the last six months, subtract 5 percent from the sales price. Ultimately, you have to attach a value or price to each difference between comparable properties and the one you're considering buying. Through a series of adjustments, you can compare the value of your target property to others that have recently sold.

Finding the information you need

When you evaluate properties, you need to put on your detective hat. If you're creative and inquisitive, you'll soon realize that this isn't a hard game to play. You can collect useful information about a property and the area in which it's located in many ways.

Begin your inquiries with the real estate agent who listed the property for sale. One thing that most agents love to do is talk and schmooze. Try to understand why the seller is selling. This will help you negotiate an offer that's appealing to the seller.

As for specifics on the property's financial situation, as we explain earlier in this chapter, ask the sellers for independent documents, including Form T776 from their tax return. Hire inspectors (we explain hiring inspectors in Chapter 12) to investigate the property's physical condition.

Local government organizations possess treasure troves of details about their communities. See the other recommended sources in Chapter 10 as well as the sources we suggest earlier in this chapter.

Should you form a real estate corporation?

When you invest in and manage real estate with at least one other partner, you can set up a company through which both of you collectively own the property.

The main reason why you may want to consider forming a real estate corporation is liability protection. A corporation can reduce the chances of lenders or tenants suing you.

To find out more about the pros and cons of incorporating and the different entities under which you can do business, see Chapter 14.

Digging for a good deal

Everyone likes to get a deal or feel like they bought something at a really good price. How else can you explain the retail practice of sales? Merchandise is overpriced so that store owners can then mark it down to create the illusion that you're getting a bargain! Some real estate sellers and agents do the same thing. They list property for sale at an inflated price and then mark it down after they realize that no one will pay the freight. "$30,000 price reduction!" the new listing screams. Of course, this reduction isn't a deal.

Purchasing a piece of real estate at a discount is possible. Without doing a lick of work, you can make money simply by purchasing a property at a discount — one of the ultimate thrills of being a capitalist!

Scores of books claim to have the real estate investment strategy that can beat the system. Often these promoters claim that you can become a multi-millionaire through investing in *distressed* properties. A common strategy is to purchase property that a seller has defaulted on or is about to default on. Or maybe you'd like to try your hand at investing in a property that has been condemned or has toxic waste contamination!

It is possible to get a good buy and purchase a problem property at a discount larger than the cost of fixing the property. However, these opportunities are hard to find, and sellers of such properties are often unwilling to sell at a discount that's big enough to leave you much room for profit. If you don't know how to thoroughly and correctly evaluate the property's problems, you can end up overpaying.

In some cases, real estate gurus advocate strategies that involve taking advantage of people's lack of knowledge. If you can find a seller in dire financial straits and desperate for cash, you may get a bargain buy. (You may or may not struggle with the moral issues of buying property cheaply this way, but that's one of the not-so-ultimate thrills of capitalism.)

Other methods of finding discounted property take lots of time and digging. Some involve cold-calling property owners to see whether they're interested in selling. This method is a little bit like trying to fill a job opening by inter-viewing people you run into on a street corner. Although you may eventually find a good candidate this way, if you factor in the value of your time, deals turn from bargains to pigs in a poke.

Without making things complicated or too risky, you can use some of the following time-tested and proven ways to buy real estate at a discount to its fair market value:

✔ **Find a motivated seller.** Be patient and look at lots of properties, and sooner or later you'll come across one that someone needs to sell (and these aren't necessarily the ones advertised as having a motivated seller). Perhaps the seller has bought another property and needs the money from this one to close on the recent purchase. Having access to sufficient financing can help secure such deals.

✔ **Buy unwanted properties with fixable flaws.** The easiest problems to correct are cosmetic. Some sellers and their agents are lazy and don't even bother to clean a property. One single-family home that Eric bought had probably three years' worth of cobwebs and dust accumulated. It seemed like a dungeon at night because half the light bulbs were burned out.

Painting, tearing up old, ugly carpeting, refinishing hardwood floors, and putting new plantings in a yard are relatively easy jobs. They make the property worth more and make renters willing to pay higher rent. Of course, these tasks take money and time, and many buyers aren't interested in dealing with problems. If you have an eye for improving property and are willing to invest the time that coordinating the fix-up work requires, go for it! Just make sure to hire someone to conduct a thorough property inspection before you buy. (See Chapter 12 for more details.)

Be sure to factor in the loss of rental income if you can't rent a portion of the property during the fix-up period. Some investors have gone belly up from the double cash drain of fix-up expenses and lost rents.

✔ **Buy when the real estate market is depressed.** When the economy takes a few knocks and investors rush for the exits, it's time to wheel out your shopping cart of cash. Buy real estate when prices and investor interest are down. During times of depressed markets, obtaining properties that produce a positive cash flow (even in the early years) is easier. In Chapter 10 we explain how to spot a depressed market.

✔ **Check for zoning opportunities.** Sometimes you can make more productive use of a property. For example, you can legally convert some multi-unit apartment buildings into condominiums. Some single-family residences may include a rental unit if local zoning allows for it. A good real estate agent, contractor, and the local planning office can help you identify properties that you can convert. If you're not a proponent of development, then you probably won't like this strategy.

If you buy good real estate and hold it for the long term, you can earn a healthy return on your investment. Over the long haul, having bought a property at a discount becomes an insignificant issue. You make money from your real estate investments as the market appreciates and as a result of your ability to manage your property well. So don't obsess over buying property at a discount and don't wait for the perfect deal, because it won't come along.

Recognizing Generally Lousy Real Estate "Investments"

Some supposedly "simple" ways to invest in real estate rarely make sense because they're near-certain money losers. In this section we discuss real estate investments that you should generally (but not always) avoid.

Second/vacation homes

An idyllic notion and an expanded part of the Canadian dream is the weekend cottage, cabin, or condo — a place where you can retreat when crowded urban or suburban living conditions get on your nerves. And when it's not in use, you may rent out your vacation home and earn some income to help defray part of the maintenance expenses.

 If you can realistically afford the additional costs of a second, or vacation, home, we're not going to tell you how to spend your extra cash. Investment real estate is property that you rent out 90 percent or more of the time. Most second-home owners we know rent their property out very little — 10 percent or less of the time. As a result, second homes are usually money drains. Even if you do rent your second home most of the time, high tenant turnover decreases your net rental income.

 If you don't rent out a second home property most of the time, ask yourself whether you can afford such a luxury. Can you accomplish your other financial goals — saving for retirement, paying for the home in which you live, and so on — with this added expense? Keeping a second home is more a consumption than an investment decision.

Time shares

Time shares are near-certain money losers. With a time share, you buy a week or two of ownership or usage of a particular unit, usually a condominium, in a resort location. If you pay $8,000 for a week of "ownership," you pay the equivalent of more than $400,000 a year for the whole unit ($8,000/week x 52 weeks). However, a comparable unit nearby may sell for only $150,000. All the extra mark-up pays the salespeople's commissions, administrative expenses, and profits for the time-share development company. (This little analysis also ignores the not so inconsequential ongoing time-share maintenance fees, which can easily run $200 to $300 per year or more.) People usually get hoodwinked into buying a time share when they're enjoying a vacation someplace. Vacationers are easy prey for salespeople who, often using high-pressure sales tactics, want to sell them a souvenir of the trip. The cheese in the mousetrap is an offer of something free (for example, a free night's stay in a unit) for going through the sales presentation. As one person said about their decision to accept an invitation to listen to the one-hour pitch, "I went in for a free Pina Colada and came out with a condo!"

The time-share concept, unfortunately, was imported into North America in the early 1970s and has stuck ever since. Even large and otherwise reputable companies, such as Disney, Marriott, and Hilton, have moved into this business in recent years. Selling lousy time-share investments to the public is a good business for them — but now you won't become another of their victims!

If you can't live without a time share, consider buying a used one. Many previous buyers, who have almost always lost much of their original investment, try to dump their time shares. (This fact alone tells you something about time shares.) You may be able to buy a time share from an existing owner at a fair price, but why commit yourself to taking a vacation in the same location and building at the same time each year? Many time shares let you trade your weeks; however, doing so is a hassle, and you're limited by what time slots you can trade for, which are typically dates other people don't want. Most of these open time slots are undesirable — that's why people trade them! You may also be charged an extra fee for swapping.

Limited partnerships

In Chapter 1 we give you good reasons to avoid limited partnerships. High sales commissions and ongoing management fees burden limited partnerships sold through stockbrokers and financial planners who work on commission. Quality real estate investment trusts (REITs), which we discuss earlier in this chapter, are infinitely better alternatives. REITs, unlike limited partnerships, are also completely liquid.

Scams

Wanting to make a lot of money in a hurry is naturally quite appealing. Real estate investors with lofty expectations for high returns become bait for various hucksters who promise these investors great riches. It's bad enough when the deck is stacked against you. Even worse is to put your money into scams.

First Pension was a U.S. outfit run by loan broker William Cooper that bilked investors out of more than $100 million. First Pension was sold as a limited partnership that invested in mortgages. Using a Ponzi-type (pyramid) scheme, Cooper used the money from new investors to pay dividends to earlier investors.

Another real estate investment vehicle is second mortgages. The allure of lending your money to a property buyer is the double-digit returns. As we discuss in Chapter 7, the only way to charge interest rates of 10 percent or higher is to lend your money to higher-risk borrowers. Even worse than the high risk that comes with higher interest rates is the problem that some second mortgage investments are hypes and scams.

Liz Pulliam reported in the *Orange County Register* that Irvine Mortgage Corporation promised second mortgage investors 14 percent returns by investing in properties with at least 30 percent equity. It also boasted no investor losses over 25 years.

When the real estate market softened in California in the early 1990s, some of these second mortgages defaulted. Investors, many of whom placed their retirement dollars with the Irvine Mortgage Corporation, later discovered that some of the properties they had lent money on never had their mortgage recorded against it. These properties ended up in default.

Time shares, an often truly terrible investment that we discuss in this chapter, have also been subject to bankruptcy and fraud problems.

Hundreds of thousands of viewers fall prey annually to infomercial hucksters. Among the more infamous real estate infomercial promoters is Tom Vu. At his seminars, according to *The Los Angeles Times*, he says, "Well, if you make no money with me, you a loser." Vu, who came to the United States from Vietnam in the mid-1970s, claims to have made a fortune investing in real estate by using a fairly simple system. He says that he searches for property owners who are in debt up to their eyeballs and offers to buy their properties with no money down. By finding desperate buyers, he says, you can buy real estate at a big discount from its fair market value.

Vu makes his money from running high-priced seminars to teach you basic real estate techniques that you can read in a book for about $20. Vu, however, charges up to $15,000 for a five-day seminar! As if overpaying this much isn't enough, Vu's former "students," who have filed a number of lawsuits that include a class action suit, say that his methods don't work and that he reneged on his promises to go into partnership on properties they identified. A number of states have investigated or are currently investigating Vu's practices, have barred further Vu seminars in their state, and are seeking compensation for victims. Unfortunately, Vu appears to have moved much of his money overseas. Other real estate seminar hucksters such as Robert Allen and Ed Buckley saw their seminar enterprises end up in bankruptcy, sunk by the claims of their unhappy students.

Other scams also abound. Stephen Murphy was a real estate investor who claimed to make a fortune by buying foreclosed commercial real estate and wrote and self-published a book to share his techniques with the public. Murphy's organization called the people who bought his book and pitched them into collaborating with him on property purchases that supposedly would return upwards of 100 percent or more per year. However, Murphy had other ideas, and he siphoned off nearly two-thirds of the money for himself and for promotion of his books! He even hoodwinked Donald Trump to write praise for his book and work: "I really admire Steve Murphy. . . . Steve commands some very wise, intelligent . . . and unique purchasing strategies." We'll say!

New York attorney Alan Harris also defrauded real estate investors (including actress Shirley Jones) out of millions of dollars when he pocketed money that was set aside for property investments. The lure: Harris promised investors far higher yields than they could get elsewhere.

If an investment "opportunity" sounds too good to be true, it is. If you want to invest in real estate, avoid the hucksters and invest directly in properties you can control or invest through reputable REITs (or REIT mutual funds).

Chapter 12

Real Estate Dilemmas and Decisions

*I*n Chapter 10 we cover what you need to know to purchase a home, and in Chapter 11 we review the fundamentals of investing in real estate. In this chapter, we discuss issues such as understanding and selecting mortgages, working with real estate agents, negotiating, and other important details that help you actually put a real estate deal together. We also provide some words of wisdom about taxes and selling your property that may come in handy down the road.

Financing 101

Unless you're affluent or buying a low-cost property, you likely need to borrow some money, via a mortgage, to finance your property acquisition. If you can't line up financing, your deal may fall apart. If you don't shop correctly for a good mortgage, you can spend thousands, perhaps even tens of thousands, of dollars in extra interest and fees. Even worse, you can get saddled with a loan that you someday can't afford, and you may end up in bankruptcy.

Understanding the differences between short-term and long-term mortgages

Most mortgage lenders offer you the option of taking out a home loan for anywhere from six months to five years. You can even take a mortgage for seven or even ten years, but these are less common.

The period of time you arrange to borrow money for your home is called the *term*. When your term is up, your loan agreement comes to an end, or *matures*. The term of your mortgage is completely separate from the *amortization* you choose — the number of years over which you spread out the repayment of your principal and the interest charges. Most mortgages are amortized over 25 years.

When your term is up, you have the choice of renewing with your existing lender or taking your mortgage elsewhere. Each time your mortgage matures, you're also free to choose whatever term you wish for your new loan. You can stick with the same term, or choose a longer or shorter term. In general, the shorter the term, the lower the interest rate you'll pay. For instance, your lender might offer you an interest rate of 6 percent on a six-month term, 6.75 percent on a three-year term, and 7.50 percent on a five-year term.

Choosing a longer term of four or five years means you don't have to concern yourself about what happens to interest rates for a while, at least as they affect your home loan. Your payments are set and guaranteed for the entire period. That makes longer-range budgeting easier , as it removes uncertainty from that part of your required expenses, which for many people is a frequent source of stress. The drawback is that, as noted above, you'll pay a higher interest rate. Think of it as an insurance premium.

A short-term mortgage that lasts, say, only six months or one year puts you at the whim of interest rate fluctuations much more frequently. If rates trend upwards, each time your mortgage renews you'll be hit by higher payments. Conversely, if rates are falling, you'll be able to enjoy lower payments much sooner than those who lock into longer terms.

Choosing between a short-term and long-term mortgage

Whether to go for a short- or long-term loan is an important decision in the real estate buying process. You need to weigh the pros and cons of each and decide what's best for your situation *before* you go out to purchase real estate or refinance.

In the real world, most people ignore this sensible advice. The excitement of purchasing a home or other piece of real estate tends to cloud judgment. In our experience, few buyers look at their entire financial picture before they make a major real estate decision.

Unfortunately, too many people let their interest rate crystal ball dictate whether they should take a short- or long-term mortgage. For example, those who think interest rates can only go up find long-term mortgages attractive.

You can't predict the future course of interest rates. Even the professional financial market soothsayers and investors can't accurately predict where rates are heading. If you could foretell this information, you could make a fortune investing in bonds and interest-rate futures and options. So cast aside your crystal ball, consider the following information, and then ask yourself the vital question that follows to help you decide whether a short-term or long-term mortgage will work best for you.

Assessing the cost

When many people are trying to decide between a short- and long-term mortgage, they focus on how much they can save over the next little while, and then factor in their sense of whether interest rates will rise in the future.

Much more important, though, is to get a sense of each option's total cost over the full life of your loan. Several studies have assessed how homeowners would have fared if they either continually renewed a short-term mortgage or stuck with five-year terms. Going back to 1980 when short-term mortgages were first made available, the studies found that, for 85 to over 90 percent of the time, the least expensive choice was to continually roll over a short-term mortgage. One study found that, for a $200,000 mortgage, the average cost of five-year terms versus a series of one-year terms was an extra $2,000 of interest a year.

Continually renewing a five-year term costs more because short-term rates are almost always lower than long-term rates. In order for a series of short-term mortgages to cost more than a five-year term, interest rates over that time must rise enough so that the one-year rate increases beyond the five-year rate, and stays there for a good percentage of that time.

Of course, that's just the numbers side of your decision. You also need to consider how comfortable you are with the extra uncertainty that choosing short-term mortgages brings.

How comfortable are you with taking risk?

How much of a gamble can you take with the size of your monthly mortgage payment? For example, if your job and income are unstable and you need to borrow an amount that stretches your monthly budget, you can't afford much risk. If you're in this situation, you may want to stick with a long-term mortgage. You may also sleep better with a long-term mortgage if you're buying your first home and have little savings to fall back on should interest rates rise in a year or two and hit you with much higher monthly payments.

If you're in a position to take the financial risks associated with mortgage payments that may change every six months or year, you have a better chance of saving money with a shorter-term mortgage. Your interest rate starts lower and stays lower if the overall level of interest rates stays unchanged. Even if rates go up, there's a good possibility they will come back down over the life of your loan. If you can stick with your short-term mortgage for better and for worse, you'll likely come out ahead in the long run.

A short-term mortgage makes more sense if you borrow less than you're qualified for. Or perhaps you can save a sizable chunk — more than 10 percent — of your monthly income. If your income significantly exceeds your spending patterns, you may feel less anxiety about fluctuating interest rates. If you do choose a short term, you may feel more financially secure if you have a hefty financial cushion (at least six months' to as much as a year's worth of expenses reserved) that you can access if rates go up.

Don't take a short-term mortgage because the lower interest rate allows you to afford the property you want to buy (unless you're absolutely certain your income will rise to meet possible future payment increases). Try setting your sights on a property you can afford to buy with a longer-term mortgage.

Understanding the differences between open and closed mortgages

Locking into closed mortgages

A *closed mortgage* means that you've agreed to the specific conditions and interest rate on your loan for the entire term of your loan. If interest rates drop significantly in the meantime, you may be prevented from *refinancing* — ending your agreement and working out a new loan. Where you're permitted to refinance, you'll likely have to pay a financial penalty that compensates the lender for the extra interest they give up by allowing you to renegotiate your agreement. In most cases, this penalty will eliminate any gain from negotiating a new mortgage at the prevailing lower interest rates.

Open mortgages

In contrast, an *open mortgage* gives you the right to pay off some or all of the loan whenever you wish without incurring any penalties. This can be useful if interest rates are falling rapidly and you want to take advantage of them. An open mortgage is also a good idea if you know you'll be coming into a significant sum that will allow you to pay off your mortgage, or if you'll be selling your home in the near future. Because of this extra flexibility, open mortgages have higher interest rates than closed mortgages.

Choosing between an open, closed, or convertible mortgage

If you know you'll be paying off your mortgage, or selling your property, in the near future, an open mortgage makes sense because of the flexibility to end your loan whenever you want without penalty.

In most other cases, paying higher interest rates for an open mortgage usually doesn't put you ahead. If you're going to be coming into a large sum of money, you could simply choose a short term and pay down your principal when the term is up. Even if you choose a longer term, most lenders allow you to pay off a reasonable chunk of your loan — typically 10 percent — once a year. If you're considering an open mortgage because interest rates appear to be heading steadily downward, you can simply select a short term — say six months or a year — so that you can soon renew at (hopefully) a lower interest rate and with lower monthly payments.

If you're like most people, you want to pay as little as you can but want some protection against a sudden and large jump in rates. In that case, a good choice is a *convertible mortgage*. Convertible mortgages vary slightly from lender to lender, but the basic concept is the same. You agree to a short-term closed mortgage — either six months or one year, usually at or close to the same interest rate as a closed mortgage for the same term. However, at any point during the term, you can convert your loan to a different term. For instance, if you choose a six-month term and rates start rising rapidly, you can simply lock in a five-year rate at the prevailing level to protect yourself against rates being much higher by the time your existing term ends.

The attraction of a convertible mortgage is it allows you to avoid paying the premium for longer-term fixed rates. At the same time, you're protected against rapidly rising rates because you can lock in for a longer term at any point, instead of either having to wait until your current term expires or paying a hefty penalty to refinance early. If rates are the same or lower when your current mortgage matures, you can just sign up for another six-month or one-year convertible mortgage.

It's important, though, to check the fine print. For instance, if you choose to convert to a different term, your lender may restrict you to a five-year term. The major drawback to a convertible mortgage is that if you do decide to convert while the mortgage is in existence, you can't change lenders, which eliminates much of your ability to bargain for a better rate. Unless you work out a rate discount ahead of time, when you convert you'll have to pay the going or posted rate for the new term you select. This means your rate will likely be anywhere from a quarter to three-quarters or more of a percent higher than you could otherwise negotiate.

Finding the best lenders

You can easily save thousands of dollars in interest charges and other fees if you shop around for a mortgage deal. It doesn't matter whether you do so on your own or hire someone to help you, but you should shop because so much money is at stake!

Shopping yourself

Many mortgage lenders compete for your business. Although having a large number of lenders to choose from is good for keeping interest rates lower, it also makes shopping a chore.

Most financial institutions, including the big banks and trust companies as well as smaller credit unions and even newcomers to the financial world such as President's Choice Financial and ING, offer mortgages. Begin by approaching the institution you currently bank with and talk to the manager about your needs. Just remember that you're under no obligation to take out your mortgage with them. Consider this your starting point, but be sure to approach several other financial institutions. Real estate agents can refer you to lenders with whom they've done business. Those lenders don't necessarily offer the most competitive rates — the agent may have simply done business with them in the past or received client referrals from them.

Look in the real estate section of a large, local weekend newspaper for charts of selected lender interest rates. Just as with Internet sites that advertise lender rates, these tables are by no means comprehensive or reflective of the best rates available. In fact, many of these rates are sent to newspapers for free by firms that distribute mortgage information to mortgage brokers. Use them as a starting point and call the lenders that list the best rates.

Shopping through a mortgage broker

A competent mortgage broker can be a big help in getting you a good loan and closing the deal, especially if you're too busy or disinterested to dig for a good deal on a mortgage. A good mortgage broker also keeps abreast of the many different mortgages in the marketplace. He or she can shop among lots of lenders to get you the best deal available. The following list presents some additional advantages to working with a mortgage broker:

- ✔ An organized and detail-oriented mortgage broker can help you through the process of completing all those tedious documents that lenders require.

- ✔ Mortgage brokers can help polish your loan package so that the information you present is favourable yet truthful.

- ✔ The best brokers can help educate you about various loan options and the pros and cons of available features.

- ✔ Brokers can also help get your loan approved if you anticipate that lenders may be skittish about offering you a loan. Problems on your credit report make lenders uncomfortable. If you want to borrow a large amount (90 percent or more) of the value of a property, many lenders aren't interested. Certain types of properties, such as co-ops and tenancies-in-common, give many lenders cold feet because these buildings tend to give them more problems.

Be careful when you choose a mortgage broker, because some brokers are lazy and don't shop the market for the best current rates. Even worse, some brokers may direct their business to specific lenders so that they can take a bigger cut or commission.

A mortgage broker typically gets paid a percentage, usually 0.5 to 1 percent, of the loan amount. This commission is completely negotiable, especially on larger loans that are more lucrative.

You need to ask what the commission is on loans that a broker pitches. Some brokers may be indignant that you ask — that's their problem. You have every right to know — it's your money.

Even if you plan to shop on your own, talking to a mortgage broker may be worthwhile. At the very least, you can compare what you find with what brokers say they can get for you. Again, be careful. Some brokers tell you what you want to hear — that is, that they can beat your best find — and then aren't able to deliver when the time comes.

If your loan broker quotes you a really good deal, make sure to ask who the lender is. (Most brokers refuse to reveal this information until you pay the necessary fee to cover the appraisal and credit report.) You can check with the actual lender to verify the interest rate and points that the broker quotes you and to make sure you're eligible for the loan.

Understanding other mortgage fees

In addition to the ongoing interest rate, lenders tack on all sorts of other upfront charges in processing your loan. Get an itemization of these other fees and charges in writing from all lenders that you're seriously considering. You need to know the total of all lender fees so that you can accurately compare different lenders' loans and determine how much closing on your loan will cost you.

Other mortgage fees can pile up in a hurry. Here are the common ones:

✔ **Application and processing fees.** Some lenders charge a few hundred dollars to work with you to complete your paperwork and funnel it through their loan evaluation process. Should your loan be rejected, or if it's approved and you decide not to take it, the lender needs to cover its costs. Some lenders return this fee to you upon closing with their loan.

✔ **Credit report.** Most lenders charge you for the cost of obtaining your credit report, which tells the lender whether you've repaid other loans on time.

✔ **Appraisal.** The property for which you borrow money needs to be valued. If you default on your mortgage, a lender doesn't want to get stuck with a property that's worth less than you owe. The cost for an appraisal typically ranges from several hundred dollars for most residential properties to as much as $1,000 or more for larger investment properties.

Some lenders offer loans without lender charges. Remember: If they don't charge fees, they may charge a higher interest rate on your loan to make up the difference. Such loans may make sense for you when you lack the cash to close a loan or when you plan to hold on to the loan for just a few years.

To minimize your chances of throwing money away on a loan that you may not qualify for, ask the lender if there's any reason your loan request may be denied. Be sure to disclose any problems on your credit report or any problems with the property you're aware of. Lenders may not take the time to ask about these sorts of things in their haste to get you to complete their loan applications.

Dealing with loan problems

Even if you have perfect or near-perfect credit, you may encounter financing problems with some properties. And, of course, not all real estate buyers have a perfect credit history, tons of available cash, and no debt. If you're one of those borrowers who end up jumping through more hoops than others to get a loan, don't give up hope. Few borrowers are perfect from a lender's perspective, and many problems aren't that difficult to fix.

The best defence against loan rejection is avoiding it in the first place. You can sometimes disclose to your lender anything that may cause a problem before you apply for the loan to head off potential rejection. For example, if you already know that your credit report indicates some late payments from when you were out of the country for several weeks five years ago, write a letter that explains this situation.

Lacking down payment money

Most people, especially when they make their first real-estate purchase, are strapped for cash. In order to qualify for the most attractive financing, lenders typically require that your down payment be at least 25 percent of the property's purchase price. In addition, you need reserve money to pay for other closing costs, such as the land transfer tax and legal fees.

If you don't have at least 25 percent of the purchase price available, don't panic and don't get depressed — you can still own real estate. One approach is to take out a mortgage of more than 75 percent of the value of the property, known as a *high-ratio* mortgage. Another option is to use the money you have tucked away in your RRSP. We discuss the pros and cons of these options below.

If you don't want the cost and strain of extra fees and bad mortgage terms, you can also postpone your purchase. Go on a financial austerity program and boost your savings rate. You may also consider lower-priced properties. Smaller properties and ones that need some work can help keep down the purchase price and the required down payment.

If lower-priced properties don't meet your needs, you may be able to find a partner. Make sure to write up a legal contract to specify what happens if a partner wants out. Family members sometimes make good partners. Your parents, grandparents, and maybe even your siblings may have some extra cash they'd like to loan, invest, or even give to you as a gift!

High-ratio mortgages

Some lenders may offer you a mortgage even though you may only be able to put down as little as 5 percent of the purchase price. However, as required by law under the National Housing Act, for any mortgage higher than 75 percent of the value of the property (a high-ratio mortgage) you'll have to purchase mortgage insurance for your loan. Mortgage insurance protects your lender in the event that you can't make your payments and default on your mortgage.

Your premium is calculated on the full value of your mortgage — not just the amount beyond 75 percent of the property's value that you can borrow under a regular mortgage. You can choose to pay the premium as a lump sum, or have it added to your mortgage amount. Adding it to your mortgage means you'll pay the premium several times over due to the extra interest you'll incur.

There's also usually an application fee that can be as high as a few hundred dollars. Mortgage insurance is available from the federal government's CMHC (Canada Mortgage and Housing Corporation) and its private sector competitor, GE Mortgage Insurance Canada.

The rate you'll pay is determined by the size of your down payment compared with the value of the property. Recently, both CMHC and GE Capital were charging 1.0 percent if you were borrowing more than 75 percent of the purchase price up to and including 80 percent. Beyond that, borrowing up to and including 85 percent of the purchase price, the rate was 1.75 percent, up to and including 90 percent was 2.0 percent, and up to and including 95 percent was 3.25 percent. For updated rates, visit the CMHC site at www.cmhc.ca and GE Mortgage Insurance Canada at www.gemortgage.ca.

"No money down" mortgages

Until recently, mortgage insurance providers required you to come up with a minimum of 5 percent of the purchase price out of your own funds. While that 5 percent minimum is still a requirement, now the money doesn't have to come out of your own savings. You can borrow it from other sources, including family members, friends, or a bank, and it doesn't have to be secured by the property. The money can even come from lender cash-back programs, where a bank or other mortgage provider gives you money back in return for your mortgage business. Both CMHC and GE — through arrangements with several of the big banks — offer this option. The only restriction is that the money can't come from a party who's related to your home purchase transaction. For instance, the builder of the home you're buying can't lend you the money.

If your cash flow is healthy and you can easily take care of the mortgage, this option may make sense in certain situations. If you've just come through a year or two of extraordinary (as in *extra*ordinary) expenses, have more than enough cash flow to cover the mortgage payments, and have an emergency fund, this option may be a way to buy a property.

However, you have to ask yourself why you don't have any money of your own for a down payment. If it's because you're living close to your means, or you have poor spending habits, buying a home with no money down is only going to make your financial situation even more precarious.

Also, you have to have access to money for all the associated costs, from legal fees and moving to home maintenance and repair bills, that will inevitably arise. You'll also pay more for mortgage insurance — the rate was recently around 3.4 percent, and that's on the entire amount of your loan. Another major factor is that you may be forced to accept some lenders' "posted" interest rate, which could be anywhere from 0.5 to 1 percent or more higher than the rate you'd get after a little negotiating or by working through a mortgage broker.

Unless you've found the home of your dreams, have crunched the numbers to know that you are comfortable with the payments and other housing costs, and have an emergency fund built up, you're better off waiting until you can comfortably afford to make a down payment of your own.

The Home Buyers' Plan

Another way to raise the level of your down payment funds is to dip into your RRSP. Under the federal government's Home Buyers' Plan, you can borrow up to $20,000 from your RRSP to buy (or build) a home. Your spouse can also borrow an additional $20,000 from his or her RRSP, meaning you can take out a combined maximum of $40,000 if you're jointly purchasing a property.

The program is open to you only if you haven't owned a home and lived in it for the last five years. You're also ineligible if your spouse has owned a home in which you've lived over the same period.

Any money you borrow under the plan is treated as an interest-free loan you're making to yourself. The money doesn't have to be included in your income for that year, and you don't have to pay any tax on the withdrawal.

You have to start repaying the money you borrowed in the second year after you borrowed it. You must repay the full amount over fifteen years, and are required to repay at least one-fifteenth each year. If you miss a payment or part of a payment, that amount is included in your taxable income for that year, and you'll have to pay tax on it at your full marginal tax rate (the rate you pay on the highest, or last dollars of income in any year).

While it can offer a way to pull together a down payment, the Home Buyers' Plan has some significant costs that may not be readily apparent. If making RRSP contributions is already a challenge, you may find it tough to make your repayments. In addition, you don't get a tax deduction for the repayments, since you're simply replacing money the government let you borrow interest-free — and tax-free — from your plan. If the tax savings from your RRSP contributions are an important factor in your finances, you need to consider the impact on your cash flow of having to replace that money as well as having to come up with the money to repay your loan.

Another problem with the plan is that it can do some significant damage to the long-term growth of your RRSP. When you withdraw money, you lose all its potential tax-free compounding until it's repaid to your plan. In addition, if you feel you'll only be able to just get together the required repayments, you will also lose out on the tax savings and compound growth of the new RRSP contributions you could have used that money for. The younger you are, the more costly this lost growth becomes. While your home's appreciation will likely offset the loss, it won't boost your retirement income unless you sell your property and move to a less expensive home, or take out a *reverse mortgage*.

A reverse mortgage allows you to tap the equity in your home via a series of payments to yourself. The money you receive, along with interest charges, is eventually paid back using the proceeds from the sale of your home, usually after you and your spouse die.

Before tapping your retirement savings, get hold of a financial planning calculator (these are included with most personal finance planning software, and are also available at many Web sites) and calculate how much using the Home Buyers' Plan will decrease the future value of your RRSP. We address retirement planning issues in more detail in Chapter 3.

Clearing up credit history blemishes

Late payments, missed payments, or debts that you never bothered to pay can tarnish your credit report and squelch a lender's desire to offer you a mortgage. If you're turned down for a loan because of your less-than-stellar credit history, request (at no charge to you) a copy of your credit report from the lender that turned down your loan.

Explain credit report problems to your lender. If the lender is unsympathetic, try calling other lenders. Tell them your credit problems upfront and see whether you can find one willing to offer you a loan. Mortgage brokers may also be able to help you shop for lenders in these cases.

Sometimes you may feel that you're not in control when you apply for a loan. In reality, you can fix a number of credit problems yourself. And you can often explain those that you can't fix. Remember that some lenders are more lenient and flexible than others. Just because one mortgage lender rejects your loan application doesn't mean that all the others will as well.

As for erroneous information listed on your credit report, get on the phone to the credit bureaus and start squawking. If specific creditors are the culprits, call them too. Keep notes from your conversations and make sure to put your case in writing and add your comments to your credit report. If the customer service representatives you talk with are no help, send a letter to the president of each company. Let the head honcho know that his or her organization caused you problems in obtaining credit.

Another common credit problem is having too much consumer debt at the time you apply for a mortgage. The more credit card, auto loan, and other consumer debt you rack up, the less mortgage you qualify for. If you're turned down for the mortgage, consider it a wake-up call to get rid of this high-cost debt. Hang on to the dream of buying real estate and plug away at paying off your debts before you make another foray into real estate.

Dealing with low appraisals

Even if you have sufficient income, a clean credit report, and an adequate down payment, the lender may turn down your loan if the appraisal of the property you want to buy comes in too low. It's unusual for a property not to appraise for what a buyer agrees to pay — odds are that the real market value of the property is less than what you agreed to pay.

Not producing enough income

If you're self-employed or have changed jobs, your current income may not resemble your past income or, more important, your income may not be what a mortgage lender likes to see with respect to the amount you want to borrow. A simple (but often not possible) way around this problem is to make a larger down payment. For example, if you put down 30 percent or more, you may be able to get a no-income-verification loan. If you can make that large a down payment, lenders probably don't care what your income is — they'll simply repossess and then sell your property if you default on the loan.

If you can't make a large down payment, another option is to get a co-signer for the loan — your relatives may be willing. As long as they aren't over extended themselves, they may be able to help you qualify for a larger loan than you can get on your own. As with partnerships, put your agreement in writing so that no misunderstandings occur.

When to consider a home equity loan

Home equity loans, also known as second mortgages, allow you to borrow against the equity in your home in addition to the mortgage that you already have (a first mortgage).

A home equity loan may benefit you if you need more money for just a few years, or if your first mortgage is at such a low interest rate that refinancing it to get more cash would be too costly. Otherwise, we advise you to avoid home equity loans.

If you need a larger mortgage, why not refinance the first one and wrap it all together? Home equity loans generally have higher interest rates than comparable first mortgages. They're riskier from a lender's perspective because the first mortgage lender gets first claim against your property if you file bankruptcy or you default on the mortgage.

One attraction of a home equity loan is that when you use your home as the security for a line of credit, the interest rate is usually the lowest available for consumer loans. You can borrow only the amount you need at the time you need it, and you can repay any or all of your borrowings at any time. These features mean you pay interest only on money you actually need, and can cut your interest charges as soon as you have money available to pay down your loan.

Working with Real Estate Agents

When you purchase real estate, if you're like most people, you enlist the services of a real estate agent. A good agent can help screen property so that you don't spend all your free time looking at potential properties to buy, negotiating a deal, helping coordinate inspections, and managing other preclosing items.

Recognizing agent conflicts of interest

But all agents, good, mediocre, and awful, are subject to a conflict of interest because of the way they're compensated — on commission. We must say that we respect real estate agents for calling themselves what they are. Real estate agents don't hide behind an obscure job title, such as "shelter consultant." (Many financial "planners," "advisers," and "consultants," for example, actually work on commission and sell investments and life insurance and, therefore, are really stockbrokers and insurance brokers, not planners or advisers.)

Real estate agents aren't in the business of providing objective financial counsel. They don't tell you to spend less money on a home because you aren't saving enough for retirement. They also won't tell you to rent because of your current financial circumstances and the state of the real estate market. Just as car dealers make their living selling cars, real estate agents make their living selling real estate. Never forget this fact as a buyer. The pursuit of a larger commission may encourage an agent to get you to do things that aren't in your best interests, such as the following:

- ✔ **Buy, and buy sooner rather than later.** If you don't buy, your agent doesn't get paid for all the hours he or she spends working with you. The worst agents fib and use tricks to motivate you to buy. They may say that other offers are coming in on a property that interests you, or they may show you a bunch of dumps and then one good listing to motivate you to buy the one good listing.

- ✔ **Spend more than you should.** Because real estate agents get a percentage of the sales price of a property, they have a built-in incentive to encourage you to spend more on a property than what fits comfortably with your other financial objectives and goals. An agent doesn't have to consider or care about your other financial needs.

- ✔ **Buy their company's listings.** Agents also have a built-in incentive (higher commission) to sell their own listings.

- ✔ **Buy in their territory.** Real estate agents typically work a specific territory. As a result, they usually can't objectively tell you the pros and cons of the surrounding region.

- ✔ **Use people that scratch their backs.** Some agents refer you to lenders, inspectors, and title insurance companies that have referred customers to them. Some agents also solicit and receive referral fees (or bribes) from mortgage lenders, inspectors, and contractors to whom they refer business.

Finding a good agent

A mediocre, incompetent, or greedy agent can be a real danger to your finances. Whether you're hiring an agent to work with you as a buyer or seller, you want someone who's competent and with whom you can get along. Working with an agent costs you a lot of money, so make sure you get your money's worth.

Interview several agents. Check references. Ask agents for the names and phone numbers of at least three clients with whom they've worked in the past six months in the geographical area in which you're looking. By narrowing the period during which they worked with references to six months, you maximize the chances of speaking with clients other than the agent's all-time favourite clients.

As you speak with an agent's references, look for these traits in any agent that you work with, whether as a buyer or seller:

- ✔ **Full-time employment.** Some agents work in real estate as a second or even third job. Information in this field changes constantly — and keeping track of it is hard enough on a full-time basis. So it's difficult to imagine a good agent being able to stay on top of the market while moonlighting elsewhere.

- ✔ **Experience.** Hiring an agent with experience doesn't necessarily mean looking for someone who's been around for decades. Many of the best agents come into the field from other occupations, such as business and teaching. Agents can acquire some sales, marketing, negotiation, and communication skills in other fields, but experience in real estate does count.

- ✔ **Honesty and integrity.** You need to trust your agent with a lot of information. If he or she doesn't level with you about what a neighbourhood or particular property is really like, you suffer the consequences.

✔ **Interpersonal skills.** An agent must get along not only with you but also with a whole host of other people who are involved in a typical real estate deal: other agents, property sellers, inspectors, mortgage lenders, and so on. An agent needs to know how to put your interests first without upsetting others.

✔ **Negotiation skills.** Putting a real estate deal together involves negotiation. Is your agent going to exhaust all avenues to get you the best deal possible? Most people don't like the sometimes aggravating process of negotiation, so they hire someone else to do it for them. Be sure to ask the agent's former client references how the agent negotiated for them.

✔ **High quality standards.** Sloppy work can lead to big legal or logistical problems down the road. If an agent neglects to recommend an inspection, for example, you may get stuck with undiscovered problems after the deal is done.

Some agents who pitch themselves as buyers' brokers claim that they work for your interests. Agents who represent you as buyers' brokers still get paid only when you buy. And agents still get paid a commission that's a percentage of the purchase price. So they still have an incentive to sell you a piece of real estate that's more expensive because their commission increases.

Agents sometimes market themselves as *top producers,* which means they sell a relatively larger volume of real estate. This title doesn't count for much for you, the buyer. In fact, you may treat it as a red flag for an agent who focuses on completing as many deals as possible. Such an agent may not be able to give you the time and help you need to get the house you want.

When you buy a home, you need an agent who's patient. The last thing you need or want is someone who tries to push you into making a deal. You need an agent who allows you the necessary time to educate yourself and who helps you make the decision that's best for you.

You also need an agent who's knowledgeable about the local market and community. If you want to buy a home in an area in which you don't currently live, an informed agent can have a big impact on your decision.

Finding an agent with financing knowledge is a plus for buyers, especially first-time buyers or those with credit problems. Such an agent may be able to refer you to lenders that can handle your type of situation, which can save you a lot of legwork.

Buying without a real estate agent

You can purchase property without an agent if you're willing to do some additional legwork. You need to do the things that a good real estate agent does, such as searching for properties, scheduling appointments to see them, determining fair market value, negotiating the deal, and coordinating inspections.

If you don't work with an agent, have a lawyer review the various contracts. Having someone else not vested in the transaction look out for your interests helps your situation.

One possible drawback to working without an agent is performing the negotiations yourself. Negotiating can be problematic if you lack these skills or get too caught up emotionally in the situation.

Closing the Deal

After you locate a property you want to buy and understand your financing options, the real fun begins. Now you have to put the deal together. The following sections discuss key things to keep in mind.

Negotiating 101

When you work with an agent, he or she usually carries the burden of the negotiation process. Even if you delegate responsibility for negotiating to your agent, you still need to have a plan and strategy in mind. Otherwise, you may overpay for real estate.

Find out about the property and the owner before you make your offer. How long has the property been on the market? What are its flaws? Why is the owner selling? The more you understand about the property you want to buy and the seller's motivations, the better able you are to draft an offer that meets everyone's needs. Some listing agents love to talk and will tell you the life history of the seller. Either you or your agent may be able to get them to reveal helpful information about the seller.

Also, bring facts to the bargaining table. Get comparable sales data to support your price. Too often, homebuyers and their agents pick a number out of the air when they make an offer. If you were the seller, would you be persuaded to lower your asking price? Pointing to recent and comparable home sales to justify your offer price strengthens your case.

Remember that price is only one of several negotiable items. Sometimes sellers fixate on selling their homes for a certain amount; perhaps they want to get at least what they paid for it themselves several years ago. You may, however, get a seller to pay for certain repairs or improvements or to offer you an attractive loan without all the extra fees that a bank charges. Also, be aware that the time for closing on the purchase is a bargaining point. Some sellers may need cash soon and may concede other terms if you can close quickly. Likewise, the real estate agent's commission is negotiable too.

Finally, try as best you can to leave your emotions out of any property purchase. This is easier said than done and hardest to do when you purchase a home in which you'll live. Try, as best you can, not to fall in love with a property. Keep searching for other properties even when you make an offer because you may be negotiating with an unmotivated seller.

Inspecting the property

When you buy a property, you're probably making one of the biggest financial purchases and commitments of your life. Unless you've built homes and other properties and performed contracting work yourself, you probably have no idea what you're getting yourself into when it comes to furnaces and termites.

Spend the money and time to hire inspectors and other experts to evaluate the major systems and potential problem areas of the home. Because you can't be certain of the seller's commitment, we recommend that you do the inspections *after* you've successfully negotiated and signed a sales contract. Although you won't have the feedback from the inspections to help with this round of negotiating, you can always go back to the seller with the new information. Make your purchase offer contingent on a satisfactory inspection.

Hire people to help you inspect the following features of the property:

- ✔ Overall condition of the property. For example, is the paint peeling, are the floors level, are appliances present and working well, and so on?
- ✔ Electrical, heating and air conditioning, and plumbing systems
- ✔ Foundations
- ✔ Roofs
- ✔ Pest control and dry rots
- ✔ Seismic/slide/flood risks

(With multiunit rental property, be sure to read Chapter 11 for other specifics you need to check out, such as parking.)

Inspection fees often pay for themselves. If you uncover problems that you weren't aware of when you negotiated the original purchase price, the inspection reports give you the information you need to go back and ask the property seller to fix the problems or reduce the property's purchase price.

Never accept a seller's inspection report as your only source of information. When a seller hires an inspector, he or she may hire someone who isn't as diligent and critical of the property. Review the seller's inspection reports if available, but get your own as well. Also, beware of inspectors who are popular with real estate agents. They may be popular because they're soft touches and don't bother to document all the property's problems.

As with other professionals whose services you retain, interview a few different inspection companies. Ask which systems they inspect and how detailed a report they will prepare for you. Consider asking the company that you're thinking of hiring for customer references. Ask for names and phone numbers of three people who used the company's services within the past six months. Also, request from each inspection company a sample of one of its reports.

The day before you close on the purchase of your home, take a brief walk-through of the property to make sure that everything is still in the condition it was before and that all the fixtures, appliances, curtains, and other items the contract lists are still there. Sellers sometimes ignore or don't recall these things, and consequently they don't leave what they agreed to in the sales contract.

Selling Real Estate

You should buy and hold real estate for the long term. If you do your homework and buy in a good area and work hard to find a fairly priced or underpriced property, why sell it in a few years and incur all the selling costs, time, and hassle to locate and negotiate another property to purchase?

Some real estate investors like to buy properties in need of improvement, fix them up, and then sell them and move on to another. Unless you're a contractor and have a real eye for this type of work, don't expect to make a windfall or even to earn back more than the cost of the improvements. In fact, it's more likely that you'll erode your profit through the myriad costs of frequent buying and selling. The vast majority of your profits should come from the long-term appreciation of the overall real estate market in the communities you own property in.

Use the reasons that you bought in an area as a guide if you think you want to sell. Use the criteria that we discuss in Chapter 11 as a guideline. For example, if the schools in the community are deteriorating and the planning department is allowing development that will hurt the value of your property and the rents you can charge, you may have cause to sell. Unless you see significant problems like these in the future, holding good properties over many years is a great way to build your wealth and minimize transaction costs.

Negotiating real estate agents' contracts

Most people use an agent to sell real estate. As we discuss in the "Finding a good agent" section earlier in this chapter, selling and buying a home demand agents with different strengths. When you sell a property, you want an agent who can get the job done efficiently and for as high a sales price as possible.

As a seller, you should seek agents who have marketing and sales expertise and who are willing to put in the time and money necessary to sell your house. Don't be impressed by an agent just because he or she works for a large company. What matters more is what the agent can do to market your property.

When you list your house for sale, the contract you sign with the listing agent includes specification of the commission you'll pay the agent if he or she succeeds in selling your property. In most areas of the country, agents usually ask for a 6 percent commission. In an area that maintains lower-cost housing, agents may ask for 7 or even 8 percent. The standard rate is 8 percent in Quebec.

Regardless of the commission an agent says is "typical," "standard," or "what my manager requires," always remember that you can negotiate commissions. Because the commission is a percentage, you're better able to get a lower commission on a higher-priced property. After all, if an agent makes 6 percent selling both a $200,000 and a $100,000 property, he or she makes twice as much on the higher-priced property, usually without twice the work.

If you live in an area with higher-priced properties, you may be able to negotiate a 5 percent commission. For expensive properties, a 4 percent commission is reasonable. You may find, however, that you're best able to negotiate a lower commission when an offer is on the table. Because of the cooperation of agents who work together through the multiple listing service (MLS), if you list your real estate for sale at a lower commission than most other properties, some agents won't show it to prospective buyers. For this reason, you're better off having your listing agent cut his take instead of cutting the commission you pay to a real estate agent who brings a buyer for your property to you.

In terms of the length of the listing agreement, three months is reasonable. If you give an agent too long to list your property (6 to 12 months), the or she may simply toss the listing into the multiple listing book and not expend much effort to get your property sold. Practically speaking, you can fire your agent whenever you want, regardless of the length of the listing agreement, but a shorter listing may motivate your agent more.

Selling without a real estate agent

When people are tempted to sell real estate without an agent it's usually to save the commission that an agent deducts from the property's sale price. If you have the time, energy, and marketing experience, you can sell sans agent and possibly save some money. There are also some middle-of-the-road alternatives. In Ontario, for example, the listing fee charged by RealtySellers (www.realtysellers.com) is half the norm — 1.25 instead of 2.5 percent. On a $350,000 home, that saves you $4,375.

The major problem with attempting to sell real estate on your own is that you can't easily list it in the MLS, which, in most areas, only real estate agents can access. If you're not listed in the MLS, many potential buyers never know your home is for sale. Agents who work with buyers don't generally look for or show their clients properties for sale by owner or listed with discount brokers. This is starting to change, however. RealtySellers — run by Stephen Moranis, a former president of the Toronto Real Estate Board and a former director of the Canadian Real Estate Association — allows you to list on the system through them for a set fee of around $700.

Besides saving you time, a good agent can help ensure that you're not sued for failing to disclose known defects of your property. If you decide to sell on your own, have access to a legal adviser who can review the contracts. Take the time to educate yourself about the many facets of selling property for top dollar.

Part IV
There's No Business Like Small Business

The 5th Wave   By Rich Tennant

"Here's my business plan for the Jazz Store. I think we should just fake the budget, improvise the marketing and make up the long range goals as we go along."

In this part . . .

Although the businesses may be small, the potential for earning profits and finding a fulfilling career isn't. Here, we explain such things as how to develop a business plan, identify marketable products or services, find customers, and wallop the competition! If setting up your own shop seems either too overwhelming or too uninspiring, you also find out how to buy an existing business.

Chapter 13

Starting Your Own Business

· ·

In This Chapter

▶ Knowing what it takes to be a successful entrepreneur

▶ Exploring alternatives to starting your own company

▶ Looking at small-business investment options

▶ Mapping out your small business plans

· ·

*M*any people dream about running their own company, and for largely good reasons. For starters, you can pursue something you're passionate about and can have control over. Successful business owners can reap major economic bounties.

But tales of entrepreneurs becoming multimillionaires focus attention on the financial rewards without revealing the business and personal challenges and costs associated with being in charge. Consider what your company has to do well in order to survive and succeed in the competitive business world:

✔ Develop products and services that the marketplace purchases.

✔ Price your offerings properly and promote them. What good are your products and services if others don't know about and buy them?

✔ Deal with the competition. Your success will likely spur imitators.

✔ Manage the accounting. You'll be confronted with tracking revenue and expenses, making tax payments, and perhaps handling a payroll.

✔ Interpret lease contracts and evaluate office space.

✔ Keep current with changes in your field. Reading trade and professional journals can help you do this.

✔ Manage employees. You need to know the right ways to hire, train, and retain good employees. You may soon become an expert on insurance and other employee benefits.

Business owners also face personal and emotional challenges, which rarely get airtime among all the glory of the rags-to-riches tales of multimillionaire entrepreneurs. Major health problems, divorces, fights and lawsuits among family members who are in business together, the loss of friends, and even suicides have been attributed to the passions of business owners who are consumed with winning or become overwhelmed by their failures.

Heard enough already? We're not trying to scare you, but we do want you to be *realistic* about starting your own business. Maybe you do have the right stuff to run your own company, but most people don't.

Testing Your Mettle

The keys to success and enjoyment as an entrepreneur vary as much as the businesses do. But if you can answer yes to most of the following questions, you probably have the qualities and perspective needed to succeed as a small-business owner.

Don't be deterred by the questions you can't answer in the affirmative. A perfect entrepreneur doesn't exist. Part of succeeding in business is knowing what you can't do as well as what you can do and finding creative ways (or people) to help you.

1. Are you a self-starter? Do you like challenges? Are you persistent? Are you willing to do research to solve problems?

Running your own business isn't glamorous most of the time, especially in the early years. You have lots of details to mind and things to do. Success in business is the result of doing lots of little things well. If you're accustomed to (and like) working for larger organizations where much of the day is spent attending meetings and keeping up on office politics and gossip, with little accountability, you probably won't enjoy or succeed at running your own business.

2. Do you value independence and self-control?

Particularly in the early days of your business, you need to enjoy working on your own. If you're a people person, however, many businesses offer lots of contact. But you must recognize the difference between socializing with co-workers and networking with business contacts and customers. When you leave a company environment and work on your own, you give up a lot of socializing. Of course, if you work in an unpleasant environment or with people you don't really enjoy socializing with, venturing out on your own may be a plus.

3. Can you develop a commitment to an idea, product, or principle?

Most entrepreneurs work about 50 hours per week, 50 or so weeks a year — that's about 2,500 hours per year. If your product, service, or cause doesn't excite you, and you can't motivate others to work hard for you, it's going to be a long year!

One of the worst reasons to start your own business is for the pursuit of great financial riches. Don't get us wrong — if you're good at what you do and you know how to market your services or products, you may make more money working for yourself. But for most people, money isn't enough of a motivation, and many people make the same or less money on their own than they did working for a company.

4. Are you willing to make financial sacrifices and live a reduced lifestyle before and during your early entrepreneurial years?

"Live like a student, before and during the start-up of your small business" was the advice that Eric's best business school professor, James Collins, gave him before he started his business. With most businesses, you expend money during the start-up years and likely have a reduced income compared with the income you receive while working for a company.

In order to make your entrepreneurial dream a reality, you need to live well within your means both before and after you start your business. But if running your own business really makes you happy, sacrificing expensive vacations, overpriced luxury cars, the latest designer clothing, and $3 lattes at the corner café shouldn't be too painful.

5. Do you recognize that, when you run your own business, you must still report to bosses?

Besides the allure of huge profits, the other reason some people mistakenly go into business for themselves is that they're tired of working for other people. Obnoxious, evil bosses can make anyone want to become an entrepreneur. We understand — we've both been there. Take Eric's experience when he worked at a consulting firm. He had a boss — we'll call him Goofus

— whom he positively detested. Although the team Eric led had many weeks to prepare client presentations, Goofus didn't really focus on their material until a couple of days before the presentation. Goofus then made massive changes, causing the entire team, as well as the production department that produced the presentation, to work 16-hour days and into the wee hours of the morning. Goofus also made himself inaccessible for input and advice and ignored voice mails until he got into crisis mode. He never apologized for his behaviour and couldn't have cared less about people's personal lives. Because of people like Goofus, employees who wanted some semblance of control in their professional and personal lives left the consulting business.

When you run your own business, you have customers and other bosses just like Goofus who are miserable to deal with. If you have enough customers, you can simply decide not to do business with such jerks. Fortunately, the worst customers usually can't make your life anywhere near as miserable as bosses like Goofus.

6. Can you withstand rejection, naysayers, and negative feedback?

"I thought every *no* that I got when trying to raise my funding brought me one step closer to a yes," says Alex Popov, an entrepreneur. Unless you come from an entrepreneurial family, don't expect your parents to endorse your "risky, crazy" behaviour. Even other entrepreneurs can ridicule your good ideas. Two entrepreneurs we know of were critical of each other's idea, yet both have succeeded! Some people (especially parents) simply think that working for a giant company makes you safer and more secure (which, of course, is a myth, because corporations can lay you off in a snap). It's also easier for them to say to their friends and neighbours that you're a big manager at a well-known corporation (such as IBM, GE . . . or Enron or WorldCom!) instead of explaining that you're working on some kooky business idea out of a spare bedroom. (How secure do you think those former employees of Enron and WorldCom felt after having lost their jobs at their former large — and supposedly sound and stable — company?)

7. Are you able to identify your shortcomings and hire or align yourself with people and organizations that complement your skills and expertise?

To be a successful entrepreneur, you need to be a bit of a jack-of-all-trades: marketer, accountant, customer service representative, administrative assistant, and so on. Unless you get lots of investor capital, which is rare for a true start-up, you can't afford to hire help in the early months, and perhaps even years, of your business.

Partnering with or buying certain services or products rather than trying to do everything yourself may make sense for you. And over time, if your business grows and succeeds, you should be able to afford to hire more help. If you can surround and partner yourself with people whose skills and expertise complement yours, you'll have a winning team!

8. Do you deal well with ambiguity? Do you believe in yourself?

When you're on your own, determining when and if you're on the right track is difficult. Some days, things don't go well. If you *are* the company, bad days are much harder to take. Therefore, being confident, optimistic, and able to work around obstacles are necessary skills.

9. Do you understand why you started the business or organization and how you personally define "success"?

Many business entrepreneurs define success by such measures as sales revenue, profits, number of branch offices and employees, and so on. These are fine measures, but other organizations, particularly non-profits, have other measures. For example, the Sierra Club of Canada seeks to "develop a diverse, well-trained grassroots network working to protect the integrity of our global ecosystems." The following is a passage from the Sierra Club of Canada's materials focusing on one of what it calls the five overriding threats, namely "the ever-growing presence of toxic chemicals in all living things":

> *With high odds of developing breast cancer (one in nine in Canada), women need to know how to better their chances for prevention. An extensive search of the literature supports that exposure to commonly used organochlorine pesticides, especially those which are persistent and estrogen-mimickers, should be avoided as a preventative measure. . . . Avoidance of unnecessary use of pesticides and promotion of lactation are important public health issues, and persistent estrogenic chemicals should be classed as toxic in Canada, as they are already in the U.S.*

In order to accomplish such goals as affecting public policy and public opinion about the environment and health, money is necessary, but such a cause-focused organization has a very different "bottom line" than a for-profit organization.

10. Can you accept lack of success in the early years of building your business?

A few, rare businesses are instant hits, but most businesses take time — years, perhaps even decades — to build momentum. Some successful corporate people suffer from anxiety when they go out on their own and encounter the inevitable struggles and lack of tangible success as they build their company.

Myths of being an entrepreneur

Many myths persist about what it takes to be an entrepreneur, partly because those who aren't entrepreneurs tend to hang out with others who aren't. The mass media's popularization of "successful" entrepreneurs such as Bill Gates, Ted Turner, and Oprah Winfrey leads to numerous misperceptions and misconceptions.

One myth is that you must be well connected or know "important" people to succeed as an entrepreneur. However, we think that being a decent human being is far more important. Enough rude, inconsiderate, and self-centred people are in the business world (and, yes, some of them do succeed despite their character flaws), and if you're not that way, you'll be able to meet people who can help you in one way or another. But remember that looking in the mirror shows you your best and most trusted resource.

Another myth is that you need to be really smart and have an M.B.A. or some other fancy degree. Many successful entrepreneurs — Bill Gates and Steve Jobs, for example — don't even have college degrees, for goodness' sakes. Perusing *Forbes* magazine's list of the 200 most financially successful small companies shows that about one in six of the CEOs didn't earn a college degree and about half don't have advanced degrees! These statistics are even more amazing when you consider that a relatively large number of entrepreneurs with humble backgrounds leave, sell, or are forced out of the successful enterprises they started.

We're not saying that a good education isn't worthwhile in general and that it can't help you succeed in your own business. (For example, Ivy Leaguers run about 6 percent of the 200 best small businesses, yet Ivy League college grads make up less than 1 percent of all graduates.) But a formal education isn't necessary.

As for intelligence, which is admittedly a difficult thing to measure, the majority of entrepreneurs have IQs under 120, and a surprising percentage have IQs under the average of 100 — more entrepreneurs, in fact, have IQs under 100 than have IQs greater than 130!

Another commonly held belief is that you must be a gregarious, big-egoed extrovert to succeed as an entrepreneur. Although some studies show that more entrepreneurs are extroverted, many entrepreneurs are not.

A final myth to dispel is the notion that starting your own business is risky. Some people focus on the potential for failure. Consider the worst-case scenario — if your venture doesn't work out, you can often go back to a job similar to the one you left behind. Also, recognize that risk is a matter of perception, and as with investments, people completely overlook some risks. What about the risk to your happiness and career if you stay in a boring, claw-your-way-up-the-corporate-ladder kind of job? You always risk a layoff when you work for a company. An even greater risk is that you'll wake up in your 50s and 60s and think it's too late to do something on your own and wish you had tried to sooner.

Considering Some Alternatives to Starting Your Own Company

Sometimes, entrepreneurial advocates imply that running your own business or starting your own non-profit is the greatest thing in the world and that all people would be happy owning their own business if they just set their mind to it. The reality is that some people won't be blissful as entrepreneurs. If you didn't score highly on our ten-question entrepreneur assessment in the preceding section, don't despair. You can probably be happier and more successful doing something other than starting your own business.

Some people are better off working for a company; for-profit or non-profit. Others do well buying an existing small business instead of trying to start one from scratch. Consider the following options.

Being an entrepreneur inside a company

A happy medium is available for people who want the challenge of running their own show without giving up the comforts and security that come with a company environment — for example, you can manage an entrepreneurial venture at a company. That's what John Kilcullen, president and chief executive officer of IDG Books Worldwide (former publisher of the Dummies books), did when he helped launch the book publishing division of IDG in 1990. (IDG Books was subsequently bought by John Wiley & Sons, Inc., in 2001.)

Kilcullen had publishing industry experience and wanted to take on the responsibility of growing a successful publishing company. But he also knew that being a player in the book publishing industry takes a lot of money and resources. Because he was a member of the founding team of the new IDG Books division, Kilcullen had the best of both worlds.

Kilcullen always had a passion to start his own business but found that most traditional publishers weren't interested in giving autonomy and money to a division and letting it run with the ball. "I wanted the ability to build a business on my own instincts . . . the appeal of IDG was that it was decentralized. IDG was willing to invest and provide the freedom to spend as we saw fit."

If you're able to secure an entrepreneurial position inside a larger company, in addition to significant managerial and operational responsibility, you can also negotiate your share of the financial success you helped create. The parent company's senior management wants you to have the incentive that comes from sharing in the financial success of your endeavours. Bonuses, stock options, and the like are often tied to the performance of a division.

Investing in your career

Some people are happy or content as employees. Companies need and want lots of good employees, so you can find a job if you have skills, a work ethic, and the ability to get along with others.

You can improve your income-earning ability and invest in your career in a variety of different ways:

- ✔ **Work.** Be willing to work extra hours and take on more responsibility, but do so within reason. Those who take extra initiative and then deliver really stand out in a company where many people working on a salary have a time-clock, 9-to-5 mentality. But be careful that the extra effort doesn't contribute to workaholism, a dangerous addiction that causes too many people to neglect important personal relationships and their own health. Don't bite off more than you can chew — otherwise, your supervisors won't have faith that they can count on you to deliver. Find ways to work smarter, not just longer, hours.

- ✔ **Read.** One of the reasons why you don't need a Ph.D., a master's, or even an undergraduate degree to succeed in business is that you can find out a lot on your own. You can gain insight by doing, but you can also gain expertise by reading a lot. A good bookstore has no entrance requirements — you just have to walk through the doors. A good book isn't free, but it costs a heck of lot less than taking more university or graduate courses!

- ✔ **Study.** If you haven't completed your university or graduate degree and the industry you're in values those who have, investing the time and money to finish your education may benefit you. Speak with others who have taken that path and see what they have to say.

Exploring Small-Business Investment Options

Only your imagination limits the ways you can make money with small businesses. Choosing the option that best meets your needs is not unlike choosing other investments, such as in real estate or in the securities markets. Following are the major ways you can invest in small business along with information on what's attractive, and not, about each option.

Starting your own business

Of all your small-business options, starting your own business involves the greatest amount of work. Although you can perform this work on a part-time basis in the beginning, most people end up working in their business full time — it's your new job, career, or whatever you want to call it.

For most of our working years, we've both run our own businesses, and overall, we really like it. (However, that's not to say that running our own businesses doesn't have its drawbacks and down moments.) We've seen many people of varied backgrounds, interests, and skills achieve success and happiness running their own businesses.

Most people perceive starting their own business as the riskiest of all small-business investment options. But if you get into a business that utilizes your skills and expertise, the risk isn't nearly as great as you may think. Suppose you teach and make $50,000 per year and you want to set up your own tutoring service making a comparable amount of money. If you find through your research that others who perform these services charge $50 per hour, you need to actually tutor about 20 or so hours per week, assuming you work 50 weeks per year. Because you can run this business from your home (which can possibly generate small tax breaks) without purchasing new equipment, your expenses should be minimal.

Instead of leaving your job cold turkey and trying to build your business from scratch, you can start moonlighting as a tutor. Over a couple of years, if you can average ten hours per week, you're halfway to your goal. If you leave your job and focus all your energies on your tutoring business, getting to 20 hours per week of billable work shouldn't be a problem. Still think starting a business is risky?

Many businesses can be launched with low start-up costs, by leveraging your existing skills and expertise. If you have the time to devote to building "sweat equity," you can build a valuable company and job. As long as you check out the competition and offer a valued service at a reasonable cost, the principal risk with your business is that you won't do a good job marketing what you have to offer. If you can market your skills, you should succeed.

Don't start a business for tax write-offs

"Start a small business for fun, profit, and huge tax deductions," a financial advice book declares, adding that "the tax benefits alone are worth starting a small business." A seminar company offers a course entitled "How to Have Zero Taxes Deducted from Your Pay Cheque." This tax seminar tells you how to solve your tax problems: "If you have a sideline business, or would like to start one, you're eligible to have little or no taxes taken from your pay."

All this sounds too good to be true — and of course it is. Not only are the strategies sure to lead to Canada Revenue Agency audit purgatory, but such books and seminars may seduce you to pony up $100 or more for audiotapes or notebooks of "inside information."

Unfortunately, many self-proclaimed self-help gurus claim that you can slash your taxes simply by finding a product or service you can sell on the side of your regular employment. The problem, they argue, is that as a regular wage earner who receives a pay cheque from an employer, you can't write off many of your other (personal) expenses. Open a sideline business, they say, and you can deduct your personal expenses as business expenses.

The pitch is enticing, but the reality is something quite different. You have to spend money to get tax deductions, and the spending must be for legitimate purposes of your business in its efforts to generate income. If you think taking tax deductions for your hobby is worth the risk because you won't get caught unless you're audited, the odds are stacked against you. Canada Revenue Agency audits an extraordinarily large portion of small businesses that show regular losses. The bottom line is that you need to operate a real business for the purpose of generating income and profits, not tax deductions.

It used to be that the Canada Revenue Agency placed a lot of importance on whether an undertaking had "a reasonable expectation of profit." The problem is that the test was done after the fact. It wasn't uncommon for people to be turned down when they tried to claim their losses as legitimate deductions, since on hindsight it's a lot easier to see why a failed business didn't have a fighting chance in the first place.

More importantly, the rule set a much higher standard for entrepreneurs than it did for larger companies, who regularly deduct the cost of misguided blunders, ill-advised takeovers, and pie-in-the-sky planning. And, of course, many of today's successful businesses would have never have got off the ground if the entrepreneurs behind them had listened to all the reasons they were "bound to fail" offered up by naysayers. Sometimes, too, businesses launched on a foolhardy premise manage to survive and often thrive thanks to good luck and fortuitous timing.

The good news for entrepreneurs is that in 2002, the Supreme Court greatly reduced the importance of the "reasonable expectation of profit" test, making it just one of many factors that the tax department considers when assessing the commercial viability of an enterprise. At the same time, the Court emphasized that a taxpayer's business smarts — or complete commercial naïveté — are not to be considered when assessing whether expenses qualify as business losses.

If you have rung up losses for three years or more, and want to continue to claim your future losses, you may still have to convince Revenue Canada that you're seriously trying to make a profit and run a legitimate business. The bottom line is that you need to operate a real business for the purpose of generating income and profits, not tax deductions. And remember that deducting any expenses that aren't directly applicable to your business is illegal.

Buying an existing business

If you don't have a specific idea for a business you want to start but you have business management skills and an ability to improve existing businesses, you may consider buying an established business. Although you don't have to go through the riskier start-up period if you take this route, you'll likely need more capital to buy a going enterprise.

You also need to be able to deal with stickier personnel and management issues. The history of the organization and the way things work predates your ownership of the business. If you don't like making hard decisions, firing people who don't fit with your plans, and coercing people into changing the way they did things before you arrived on the scene, buying an existing business likely isn't for you. Also realize that some of the good employees may be loyal to the old owner and his style of running the business, so they may split when you arrive.

Some people perceive that buying an existing business is safer than starting a new one, but buying someone else's business can actually be riskier. You'll have to shell out far more money up front, in the form of a down payment, to buy a business. If you don't have the ability to run the business and it does poorly, you may lose much more financially. Another risk is that the business is for sale for a reason — it's not very profitable, it's in decline, or it's generally a pain in the posterior to operate.

Good businesses that are for sale don't come cheap. If the business is a success, the current owner has removed the start-up risk from the business, so the price of the business should include a premium to reflect this lack of risk. If you have the capital to buy an established business and you have the skills to run it, consider going this route. Chapter 15 discusses how to buy a good business.

Investing in someone else's business

If you like the idea of profiting from successful small businesses but don't want the day-to-day headaches of being responsible for managing the enterprise, you may want to invest in someone else's small business. Although this route may seem easier, fewer people are actually cut out to be investors in other people's businesses.

Investing for the right reasons

Consider investing in someone else's business if you meet the following criteria:

✔ You have sufficient assets so that what you invest in small privately held companies is a small portion (20 percent or less) of your total financial assets.

✔ You can afford to lose what you invest. Unlike investing in a diversified stock mutual fund (Chapter 8), you may lose all your investment when you invest in a small, privately held company.

✔ You're astute at evaluating corporate financial statements and business strategies. Investing in a small privately held company has much in common with investing in a publicly traded firm. The difference is that private firms aren't required to produce comprehensive, audited financial statements that adhere to certain accounting principles the way that public companies are. Thus, you have a greater risk of not receiving sufficient or accurate information when you evaluate a small private firm.

Putting money into your own business (or someone else's) can be a high-risk — but potentially high-return — investment. The best options to pick are those you understand well. If you hear about a great business idea or company from someone you know and trust, do your research and make your best judgment. That company or idea may well be a terrific investment.

Before you invest in a project, ask to see a copy of the business plan and compare it with the business plan model that we suggest later in this chapter. Thoroughly check out the people running the business. Talk to others who don't have a stake in the investment and benefit from their comments and concerns. But don't forget that many a wise person has rained on the parade of what turned out to be a terrific business idea.

Avoiding investing mistakes

Although some people are extra careful when they invest other people's money, you need to know that many small-business owners seek investors' money for the wrong reasons. Some business owners are impatient and perhaps don't understand the feasibility of making do with a small amount of capital (a process called bootstrapping, which we discuss in Chapter 14).

Other businesses need money because they're in financial trouble. Take the small furniture retailer that conducted a stock offering to raise money. On the surface, everything seemed fine, and the company made it onto the *Inc.* 500

list of fast-growing small companies. But it turns out that the company wanted to issue stock because it expanded too quickly and didn't sell enough merchandise to cover its high overhead. The company ended up in bankruptcy.

Another problem with small businesses that seek investors is that many small-business owners may take more risk and do less up-front planning and homework with other people's money. Many well-intentioned people fail at their businesses. Consider the M.B.A. from a top business school — we'll call him Jacob — who convinced an investor to put up about $300,000 to purchase a small manufacturing company. Jacob put a small amount of his own money into the business and immediately blew about $100,000 on a fancy-schmancy computer scheduling and order-entry system.

Likewise, Jacob wasn't interested much in sales (a job that the previous owner managed), so he hired a sales manager. The sales manager he hired was a disaster — many of the front-line salespeople fled to competitors, taking key customers with them. By the time Jacob came to his senses, it was too late — the disaster had unfolded. He tried to cut costs, but doing so hurt the quality and timeliness of the company's products. The business dissolved, and the investor lost everything.

Drawing Up the Business Plan

If you're motivated to start your own business, the next step is to figure out what you want to do and how you're going to do it. You don't need a perfectly detailed plan that spells out all the minutiae. Making such an involved plan is a waste of your time because things change and evolve over time.

However, you do need a general plan that helps you define what you think you want to do and the tasks you need to perform to accomplish your goal. The business plan should be a working document or blueprint for the early days, months, and years of your business.

The amount of detail that your plan needs depends on your goals and the specifics of your business. A simple, more short-term focused plan (ten pages or so) is fine if you don't aspire to build an empire. However, if your goal is to grow, hire employees, and open multiple locations, then your plan needs to be longer (20 to 50 pages) to cover longer-term issues. If you want outside investor money, a longer business plan is a necessity.

As you put together your plan and evaluate your opportunities, open your ears and eyes. Expect to do research and to speak with other entrepreneurs and people in the industry. Many people will spend time talking with you as long as they realize that you don't want to compete with them.

Identifying your business concept

What do you want your business to do? What product or service do you want to offer? Maybe your business goal is to perform tax-preparation services for small-business owners. Or, perhaps you want to start a consulting firm, open a restaurant that sells healthy fast food, run a gardening service, or manufacture toys.

Your concept doesn't need to be unique to survive in the business world — witness the legions of self-employed consultants, plumbers, tax preparers, and restaurant owners. The existence of many other people who already do what you want to do validates the potential for your small-business ideas. We know many wage slaves who say they'd love to run their own business if they could only come up with "the idea." Most of these people still dream about their small-business plans as they draw their Canada Pension Plan cheques. Being committed to the idea of running your own business is more important than developing the next great product or service. In the beginning, the business opportunities you pursue can be quite general to your field of expertise or interest. What you eventually do over time will evolve.

We're not saying that an innovative idea lacks merit. A creative idea gives you the chance to hit a big home run, and the first person to successfully develop a new idea can achieve big success.

Even if you aspire to build the next billion-dollar company, you can put a twist on older concepts. Suppose you're a veterinarian but you don't want a traditional office where people must bring their cats and dogs for treatment. You believe that because many people are starved for free time, they want a vet who makes house calls. Thus, you open your Vet on Wheels business. You may also want to franchise the business and open locations around the country. However, you can also succeed by doing what thousands of other vets are now doing and have done over the years with a traditional office.

Wet blankets through history

"This 'telephone' has too many shortcomings to be seriously considered as a means of communication. The device is inherently of no value to us." — Western Union internal memo in response to Alexander Graham Bell's telephone, 1876.

"The concept is interesting and well formed, but in order to earn better than a C, the idea must be feasible." — A Yale University management professor in response to Fred Smith's paper proposing reliable overnight delivery service. Smith went on to found Federal Express Corporation.

"We don't tell you how to coach, so don't tell us how to make shoes." — A large sporting shoe manufacturer to Bill Bowerman, inventor of the waffle shoe and cofounder of NIKE, Inc.

"So we went to Atari and said, 'Hey, we've got this amazing thing, even built with some of your parts, and what do you think about funding us? Or we'll give it to you. We just want to do it. Pay our salary, we'll come work for you.' And they said, 'No.' So then we went to Hewlett-Packard, and they said, 'Hey, we don't need you. You haven't got through college yet.'" — Steve Jobs, speaking about attempts to get Atari and Hewlett-Packard interested in his and Steve Wozniak's personal computer. Jobs and Wozniak founded Apple Computer.

"'You should franchise them,' I told them. 'I'll be your guinea pig.' Well, they just went straight up in the air! They couldn't see the philosophy. . . . When they turned us down, that left Bud and me to swim on our own." — Sam Walton, describing his efforts to get the Ben Franklin chain interested in his discount retailing concept in 1962. Walton went on to found Wal-Mart.

"We don't like their sound, and guitar music is on the way out." — Decca Recording Company in rejecting The Beatles, 1962.

In 1884, John Henry Patterson was ridiculed by his business friends for paying $6,500 for the rights to the cash register — a product with "limited" or no potential. Patterson went on to found National Cash Register (NCR) Corporation.

"What's all this computer nonsense you're trying to bring into medicine? I've got no confidence at all in computers and I want nothing whatsoever to do with them." — A medical professor in England to Dr. John Alfred Powell, about the CT scanner.

"That is good sport. But for the military, the airplane is useless." — Ferdinand Foch, Commander in Chief, Allied Forces on the Western Front, World War I.

"The television will never achieve popularity; it takes place in a semidarkened room and demands continuous attention." — Harvard professor Chester L. Dawes, 1940.

These quotes were reprinted with permission from *Beyond Entrepreneurship, Turning Your Business into an Enduring Great Company,* James C. Collins and William C. Lazier, Prentice Hall.

Outlining your objectives

The reasons for starting and running your own small business are as varied as the entrepreneurs behind their companies. Before you start your firm, it's useful to think about what you're seeking to achieve. Your objectives need not be cast in concrete and will surely change over time. If you like, you can write a short and motivating mission statement.

When you ask an M.B.A., especially one from a big-name school, to think about objectives, he or she usually says something like, "My goal is to run a $20 million company in seven years." Financial objectives are fine, but don't make your objectives strictly financial, unless money is the only reason why you want to run your own business.

Introductory economics courses teach students that the objective of every for-profit firm is to maximize profits. As with many things taught in economics courses, this theory has one problem — it doesn't hold up in reality. Most small-business owners we know don't manage their businesses maniacally in the pursuit of maximum profits. The following list gives you some other possible objectives to consider:

- ✔ **Working with people you like and respect.** Some customers may buy your products and services, and some employees and suppliers may offer you their services for a good price, but what if you can't stand working with them? If you have sufficient business or just have your own standards, you can choose whom you do business with.

- ✔ **Educating others.** Maybe part of your business goal is to educate the public about something you're an expert in. We know that when we started businesses, we saw education as a core part of our companies' purpose.

- ✔ **Improving an industry/setting a higher standard.** Perhaps part of your goal in starting your business is to show how your industry can better serve its customers. Having an ideal and putting it into practice can be very rewarding and a terrific motivator that helps you get through tough stretches.

Of course, you can't accomplish these objectives without profits, and doing these things isn't inconsistent with generating greater profits. But if your objectives are more than financial or your financial objectives are not your number-one concern, don't worry — that's usually a good sign.

Research model companies

If your business provides products or services similar to those that other companies offer, identify two or three of your competitors that do a good job or seem most similar. Which of these companies' practices do you want to emulate? In what areas can you improve upon or differentiate your offerings?

Even if you have an innovative and apparently unique concept, examine companies in related and even dissimilar fields to identify those you want to emulate. Identify traits and characteristics from several of them so that you can build these into the composite of your own firm.

For the model companies that you examine, find information about the following:

- ✔ Why they chose their location.

- ✔ How they promote their services and products.

- ✔ How they provide or manufacture their products and services.

- ✔ What types of customers they attract.

- ✔ What their revenues, expenses, and profitability are.

- ✔ How they've expanded their locations over time (if this is your goal).

Analyzing the marketplace

The single most important area to understand is the marketplace in which your business competes. To be successful, your business must not only produce a good product or service but also reach customers and convince them to buy your product. You should discern what the competition has to offer as well as its strengths and vulnerabilities. In most industries, you also need to understand government regulations that affect the type of business you're considering.

Meeting customer needs

If market analysis is the most important part of the business plan, then understanding your customers is the most important part of your market analysis. If you don't understand your desired customers and their needs, don't expect to have a successful business.

If you're in a business that sells to consumers, consider your customers' gender, age, income, geographic location, marital status, number of children, education, living situation (rent or own), and the reasons they want your product or service. Who are your prospective customers? Where do they live, and what do they care about? If you sell to businesses, you need to understand similar issues. What types of businesses may buy your product or services? Why?

The best way to get to know your potential customers is to get out and talk to them. In-person interviews and paper-based surveys both have their benefits. Although more time consuming, live interviews allow you to go with the flow of the conversation, improvise questions, and probe more interesting areas. Although you can mail or fax paper-based surveys to many people with a minimal investment of your time, the response rate is usually quite low and the answers are usually not as illuminating. Offer a product or service sample or some other promotional item to those who help you with your research. Doing so attracts people who are interested in your product or service, which helps you define your target customers.

Also, try to get a sense of what customers pay and will pay for the products or services you offer. Analyzing the competition's offerings helps, too. Some products or services also require follow-up or additional servicing. Understand what customers need and what they'll pay for your services.

 If you want to raise money from investors, include some estimates as to the size of the market for your product or services. Of course, such numbers are ballpark estimates, but sizing the market for your product helps you estimate profitability, the share of the market needed to be profitable, and so on.

Besting the competition

Always examine the products, services, benefits, and prices that competitors offer. Otherwise, you go on blind faith that what you offer stacks up well against the alternatives in the industry.

You first need to decide whether you have a realistic chance of winning the consumer choice battle. We think you'll agree that going into the same discount warehouse retailing business and competing head-to-head with Wal-Mart, Costco, or Home Depot is crazy — you'll likely lose.

Examine your competitors' weaknesses so that you can exploit them. Rather than trying to beat them on their terms, maybe you've identified a need for a neighbourhood pet supply store that offers a much broader and specialized range of pet supplies than the big-selling brands of dog and cat food that warehouse stores sell. Providing knowledgeable customer sales representatives to answer customer questions and make product suggestions can also give you a competitive edge.

Thus, you may be able to surpass the warehouse stores on three counts: convenience of location for people in your neighbourhood, breadth of product offerings, and customer assistance. Offering only economy sizes of the best-selling brands of pet food to compete with warehouse stores would be foolish. Your prices may have to be higher because you can't negotiate the volume discount purchases that they can. You may also have greater overhead (not in absolute dollars but as a percentage of your revenue) running a small business.

However, that's not to say your neighbourhood pet supply store can't offer some best-selling pet food. As we're sure you know, customers of convenience stores often pay top dollar for smaller bags of supplies that they can purchase close to home or after normal shopping hours.

If you want to open a neighbourhood pet supply store, evaluate a number of different locales to see where other similar stores are located. Visit those stores and observe their strengths and weaknesses. If you're discreet, you may be able to interview some customers outside the stores to see what they like and don't like about the competition.

Don't make the mistake of thinking that even if you have a completely innovative product or service that no other business currently offers, you don't have competitors. All businesses have competitors. In the highly unlikely event that you've developed something truly unique that has little competition, your success will surely breed competition as imitators follow or attempt to leapfrog your lead.

Complying with regulations

Most businesses are subject to some sort of regulation. If you want to start a retail business, for example, few communities permit you to run it out of your home. If you lease or purchase a private location, the zoning laws in that location may restrict you. Therefore, you need to check what you can and can't sell at that location. Check with the zoning department of your city or town — don't simply believe a real estate broker or property owner who says, "No problem!" The goal of that person, after all, is to sell the property.

If you were going to start a veterinary practice, you'd quickly discover that special zoning is required to use a piece of real estate for a vet's office. Convincing a local zoning board to allow a new location such special zoning is quite difficult, if not impossible, in some areas. With some businesses, other licences and filings with local, provincial, or even the federal government are required.

If you enter an industry you're relatively new to, ask questions and open your ears to start finding out more about the location and function of your business. Speak to people who are currently in the field and your local Chamber of Commerce or Board of Trade to see what, if any, licences or filings you must complete. Also, check out your local bookstore. If running a plumbing business interests you, read books on the subject. Also, check the newsstand and local library for trade magazines that may deal with your questions. Libraries have books and online services that can help you locate specific articles on topics that interest you.

Delivering your service or product

Every business has a product or service to sell. How are you going to provide this product or service? Suppose you want to start a business that delivers groceries and runs errands for busy people or older and disabled people who can't easily perform daily tasks for themselves.

Delineate the steps you'll take to provide the service. When potential customers call you to inquire about your business, what kinds of information do you want to record about their situation? Create a pricing sheet and other marketing literature (discussed in the next section) that you can mail curious customers.

After someone calls and says "I want to hire you," you need to collect more details. Try drawing up an information sheet that prompts you for the information you need (for example, address, promised delivery time, desired items, and so on).

If you want to be a tax preparer, you need forms or a filing system to give your customers to help them organize the information they give you. The point of these examples is to map out in advance a system that you can work with. Your system will evolve over time — you can be guaranteed of that — but a tentative game plan has great value.

If you want to manufacture a product, you definitely need to scope out the process you're going to use. Otherwise, you have no idea how much time the manufacturing process may take or what the process may cost.

As your business grows and you hire employees to provide services or create your products, the more you codify what you do and the better your employees can replicate your good work.

Marketing your service or product

After you get more in-depth information about your company's services or products, you need to find more specific information about the following:

- **How much will you charge for your services and products?** Look at what competing products and services cost. Also, estimating your costs helps you figure out what you need to charge to cover your costs and make a reasonable profit.

- **How will you promote and advertise?** Having a great product or service isn't enough if you keep it a secret — you gotta get the word out. And you're unlikely to have the budget or even the desire to reach the same region that television and radio reach.

Start marketing your product to people you know. Develop a punchy, informational one-page letter that announces your company's inception and the products or services it offers, and mail it to your contacts. Include an envelope with a reply form that allows recipients to provide the addresses of others who may be interested in what you have to offer. Send these folks a mailing as well, referencing who passed their name along to you.

Finding and retaining customers is vital to any business that wants to grow and keep its costs in line. One simple, inexpensive way to stay in touch with customers you've dealt with or others who've made inquiries and expressed interest in your company's offerings is via a mailing list. Once a quarter, once a year, or whatever makes sense for your business, send out a simple, professional-looking postcard or newsletter announcing new information about your business and what customer needs you can fulfill. Such mailings also allow you to remind people that you're still in business and that you provide a wonderful product or service. Computer software gives you a fast, efficient way to keep a customer mailing list up to date and to print mailing labels.

E-mailing this information has the attraction of no out-of-pocket expenses. However, due to the deluge of junk e-mail most people get, your e-mail is likely to be deleted with other spam e-mail without being opened. At least a snail-mailed postcard will get prospective customers' attention, even if only for a brief period.

✔ **How will you position your product and services against the competition?** Remember the local pet supply store example that we mention earlier in this chapter? It positions itself as a convenient store equipped with a broad selection and knowledgeable customer assistance. Books similarly position themselves in the book marketplace. We hope, in your mind, that our financial books are down-to-earth, practical, answer-oriented, and educational.

✔ **Where will you sell your product or service?** Business consultants label this decision the *distribution channel* question. For example, if you're going to go into the hula hoop manufacturing business, you may consider selling via mail order and the Internet, through toy stores, or through discount warehouse stores. Selling through each of these different distribution channels requires unique marketing and advertising programs. If you market a product or service to companies, you need to find out who the key decision makers are at the company and what will convince them to buy your product or service.

Organizing and staffing your business

Many small businesses are one-person operations. So much the better for you — you have none of the headaches of hiring, payroll, and so on. You only have to worry about you — and that may be a handful in itself!

But if you want to manage the work being done instead of doing all the work yourself, and if you hope to grow your business, you'll eventually want to hire people. (We explain the best way to fill your personnel needs in Chapter 14.) If hiring is your goal, give some thought now to the skills and functional areas of expertise that future hires need. If you want to raise money, the employment section of your business plan is essential to show your investors that you're planning long term.

Maybe you'll want an administrative assistant, researcher, marketing person, or sales representative. What about a training specialist, finance person, or real estate person if your company expands to many sites? Consider the background you're looking for in those you hire, and look at the types of people that similar companies select and hire.

You should also consider what legal form of organization — for example, a sole proprietorship, partnership, incorporated business, and so on — your business will adopt. We address this topic in Chapter 14.

Projecting finances

An idea often becomes a bad idea or a business failure if you neglect to consider or are unrealistic about the financial side of the business you want to start. If you're a creative or people-person type who hates numbers, the financial side may be the part of the business plan you most want to avoid. Don't — doing so can cost you perhaps tens of thousands of dollars in avoidable mistakes. Ignoring the financial side can even lead to the bankruptcy of a business founded with a good idea.

Before you launch your business, you should do enough research so that you can come up with some decent financial estimates to address these issues. Financial projections are mandatory, and knowledgeable investors will scrutinize them if you seek outside money. You also need to think through how and when investors can cash out.

Start-up and development costs

Spending money to get your business from the idea stage to an operating enterprise is inevitable. Before the revenue begins to flow in, you'll incur expenditures to develop and market your products and services. Therefore, you need to understand what you must spend money on and the approximate timing of the needed purchases.

If you were going to build a house, you'd develop a list of all the required costs. How much are the land, construction, carpeting, landscaping, and so on, going to cost? You can try to develop all these cost estimates yourself, or you can speak with local builders and have them help you. Likewise, you can hire a business consultant who knows something about your type of business. But we think you're best served by doing the homework yourself — you discover a lot more, and it's cheaper.

If you're going to work in an office setting, at home or in an outside space, you need furniture (a desk, chair, filing cabinets, and so on), a computer, a printer, and other office supplies. Don't forget to factor in the costs of any licences or government registrations you may need.

If you run a retailing operation, you need to estimate your initial inventory costs. Remember, selling your inventory takes time, especially when you first start up. And as a new business, suppliers won't give you months on end to pay for your initial inventory. Be realistic — otherwise the money you tie up in inventory can send you to financial ruin.

Income statement

Preparing an estimated *income statement* that summarizes your expected revenue and expenses is a challenging and important part of your business plan. (We explain the elements of an income statement in Chapter 6.) Preparing an income statement is difficult because of all the estimates and assumptions that go into it. As you prepare your estimated income statement, you may discover that making a decent profit is tougher than you thought. This section of your business plan helps you make pricing decisions.

Consider the Vet on Wheels business idea that we discuss in the "Identifying your business concept" section earlier in this chapter. What range of veterinary services can you provide if you make house calls? You can't perform all the services that you can in a larger office setting. What equipment do you need to perform the services? How much should you charge for the services? You need to estimate all these things to develop a worthwhile income statement. You should be able to answer these questions from the information and insights you pulled together regarding what customers want and what your competitors are offering.

With service businesses in which you or your employees sell your time, be realistic about how many hours you can bill. You may end up being able to bill only a third to half of your time, given the other management activities you need to perform.

Because building a customer base takes several years, try to prepare estimated income statements for the first three years. In the earlier years, you have more start-up costs. In later years, you reap more profits as your customer rolls expand. Doing income statements over several years is also essential if you're seeking investor money.

Balance sheet

An income statement measures the profitability of a business over a span of time, such as a year, but it tells you nothing of a business's resources and obligations. That's what a *balance sheet* does. Just as your personal balance sheet itemizes your personal assets (for example, investments) and liabilities (debts you owe), a business balance sheet details a company's assets and liabilities.

If you operate a cash business — for example, you provide a service and are paid for that service, and you don't hold an inventory — a balance sheet has limited use. An exception is if you're trying to get a bank loan for your service business.

A complete balance sheet isn't as important as tracking the available cash, which will be under pressure in the early years of a business because expenses can continue to exceed revenue for quite some time.

A complete balance sheet is useful for a business that owns significant equipment, furniture, inventory, and so on. The asset side of the balance sheet provides insight into the financial staying power of the company. For example, how much cash does your business have on hand to meet expected short-term bills? Conversely, the liability side of the ledger indicates the obligations, bills, and debts the company has coming due in the short and long term.

See Chapter 6 for more information on all the elements of a balance sheet.

Writing an executive summary

An *executive summary* is a two- to three-page summary of your entire business plan that you can share with interested investors who may not want to wade through a 40- to 50-page plan. The executive summary whets the prospective investor's appetite by touching on the highlights of your entire plan. Because this summary should go at the front of your plan document, you may find it odd that we list this element last. We have a reason for doing so: You're not going to be able to write an intelligent summary until you flesh out the body of your business plan.

Chapter 14

Running Your Small Business

*A*fter you research and evaluate the needs of your business, at some point you need to decide whether to actually start your business. In reference to his business plan, Alex Popov — founder of Smart Alec's, a healthy fast-food restaurant — says, ". . . something just clicked one day, and I said to myself, 'Yes, this is a business that is viable and appropriate now.'"

Most entrepreneurs experience this sudden realization, including the two of us — we've experienced it with every business we've ever started. If you really want to, you can conduct and analyze market research and crunch numbers until the cows come home. Even if you're a linear, logical, analytic, quantitative kind of person, you need to make a gut-level decision in the final analysis: Do you want to jump in the water and start swimming, or do you want to stay on the sidelines and remain a spectator? In our opinion, watching isn't nearly as fun as doing. If you feel ready but have some trepidation, you're normal — just go for it!

Starting Up: Your Preflight Check List

When you decide to launch yourself into the world of small business ownership, you also need to ponder and make some decisions about a number of important issues. Just like a pilot before he or she launches an airplane into flight, you need to make sure that all systems are in order and ready to do the job. If your fuel tanks aren't adequately filled, your engines clean and in working order, and your wing flaps in the proper position, you may never get your business off the ground.

Preparing to leave your job

The two top reasons why wannabe entrepreneurs remain wannabe entrepreneurs are psychological and financial. You may never discover that you have the talent to run your own business, and perhaps a good idea to boot, unless you prepare yourself fiscally and emotionally to leave your job. Money and mind issues cause many aspiring entrepreneurs to remain their employers' indentured servants and cause those who do break free to soon return to their bondage.

The money side of this self-exploration is easier to deal with than your mind, so we'll start with that. A net reduction in the income you bring home from your work — at least in the early years of your business — is a foregone conclusion for the vast majority of small-business opportunities you may pursue. Accept this fact and plan accordingly.

Do all that you can to reduce your expenses to a level that fits the entrepreneurial life you want to lead. You must examine your monthly spending patterns now to make your budget lean, mean, and entrepreneurially friendly. Determine what you spend each month on your rent (or mortgage), groceries, eating out, telephone calls, insurance, and so on. Unless you're one of those organized computer geeks — someone who keeps all this data detailed in a software package — you need to whip out your chequebook register, ABM receipts, credit card statements, and anything else that documents your spending habits. Don't forget to estimate your cash purchases that don't leave a trail, like when you eat lunch out or drop a $20 bill on gas and a Tim Hortons double-double.

Don't tell us that everything you spend your money on is a necessity and that you can't cut anywhere. Question your expenditures! If you don't, continuing to work as an employee will be a necessity, and you'll never be able to pursue your entrepreneurial dream.

Beyond the bare essentials of food, shelter, health care, and clothing, most of what you spend money on is discretionary — that is, you spend money on luxuries. Even the amount you spend on the necessities, such as food and shelter, is part necessity and a fair amount of luxury and waste. If you need a helping hand and an analyst's eye in preparing and developing strategies for reducing your spending, pick up a copy of the latest edition of our book *Personal Finance For Canadians For Dummies* (published by John Wiley & Sons Canada, Ltd.).

Reduce your expenses to the level they were at when you lived at home or when you were a university student — remember those enjoyable days? Spending more doesn't make you happy; you'll be miserable over the years if your excess spending makes you feel chained to a job you don't like. Life is too short to spend most of it working at a full-time job that makes you unhappy.

If reducing your spending is the most important financial move you can make before and during the period in which you start your business, the second-best thing you can do is to spend some time figuring how you'll manage the income side of your personal finances. Here are some good strategies to ensure that you'll earn enough income to live on:

- ✔ **Transition gradually.** One way to pursue your entrepreneurial dreams (and not starve while doing so) is to continue working part time in a regular job while you work part time at your own business. If you have a job that allows you to work part time, seize the opportunity. Some employers may even allow you to maintain your benefits.

  In addition to ensuring a steady source of income, splitting your time allows you to adjust to a completely new way of making a living. Some people have a hard time adjusting to their new lifestyle if they quit their job cold turkey and immediately plunge headfirst into full-time entrepreneurship.

  Another option is to completely leave your job but line up a chunk of work that provides a decent income for at least some of your weekly work hours. Consulting for your old employer is a time-tested first "entrepreneurial" option with low risk.

- ✔ **Get/stay married.** Actually, as long as you're attached to someone who maintains a regular job and you manage your spending so that you can live on that person's income alone, you're golden! Just make sure to talk things through with the love of your life to minimize misunderstandings and resentments. Maybe someday you can return the favour — that's what Eric and his wife did. She was working in education (no big bucks there!) when he started an entrepreneurial venture after business school. They lived a Spartan lifestyle and made do just fine on her income. Several years later, when things were going swimmingly for Eric, she left her job to work on her own business.

Valuing and replacing your benefits

One of the money dilemmas you may encounter is the loss of benefits your employer provides. For many people, walking away from these benefits is both financially and psychologically challenging. Benefits are valuable, but you may be surprised how quickly you can replicate them in your own business.

Health insurance

Some prospective entrepreneurs fret over finding new health insurance. But unless you have a significant existing medical problem (known in the insurance business as a *pre-existing condition*), getting health insurance as an individual isn't difficult.

The first option to explore is whether your existing coverage through your employer's group plan can be converted into individual coverage. If it can be, great, just don't act on this option until you've explored other extended health plans on your own, which may offer similar benefits at lower cost. Also, get proposals for individual coverage from Blue Cross, Liberty Health, Ingle Health, and other major health plan offerers in your area. Investigate joining your local Chamber of Commerce or Board of Trade, which often offer insurance plans to their members. Take a high deductible, if available, to keep costs down.

Long-term disability insurance

For most people, their greatest asset is their ability to earn money. If you suffer a disability and can't work, how would you manage financially? Long-term disability insurance protects your income in the event of a disability.

Before you leave your job, secure an individual long-term disability policy. After you leave your job and are no longer earning steady income, you won't qualify for a policy. Most insurers want to see at least six months of self-employment income before they'll write you a policy. If you become disabled during this time, you're uninsured and out of luck — that's a big risk to take!

Check with any professional associations you belong to or could join to see whether they offer long-term disability plans. As with many employer-based programs, association plans are sometimes less expensive because of the group's purchasing power.

Life insurance

If you have dependents who count on your income, you need life insurance. And, unlike disability insurance, in the vast majority of cases you can purchase a life insurance policy at a lower cost than the additional coverage you could get through your employer.

Retirement plans

If your employer offers a retirement savings program, such as a pension plan or a deferred profit sharing plan, don't despair about not having these in the future. (Of course, what you've already earned and accumulated while employed is yours as long as you've been in the plan the required amount of time to own the benefits, known as *vesting*.) When you're self-employed you can continue — or start — putting away money into an RRSP. As long as you earn a profit from your enterprise, you'll be able to take advantage of RRSPs, which allow you to sock away a hefty chunk of your earnings on a tax-deductible basis.

Other benefits

Yes, employers offer other benefits that you may value. For example, you *seem* to get paid holidays and vacations. In reality though, your employer simply spreads your salary over all 52 weeks of a year, thus paying you for actually working the other 47 weeks or so out of the year. You can do the same by building the cost of this paid time off into your product and service pricing.

Another "benefit" of working for an employer is that it pays for half of your Canada Pension Plan contributions. When you're self-employed, you must pay the entire amount yourself. However, Canada Revenue Agency allows you a deduction for half of the amount — which, along with the resulting provincial credit and depending on your marginal tax rate, reduces your taxes by anywhere from 24 to 45 percent of the deduction, so the tax isn't as painful as you think. As with vacations and holidays, you can build the cost of this tax into your product and service pricing. Just think: Your employer could pay you a higher salary if it wasn't paying CPP on your behalf.

Some employers offer other insurance plans, such as dental or vision care plans. Typically, these plans cover small out-of-pocket expenditures that aren't worth insuring for. Don't waste your money purchasing such limited policies, especially when you're self-employed. If you want this sort of coverage, look for a plan that includes it as part of a wider range of health coverage. Whether you're self-employed or incorporated, the premiums for health and dental insurance are generally deductible.

Financing Your Business

When you create your business plan (which we explain how to do in Chapter 13), you should estimate your start-up and development costs. You can start many worthwhile small businesses with little capital. The following sections explain methods for financing your business.

Bootstrapping

Making do with a small amount of capital and spending it as you can afford to is known as *bootstrapping*. Bootstrapping is just a fancy way of saying that a business lives within its means. This forces a business to be resourceful and less wasteful. Bootstrapping is also a great training mechanism for producing cost-effective products and services. It offers you the advantage of getting into business in the first place with little capital.

Millions of successful small companies were bootstrapped at one time or another. Like small redwood saplings that grow into towering trees, small companies that had to bootstrap in the past can eventually grow into hundred-million and even multibillion-dollar companies. For example, Ross Perot started EDS with a mere $1,000, and Hewlett-Packard's founders started their company out of a garage in Palo Alto, California. Motorola, Sony, and Disney were all bootstrapped, too.

Whether you want to maintain a small shop that employs just yourself, hire a few employees, or build the next Canadian Tire, you need capital. However, misconceptions abound about how much money a company needs to achieve its goals and sources of funding.

"There's an illusion that most companies need tons of money to get established and grow," says James Collins, former lecturer at the Stanford Graduate School of Business and co-author of the best sellers *Built to Last* and *Good to Great: Why Some Companies Make the Leap . . . and Others Don't*. "The Silicon Valley success stories of companies that raise gobs of venture capital and grow 4,000 percent are very rare. They are statistically insignificant but catch all sorts of attention," he adds.

Studies show that the vast majority of small businesses obtain their initial capital from personal savings and family and friends rather than outside sources such as banks and venture capital firms. A Harvard Business School study of the *Inc.* 500 (500 large, fast-growing private companies) found that more than 80 percent of them were launched with funds from the founder's personal savings. The median start-up capital was a modest $10,000 — and these are successful, fast-growing companies! Slower-growing companies tend to require even *less* capital.

Even among high-technology firms, which tend to be more capital intensive, 79 percent are initially funded through the founder's personal savings and family and friends, according to a study by Edward B. Roberts, author of *Entrepreneurs in High Technology* (Oxford Press).

With the initial infusion of capital, many small businesses can propel themselves for years after they develop a service or product that brings in more cash flow. Jim Gentes, the founder of Giro, the bike helmet manufacturer, raised just $35,000 from personal savings and loans from family and friends to make and distribute his first product and then used the cash flow for future products.

Eventually, a successful, growing company may want outside financing to expand faster. Raising money from investors or lenders is much easier after you demonstrate that you know what you're doing and that a market exists for your product or service.

As we explain in the "Preparing to leave your job" section earlier in this chapter, aspiring entrepreneurs must examine their personal finances for opportunities to reduce their own spending. If you want to start a company, the best time to examine your finances is years before you want to hit the entrepreneurial path. As with other financial goals, advance preparation can go a long way toward starting a business. The best funding source and easiest investor to please is you.

Alan Tripp, founder and CEO of Score Learning, a chain of storefront interactive learning centres, planned for seven years before he took the entrepreneurial plunge. He funded his first retail centre fully from personal savings. He and his wife lived frugally to save the necessary money — and worked as caretakers for two years in order to save even more money. Tripp's first centre proved the success of his business concept: retail learning centres where kids can use computers to improve their reading, math, and science skills. With a business plan crafted over time and with hard numbers to demonstrate the financial viability of his operation, Tripp successfully raised funds from investors to open many more centres. (His company was ultimately bought out by Kaplan Inc.)

Some small-business founders put the cart before the horse and don't plan and save for starting their business the way Tripp did. And in many cases, small-business owners want capital but don't have a clear plan or need for it.

Borrowing from banks

If you're starting a new business or have been in business for just a few years, borrowing, particularly from banks, may be difficult. Borrowing money is easier when you don't really need to do so. No one knows this fact better than small-business owners.

Small-business owners who successfully obtain bank loans do their homework. To borrow money from a bank, you generally need a business plan, three years of financial statements and tax returns for the business and its owner, and projections for the business. Hunt around for banks that are committed to and understand the small-business marketplace.

The Canada Small Business Financing (CSBF) program guarantees some small-business loans provided by banks, credit unions, and many trust, loan, and insurance companies. Many of these loans would not otherwise granted because of the business's risk and lack of collateral. In addition to guaranteeing loans for existing businesses, the CSBF backs loans to start-ups. The loans, which can go as high as $250,000, can be used to finance the purchase of assets, leasehold improvements, computer acquisitions, and so on, and are available to sole proprietorships, partnerships, and incorporated companies. If you choose a floating-rate loan, the interest rate can't be more than 3 percent above the lender's *prime lending rate*, the rate they charge their lowest-risk corporate borrowers. You can also choose a fixed-rate loan: In this case, the interest rate can't be greater than 3 percent over the lender's residential mortgage rate for a similar term. For more information, call the Small Business Loans Administration branch of Industry Canada at 613-954-5540, or visit their Web site at http://strategis.ic.gc.ca, click on "Financing" under "Strategis Guides," and select "."

Another source of funds is the Business Development Bank of Canada (BDC). For start-ups or companies in their first 12 months of ringing up sales, the BDC offers up to $100,000 in financing. You can take up to six years to repay the loan, and you have the option of seasonal or progressive payments to fit your projected cash flow. For businesses already on their way, the BDC offers working capital loans as well as loans for expanding your existing premises or constructing new facilities. They also provide financing for a range of other undertakings, including product and market research, sales planning, feasibility studies, and developing marketing and distribution plans.

The BDC is also a good place to turn for counselling and consulting services. They offer programs to assist small businesses on a number of fronts, including developing a business plan, strategic planning, human resources, finance, and assessing opportunities for growing your business.

To get more information on BDC's services and how to contact a local office, call 1-888-463-6232. They also have an informative Web site at www.bdc.ca.

In addition to CSBF-backed loans or financing arranged with the BDC, banks, trust companies, and credit unions are often willing to make personal loans to individuals. Borrowing against the equity in your home or other real estate can ease your access to capital, because it acts as security on your loan and allows you to get a lower interest rate.

You can use your RRSP as another potential source of capital. However, any money you take out of your plan will be taxed as income at your full marginal tax rate (the rate you pay on your highest, or last dollar of income in the year). If you do withdraw money from your RRSP, your plan administrator has to retain some of the money to help pay the tax on the withdrawal. This is known as a *withholding tax*. The tax is 10 percent on amounts up to $5,000, 20 percent on withdrawals of between $5,001 and $15,000, and 30 percent on amounts over $15,000. In Quebec, the combined federal and Quebec withholding tax rates are 21, 30, and 35 percent, respectively.

If you do decide to draw on your RRSP savings, you'll increase your cash flow by taking out several smaller chunks rather than one large amount. For instance, if you need to take $9,000 out of your RRSP, instead of taking it out as one lump sum, make two withdrawals, one for $5,000 and one for $4,000.

There are two points to consider before you plunder your retirement plan. First, the withholding tax will often not be enough to cover the total tax bill on your withdrawal. That means the following spring you may need to find extra money in order to pay the outstanding tax on your withdrawal. Far more importantly, taking money out of your plan can be an expensive way to fund your business. For example, say you borrow $20,000 from your RRSP. If you left that money in your plan and it compounded annually by 10 percent, it would grow to almost $135,000 in 20 years' time.

If you've got the itch to get your business going but can't wait to save the necessary money and lack other ways to borrow, the plastic in your wallet may be your ticket to operation. You can acquire many credit cards at interest rates of 10 percent or less. Because credit cards are unsecured loans, if your business fails and you can't pay back your debt, your home equity and assets in retirement accounts aren't at risk.

Credit unions can be another source of financial help. They're often more willing to make personal loans to individuals. Borrowing against the equity in your home or other real estate is also advantageous because loans made with real estate backing up your borrowing generally have the lowest available interest rates.

No matter what type of business you have in mind and how much money you think you need to make it succeed, be patient. Start small enough that you don't need outside capital (unless you're in an unusual situation where your window of opportunity is now, but will close if you don't get funding soon). Starting your business without outside capital instills the discipline required for building a business piece by piece over time. The longer you can wait to get a loan or equity investment, the better the terms will be because the risk is lower for the lender or investor.

Borrowing from family and friends

Because they know you and hopefully like and trust you, your family and friends may seem like a good source of investment money for your small business. They also have the advantage of offering you better terms than a banker, wealthy investor, or a venture capitalist.

But before you solicit and accept money from those you love, consider the pitfalls. First, defaulting on a loan made by a large, anonymous lender if your business hits the skids is one thing, but defaulting on a loan from your dear relatives can make future Thanksgiving meals mighty uncomfortable!

Second, most entrepreneurs receive surprisingly little encouragement from those they're close to. Most parents, for example, will think you've severed some of your cerebral synapses if you announce your intention to quit your job with its lofty job title, decent pay, and benefits. And this lack of emotional support can discourage you far more than the lack of financial support.

From the entrepreneurs we've observed, family investments in a small business work best under the following conditions:

- You prepare and sign a letter of agreement that spells out the terms of the investment or loan as if you were doing business with a banker or some other investor you know for business purposes only. As time goes on, people have selective recall. Putting things in writing reminds everyone what was agreed to.
- You're quite certain that you can repay the loan.
- You can start your business with an equity investment. With an equity investment, a person is willing and able to lose all the money invested but hopes to hit a home run while helping you with your dream.

Courting investors and selling equity

Beyond family members and friends, private individuals with sufficient money — also known as wealthy individuals — are your next best source of capital if you want an equity investor (and not a loan from a lender). Before you approach wealthy people, you must have a good business plan, which we explain how to prepare in Chapter 13.

Although you want such people to care about your business, it's best if their investment in your business is no more than 5 to 10 percent of their total investment portfolio. No one wants to lose money, but doing so is less painful if you diversify well. A $10,000 loan from a millionaire is 1 percent of his portfolio.

Finding people who may be interested in investing isn't difficult, but you need to be persistent and creative. Tax advisers and lawyers you know may have contacts. Networking with successful entrepreneurs in similar fields may produce an investor or two. Also, consider customers or suppliers of your business who like your business and believe in its potential.

Finding your way to wealthy individuals who don't know you may prove fruitful as well. Alex Popov, whom we introduce at the beginning of this chapter, sent hundreds of letters to people who lived in upscale neighbourhoods. The letter, a one-page summary of Alex's investment opportunity, got an astounding 5 percent response from people interested in receiving a business plan. Through this search method, Popov ultimately found one wealthy investor who funded his entire deal.

Determining how much of the business you're selling for the amount invested is not easy. Basically, the equity percentage should hinge on what the whole business is worth (see Chapter 15 for details on how to value a business). If your whole business is worth $500,000 and you're seeking $100,000 from investors, that $100,000 should buy 20 percent of the business.

New businesses are the hardest to value — yet another reason why you're best off trying to raise money after you demonstrate some success. The farther along you are, the lower the risk to an investor and the lower the cost to you (in terms of how much equity you must give up) to raise money.

Deciding Whether to Incorporate

Most businesses operate as sole proprietorships. The term *sole proprietorship* doesn't mean that only one person owns the business, but rather that for legal and tax purposes, your business is not a corporation. If you run a sole proprietorship, you report your business income and costs on your tax return on the Statement of Business Activities (Form T2124). Certain professionals such as doctors, lawyers, and engineers are required to use the Professional Income and Expenses form (T2032). You attach these to your personal income tax return, the T1 General.

Incorporating, which establishes a distinct legal entity under which you do business, takes time and costs money. Therefore, incorporation must offer some benefits. A major reason to consider incorporation is liability protection. Incorporation effectively separates your business from your personal finances, which offers some protection of your personal assets from lawsuits that may arise from your business.

Before you incorporate, ask yourself (and perhaps others in your line of business or advisers — legal, tax, and so on — who work with businesses like yours) what can or may cause someone to sue you. Then see if you can purchase insurance to protect against these potential liabilities. Insurance is superior to incorporation because it pays claims, and people can still sue you even if you're incorporated. If you incorporate and someone successfully sues you, your company must cough up the money for the claim, and doing so may sink your business. Only insurance can cover such financially destructive claims.

People can also sue you if they slip and break a bone or two while on your property. To cover these types of claims, you can purchase a property or premises liability policy from an insurer.

Accountants, doctors, and a number of other professionals can buy liability insurance. A good place to start searching for liability insurance is through the associations for your profession. Even if you're not a current member, check out the associations anyway — you may be able to access the insurance without membership, or you can join the association long enough to sign up. (Associations also sometimes offer competitive rates on disability insurance.)

Because corporations are legal entities distinct from their owners, they offer other features that a proprietorship or partnership doesn't. For example, corporations can have shareholders who own a piece or percentage of the company. These shares can be sold or transferred to other owners, subject to any restrictions in the shareholder's agreement. Corporations also offer *continuity of life*, which simply means that they can continue to exist despite an owner's death or the owner's transfer of his or her stock in the company.

Don't waste your money incorporating if you simply want to maintain a corporate-sounding name. If you operate as a sole proprietor, you can choose to operate under a different business name ("doing business as," or d.b.a.) without the cost and hassles of incorporating.

Paying corporate taxes

Aside from the different tax treatment of insurance and other benefits, the government taxes a corporation's profits differently from those realized in a sole proprietorship. Starting in 2004, the general federal corporate tax rate is 22 percent. In addition, corporations pay provincial tax of around 13 percent.

If you meet certain requirements as a small business, the tax rates are a good deal lower. To qualify, your business must be deemed a *Canadian-controlled private corporation*, meaning it is resident in Canada and not controlled by non-residents and/or public corporations. If you meet the criteria, for 2004 the federal tax rate is 13 percent on the first $250,000 of income. (In 2003 the amount of income that was taxed at the lower rate was $225,000. For 2005 it rises to $275,000, and for 2006, $300,000.) Except for Quebec, the provinces also have reduced small-business tax rates for the first few hundred thousand dollars of income.

Whether incorporating makes sense depends on your situation. Suppose your business performs well and makes lots of money. If it isn't incorporated, the government taxes all profits from your business on your personal tax return in the year that your company earns those profits. If you intend to use these profits to reinvest in your business and expand, incorporating can potentially save you some tax dollars.

Resist the short-term temptation to incorporate just so that you can have money left in the corporation taxed at a lower rate. If you want to pay yourself the profits in the future, you can end up paying more taxes. Why? Because you first pay taxes at the corporate tax rate in the year that your company earns the money, and then you pay taxes again on your personal income tax return when the corporation pays you.

Another reason not to incorporate, especially in the early months of a business, is that you can't immediately claim the losses for an incorporated business on your personal tax return. Because most businesses produce little revenue in their early years and have all sorts of start-up expenditures, losses are common.

Making the decision

If you're totally confused about whether to incorporate because your business is undergoing major financial changes, it's worth getting competent professional help. The hard part is knowing where to turn, because finding one adviser who can put all the pieces of the puzzle (financial, legal, and taxes) together is challenging. Also be aware that you may get wrong or biased advice.

Lawyers who specialize in advising small businesses can help explain the legal issues. Tax advisers who perform a lot of work with business owners can help explain the tax considerations. Although most lawyers and tax advisers don't understand the business side of business, try to find one who does, or you may also need a business adviser.

If you've weighed the factors and you still can't decide, our advice is to keep your business simple — don't incorporate. Why? Because, after you incorporate, unincorporating takes time and money. Start your business off as a sole proprietorship and take it from there. Wait until the benefits of incorporating your business clearly outweigh the costs and drawbacks.

Finding and Keeping Customers

When you write your business plan (see Chapter 13), you need to think about your business's customers. Just as the sun is the centre of our solar system, everything in your business revolves around your customers. If you take care of your customers, they'll take care of you and your business for many years.

The first thing we recommend doing is putting together a mailing list of people you know who may be interested in what you're offering. Draft and mail an upbeat, one-page letter that provides an overview of what your business offers. As you have news — successes to report, new products and services, and so on — do another mailing. Your letter doesn't need to be a colour, multi-page newsletter-type thing, although you can do those if your budget and desire allow. A short letter gets read more than something that looks like another glossy, advertorial or multi-page newsletter. Most people are busy and don't care about your business enough to read something lengthy.

In addition to mailings, other successful ways to get the word out and attract customers are limited only to your imagination and resourcefulness. Consider the following ideas:

✔ If your business idea is indeed innovative or somehow different, or if you have grand expansion plans, add some local media people to your mailing list and send them the one-page updates on your business, too. Newspaper, radio, and even television business reporters are always looking for story ideas. Just remember to make your press releases informational and not an advertisement.

✔ If your business seeks customers in a specific geographic area, blanket that area by mailing your one-page letter or delivering it door to door. You can include a coupon that offers your products or services at a reduced cost (perhaps at your cost) to get people to try them. Make sure people know that this is a special opening-for-business bargain.

After you attract customers, don't treat them as if business is a one-night stand. Treat your customers as you'd like to be treated by a business. If customers like your products and services, they not only come back to buy more when the need arises but they also tell others. Satisfied customers are every business's best cost-effective marketers.

Although good customer service is just good common sense, we never cease to be amazed by how many businesses have mediocre or poor customer service. One reason for poor service is that, as your business grows, your employees are on the customer service front lines. If you don't hire good people and give them the proper incentives to service customers, many of them won't do it. For most employees on a salary, the day-to-day servicing of customers may be just an annoyance. The Internet is also responsible for a great drop in service by many companies. It's often much cheaper and more efficient for companies to direct you to their Web site than to have a real live human being answer the phone and help answer your questions or direct you to the resources you're looking for. But like us, you've probably learned that most Web sites are poorly designed, difficult to navigate, and can eat up loads of time before you find what you're looking for . . . if you find it at all.

One way to make your staff care about customer service is to base part of their pay on the satisfaction of the customers they work with. Tie bonuses and increases at review time to this issue. You can easily measure customer satisfaction with a simple survey form.

Think about your own experiences with poor customer service. For example, not having a green thumb, Eric hired a gardening company to install a garden. The company did a decent job in the early days of the project and expressed interest in providing ongoing maintenance. Within days of the garden installation, some problems (minor from his perspective) surfaced. A large jasmine vine that had survived for more than a year under his care started to die a few days after the new garden was installed. One worker thought that the vine could be dying because some roots were inadvertently cut during installation, but no one ever came out to look at the vine or suggest what to do. A number of plants were poorly placed and quickly encroached onto the lawn. Again and again he asked someone to come out and take a look, but no one did.

Unfortunately, Eric figured out that because he had already paid for the job, the company wasn't interested in addressing the problems. Even though the company's workers did a good job with the project overall, the lack of follow-up left a bad taste in his mouth and caused him to not recommend the company.

Treating the customer right starts the moment that the selling process begins. Honesty is an often underused business tool. More than a few salespeople mislead and lie in order to close a sale. Many customers discover after their purchase that they've been deceived, and they get angry. These unethical businesses not only likely lose future business from customers but also surely — and justifiably — lose referrals.

If your business doesn't perform well for a customer, apologize and bend over backward to make the customer happy. Offer a discount on the problem purchase or, if possible, a refund on product purchases. Also, make sure that you have a clear return-and-refund policy. Bend that policy if doing so helps you satisfy an unhappy customer or rids you of a difficult customer.

Setting Up Shop

No matter what type of business you have in mind, you'll need space to work from, whether it's your bedroom, a spare room in your home, or a small factory. You also need to outfit that space with the tools of your trade. This section explains how to tackle these tasks.

Finding business space and negotiating a lease

Unless you can run your business from your home, you may be in the market for office or retail space. Finding good space and buying or leasing it take tons of time if you do it right.

In the early months and years of your business, buying an office or a retail building generally doesn't make sense. The down payment consumes important capital, and you may end up spending lots of time and money on a real estate transaction for a location that may not interest you in the long term. Buying this type of real estate rarely makes sense unless you plan to stay put for five or more years.

Leasing a space for your business is far more likely. Renting office space is simpler than renting retail space because a building owner worries less about your business and its financial health. Your business needs more credibility to rent retail because your retail business affects the nature of the strip mall or shopping centre where you lease. Owners of such properties don't want quick failures or someone who does a poor job of running his business.

Because renting retail space is harder, if you and your business don't have a track record with renting space, getting references is useful. If you seek well-located retail space, you must compete with chains like Starbucks, so you'd better have an A+ credit rating and track record. Consider subletting — circulate flyers to businesses that may have some extra space in the area where you want to locate your business. Also prepare financial statements that show your creditworthiness (personally and in business).

Brokers list most spaces for lease. Working with a broker can be useful, but the same conflicts exist as with residential brokers (see Chapter 12). You should also examine spaces for lease without a broker, where you deal with the landlord directly. Such landlords may give you a better deal, and they don't worry about recouping a brokerage commission.

The biggest headaches with leasing space are understanding and negotiating the lease contract. Odds are good that the lessor presents you with a standard, pre-printed lease contract that he or she says is fair and the same lease that everyone else signs. Don't sign it! This contract is the lessor's first offer — have an expert review it and help you modify it. Find yourself a lawyer who regularly deals with such contracts.

Office leases are usually simpler than retail leases — they can be full service, which includes janitorial benefits. Retail leases, however, are *triple-net,* which means that you as the tenant pay for maintenance (for example, resurfacing the parking lot, cleaning, and gardening), utilities, and property taxes. You're correct to worry about a triple-net retail lease, because you can't control many of these expenses. If the property is sold, property taxes can also jump. Your lease contract needs to include a cap for the triple-net costs at a specified limit per square foot. Also compare your site's costs with other sites to evaluate the deal that the lessor offers you.

Try to exclude from the lease contract removal costs for any toxic waste you may discover during your occupation. Also exclude increased property taxes that the sale of the property may cause. If feasible, get your landlord to pay for remodelling — it's cheaper for the landlord to do it and means fewer hassles for you. With retail leases, get an option for renewal — this is critical in retail, where location is important. The option should specify the cost — for example, something like 5 percent below market, as determined by arbitration. Also get an option whereby the lease can be transferred to a new owner if you sell the business.

If you really think you want to purchase (not lease) because you can see yourself staying in the same place for at least five years, read Chapter 11.

Should you work from home?

You may be able to run a relatively simple small business from your home. If you have the choice of running your business out of your home versus securing outside office space, consider the following issues:

✔ **Cost control.** As we discuss earlier in the chapter, bootstrapping your business can make a lot of financial and business sense. If you have space in your home that you can use, then you've found yourself a rent-free business space. (If you consider buying a larger home to have more space, then you can't really say that your home office is rent free.)

✔ **Business issues.** What are the needs of your business and customers? If you don't require fancy office space to impress others or to meet with clients, work at home. If you operate a retail business that requires lots of customers coming to you, getting outside space is probably the best (and legally correct) choice. Check with the governing authorities of your town or city to find out what local regulations exist for home-based businesses.

✔ **Discipline.** At home, do you have the discipline to work the number of hours that you need and want, or will the kitchen goodies tempt you to make half a dozen snack trips? Can you refrain from turning on the television every hour for late-breaking news? The sometimes amorphous challenge of figuring out how to grow the business may cause you to focus your energies elsewhere.

✔ **Family matters.** Last, but not least, your home life should factor into where you decide to work. If you're single and living alone, home life is less of an issue. One advantage to working at home when you have children is that you can be a more involved parent. If nothing else, the one to two hours per day that many people spend commuting can be time spent with your kids! Just make sure to set aside work hours during which your office is off limits.

Ask other family members how they feel about your working at home. Be specific about what you plan to do, and where, when, and how. Will clients come over? What time of day and where in the home will you meet with them? You may not think that your home office is an imposition, but your spouse may. Home business problems come between many couples.

Equipping your business space

You can easily go overboard spending money when you're leasing or buying office space and outfitting that space. The most common reason why small-business owners spend more than they should is the attempt to project a professional, upscale image. You can have an office or retail location that works for you and your customers without spending a fortune if you observe some simple rules:

- ✔ **Buy — don't lease or finance — equipment.** Unless you're running a manufacturing outfit where the cost of buying equipment outright is prohibitive, try to avoid borrowing and leasing. If you can't buy office furniture, computers, cash registers, and so on with cash, then you probably can't afford them! Buying such things on credit or leasing them — leasing is invariably the most expensive way to go — encourages you to spend beyond your means.

- ✔ **Consider buying used equipment, especially furniture, that takes longer to become obsolete.** The more other businesses use a piece of equipment, the more beneficial it is for you to purchase rather than lease: Many other businesses using the equipment should make it easier for you to unload it if you want to sell it down the road. Leasing may make more sense with oddball-type equipment that's more of a hassle and costly for you to unload after a short usage period.

- ✔ **Don't get carried away with technological and marketing gadgets.** We know it's hard to imagine, but the business world worked just fine (and in some respects better) before faxes, e-mail, and the growth of the Internet. Many small-business owners we speak with spend all sorts of money on such things because they feel the need to be "competitive" and "current." Think of a Web site as buying an expensive online Yellow Pages ad, because that's what it often is for most businesses.

- ✔ **Voice mail is one device that many small-business owners find worth spending money on.** Voice mail sounds more professional than an answering machine and can handle simultaneous calls with ease. Best of all, voice mail can save you money on administrative help.

Bootstrap-equipping your office makes sense within certain limits (see "Bootstrapping" earlier in this chapter). If customers come to you, of course, you don't want a shabby-looking store or office. But that doesn't mean you have to purchase the Rolls-Royce equivalent of everything you need for your office. For example, neither of us bought a fax machine until several years after we'd started our businesses — and we both wish we had waited even longer, because their presence encourages people we work with to procrastinate sending us things!

Accounting for the Money

One of the less glamorous aspects of running your own business is dealing with accounting. Unlike when you work for an employer, you must track your business's income, expenses, and taxes (for you *and* your employees). Even if you can afford to hire others to help with these dreary tasks, you must know the inner workings of your business to maintain control over it, to stay out of trouble with the tax authorities, and to minimize your taxes. The following sections show you how to handle the accounting aspect of your business.

Tax record keeping and payments

With revenue hopefully flowing in and expenses surely heading out, you must keep records to help satisfy your tax obligations and to keep a handle on the financial status and success of your business. You can't accurately complete the necessary tax forms if you don't properly track your income and expenses. And, should the Canada Revenue Agency audit you — the likelihood of which is about four times higher as a small-business owner than as an employee at a company — you'll need to prove some or even all your expenses and income.

In order to keep your sanity, and keep the tax collectors at bay, make sure you do the following:

✔ **Pay your taxes each quarter and on time.** When you're self-employed, you're responsible for the accurate and timely filing of all taxes that you owe on your income on a quarterly basis. You must pay taxes by the 15th of March, June, September, and December (unless the 15th falls on the weekend, in which case the payment is due the Monday that follows the 15th). To pay correctly, call the Canada Revenue Agency — you'll find the number for your local office in the blue pages of your telephone book — and ask for Form T1033-WS (Instalment Payment Calculation Worksheet). This form includes an easy-to-use estimated tax worksheet to help you calculate your quarterly tax payments. Mark the due dates for your quarterly taxes on your calendar so that you don't forget!

If you have employees, you need to withhold taxes from each pay cheque they receive. You must use the money that you deduct from their pay cheques to make timely payments to the Canada Revenue Agency. In addition to income tax, you need to withhold and send in Canada Pension Plan (or Quebec Pension Plan) and Employment Insurance premiums. Pay these premiums immediately and *never* use the money to fund your business needs. We recommend using a payroll service to make sure your payments are made on time and correctly to all the different places these tax filings need to go.

✔ **Keep your business accounts separate from your personal accounts.**
The Canada Revenue Agency knows that small-business owners, as a
group, cheat more on their tax returns than do company employees.
One way that dishonest entrepreneurs cheat is by hiding business
income and inflating business expenses. Thus, the Canada Revenue
Agency looks with a jaundiced eye at business owners who use and
commingle funds in personal chequing and credit card accounts for
business transactions.

Although you may find opening and maintaining separate business
accounts troublesome, do so. And remember to pay for only legitimate
business expenses through your business account. You'll be thankful
come tax preparation time to have separate records. Having separate
records can also make the Canada Revenue Agency easier to deal with if
and when you're audited.

✔ **Keep good records of your business income and expenses.** You can use
file folders, software, or a shoebox to collect your business income and
expenses — all that matters is that you do it! When you need to file your
annual return, you want to be able to find the documentation that allows
you to figure your business income and expenses. For most people, the
file folder system works best. If your business is small, one folder for
income and one for your expenses will do. Computer software can help
you with this drudgery as well. Because you must go through the hassle
of entering the data, software is more useful with larger small businesses
and in those businesses that process lots of cheques or expenses.

Charging expenses on a credit card or writing a cheque can make the
documentation for most businesses easier. These methods of payment
leave a paper trail that simplifies the task of tallying up your expenses
come tax time and makes the Canada Revenue Agency auditor less
grumpy in the event that he or she audits you. (Just make sure that you
don't overspend, as many people do with credit cards!)

How to (legally) pay lower taxes

Every small business must spend money, and spending money in your
business holds the allure of lowering your tax bill. But don't spend money on
your business just for the sake of generating tax deductions. Spend your
money to make the most of the tax breaks that you can legally take. The
following are some examples of legal tax breaks:

✔ **Appreciate depreciation.** If you purchase furniture, computers, and other
equipment — called *capital assets* — you can't simply deduct the price as
a business expense. Instead, you spread the cost over a number of years.
You're allowed annual deductions for the decreasing value — the wear
and tear — on the equipment purchases (for example, computers, desks,
chairs — even that funky espresso machine) you use in your business.
The income tax system refers to this as *capital cost allowance*, or *CCA*.

Normally, equipment for your business is *depreciated* over a number of years. With depreciation, you claim a yearly tax deduction for a portion of the total purchase price of the equipment. Different types of equipment are grouped into different CCA classes, which have different allowable rates of depreciation. For instance, computer hardware can be depreciated at 30 percent annually, while furniture can be depreciated at 20 percent annually. Each year, your maximum deduction is equal to the allowable depreciation, or *CCA rate*, times the remaining undepreciated value of the assets. In addition, in the year you purchase an asset, you can claim a deduction of only one-half of the regular CCA.

For example, say you buy a new desk and chair for $4,000. Furniture can be depreciated at 20 percent, so you'd normally get a deduction for $800. However, in the first year, you can claim only half that, or $400. The next year you can claim a deduction worth 20 percent of the remaining undepreciated value of $3,600 ($4,000 – $400), worth $720.

You're not required to claim the maximum allowable CCA each year. The undepreciated amount simply gets carried ahead to the next year. This can be a profitable strategy. Consider that in the early years of most businesses, profits are low. When your business is in a low tax bracket, the value of your deductions is low. If your business grows, you may come out ahead if you don't claim some or all of the allowable deduction for some of your early-year big-ticket purchases, instead postponing claiming the expenses until your income — and therefore your marginal tax rate — is higher.

✔ **Make the most of your auto deductions.** If you use your car for business, you can claim a deduction for a portion of the expenses, usually based on the kilometres you drive for business compared with the overall kilometres you put on your vehicle. You can also claim a deduction for the depreciation (capital cost allowance), again using the same percentage. However, Canada Revenue Agency puts a ceiling on the purchase cost you can use when doing your calculations. The maximum price you can use for calculating your CCA is $26,000 for cars bought in 1998 or 1999, $27,000 for cars bought in 2000, and $30,000 for cars bought in 2001 through 2003. If you borrow money to purchase a vehicle, the maximum interest expense allowed before you calculate your business portion is $300 a month. For cars bought in 1997 through 2000, the limit is $250.

✔ **Deduct travel, meal, and entertainment expenses.** For Canada Revenue Agency to consider your expenses deductible, your travel and other related expenses must be for a bona fide business purpose. There are also certain restrictions you need to be aware of. For instance, say you live in Winnipeg and fly to Honolulu for a week for a convention. You spend three days at a seminar for business purposes, and then the other four days snorkelling and getting skin cancer on Waikiki Beach. You can deduct the expenses for only the three days of your trip that you devoted to business. In most cases, however, you can deduct the full cost of getting there and back. Note that you're allowed to deduct only the cost of a maximum of two conventions a year. Further, the convention has to be held in a location that's part of the normal area of the sponsoring organization.

Don't waste your money on meal and entertainment expenses, since you can deduct only 50 percent of these. By all means, take that 50 percent deduction when you can legally do so, but don't spend frivolously on business trips and think you can deduct everything. Even if you're out of town at a convention, you can deduct only 50 percent of the cost of any meals.

Canada Revenue Agency doesn't allow business deductions for club dues, such as for health, business, airport, or social clubs, or entertainment such as executive boxes at sports stadiums. If you entertain others for business purposes at a club, the cost can be deducted subject to the limitations noted above.

Keeping a Life and Perspective

David Packard, co-founder of Hewlett-Packard, said, "You are likely to die not of starvation for opportunities, but of indigestion of opportunities."

Most small businesses succeed in keeping their owners more than busy — in some cases, too busy. If you provide needed products or services at a fair price, customers will beat a path to your door. You'll grow and be busier than what you can personally handle. You may need to start hiring people. I know small-business owners who work themselves into a frenzy and put in 80 or more hours a week.

If you enjoy your work so much so that it's not really work and you end up putting in long hours because you enjoy it, terrific! But success in your company can lead you to put less energy into other important aspects of your life that perhaps don't come as easily.

Although careers and business successes are important, don't place these successes higher than fourth on your overall priority list. You can't replace your health, family, and friends — but you can replace a job or a business.

Chapter 15

Purchasing a Small Business

. . . .

In This Chapter

▶ Evaluating the pros and cons of buying a small business

▶ Examining the skills you need to buy a small business

▶ Selecting the right business for yourself

▶ Considering franchises and multilevel marketing companies

▶ Checking out and negotiating a successful purchase

. . . .

*E*ach year, hundreds of thousands of small businesses change hands. This chapter is for those of you who want to run or invest in an existing small business but don't want to start the business yourself. And, of course, this chapter can also show you how to make good money and have fun along the way!

Looking at the Advantages of Buying a Business

When you decide to purchase a home, you can choose between buying an existing one (that someone has more than likely lived in) or building one from scratch. Purchasing an already-built home makes the vast majority of people happy. Why? Because building a home requires a lot of work, takes a lot of time, and has a lot of potential for screw-ups.

We don't want to scare you off if you want to start a business. However, as with buying an existing home, buying someone else's business works better for some people than others. The following list reflects the main advantages of buying a business:

✔ **You avoid start-up hassles and headaches.** Starting a business from scratch requires dealing with a lot of stuff — just take a look at Chapters 13 and 14 for starters. In the early years of starting a business, beyond formulating a plan, you must deal with a variety of issues, such as developing a marketing plan, finding customers, locating space, hiring employees, and incorporating. Although you still need a game plan for a business that you buy and you need to fix any problems it has, if you buy a good business, part of what you buy is a more-finished entity.

- ✔ **Think about the learning curve for the type of business you're considering purchasing.** Buying an existing business makes more sense if the business is complicated. For example, purchasing a business that manufactures musical instruments makes more sense than purchasing a plumbing business that requires plumbing know-how and a few tools to start up. Unless you've built musical instruments before and understand the intricacies of the production process, starting such a business from scratch is quite risky and perhaps foolhardy. (However, purchasing an existing plumbing business may still make sense if you don't want to build a stable of customers from scratch.)

- ✔ **You don't have to come up with an idea for a product or service.** Starting a business is hard if you lack an idea for a product or service to sell. If nothing new strikes your fancy, you have a good reason to buy an existing business.

- ✔ **You reduce risk.** After a business has an operating history and offers a product or service with a demonstrated market, some of the risk in the company is removed. Although investing in something that's proven is far from a sure thing, your risk may be significantly lower than that involved in a start-up. Looking at past financial statements also helps you make more accurate financial forecasts than you could make with a start-up venture.

- ✔ **You enhance your ability to attract investor or lender money.** You should have less difficulty raising money from investors and lenders for your business than with a start-up. Attracting most investors to something that's more than an idea is easier. And for the amount they put up, investors demand a smaller piece of an existing business than they would investing in an idea.

- ✔ **Buying into an existing business is your only ticket into some businesses.** You can enter some businesses — such as bottlers or car dealerships — only through your purchase of a business that already exists.

- ✔ **You can find businesses where you can add value.** Some entrepreneurs who start businesses don't see the potential for growth or don't want to grow their business — they may be burned out, content with their current profit, or simply ready to retire. Finding businesses where the potential exists to improve operating efficiency and to expand into new markets isn't too hard. Relative to investing in stocks or real estate, finding small companies that are undervalued relative to their potential is easier for a business-minded person.

✔ **Just because you see the potential to improve a business, don't pay a high price based on your high expectations.** You can be wrong — you may be looking at the business through rose-coloured glasses. Even if you're correct about the potential, don't pay the current owner for the hard work and ingenuity you'll bring to the business if you purchase it. Offer a fair price based on the value of the business *now* — we explain how to figure this value in the "Evaluating a Small Business" section later in this chapter.

Understanding the Disadvantages of Buying a Business

Just as everyone doesn't enjoy running or cooking, some people don't enjoy the negatives that come with buying an existing business. If the following issues don't turn you off, purchasing an existing business may be right for you:

✔ **You buy the baggage.** When you buy an existing business, the bad comes with the good. All businesses include their share of the bad. The company may employ problem employees, for example, or it may have a less-than-stellar reputation in the marketplace. Even if the employees are good, they and the culture of the company may not mesh with where you want to take the company in the future.

✔ **Are you able to motivate people to change or to fire them?** Do you have the patience to work at improving the company's products and reputation? You need these types of skills and traits in order to run and add value to a company. Some people thrive on such challenges, and others toss and turn in their sleep from the pressure. Think back on your other work experiences for clues as to what challenges you've tackled and how you felt about them.

✔ **You need to do a lot of inspection.** If you think buying a company is easier than starting one, think again. You must know what you're buying *before* you buy. So you need to do a thorough inspection, perform due diligence, kick the tires, or whatever you want to call it. For example, you need to rip apart financial statements to ascertain whether the company is really as profitable as it appears and to determine its financial health.

✔ **After you close the deal and the cheques and/or money are transferred, you can't change your mind.** Unless a seller commits fraud or lies (which is difficult and costly for a buyer to prove in a court of law), it's "buyer beware" about the quality of the business you're buying. In "Evaluating a Small Business" later in this chapter, we cover the homework you need to do before you buy.

✔ **You need more capital.** Existing businesses have value, which is why you generally need more money to buy a business than to start one. If you're short of cash, starting a company is generally a lower-cost path.

✔ **Lower risk means lower returns.** If you purchase a good business and run it well, you can make decent money. In some cases you can make a lot of money. But you generally have less upside and potential for hitting it really big than with a business you start. Those who have built the greatest wealth from small business are usually those who have started them rather than those who buy existing ones.

✔ **You don't get the satisfaction of creating a business.** Whether for your ego or your psyche, entrepreneurs who build their own businesses get a different experience from those who buy someone else's enterprise. You can make your mark on a business that you buy, but doing so takes a number of years. Even then, the business is never completely your own creation.

Prerequisites to Buying a Business

Not everyone is cut out to succeed when buying an existing business. Even if you have sufficient funds for the purchase, you may be blind to a whole host of problems and pitfalls and can end up losing your entire investment. Later in this chapter we introduce you to some small-business buyers who did just that.

Conversely, some people with little money for buying a business succeed wildly. You can purchase a good small business with little and, in rare cases, no money down. So what then are the traits common to people who successfully buy and operate an existing small business?

Business experience

First, you should have business experience and background. If you were an economics or business major in college and you took accounting and other quantitatively oriented courses, you're off to a good start.

Even better than academic learning is work experience in the type of business you want to buy. If you want to run a restaurant, go work in one. Consider the experience as paid on-the-job training.

If you've worked on business-management issues with a variety of industries, you also have a good background. However, the danger in having done only consulting is that you're usually not on the front lines where most of the serious business operational issues arise.

If none of the previous examples apply to you, we won't say that you're doomed to fail if you buy a business, but we will say that the odds are against you.

If you don't have business experience, you'll likely do far better in your first business venture after some remedial work. Get some hands-on experience, which is more valuable than any degree or credential you can earn through course work. There's no substitute for the real-life experiences of marketing to and interacting with customers, grappling with financial statements, dealing with competitive threats, and doing the business of business. However, we don't endorse not doing *any* academic course work. You may, in fact, be required to get a credential in order to do the work you want to do. If you don't need a specific credential, taking selected courses and reading good business books (we recommend some in Chapter 18) can boost your knowledge.

Financial background

To buy a business, as with buying real estate, you need to make a down payment on the purchase price. In most cases, you need to put down 25 to 30 percent. Bankers and business sellers who give loans to business buyers normally require such down payments in order to protect their loan. Small-business buyers who make such down payments are less likely to walk away from a loan obligation if the business gets into financial trouble.

If you lack significant capital for a down payment, try asking family or friends to invest. You can also set your sights on a less-expensive business or seek business owners willing to accept a small down payment. If you can find a business for sale where the owner wants less than 20 percent down, you may be on to something good. Be careful, though: An owner who accepts such a small down payment may be having a difficult time selling because of problems inherent in the business or because the business is overpriced.

You can purchase many existing small businesses with a loan from the selling owner. Also, check for loans with banks in your area that specialize in small-business loans. (See Chapter 14 for other financing ideas.)

Finding a Good Business to Buy

Unless you're extraordinarily lucky, finding a good business to buy takes a great deal of time. If you spend this time outside of your work hours, finding a quality business that's right for you can easily take a year or two. Even if you can afford the luxury of looking for a business full time, finding, analyzing, negotiating, and closing on a business can still take many months.

Above all else, it pays to be persistent, patient, and willing to spend some time on things that don't lead immediately to results. You must be willing to sort through some rubbish to find a keeper. If you require immediate gratification, you can make yourself miserable in your search or rush into a bad deal. The following sections give you the best techniques for identifying good businesses for sale that meet your needs.

Homing in on what you want

You're going to end up spinning your wheels (and likely with the wrong type of business) unless you set some boundaries for your business search. You don't need to be rigid or to precisely define every detail of the business you want to purchase, but the better you set some parameters, the sooner you can start laying the groundwork to purchase.

Each person has unique shopping criteria. The following list exemplifies some good ones to help narrow your search:

- **Size/purchase price.** Unless you're already wealthy, the money you have to invest will constrain the size of business you can afford. As a rough rule, figure that you can afford a purchase price of about three times the amount of cash you have earmarked for the business. For example, if you have $50,000 in the till, you should look at buying a business for about $150,000. Because many sellers overprice their businesses, you can probably look at businesses listed at a price above $150,000, perhaps as high as $200,000.

- **Location.** If you're already rooted and don't want to move or face a long commute, the business's location further narrows the field. Although you may be willing to look at a broader territory, maybe even nationally if you're willing to relocate, evaluating businesses long distance is difficult and costly. Unless you want a highly specialized type of company, try to keep your business search local.

- **Industry.** Industry-specific expertise that you want to use in the business you buy can help whittle the pool down further. If you don't have this expertise, we highly recommend that you focus on some particular niches in industries that interest you or that you know something about. Focusing on an industry helps you conduct a more thorough search and turn up higher-quality companies. The industry knowledge you accumulate in your search process can pay big dividends during your years of ownership in the business.

If you have a hard time brainstorming about specific industries, use this trick to jump-start your creativity — take a walk through the Yellow Pages! All the businesses known to exist in your area are listed alphabetically by type. Remember that a separate Yellow Pages directory exists for businesses that sell mainly to consumers; in larger areas, there are also "business-to-business" Yellow Pages directories. These list businesses whose customers are primarily other businesses. Look at either or both, depending on the types of business that may interest you. You also may want to buy a business in a sector that's experiencing fast growth so that you too can ride the wave. Check out *Profit* magazine's annual list of the country's 100 fastest-growing companies. In addition, the magazine now compiles a list of 50 of Canada's fastest-growing start-ups, ranked by their two-year growth rate. Also take a look at the annual *Inc.* 500 list of the fastest-growing smaller companies in the U.S.

✔ **Opportunity to add value.** Some buyers want to purchase a business with untapped opportunities or with problems that need fixing. As with real estate, however, many people are happier leaving the fixer-uppers to the contractors. Likewise, some businesses without major problems can offer significant untapped potential.

After you define your shopping criteria, you're ready to go to the marketplace. We recommend that you type up your criteria on a single page so that you can hand it to others who may put you in touch with businesses for sale. Use the following methods to uncover businesses that meet your desires.

Perusing publications

If you're focused on specific industry sectors, you may be surprised to learn that all sorts of specialty newsletters and magazines are out there. Just think of the fun you can have reading publications such as *Canadian Plastics*, *Alternative Energy Retailer, Welding Canada, Specialty Foods Merchandising, Coal Mining Newsletter,* or *Gas Turbine World*! Specialty publications not only get you into the thick of an industry, they also advertise businesses for sale or business brokers who work in the industry.

A useful U.S. reference publication that you can find in public libraries with decent business sections is a two-volume set entitled *Small Business Sourcebook* (Gale). Organized alphabetically by industry, this reference contains listings of publications, trade associations, and other information sources.

Conducting literature searches of general-interest business publications can also help you identify articles on your industry of interest. Use the *Reader's Guide to Periodicals* and online computer searches to help you find the articles. Web sites worth examining include www.bizbuysell.com and www.sba.gov.

Networking with advisers

 Speak with accountants, lawyers, bankers, and business consultants who specialize in working with small businesses. These advisers are sometimes the first to hear of a small-business owner's desire to sell. Advisers may also suggest good businesses that aren't for sale but whose owners may consider selling (see the next section).

Knocking on some doors

If you own a home and someone came to your door and said he was interested in buying it, you'd likely say you're not interested in selling. If the interested buyer said he really liked the type of property you had and that he was willing to pay you a good price, he may get a little more of your attention, but you'd still likely turn him away. But if you, as the homeowner, were considering selling anyway, you might be all ears, especially if you could sell your house directly and save paying a broker's commission.

Why would you want to go to this trouble and bother business owners? Some owners who haven't listed their business for sale may still think about selling, so if you approach enough businesses that interest you, you may luck out. You can increase your chances of finding the business you want, and you may get a good deal on it too. You also have the advantage of negotiating with the seller without having to compete with other potential buyers.

 Instead of phoning or literally knocking on the business's door, start your communications by mail. Sending a concise letter of introduction explaining what kind of business you're looking for and what a wonderful person you are demonstrates that you're investing some time in this endeavour. Follow up with a call a week or so after you send the letter.

Working with business brokers

Numerous small businesses for sale list their enterprises through business brokers. Just as a real estate agent makes a living selling real estate, a business broker makes a living selling businesses.

Business brokers generally sell smaller small businesses — those with less than $1 million in annual sales. These businesses tend to be family-owned or sole proprietorships, such as restaurants, dry cleaners, other retailers, and service firms. About half of such small businesses are sold through brokers.

One advantage of working with brokers to buy a business is that they can expose you to other businesses you may not have considered (a doughnut shop, for example). Brokers can also share their knowledge with you about some of your ideas — like the fact that you need to get up at 2 a.m. to make doughnuts. Still want to buy one?

Most business brokerage firms sell different types of businesses. Some firms, however, specialize in one industry or a few industries.

The pitfalls of working with brokers are numerous:

✔ **Commissions.** Brokers aren't your business advisers; they're salespeople. That fact doesn't make them corrupt or dishonest, but it does mean that their interests aren't aligned with yours. Their incentive is to do a deal and do it soon — and, the more you pay for your business, the more they make. Business brokers typically get paid 10 to 12 percent of the sales price of the business. Technically, the seller pays this fee, but as with real estate deals done through brokers, the buyer actually pays. Remember, if a broker isn't involved, the seller can sell for a lower price and still clear more money, and the buyer is better off too.

✔ **Undesirable businesses.** Problem businesses are everywhere, but a fair number end up with brokers when the owners encounter trouble selling on their own.

✔ **Packaging.** This problem relates to the preceding two. Brokers help not-so-hot businesses look better than they really are. Doing so may involve lying, but more typically it involves stretching the truth, omitting negatives, and hyping potential. (Owners who sell their business them-selves may do these things as well.)

✔ **You (and your advisers) need to perform the due diligence on a business that you may buy (see Chapter 14).** Never, ever trust or use the selling package that a broker prepares for a business as your sole source of information. Remember: Brokers, as well as sellers, can stretch the truth, lie, and commit fraud.

✔ **Access to limited inventory.** Unlike real estate brokers who can access all homes listed with brokers for sale in an area through a shared listing service, a business broker can generally tell you only about his office's listings. (Confidentiality is an issue because a shared listing service increases the number of people who can find out that a business is for sale and the particulars of the sale.)

✔ **If you want to work with a business broker, use more than one.** Working with a larger business brokerage firm or one that specializes in listing the type of business you're looking for can maximize the number of possible prospects that you see. Some area associations of business brokers share their listings. However, some of the larger brokerages don't include themselves because they benefit less from sharing their information.

> ✔ **Few licensing requirements.** Unlike real estate agents, the business brokerage field is not tightly regulated. The majority of regions have no requirements — anyone can hang out a shingle and work as a business broker. Some regions allow those with securities brokerage licences to operate as business brokers, whereas many require real estate licences.

You can find business brokers in the Yellow Pages under "Business Brokers". Ads for businesses for sale may lead you to a broker as well. You can also ask tax, legal, and business consultants for names of good brokers they may know. If you find a broker you think you'd like to work with, check references from other buyers who have worked with the broker. Make sure the broker works full time and has solid experience. Some business brokers dabble in it part time and make a living in other ways.

Ask the broker you're interested in for the names of several buyers of similar businesses whom they've worked with over the past six months. By narrowing down the field to only your particular business interest, the broker can't just refer you to the three best deals of his or her career. Also, check whether anyone has filed complaints against the brokerage with the local Better Business Bureau (although the BBB favours member companies) and provincial regulatory departments (consumer and commercial relations, attorney general, and so on) that oversee business brokers.

Considering a Franchise or Multilevel Marketing Company

Among the types of businesses you may buy are franchises and multilevel marketing companies. Both of these types offer more of a pre-packaged and defined system for running a business. Although both may be worth your exploration, significant pitfalls can trip you up, especially with multilevel marketing companies.

Finding a franchise

Purchasing a good franchise can be your ticket into the world of small-business ownership. Some companies expand their locations through selling replicas, or *franchises,* of their business. When you purchase a franchise, you buy the local rights to a specified geographic territory to sell the company's products or services under the company's name and to use the company's system of operation. In addition to an up-front franchisee fee, franchisors typically charge an ongoing royalty.

As a consumer, you've likely done business with franchises. Franchising makes up a huge part of the business world. Companies that franchise — such as McDonald's, Canadian Tire, Pizza Hut, H&R Block, Grand & Toy, Midas Muffler, Second Cup, Century 21 Real Estate, Holiday Inn, Avis, Subway, and Foot Locker — account for more than $1 trillion in sales annually.

Franchise advantages

When you purchase a franchise, unlike buying other businesses, you don't buy an operating enterprise. Although the parent company should have a track record and multiple locations with customers, you start with no customers if you purchase a new franchise. (You can buy existing franchises from owners who want to sell.) As the owner of a new franchise, you don't already have customers — just like starting a business, you must find them.

So why would you want to pay a good chunk of money to buy a business without customers?

- **Proven business.** A company that's been in business for a number of years and has successful franchisees proves the demand for the company's products and services and shows that its system for providing them works. The company has worked the bugs out and hopefully solved common problems. As a franchise owner, you benefit from and share in the experience that the parent company has gained over the years.

- **Name-brand recognition.** Some consumers recognize the company name of a larger and successful franchise company and may be more inclined to purchase its products and services. Some consumers feel more comfortable getting a muffler job done at franchisor Midas Muffler than hunting around and calling Discount Muffler World or Manny's Muffler Bazaar from a Yellow Pages listing. The comfort from dealing with Midas may stem from the influence of advertisements, recommendations of friends, or your own familiarity with Midas's services, perhaps in another part of the country. Most free-standing small businesses for sale in a community lack name-brand recognition.

- **Centralized purchasing power.** You would hope and expect that Midas, as a corporation made up of hundreds of locations, buys mufflers at a low price — volume purchasing generally leads to bigger discounts. As well as possibly saving franchisees money on supplies, the parent company can take the hassle out of figuring out where and how to purchase these supplies. Again, most unattached small businesses you could buy won't offer this advantage, although quality business associations can provide some of these benefits.

Franchise pitfalls

As with purchasing other small businesses, pitfalls abound in buying a franchise. Franchises aren't for everyone. Here are some common problems that may make you reconsider buying a franchise:

- ✓ **You're not the franchise type.** When you buy a franchise, you buy into an established system. People who like structure and following established rules and systems adapt more easily to the franchise life. But if you're the creative sort who likes to experiment and change things, you may be an unhappy franchisee. Unlike starting your own business where you can get into the game without investing lots of your time and money, buying a business that you end up not enjoying can make for an expensive learning experience.

- ✓ **You must buy over-priced supplies.** Centralized, bulk purchasing through the corporate headquarters supposedly saves franchisees time and money on supplies and other expenditures. Some franchisors, however, take advantage of franchisees through large mark-ups on proprietary items that franchisees must buy from the franchisors.

- ✓ **The franchise is unproven.** If the company's concept hasn't stood the test of time and other franchises, don't make yourself a guinea pig. Some franchisors show more interest in simply selling franchises to collect the up-front franchise money. Reputable franchisors want to help their franchisees succeed so that they can collect an ongoing royalty from the franchisees' sales.

- ✓ **The franchise is a pyramid scheme.** Unscrupulous, short-term-focused business owners sometimes attempt to franchise their business and sell as many franchises as they can as quickly as possible. Some push their franchisees to sell franchises. The business soon focuses on selling franchises rather than operating a business that sells a product or service well. In rare cases, franchisors engage in fraud and sell next to nothing, except the hopes of getting rich quick.

Evaluating a franchise

Make sure you do plenty of homework before you agree to buy a franchise. The following list is our catalogue of critical steps that you need to take before buying a franchise that interests you.

1. **Request and read any available disclosure documents.**

   Ontario and Alberta are the only provinces that currently require franchisors to prepare and distribute official disclosure documents. (Of course, that generally means that franchisors who operate nationally will have disclosure documents.) Don't be put off by this document's size — read it cover to cover. The Canadian Franchise Association recommends — but does not require — that its members distribute a disclosure document.

If you're looking at a franchise that also operates in the U.S., you should request the Uniform Franchise Offering Circular (UFOC). In the U.S., the Federal Trade Commission (FTC) requires all franchisors to issue this document at least ten days before a prospective franchise buyer writes a cheque or signs an agreement to purchase.

The UFOC contains a treasure trove of valuable information, such as the names and addresses of the franchisees closest to your area and a list of franchises that the company terminated, didn't renew, or bought back. The document discloses pending or settled litigation and should indicate potential or actual troubles between franchisors and franchisees. The UFOC also gives you the employment background of the franchisor's senior management, your costs to purchase a franchise, and required inventory, leases, and other costs.

2. **Determine whether the franchisors are looking for a partner or your wallet.**

   In your first interactions with the franchising company, observe the demeanour and approach of those you speak with. Although all such companies have enthusiastic salespeople, the best franchising companies want to check you out almost as much as you want to check them out. Smart franchisors don't want to sell a franchise to someone who's likely to crash and burn or tarnish the company's good reputation. Smart companies know that their interests are aligned with yours — they make more money from ongoing royalties if they sell franchises to capable franchisees who succeed.

   Run as fast as you can in the opposite direction if the franchisors tell tales of great riches from just a small investment of your time and money. Some franchisors are more interested in selling franchises than in finding and helping the most-qualified franchisees succeed. Such franchisors may also attempt to pressure you into making a quick decision to buy, and they may be evasive about providing detailed information about their business.

3. **Speak with franchisees.**

   Talk with franchisees currently with the company, as well as those who quit or were terminated. Start with the lists of franchisees you may have received with any disclosure documents — not with references the company provides. Ask the franchisees about their experiences, both good and bad, with the parent company. Those franchisees for whom things didn't work out generally tell you more about the warts of the system, but also try to identify whether some of these people were poor fits. Conversely, active franchisees may likely see their franchise experience through rose-coloured glasses, if for no other reason than to reinforce their decision to buy a franchise. Observe the happiest and most successful franchisees and see whether you share their business perspectives and traits.

4. **Understand what you're buying.**

   Good franchises can cost you a reasonable chunk of change up front. At the low end, service businesses, which you can run from your home, sell for around a $25,000 up-front franchise fee; compare that with the several hundred thousands to a million dollars or more required for the bricks-and-mortar locations of established franchisers, such as McDonald's or Canadian Tire. Additionally, ongoing franchise royalties run about 3 to 10 percent of gross revenue. The disclosure documents should detail all the up-front costs. What do you get for this up-front payment? Is the system and name brand really worth this fee? What kind of training will you receive?

5. **Look at comparable franchises.**

   Few franchises are unique. Compare the cost of what a particular franchise offers you with the cost of purchasing franchises from different companies in the same business. For example, if you're considering a coffee shop franchise, compare the terms and offerings of Tim Hortons, Timothy's, and Second Cup, three large, established, and successful coffee franchise firms.

6. **Consider the start-up alternative.**

   If you look at the "best" franchises in a particular business and think, "Hey, I can do this as well or better and at less cost on my own," then consider starting your business from scratch. Make sure you're realistic, though, because starting a business involves many hidden costs — both out-of-pocket financial costs and time costs.

7. **Check with regulators.**

   Check with government regulators to see whether any complaints are on file. You may also want to check with the Better Business Bureau in the city where the franchising company is headquartered to discover whether any information is on file (recognize, however, that if the company is a BBB member, the BBB may be less demanding and too lenient about reporting problems).

8. **Run a credit report on the company.**

   You can examine the franchisor's credit report to get another indicator of the kinds of business relationships it maintains. Just as you have a personal credit report on file, business credit reports show how a company deals with the payments and debts it owes to suppliers and creditors.

9. **Review the franchise contract.**

   If your digging makes you feel more, rather than less, comfortable with the franchise purchase, you now need to get down to the nitty-gritty of the contract. Franchise contracts are usually long and tedious. Read the contract completely to get a sense of what you're getting yourself into.

Have a lawyer who's experienced with franchising agreements review the contract as well. In addition to the financial terms, the contract should specify how the company handles disputes, what rights you have to sell the franchise in the future, and under what conditions the parent company may terminate the franchise. Make sure you can live with and be happy with the non-financial parts of the contract.

10. **Negotiate.**

    Different companies negotiate differently. Some companies offer their best deal up front and don't engage in haggling. Others don't put their best foot forward in the hope that you may simply sign and accept the inferior terms and conditions. Some naive franchise buyers see the contract as cast in stone and don't negotiate. Remember that almost everything is negotiable.

Cover all ten steps when you evaluate any franchise. You may be most tempted to cut corners in reviewing a franchise from a long-established company. Don't. You may not be right for the specific franchise, or perhaps the "successful" company has been good at keeping problems under wraps.

In the "Evaluating a Small Business" section later in this chapter, we explain the homework you should complete prior to buying an existing business. Read that section as well, especially if you want to purchase an existing franchise from another franchisee.

Work-from-home "opportunities"

"We made $18,269.56 in just 2½ weeks! Remarkable, home-based business! We do over 90 percent of the work for you! Free info: 800-555-8975."

"Earn $4,000 per month on the new instant information superhighway."

"You can be earning $4,000 to $10,000 each month in less than 30 days! We'll even help you hire agents to do the work for you . . . FREE!"

"Work from home. Company needs help. Earn $500–$900 per week. Anyone can do this — will train. Full time or part time. Call 555-8974. Only for the serious — please!"

You can find lots of ad copy like this, especially in magazines that small-business owners and wannabe small-business owners read. In most cases, these ads come from grossly over-hyped multilevel marketing companies. In other ads, no legitimate company exists; instead, a person (or two or three) simply tries to sell you some "information" that explains the business opportunity. This information may cost several hundred dollars or more. Such packages end up being worthless marketing propaganda and rarely provide useful information that you couldn't find at a far lower cost or no cost at all.

Never buy into anything like these ads that companies (or people) pitch to you through the mail or over the phone.

Considering a multilevel marketing company

A twist, and in most cases a bad one, on the franchising idea is multilevel marketing (MLM) companies. Sometimes known as network companies, MLMs can be thought of as a poor person's franchise. We know dozens of people who have been sorely disappointed with the returns from money and time they've spent on MLMs.

Some people are enthusiastic about MLMs. One book on the subject says,

> Like an elemental force of nature, network marketing has risen from the soil and roots of America's heartland, boldly promising wealth, freedom, and limitless horizons to those with the courage to seek them out.

One day Eric received a letter from a client describing an MLM opportunity. "It is the best thing I've ever seen," gushed the letter, ". . . I have friends who are making $10,000, $25,000, $70,000, and $125,000 per month! $195 starter fee gets you literally a national distributorship."

The company, which we'll call "Superhype Telemarketing," sells long-distance phone service and claims to offer rates far lower than the large telephone companies. You pay for your starter kit, go through a short training seminar, and — voilà — you're in business for yourself. Work when you want, get a share of every dollar your customers spend on long distance, recruit others as representatives, and make money off the business they bring in.

For those weary of traditional jobs, the appeal of multilevel marketing is obvious. You can work at home, part time if you want. You have no employees. You don't need any experience. Yet you're told you can still make big bucks. If your parents raised you right, however, you should be sceptical of deals like these. If you can make $10,000, $25,000, $70,000, and $125,000 per month, wouldn't everyone do it?

Superhype Telemarketing is one of many companies that use multilevel marketing. Representatives who work as independent contractors solicit customers as well as recruit new representatives, known in the industry as your "downline."

A big problem to watch out for is the business equivalent of the pyramid scheme — businesses that exist to sign up other people. A little bit of digging revealed the following about Superhype Telemarketing: Its marketing director advocates that you "sell directly to those that you have direct influence over. The system works great because you don't need to resell month after month. It's an opportunity for anybody — it's up to them how much work they want to put into it."

Any MLM examination should start with the company's product or service. In Superhype Telemarketing's case, hundreds of companies offer telephone service, so the service is hardly unique. Superhype Telemarketing claims to provide cheaper services than the large long-distance providers and local toll-call providers. Some of the company's marketing materials claim savings of as much as 50 to 75 percent. The reality: Comparing Superhype Telemarketing's rates with the big, nationally advertised, name-brand, long-distance phone services, which certainly aren't the cheapest services, shows little difference. If you make more than $10 in long-distance calls per month, Superhype Telemarketing is about 7 percent cheaper. If you place more than $50 per month in calls, Superhype's rates are about the same.

A call to the Better Business Bureau in the city where Superhype Telemarketing is headquartered revealed that the company has been the subject of dozens of filed complaints of unauthorized switching of consumers' long-distance phone service by Superhype sales representatives. Other complaints alleged misrepresentation of savings.

So what about the big money — can you make tens of thousands to a hundred thousand dollars per month or more working for Superhype? For starters, you must pay to become a Superhype representative. The fee of $195 gets you a kit that provides advice, 12 months of a corporate newsletter, and a small amount of training. If you want to get paid a $40 fee for training others who sign up with the company, you pay $395 to become a trainer.

Superhype Telemarketing put Eric in touch with one of its most successful salespeople: Big Al. "I used to be in real estate and got tired of the headaches of dealing with tenants . . . the idea of earning residual payments for everyone signed up to use a phone service appealed to me," Big Al said. Without being prompted, Big Al told Eric that he made $17,000 working part time in his first year and then, working full time, he earned $60,000, $670,000, and $1.4 million in his next three years, respectively.

Being a sceptic, Eric asked Big Al for proof. He said he'd be happy to fax him a copy of a big cheque he was presented with two years earlier. What he sent were marketing materials that showed photos of "top leaders" being presented with oversized cheques, similar to the props that companies use for public relations opportunities when they make a big contribution to charity. Big Al's big cheque (which was supposedly for one month) was for $57,000.

Not satisfied with this copy as proof, Eric asked Big Al for his monthly sales report from Superhype, which the company provides to all its representatives. He said he didn't have this information because his tax preparer was working on his return. When Eric pointed out that the month in question was from two years ago and not in the past year, he said that all his financial statements were in storage and, because he was soon heading out of town for ten days, he wouldn't have a chance to retrieve them until he got back. Eric then suggested that Big Al's tax preparer could send him Big Al's proof of income for a recent year or some other sort of proof. Eric's still waiting.

As for the company's other top producers, the company never provided proof of the hyped income claims. All this hype reminds us of the movie *Quiz Show* (we recommend you see it if you haven't yet), an eye-opening account of how television quiz shows in the 1950s were rigged to dupe the public.

Big Al, who's also one of the company's most successful recruiters, claims that the company is contractually obligated to pay residuals and can't cut sales reps out of the picture financially after they sign up others. However, according to Superhype's marketing director, "There is no guarantee of future payments. The company has the ability to change its program at any time." So if Superhype's management or a future buyer of the company decides to cut commissions, reps will be at their mercy.

Also cause for pause: Superhype's marketing packages contain a feature article (which is from a supposed business periodical) that praises the company. Buried in the fine print on the back page of the reprint of the "article," which is sandwiched around a two-page ad for the company, is the following: "Information contained in feature articles is provided by the company." Turns out that when a company like Superhype buys the space for the ad, the "story" comes with it as well! The sticker price for the ad exceeds $10,000. Rather than an independent appraisal of the company, this article is basically an ad that Superhype bought.

The bottom line on any network marketing "opportunity" is to remember that it's a job. No company is going to pay you a lot of money for little work. As with any other small-business venture, if you hope to earn a decent income, multilevel marketing opportunities require at least three to five years of low income to build up your business. Most people who buy into networks such as Superhype make little money, and many quit and move on. According to a Superhype company document, more than 60 percent of its representatives make less than $100 per month and fewer than 5 percent make more than $1,000 monthly, but you'd never know this from its advertising or sales hype.

Also, think twice before you sign up relatives, friends, and co-workers — often the first people whom network marketers encourage you to sell to. A danger in doing business with those people whom you have influence over is that you put your reputation and integrity and your friendships and family relations on the line.

Do your homework and remember that due diligence requires digging for facts and talking to people who don't have a bias or reason to sell to you. Do the same homework that we recommended for franchises in the "Evaluating a franchise" section earlier in this chapter. Be sceptical of multilevel marketing systems, unless the company has a long track record and many people who are happy. Assume that an MLM company isn't worth pursuing until your extensive due diligence proves otherwise.

Quality multilevel marketing companies are the exception

A number of network companies have achieved success over the years. Amway, Herbalife, and Mary Kay have stood the test of time and achieved significant size. Amway founders Richard De Vos and Jay Van Andel achieved multibillionaire status.

Not all multilevel companies are created equal, and few are worth a look. However, Mary Kay, which sells primarily makeup and skin care products, is an example of a successful network company with a 30-plus year history. Mary Kay has hundreds of thousands of sales representatives and does business worldwide. Although not shy about the decent money that its more successful salespeople make, Mary Kay doesn't hype the income potential. According to the company, the top 50 percent of local Canadian sales directors earn anywhere from under $20,000 to over $100,000 per year, but this income comes after many years of hard work. Mary Kay rewards top sellers with gifts, such as the famous pink Cadillac.

The ingredients for Mary Kay's success include competitive pricing, personal attention, and social interaction, which many stores don't or can't offer their customers. "We make shopping and life fun . . . we make people look and feel good," says Mary Gentry, one of Mary Kay's sales directors.

Mary Kay encourages prospective Mary Kay reps to try the products first and then host a group before they sign up and fork over the $150 to purchase a showcase of items to sell. To maximize sales, the company encourages Mary Kay representatives to keep a ready inventory because customers tend to buy more when products are immediately available. If reps want out of the business, they can generally sell their inventory back to the company at 90 cents on the dollar originally paid, a good sign that the company stands behind its product.

Quality multilevel marketing companies make sense for people who really believe in and want to sell a particular product or service and don't want to or can't tie up a lot of money buying a franchise or other business. Just remember to check out the MLM company, and realize that you won't get rich in a hurry, or probably ever.

Evaluating a Small Business

If you put in many hours, you may eventually come across a business that interests and intrigues you so much that you consider purchasing it. As with buying a piece of real estate, major hurdles stand between you and ownership of the business. You need to inspect what you want to buy, negotiate a deal, and finalize a contract — and done correctly, these processes take a lot of time.

Doing due diligence

Our legal system presumes a person is innocent until a judge or jury proves that person is guilty beyond a reasonable doubt. When you purchase a business, however, you must assume that the seller is guilty of making the business appear better than what it is (and possibly lying) until you prove otherwise.

We don't want to sound cynical, but a business owner can use more than a few tricks to make a business look more profitable, financially healthier, and more desirable than it really is. You can't decide how much inspection or due diligence to conduct on a business based on your gut-level feeling.

Because you can't guess what hidden surprises exist in a business, you must dig for them. Until you prove to yourself beyond a reasonable doubt that these surprises don't exist, don't go through with a business purchase.

When you find a business that you think you want to purchase, you absolutely, positively must do your homework before you buy. However, just as with purchasing a home, you don't want to expend buckets of money and time on detailed inspections until you can reach an agreement with the seller. What if you deal with a seller who's unrealistic about what the business is worth? You need to perform the most serious, time-consuming, and costly due diligence after you have an accepted offer to purchase a business. Make such inspections a contingency in your purchase contract (see "Contingencies" later in this chapter).

Ultimately, if you're going to buy a business, you need to follow a plan similar to, but likely shorter than, the one we present in Chapter 13. Addressing such issues in a plan goes a long way toward helping you perform your due diligence.

Here are some additional questions that you need to answer about a business you're contemplating purchasing: (Address as many of the questions as possible before you make your offer.)

- ✔ **Why is the owner selling?** Ask the owner or the owner's advisers why the owner wants to sell and why now. The answer may shed light on the owner's motivations and need to sell. Some owners want to bail when they see things getting worse.

- ✔ **What's the value of the assets you want to buy?** This value includes not only equipment but also "soft" assets, such as the firm's name and reputation with customers and suppliers, customer lists, patents, and so on. Interview key employees, customers, suppliers, advisers, and competitors. Ask key customers and key employees whether they would still be loyal to the business if you took it over.

- ✔ **What do the financial statements reveal?** Search for the same things you'd look for in a company whose stock you're considering purchasing. (See Chapter 6 for how to read financial statements and what to look for.) Don't take the financial statements at face value simply because they're audited. The accountant who did the audit may be incompetent or chummy with the seller.

One way to check for shenanigans is to ask the seller for a copy of the business's tax returns. Owners are more likely to try to minimize reported revenue and maximize expenses on their tax return to keep from paying more tax. After you have an accepted purchase offer, ask a tax adviser experienced in such matters to do an audit.

✔ **If the company leases its space, what does the lease contract say?** A soon-to-expire lease at a low rate can ruin a business's profit margins if you have to renew the lease at much less favourable terms. With a retail operation, the ability to maintain a good location is also vital. Check comparables — that is, what other similar locations lease for — to see whether the current lease rate is fair, and talk to the building owner to discover his plans for the building. Ask for and review (with the help of a legal adviser) the current owner's lease contract.

✔ **What liabilities, including those that may be hidden "off" the balance sheet, are you buying with a business?** Limit liabilities, such as environmental contaminations, through a contract. Conduct legal searches for liens, litigation, and tax problems.

✔ **What does a background check turn up on the owners and key employees?** Do they have good business experience, or do they have criminal records and a trail of unpaid debts?

Questioning profits

Don't blindly take the profit from the bottom line of a business's financial statement as gospel. As part of your due diligence, ask a tax adviser to perform an audit after you negotiate a deal.

Even if the financial statements of a business are accurate, you (and your tax adviser) must still look for subtle problems that can make the profits of the business appear better or worse than they truly are. The issues to look for when you analyze the financial statements of public companies that issue stock (explained in Chapter 6) also apply to evaluating the financial statements of small companies.

If necessary, factor out one-time events from the profit analysis. For example, if the business last year received an unusually large order that's unlikely to be repeated and hasn't been the norm in the past, subtract this amount from the profitability analysis. Also, examine the owner's salary to see whether it's high or low for the field. Owners can reduce their draw to a minimum or pay family members less than fair market salaries to pump up the profitability of their company in the years before they sell.

Also examine whether the rent or mortgage expense may change when you buy the business. Consider what will happen to profits when you factor in your expected rent or mortgage costs.

Negotiating a good deal

After you find what you think is a good business and do some homework, you're ready to make an offer. Negotiating takes time and patience. Unless you're legally savvy, find a lawyer who focuses his or her practice on small-business dealings. Have the lawyer review and work with your contract. Also consider obtaining input from a qualified tax adviser.

Good advisers can help you inspect what you're buying and look for red flags in the company's financial statements. Advisers can also help structure the purchase to protect what you're buying and to gain maximum tax benefits. If you work with a business broker, use a lawyer and accountant as well.

To get a good deal, a number of things need to fall into place.

Valuing a business

How can you buy a business if you don't know its worth? The price that a business is listed for is often in excess of — and sometimes grossly so — the business's true worth.

Look at what similar businesses have sold for as a starting point for valuing a business you want to buy. A smart home buyer or real estate investor looks at comparable properties when she's ready to make an offer on a property.

The challenging part is finding the specific sales price and other information on businesses that have sold. Small businesses are privately held, and the terms of sales aren't a matter of public record. Following are some good sources for uncovering details of small business sales:

- **Business brokers.** If you're already working with a business broker or looking at businesses listed with a business broker, he should be able to provide a comparable market analysis of similar businesses that his office has sold. Use this analysis as a starting point. Remember that the more you pay for a business, the more money brokers make. Brokers also generally have access to sales data for only the small number of similar businesses that their office has sold.

- **Businesses that you've looked at that have sold.** If your search lasts months or perhaps years, keep track of similar businesses you've considered that eventually sell. These sales are extra valuable comparables because you may have been able to see the business and obtain more details about the company's financial position.

- **Advisers.** Lawyers, tax advisers, and business consultants you work with can help provide you with comparables. If an adviser doesn't have memories of or experience with similar deals, find another adviser. You need advisers who can bring applicable experience to the negotiating table.

✔ **Business appraisers.** If you really want to buy a business and your initial investigation suggests that the seller is committed to and serious about selling, consider hiring a business valuator. The Canadian Institute of Chartered Business Valuators (416-204-3396, or www.business valuators.com) can provide you with a list of association members in your area. Also check the Yellow Pages in your area under "Business Valuators."

✔ **Research firms and publications.** A small number of companies publish comparable sales information or perform searches for a fee:

- **Bizcomps** is an annual publication that provides sales price, revenue, and other financial details for businesses sold. This compendium of sales information is available for different major regions of the United States (Western, Central, and Eastern editions). A national U.S. edition provides sales information for larger manufacturing, wholesale, and service businesses. Call 858-457-0366 for a sample of this publication. Each directory sells for $125 U.S., or you can pay an annual subscription and tap into Bizcomps database through its Web site at www.bizcomps.com.

- **Financial Research Associates (FRA)** provides balance sheet and income statement comparisons for small companies through its annual *Financial Studies of the Small Business* directory, which sells for $104 U.S. Call 863-299-3969 to receive a background package on this directory.

✔ **Trade publications.** As we recommend earlier in the chapter, trade publications can help you find information about a particular industry and how to value companies within the industry. Many publications can, for a small fee, send you past articles on the topic.

When you look at comparables, figure the multiple of earnings that these businesses sold for. In Chapter 5 we discuss how the price/earnings ratio works for assessing the value of larger, publicly traded companies. Because they're less well established and riskier from an investment standpoint, small, privately held businesses sell for a lower multiple of earnings than comparable, but larger, companies.

Some advisers and business brokers advocate using a multiple of revenue to determine the value of a business. Revenue is a poor proxy for profitability: Two businesses in the same field can have identical revenue yet quite different profitability because of how well they're run, the pricing of their products and services, and the types of customers they attract.

In addition to looking at the sales price of other businesses relative to earnings, you can consider the value of a company's assets. The so-called *book value* of a company's assets is what the assets are worth per the company's balance sheet. Check these figures to ensure that their asset values are correct. Another, more conservative way to value such assets is to consider the liquidation/replacement cost.

Using contingencies

When you purchase a home, you make your offer contingent upon satisfactory inspections, mortgage loan approval, and proof that the property seller legally holds title to the home. When you make a purchase offer for a business, you should make your offer contingent upon a number of similar issues:

- ✓ **Due diligence.** Make your purchase offer contingent upon a thorough review of the company's financial statements and interviews of key employees, customers, suppliers, and so on. Also, make sure that you can employ whomever you want to help with these evaluations. You may also want to defer paying a portion of the purchase price for 6 to 12 months to make sure that everything is as the owner/seller claims.

- ✓ **Financing.** Unless you make an all-cash offer, make finding financing at an acceptable interest rate another condition of your purchase offer. (Specify acceptable loan terms, including the maximum interest rate at which you will go ahead with the purchase.) By the time you make an offer, you should know whether the seller will loan you money for the purchase. Check with your area's banks that specialize in small-business loans and compare their terms with a loan the seller offers.

- ✓ **Limited liability.** Make sure that the seller is liable for environmental cleanup and undisclosed existing liabilities (debts).

- ✓ **Non-compete clause.** You don't want to buy the business and then have the former owner set up an identical business down the road. Insist that the owner place a non-compete clause in your purchase offer, which specifies that for, say, two years the seller can't establish a similar business. Also consider asking the owner to consult with you for 6 to 12 months to make sure that you tap all his or her valuable experience, as well as to transition relationships with key customers, employees, and suppliers. Consider making the total purchase price dependent on the future success of the company.

Allocating the purchase price

Unlike when you purchase a home and offer, say, $200,000 for it, when you offer $200,000 for a business you need to break down, or allocate, the purchase price among the assets of the business and other categories. The way you structure your purchase can save you tens of thousands of dollars in taxes.

As a buyer, you're generally better off allocating as much of the purchase price as possible to the assets of the business. Why? Because such assets can generally be depreciated (written off for tax purposes) faster than, say, land, which is not depreciable. For tax reasons, the seller's interests will likely oppose yours. You must report the purchase of the business and allocation of the purchase price among business assets to the Canada Revenue Agency.

Taking the final steps

With the help of a lawyer, you should take these additional steps prior to closing the purchase of the business:

- ✔ Notify creditors of the transfer of ownership. In areas where the company does business, a transfer of ownership notice should be published in a general circulation newspaper. If you omit this step, unsecured creditors can generally come after your business if the previous owner has outstanding debts.

- ✔ Check to make sure that no liens are filed against assets of the business and, if you're buying real estate, that the property title is clear.

- ✔ Get the seller to provide proof certifying that federal and provincial employment, sales, and other taxes are all paid up.

Part V

Investing Resources

The 5th Wave   By Rich Tennant

"You may want to talk to Phil—he's one of our more aggressive financial planners."

In this part . . .

Everywhere you turn these days, you're bombarded with investing tidbits, sound bites, trivia, advice, and opinions. In this important part, we help you to evaluate the reliability of a given source. Whether you're reading a magazine or newspaper article or book, perusing an Internet site, using software, watching television, or listening to the radio, you need to know how to evaluate what's worth considering and what to ignore.

Chapter 16

Selecting Investing Resources

● ●

In This Chapter

▶ Overcoming information and advice overload

▶ Evaluating investing resources

● ●

*I*n the past, finding financial information was much simpler and limited. You could subscribe to publications such as *Business Week* and *Forbes* magazine for general money issues and a local, big-city newspaper for daily stock prices. The hard-core, upscale investor had *The Wall Street Journal* or the *Financial Post* delivered daily.

Times have changed, though. Today's investor faces information overload. Radio, television, magazines, newspapers, books, the Internet, family, friends, neighbours, and cabdrivers . . . everywhere you turn these days, someone is offering investing opinions, tips, and advice. You can't pick up a newspaper or magazine or go channel surfing on cable or radio without bumping into articles, stories, segments, and entire programs devoted to investment issues.

You don't (directly) pay for most of this information and, unfortunately, you usually get your money's worth! Much of the financial advice out there is biased and wrong.

Sure, scores of "free" investing sites — most of which are run by investment companies or someone else with something to sell — are on the Internet. Why don't these sites charge you a fee? Gullible people think they're getting a free lunch, but what these sites give away is nothing but subtle and not-so-subtle advertising for whatever products and services they sell. If these sites charged people for frequenting their sites, few would visit.

Chosen wisely, the best investing resources can further your investment education and knowledge and enable you to make better decisions. Because investment information and advice is so widespread, we devote this chapter to helping you separate the good from the mediocre and awful. Although we name the best investment resources we're familiar with, we also explain how you can discern for yourself what's good from what's not. Because the world of investment resources is already large and continues to grow, knowing how to sift is just as important as hearing what the best resources are today.

Coming to Terms with Information Overload

In the late 1990s and early 2000s, many people who were managing their investments in a long-term, conservative fashion were feeling financially left out — and left behind. One of Eric's clients, Roseanne, called him in a near panic. "Eric, I'm not satisfied with my investments. Why are so many of my friends doubling and tripling their money in technology stocks and my mutual funds are going nowhere? Everywhere I turn, people are talking about these high-growth technology companies. I want my piece of the pie too!" Eric explained that many of her diversified mutual funds held some technology stocks as well as stocks in many other industries. He also reminded her that because she was nearing 50 she had a healthy helping of bonds in her portfolio as well.

She urged him to have her put money in some technology stocks and technology-focused funds, but Eric stood his ground. He further encouraged her to read this book (an earlier edition was out at the time), wherein we highlighted technology stocks as a bubble waiting to burst (see Chapter 5). Roseanne followed Eric's advice and now, years later, is happy she did. During the severe stock market decline that began later in the year 2000, technology stocks got clobbered but other market segments (such as bonds and value-oriented stocks) actually increased in value.

A major reason why so many people were talking about making money with technology stocks was that so many media outlets (radio, television, Web sites, and so on) were talking about these investments and other personal money management issues around the clock.

Why are everybody and his brother in the media and publishing world putting out investing information? Has money become that much more complicated over the years? Are there simply more media and publishing executives who want to help us? The following sections explain some of the reasons why investing has become such a hot topic:

✔ **Communications options are expanding.** Over the past generation, the number of television channels has mushroomed as a result of cable television. The explosion of the Internet has introduced a whole new medium. Flip through your cable channels at any hour of the day, and you see infomercials that promise to make you a real estate tycoon or stock market day trader in your spare time. Now, at a relatively low cost, anybody can publish a Web page.

The accessibility of these communications mediums now lets just about anyone with an animated personality and a few bucks appear to be an expert. These newer communications options are primarily structured around selling advertising rather than offering quality content.

✔ **Economic change breeds uncertainty.** Many factors have led to the explosion in financial information and advice that the media and publishers offer. Some are obvious: Global competition and rapid changes in technology are compelling most industries to undergo dramatic changes in much shorter periods of time. Although jobs are relatively plentiful for many with particular training and skills, fear of job loss and financial instability runs high. Economic change and widespread cynicism about the ability of our pension system to provide baby boomers with a reasonable retirement income has also led many to seek investment guidance.

✔ **Financial planners have significant conflicts of interest and are costly.** Ironically, the failure of the "financial planning" industry to meet the needs of those looking for help is one reason why so many consumers seek investment advice elsewhere. Most financial planners earn some or all of their income through commissions from products they sell. Of the small number of fee-based advisers, many primarily manage money for the affluent. And fee-based planners who also manage money have their own conflicts of interest. These planners have a bias against recommending strategies, such as paying off a mortgage or investing in real estate or a small business, that take money away from them to manage. And their hourly consulting rates, if such a service is even offered, are usually quite high.

✔ **Investment choices and responsibilities are increasing.** The difficulty in finding objective financial help is all the more frustrating as individuals face increasingly complex choices. More employees are forced to take responsibility for saving money for their retirement and deciding how to invest that money.

In the past, more employers offered company-managed pension plans with set-out payments. In these plans, the employer put aside money on behalf of employees and retained a pension manager who decided how to invest it. All the employees had to do was learn the level of benefits they had earned and when they could begin drawing a monthly cheque.

Today, there's a big trend toward so-called *defined contribution* pension plans. As the name implies, workers can contribute a set amount, with the employer sometimes also contributing on the employees' behalf. But just how much the plan will pay out in retirement pension payments isn't at all fixed. The employee typically has to make some decisions about how the money is invested. And the amount of pension each worker will receive hinges on how successful — or unsuccessful — those decisions are. Just as with individual RRSPs, employees need to educate themselves about how much money they need to save and how to invest it. In addition to mastering retirement planning and investment allocation, individuals face a dizzying number of financial products, such as the hundreds of mutual funds that are on the market.

✔ **Our society is too money focused.** The pages of tabloid papers and magazines are filled with highly paid movie and sports celebrities and wealthy corporate executives. Other warning signs abound for a society that cares more about money than people and human relationships. Some people view hiring hordes of people to raise their children as a luxury of wealth. Others spend tens of thousands of dollars on fancy, financed cars that require years of work to pay off. We don't spend enough time with our children and then are puzzled why the teen suicide rate has tripled in the past two generations and why violence in schools and elsewhere is on the rise.

Read the next section to find out how you can filter out the best information and advice and skip the rest.

Separating Financial Facts from Fiction

As the late Carl Sagan said in *The Fine Art of Baloney Detection,* "Finding the occasional straw of truth awash in an ocean of confusion and bamboozle requires intelligence, vigilance, dedication and courage. But, if we don't practice these tough habits of thought, we cannot hope to solve the truly serious problems that face us — and we risk becoming a nation of suckers, up for grabs by the next charlatan who comes along."

Just because more sources offer investing advice doesn't mean that you should read, listen to, or watch much of it. In this section we offer prescriptions for how to intelligently choose among all the available financial content.

Understanding how advertising distorts the facts

The first rule for maximizing your chances of finding the best investing information and advice is to recognize that there are no free lunches. Too many people get sucked into supposedly free resources. Click on your television, radio, or the Internet and you come across mountains of "free" stuff. In addition to more violence and sex than the world needs or wants, you'll find lots to do with the world of investing.

Of course, someone is paying for providing all this "free" content, and it's all there for some reason. In the vast majority of cases, advertising is footing the bill. And therein generally lies a huge problem.

Imagine for a moment that, instead of paying for this book, you could obtain it for free by simply visiting your favourite bookstore and legally walking out with a copy. Further suppose that this book was totally financed by advertising. Instead of being 450 pages, it would be 900 pages, with half the pages devoted to ads. Although the book would be heftier, it would be free.

If you think that's a worthwhile trade-off because you'd still get to read the same useful advice written by yours truly, you'd be mistaken — we wouldn't write such a book.

As we discuss in Chapter 18, some authors choose to write books that are the equivalent of an infomercial for something else — such as high-priced seminars — that the "author" *really* wants to sell. Such writers aren't interested in educating and helping you as much as they're seeking to sell you something. So, for example, an author might write about how complicated the investing markets are and what indicators he follows to time investments. However, at the end of such a book, the author might say that investing is simply too complicated to do on your own and that you really need a personal investment manager — which, to no great surprise, the author happens to be.

Advertising often compromises the quality of investment advice.

We won't say that you can't find some useful investment resources in mediums with lots of advertising. You can find some good investing programs on radio and television and some helpful investing sites on the Internet. However, these resources are the exception to the rule that, where there's lot of advertising, there's little valuable information and advice. Likewise, just because magazines and newspapers have quite a bit of advertising doesn't mean that some of their columnists and articles aren't worthy of your time.

Advertising can cause the following problems with the media outlets and other publications that profit from it:

- **Influencing content.** Many organizations, such as newspaper and magazine publishers and radio and television stations that accept ads, say that their ad departments are separate from their editorial departments. The truth, however, is that in most of these organizations, advertisers wield influence over the content. At a minimum, the editorial environment must be perceived as conducive to the sale of the advertiser's product.

The stock market cable television channels, for example, carry many ads from brokers catering to investors who pick and trade their own stocks. Furthermore, such stations carry ads from firms that purport to teach you how to make big bucks day trading (see Chapter 5). Not surprisingly, such stations offer many "news" segments on their shows that cater to stock traders and condone and endorse foolish strategies, such as day trading, instead of condemning them. Rather than asking themselves what's in the best interests of their viewers, listeners, and readers, executives at too many media and publishing firms ask what will attract attention and advertisers.

✔ **Corrupting content.** In too many organizations, advertisers can have a direct and adulterating influence on editorial content. Specifically, some media organizations and publishers simply won't say something negative about a major advertiser or will highlight and praise investment companies that are big advertisers.

More than a few publications have attempted to edit out critical comments we've made about companies with lousy products that turned out to be advertisers in their publications. Some editors simply say that they don't want to bite the hand that feeds them. Others are less candid about why they remove such criticism. The bottom line is still the same: Advertisers' influence squashes freedom of speech and, more important, prevents readers, viewers, and listeners from getting the truth and best advice. (By the way, we avoid writing for organizations that edit our work in such a fashion.)

✔ **Low-quality content.** Because of the previously mentioned reasons and an overall lack of concern for the value of information and advice, some investing resources cut corners on the quality of their content. Since consumers often pay nothing or next to nothing for many investment resources, the media have an incentive to sell advertising space and not to hire high-quality writers who can offer sound advice.

Recognizing quality resources

With the tremendous increase in the coverage of investing and other personal money issues, more and more journalists are writing about increasingly technical issues — often in areas in which they have no expertise. Some of these writers provide good information and advice. Unfortunately, some dish out bad advice. In fields such as medicine or the law, you wouldn't be so willing to take advice from non-experts. Why should you care any less about your money?

How can you know what's good and whom you can trust? Although we can suggest resources that we hold in high regard (and do so throughout this book, especially in Chapters 17, 18, and 19), we recognize that you may encounter many different investment resources and that you need to understand how to tell the best from the rest. The answer to the question, dear reader, rests in educating thyself. The more knowledgeable you are about sound and flawed investment strategies, the better able you are to tell good from not-so-good investment resources.

The best thing to do when you encounter a financial magazine, newspaper, Web site, or other resource for the first time is to investigate it. The following sections suggest some investigative work you should do before you take anyone's investment advice.

Follow the money

All things being equal, you have a greater chance of finding quality content when subscriber fees account for the bulk of a company's revenue and advertising accounts for little or none of the revenue. This generalization, of course, is just that — a generalization. There are, of course, exceptions.

Some publications that derive a reasonable portion of their revenues from advertising have some good columns and content. Conversely, some relatively ad-free sources aren't very good.

Figure out their philosophy and agenda

Readers of our books can clearly understand our philosophies about investing. We advocate buying and holding, not trading and gambling. We explain how to build wealth through proven vehicles, including stocks, real estate, and small-business ownership. Our guiding beliefs are clearly detailed on the Cheat Sheet in the front of this book.

Unfortunately, many publications and programs don't make it as easy for you to see or hear their operating beliefs. You may have to do some homework. For example, with a radio program, you probably have to listen to at least portions of several shows to get a sense of the host's investment philosophies. Warning signs include publications and programs that make investing sound overly complicated and that imply or say outright that you won't succeed or do as well if you don't hire a financial adviser or follow your investments like a hawk.

Just about everywhere you turn these days — radio, television, and the Internet — you can get up-to-the-minute updates on financial markets around the globe. Although most investors have a natural curiosity about how their investments are doing, from our experience, the constant barrage of updates obscures the big picture.

In many cases, publishing and media companies report what we call the "noise" rather than the news of the day. Some companies are far worse about doing so than others.

Over the next week, take a close look at how you spend your time keeping up with financial news and other information. Do the programs and publications you most heavily use really help you better understand and map out sound investment strategies, or do they end up confusing, overwhelming, and paralyzing you with bits and pieces of contradictory and often hyped noise? We're not saying you should tune these resources out completely, but we are saying that you should devote less time to the noise of the day and more time to self-education. How can you do that? Read a few good books (a topic we discuss in detail in Chapter 18).

Consider their qualifications

Examine the backgrounds, including professional work experience and education credentials, of a resource's writers, hosts, and/or anchors. If such information isn't given or easily found, that's usually a red flag. People with something to hide, or a lack of something significantly redeeming to say about themselves, usually don't promote their backgrounds.

Of course, just because someone seems to have a relatively impressive background doesn't mean that she has your best interests in mind or has honestly presented her qualifications. For example, journalist William P. Barrett was sceptical of financial author Suze Orman's publisher's claim that Orman (author of several books, including *The 9 Steps to Financial Freedom*) had 1,000 new clients per year. He investigated and presented a sobering review of Orman's stated credentials and qualifications in *Forbes* magazine — revealing that they were largely exaggerated. A writer for *The San Francisco Chronicle* later substantiated this fact.

So what's the lesson to be learned from this story? You can't accept stated credentials and qualifications at face value, for the simple reason that some people don't tell the truth. You can increase your chances of being tipped off to hucksters by being sceptical. In fact, *Forbes* journalist Barrett began his investigation of Orman based on the sheer outrageousness of the number of new clients she claimed to be getting each year.

Chapter 17

Periodical, Radio, and Television Investing Advice

In This Chapter

▶ Financial magazines and newspapers

▶ Investment newsletters

▶ Radio and television programs

*A*ll the news that's fit to print, air, or view — newspapers, magazines, newsletters, and radio and television programs — inundates us with investing information and advice. In this chapter, we explain what to look for — and what to look *out* for — when you tune in to these media sources in the hopes of finding out how to invest like the best.

In Print: Magazines and Newspapers

Visit a newsstand, and you find many investing publications as well as general-interest publications with investing columns. We've written many investing articles for various magazines and newspapers. Some of the experiences have been enjoyable, others okay, and some miserable. The best publications and editors we've written for take seriously their responsibility to provide qualify information and advice to their readers. The worst and mediocre are more concerned with their bottom line than with quality. In this section we alert you to the problems with magazine and newspaper investment articles and help you choose the best publications for your investing needs.

Oversimplifying the message

The short length of newspaper and magazine articles can easily lead writers to oversimplify complex issues and offer flawed advice. For example, many pieces on mutual funds focus on a fund's returns and investment philosophies, devoting little, if any, space to the risks or tax consequences of investing in recommended funds.

Consider a short piece entitled "Index Funds: Size Matters" in the October 12, 1998, issue of *Time* magazine. Using data from Morningstar, the article argues, "To invest in large companies, buy a low-fee index fund. But to invest in smaller stocks, it's worth paying more for an active fund manager."

According to the *Time* article, for the five-year period ending August 31, 1998, 0 percent of actively managed mutual funds investing in large company stocks were able to beat the corresponding market index — the Standard & Poor's 500 (S&P 500). By comparison, the article says, a whopping 98 percent of actively managed mutual funds investing in a mix of small-company stocks were able to beat its corresponding market index — the Russell 2000. This data does seemingly lead to the conclusion offered in the article: Use index funds for investing in large-company stocks but shun index funds and use actively managed funds when investing in small-cap stocks. The data is compelling.

There's a big problem, however, with the article's analysis of Morningstar's data: It's wrong, and wrong in a big way. Like many such articles in media publications, the genesis for this piece was an already-published piece, in this case in Morningstar's *FundInvestor* publication. Like too many reporters who cover investing these days, the *Time* reporter was too busy or (more likely) too financially ignorant to understand Morningstar's article.

What Morningstar's piece actually demonstrated was how frequently over the preceding 5 years (over the various 12-month periods) the average return for a fund in a given fund category beat the corresponding index performance for the category. However, this data is quite different from what portion of the individual funds in a given category outperformed the corresponding index over the five-year time period.

Readers who perused this *Time* piece were left with the erroneous conclusion that actively managed stock funds investing in large-cap stocks never beat the S&P 500 but that small-cap stock funds almost always beat their corresponding index — the Russell 2000. Eric asked Morningstar to compile its data the way in which *Time* presented it. For each fund category, Morningstar analyzed what portion of the funds was able to beat the comparable market index over the same five-year period.

Among large-company stock funds, just over 17 percent (a far cry from 0 percent) of them beat the S&P 500 over that five-year time span. Among small-company stock funds, about 50 percent (again, a big difference from the 98 percent cited by *Time*) beat the Russell 2000.

You should exercise great caution even in using this correct data to assert that it's better to buy index funds when investing in large-company stocks. During the five-year period study, larger-cap stocks did far better than small-cap stocks — the S&P 500 returned an annualized 18.2 percent, more than double the annual returns of the Russell 2000 of 8.1 percent. Many mutual funds focusing on small-company stocks tend, because of the large assets of the fund, to hold a portion in larger-cap stocks. Thus, many small-cap funds were able to best the Russell 2000 index, thanks to higher returns provided by large-cap holdings.

You also shouldn't simply use one period of data to determine the value (or lack thereof) of particular index funds. The results of various studies we've examined demonstrate that the majority of actively managed funds underperform the market indexes. Although a somewhat greater proportion of larger cap funds tend to fall short of their mark, small company stock index funds have value, too.

Highlighting hype and horror

Whenever the stock market suffers a sharp decline, many in the media bring out the gloom and doom. Front-page headlines, such as "The Beginning of the End," torment investors about holding on to their stocks.

Scores of articles horrify parents with the expected cost of a university education. The typical advice: Start saving and investing early so that you don't have to tell Junior that you can't afford to send him to university.

Completely overlooked and ignored are the tax and other consequences of the recommended investment strategies. For example, if parents don't take advantage of tax-deductible RRSPs, they pay more in taxes. Sound investing decisions require a holistic approach that acknowledges that people have limited money and must make these sorts of trade-offs.

Offering poor advice

Consider the gaffe made by a *Money* magazine piece entitled "Where to get safe, high yields." The title itself should have been a red flag: It's impossible to find a *safe,* high yield. To get high yields, you must be willing to accept more risk. In the *Money* article, three of the recommended investments were limited partnerships (LPs) sold through commission-based brokers. These products' high commissions and ongoing fees doomed even the luckiest of investors to mediocre or dismal investment returns.

The *Money* article even asserted that investors could earn annual returns as high as 18 percent on some LPs. Students of the financial markets know that the best ownership investments, such as stocks and real estate, return no more than 10 to 12 percent per year over the long haul. To expect more is to hold unrealistic expectations.

Quoting experts who are not

Historically, one way that journalists have attempted to overcome technical gaps in their knowledge is to interview and quote financial experts. Although this may add to the accuracy and quality of a story, journalists who aren't experts themselves sometimes have trouble discerning among self-anointed experts.

We continue to be amazed at how many newspaper and magazine financial writers quote investment newsletter writers' advice. As we discuss in the section "Investment Newsletters" later in this chapter, the predictive advice of newsletter writers is often wrong and leads investors to earn lower returns due to frequent trading than if they simply bought and held.

Focusing on noise and minutiae

In addition to not doing their homework on their sources, writers of daily financial press reports tend to make people short-sighted. Today it's common for daily newspaper charts to show the stock market's movements at five-minute intervals throughout the previous day. This focus on the noise of the day leads nervous investors to make panicked, emotionally based decisions, such as selling *after* major stock market falls.

Of course, the daily print media aren't the only ones chronicling the minutiae. As we discuss elsewhere in this chapter and this part, other media, including television, radio, and the Internet, induce many investors to lose sight of the long term and the big picture.

Making the most of newspapers and magazines

So what should you do if you want to find out more about investing but don't want to be overloaded with information? Educate yourself and be selective. If you're considering subscribing to financial publications, go to the library first and review some old issues. Was the information and advice useful and free of errors? The more you know, the easier it is to separate the wheat from the chaff.

Shy away from publications that purport to be able to predict the future — few people can, and those who can are usually busy managing money. Unfortunately, since the financial markets became more volatile in the late 1990s and early 2000s, we've witnessed more and more publications promoting columnists and headlines that attempt to prognosticate.

Read bylines and biographies and get to know writers' strengths and weaknesses. Ditto for the entire publication. Any writer or publisher can make mistakes. Some make many more than others — follow their advice at your own peril. Start by evaluating advice in the areas you know the most about. For example, if you're interested in investing in Microsoft or Nortel and are reasonably familiar with the computer industry, find out what the publications say about technology investments.

And remember that you're not going to outfox the financial markets, because they're reasonably efficient (see Chapter 4). Spend your time seeking out information and advice that helps you flesh out your goals and develop a plan with specific recommendations.

Investment Newsletters

Particularly in the newsletter business, prognosticators fill your mailbox with promotional material making outrageous claims about their returns. Private money managers, not subject to the same scrutiny and auditing requirements as mutual funds, can do the same.

Be especially wary of any newsletters that tout high returns. Stephen Leeb's *Personal Finance* newsletter, for example, claims that he's developed a brilliant proprietary model, which he calls the "Master Key Indicator." His model has supposedly predicted the last 28 upturns in the market in a row without a single miss. The odds of doing this, according to Leeb, are more than 268 million to 1! The ad goes on to claim that Leeb's "Master Key" market-timing system could have turned a $10,000 investment over 12 years into $39.1 million, a return of 390,000 percent!

Turns out that this outrageous claim was based on *backtesting,* looking back over historic returns and creating "what if" scenarios. In other words, Leeb didn't turn anyone's $10,000 into $39 million. Much too late after that ad appeared, the SEC finally charged Leeb with false advertising. Leeb settled out of court for a mere $60,000 fine (far less than he cost investors).

According to the *Hulbert Financial Digest,* a publication that evaluates financial newsletters, the worst investment newsletters have underperformed the market averages by dozens of percentage points; some would have even lost you money during a decade when the financial markets performed extraordinarily well. Newsletter purveyor Joe Granville, for example, has long been known for making outrageous and extreme stock market predictions and is often quoted in financial publications. He claims to have the number-one rated newsletter — omitting the significant detail that it was for one year (1989). Over the subsequent decade — one of the best decades ever for the stock market (with U.S. stocks more than quadrupling in value) — followers of Granville's advice *lost* 99 percent of their investment!

Be highly suspicious of investment newsletters' claims of past investment performance. Don't believe a track record unless it's been audited by a reputable accounting firm with experience doing such audits. In order to make sound investing choices, you don't need predictions and soothsayers. If you choose to follow these prognosticators and you're lucky, little harm will be done. But more often than not, you can lose lots of money following their predictions. Stay far away from publications that purport to be able to tell what's going to happen next. No one has a crystal ball.

If you're looking for ongoing advice and commentary, select newsletters that have a conservative, long-term, and anti–crystal ball philosophy. The best newsletters will admit outright that they cannot — and will not — try to predict just which stock or fund will serve up the next investing home run. Instead, they see their role as reinforcing sound investing fundamentals, providing useful background and analysis, and informing readers of significant changes or news in the areas they cover. One example of a Canadian newsletter that focuses on stocks in this manner is *The Investment Reporter.* Published weekly by MPL Communications, an annual subscription costs $297 and can be ordered by calling 800-430-1897. Another choice is *The Successful Investor,* which is published monthly. Annual subscriptions cost $72. For information, call 416-756-0888 or e-mail the editor at mckeough@idirect.com.

For mutual fund investors, good long-term advice is coupled with a decidedly realistic and grounded view of the markets in general in the *Canadian Mutual Fund Adviser.* Also from MPL, it's published every two weeks, and annual subscriptions cost $127.

Radio and Television Programs

As you move from the world of magazines and newspapers to radio and television, the entertainment component usually increases. In this section we highlight some common problems with radio and television programs and offer some recommendations for the better programs.

Looking at problems with radio and television programs

We've both been guests on many a radio and television program. Just as Dorothy discovered in *The Wizard of Oz,* seeing how things work behind the scenes tends to deglamorize these mediums. Here are the main problems we've discovered from our years observing radio and television.

You often get what you pay for

Some of the worst financial advice is brought to you, not surprisingly, for "free." Many radio stations have financial and money talk shows. Money and investing shows are proliferating on television cable channels. Because listeners don't pay for these shows, advertising often drives who and what gets on the air.

Some of these shows are "hosted" by someone who's nothing more than a financial salesperson. That person's first, and sometimes only, motivation for wanting to do the show is to pick up clients. Many local radio investing programs are hosted by a local stockbroker (who usually calls himself a financial consultant or planner). A broker who reels in just one big fish a month — a person with, say, $300,000 to invest — can generate commissions totalling $15,000 by selling investments with a 5 percent commission.

But radio suffers from more than brokers trolling for new clients, as evidenced by the case of Sonny Bloch, a New York radio personality who was indicted for fraud. The U.S. Securities and Exchange Commission found that Bloch was receiving kickbacks from investment brokers for endorsing some pretty crummy investment products on his nationally syndicated radio show. The SEC also filed a complaint against Bloch for defrauding investors of millions of dollars to supposedly purchase some radio stations. Instead, according to the SEC, Bloch and his wife used hundreds of thousands of dollars to buy a condominium. Partners in a precious metals firm (DeAngelis Brothers Collectibles) that Bloch regularly endorsed on the air were arrested for theft and ended up in bankruptcy. Again, Bloch was accused of receiving kickbacks.

We know from personal experience what too many radio stations look for in the way of hosts for financial programs. The host's integrity, knowledge, and lack of conflict of interest don't matter. Willingness to work for next to nothing helps: One radio station program director said she liked the broker who was hosting a financial talk show because the broker was willing to work for so little compensation from the radio station. Never mind the fact that the broker rarely gave useful advice and was obviously trolling for new clients. That didn't matter to the program director, who said, "We're in the entertainment business."

Information and hype overload

Picture this: The opening bell will sound in 5 minutes, 32 seconds on the floor of the New York Stock Exchange. A digital clock counts down the seconds on-screen as CNBC reporter Maria Bartiromo crams sound bite after sound bite into her monologue.

The previous day, U.S. Federal Reserve Board Chairman Alan Greenspan made an unexpected 0.25 percent cut in the Fed Discount Rate, and stocks jumped sharply. Now, on the morning after, CNBC tries to pump this short-term excitement for all it's worth. Bartiromo talks so frenetically that she has to continually brush her hair back after every time she whips her head around. Like a runner near the end of a sprint, she's practically out of breath. Although Bartiromo is technically reporting, her real job is to keep CNBC viewers glued to their TV screens for the opening of the world's biggest stock market.

At 9:30 a.m. EST the market opens, and transactions start streaming across the bottom of the television screen. Changes in the major market indexes — the Dow Jones Industrial Average, the S&P 500, and the NASDAQ index — also flash on the screen. In fact, these indexes are updated almost every five *seconds* on the screen. Far more exciting than a political race or sporting event, this event never ends and offers constant change and excitement. Even after the markets close, reporting of still-open overseas markets continues.

Does all this reporting and data make us better investors? Of course not. But the conventionally accepted notion is that this information overload levels the playing field for the individual investor. We know too many investors who make emotionally based decisions prodded by all this noise, prognostication, opinion, and hearsay.

Poor method of guest selection

Some journalists, often in an effort to overcome their own lack of knowledge, like to interview "experts." However, as noted above, journalists who are themselves not experts sometimes have trouble discerning among the self-anointed experts. A classic example of this problem is the media exposure that author Charles Givens used to receive. Givens became a darling of the media and the public following unprecedented, consecutive three-day appearances on NBC's *Today* show.

"When Charles Givens talks, everyone listens," said Jane Pauley, then co-host of the *Today* show. Bryant Gumbel, the other co-host, said of Givens, "Last time he was here, the studio came to a complete stop. . . . Everyone started taking notes, and I was asking for advice." Givens regularly held court on the talk show circuit with the likes of Larry King, Oprah Winfrey, and Phil Donahue.

The Givens example highlights some of the media's inability to distinguish between good and bad experts. It's relatively easy for the financially sophisticated to see the dangerous, oversimplified, and biased advice that Givens offers in his books. In his first best-seller, *Wealth Without Risk,* Givens recommended investing in limited partnerships and provided a phone number and address of a firm, Delta Capital Corporation in Florida, through which to buy the partnerships. Those who bought these products ended up paying hefty sales commissions and owning investments worth half or less of their original value. Besides the problematic partnerships he recommended, court proceedings against Givens in a number of states eventually uncovered that he owned a major share of Delta Capital.

Other investing advice from Givens that gives cause to pause: In his chapters on investing, he says that the average yearly return you'll earn investing in mutual funds will be 25 or 30 percent on discounted mortgages. The reality: An investor would be fortunate to earn half of these inflated returns.

So how did Givens get on all these national programs? He had a shrewd publicist, and the show producers either didn't read his books or were themselves financially illiterate. Talk shows and many reporters often don't take the time to check out people like Givens. We know this for a fact because we've been on dozens of radio and television programs and understand how they work. Most of the time, the books are never read. Producers, who themselves are often financially illiterate, often decide to put someone on the air on the basis of a press kit or a call from a publicist.

Picking the best radio and television investing programs

Even though we warn you about problems associated with radio and television investing advice, you can find some good programs and hosts among the bad apples — and, yes, some of the good ones are Canadian. The following are our picks for the best of the lot:

✔ *Venture.* This CBC program offers a look at the trials and tribulations of entrepreneurs and other business owners, following them as they struggle through the stages of founding or growing a business. It offers a real-life view of the challenges — and the rewards — offered by going into business for oneself. *Venture* airs on both CBC TV and Newsworld on Sunday evenings.

✔ *CBC News Business Weekly.* This magazine-style show offers a mix of personal finance and stock market advice and analysis, and also recaps the week's business news. Catching the program is a good way to keep abreast of significant business or economic news without getting caught up in the daily noise of the marketplace. The program airs several times on Newsworld each weekend.

✔ *Street Cents.* *Street Cents* is a rarity. While not an investing show, it offers young people valuable advice and insights into money and the world of business, all while teaching them how to be smart consumers. It profiles young people who are starting or actually running their own small business, and also regularly puts to the test the marketing hype targeted at young people.

Many other programs are out there. Worthy of honourable mention are CBC's *Marketplace, The Wall Street Journal*'s syndicated television show, and *Louis Rukeyser's Wall Street.*

Chapter 18

Investing Books: The Best and the Rest

. . . .

In This Chapter

▶ Recognizing that some books advertise more than they educate

▶ Being sceptical about authors' claimed historic returns

▶ Presenting our favourite investing books

. . . .

O ver the years, we've read hundreds of investing and financial books. We hope you haven't subjected yourself to this task!

Although most investing books have something to offer, too many are burdened with wrongheaded advice and misinformation. As a non-expert, you may have a hard time sifting through the dung heap for the tidbits of treasure. The bad stuff can pollute your otherwise intelligent thinking and lead you to make the same investing mistakes that millions have made before you.

We hope we're not the first to tell you not to believe everything you read. Publishing is no different from any other business — companies are in it to make money. As with other industries, the short-sighted desire to reap quick profits motivates some companies to publish content that seems attractive in the short term but is toxic to readers in the long term. In this chapter we help you sift through the confusion to find books worth reading.

Beware Infomercials Disguised as Books

The worst books tend to confuse more than they convey. Why would an author want to do that? Well, some authors have an incentive to make things complicated and mysterious. Their agenda may be to sell you a high-priced newsletter or convince you to turn your money over to them to manage.

Here's what one book author admitted: "Royalties, schmoyalties . . . I write books to hook people into my monthly newsletter. I can make $185 per year off of a $195 newsletter sale. You can't do that with a book." You sure can't, but this author's books are short on information and advice and say that you need to keep up with the latest developments to make the right investments. Worse, when you subscribe to his newsletter, you're told that the financial markets are so complicated and rapidly changing that the newsletter is really no substitute for using his money-management service!

The worst books steer you toward purchasing a crummy investment product that the author has a vested interest in selling you. Unfortunately, most publishers don't do their homework to check out prospective authors. Most publishers don't care what the author is up to, or if the author is indeed an expert on the topic, as long as he or she is willing and able to write a saleable book. Authors who run around the country conducting seminars are a plus to the publisher.

For one *extremely* cautionary tale, we offer you the story of Wade Cook. In his books and seminar promotional materials, Cook claims to be able to teach people how to earn monthly returns of 20 percent or more (that's right — *monthly*, not yearly) by using his stock market investing strategies.

Cook's self-published best-selling books are short on specifics and are largely infomercials for his high-priced seminars. His get-rich-quick investment seminars — many of which cost a whopping $4,695 U.S. — were so successful at attracting attendees that his company, Profit Financial Corporation, went public and generated more than $100 million in revenues annually! Cook wasn't shy about promising people they can get rich quick without much effort. Here's a passage from his book *Stock Market Miracles:*

> I want millions of dollars and I don't want to have to work a 9 to 5 job to get them. Boy, that's a conundrum. It's almost impossible to work a typical American job, with average income and accumulate millions. Yes, in 40 to 50 years maybe, but who wants to wait that long? That's the rub —accomplishing the task of having millions without having to work for millions.

> You see my method is simple. I want to use a small amount of money — risk capital if you will — to generate cash flow which will exponentially generate more income.

Cook promised his followers several hundred percent annualized returns by teaching them how to successfully gamble (not invest) in the stock market. His "techniques" included trading in and out of stocks and options on stocks after short holding periods of weeks, days, or even hours.

His trading strategies were loosely based on technical analysis — that is, examining a stock's price movements and volume history through charting. (See Chapter 6 for more details on the general foolishness of technical analysis.) More best-selling books have appeared in recent years touting how people can get rich day trading stocks, which is quite similar to Cook's recommended approach.

With the booming stock market during the 1990s, some people earned higher-than-average (10 percent) annualized returns. But Cook's investment seminars, which were offered in cities throughout the country, were marketed to folks this way: "If you aren't getting 20 percent per month, or 300 percent annualized returns on your investments, you need to be there."

Steven Thomas, a truck driver, went to a seminar with his wife so that both of them could follow and implement Cook's strategies. In addition to spending $4,695 on the seminar, they spent another $2,000 on audiotapes and videotapes. Six months later, he spent $1,500 on a paging system from Cook's company. The results: Thomas eventually lost $36,000 on investments made following Cook's strategies, which he borrowed against his home's equity. "I saw this as an opportunity to quit my job and just invest in the stock market," says Thomas. "This has had a terrible impact on my family, and I'm super depressed."

Of course, if Cook were indeed earning the 300 percent annual returns his seminars claim to be able to teach the masses how to achieve, he would, in about a decade, become the world's wealthiest individual if he invested just 1 million of the dollars he supposedly earned in real estate. Look out, Bill Gates and Warren Buffett! Any investor starting with just $10,000 would vault to the top of the list of the world's wealthiest people in about 15 years if Cook's teachings really worked. So how did he get his start in the investing world? Here's what his Web site says:

> He was a taxicab driver in the '70s. Borrowing $500 from his father, Wade Cook started buying real estate. His innovative ideas and gutsy follow-through enabled him to turn that $500 into several million. But that's nothing compared with what he's doing on Wall Street. Starting with $1,300, using his "Rolling Rock" and "Range Rider" methods, he's showing students how to create millions. Why is Wade so smart? He says he's "street smart." What he discovered driving a cab changed his life forever. While his fellow cabbies were out looking for the big runs, Wade was taking every little run he could find — $4 here, $5 here. You see it costs $2 just to get into a cab (something called a meter drop) even if you only go two blocks. At the end of a month, Wade made three times what every other taxicab driver made. Now, Wade applies his "meter drop" technique to his stock market investment business — making a ton of money on a lot of little deals.

What was the real story behind Cook's wealth? Although his investment return expectations were completely unrealistic, he got away with claiming hyped and undocumented returns for many years because he doesn't manage money for others. In the U.S., seminar promoters and newsletter writers face no scrutiny by the U.S. Securities and Exchange Commission (the SEC) of their inflated performance claims or what they do in their seminars as long as no securities laws are violated. The SEC refers to such organizations as "nonregulated entities."

Of course, Cook isn't the first person to profit in this fashion. Numerous other seminar promoters and authors (some are discussed later in this chapter) have cleaned up as well, including the Beardstown Ladies investment club, which could not document their supposedly market-beating returns of 23+ percent per year (see the next section for details). And there's more to Cook's past than simply driving a taxi. According to *Smart Money* magazine, his dubious business practices had him in trouble throughout the 1980s. At the end of his real estate seminars, which touted that average people could become millionaires by buying property with little money down, he began peddling stock in his own business ventures.

By 1990, securities regulators in six states — Missouri, Utah, Minnesota, Illinois, Oregon, and Arizona — issued him cease-and-desist orders for selling securities without a licence, selling unregistered securities, and omission of material facts — like the fact that he'd declared bankruptcy in 1987. In fact, Arizona charged that Cook had duped $390,841 out of 150 investors by selling unregistered securities, funnelling $48,000 of that money into a Scottsdale home purchase and federal income tax payments. The state ordered him to pay back the money and slapped him with a $150,000 penalty.

Cook answered by filing bankruptcy (again). Arizona shot back by indicting him on 18 counts of securities fraud. The case has been battled all the way to the Supreme Court. Most of the counts were dismissed on a technicality (double jeopardy); the rest were settled when he paid $70,500 in restitution.

Cook then moved back up to his home state of Washington, where he didn't lay low for long. His new company, Profit Financial Corporation, has become wildly successful by selling his Wall Street Workshop seminars and publishing his two stock-picking books. The attorneys general of several states sought millions of dollars in consumer refunds and sued the company. The states alleged that the company lied about its investment track record. (Now that's a big surprise — this company claimed you'd make 300 percent per year in stocks!) Cook's company settled the blizzard of state and Federal Trade Commission (FTC) lawsuits against his firm by agreeing to accurately disclose its trading record in future promotions and to give refunds to customers who were misled by past inflated return claims.

Although Profit Financial Corporation is a public company, SEC documents show that it's not exactly shareholder-friendly. Cook has set up a rather clever business structure whereby the public company (of which he is the majority owner) must pay him for the right to print his words and teach his methods. This enables him to funnel much of the revenue stream directly into his pockets before it ever gets to the shareholders. According to SEC filings, Cook's total corporate compensation in one year exceeded $8 million! According to a recent news report by Bloomberg News, his firm lost a whopping 89 percent of its own money trading in 2000. As Deb Bortner, director of the Washington State Securities Division and president of the North American Securities Administrators Association, observed, "Either Wade is unable to follow his own system, which he claims is simple to follow, or the system doesn't work."

Be highly suspicious of investing books that direct you to high-priced seminars and other expensive products and services from the author. The best investing books, which we recommend later in this chapter, seek to instruct and educate.

Ignore Unaudited Performance Claims

Book authors avoid careful scrutiny of claims of especially high returns. Some book publishers are happy to look the other way or even to solicit and encourage great boasts that they use in the packaging to sell books. Consider these two recent books: *The Beardstown Ladies' Common-Sense Investment Guide: How We Beat the Stock Market — And How You Can, Too* and *The Whiz Kid of Wall Street's Investment Guide* by Matt Seto.

The Beardstown investment club claimed a whopping 23.4 percent annual return since the club's inception in 1983. In the book, the authors advocate forming an investment club, pooling your money, and using a simple stock selection method to beat the pants off the market and the suspendered managers of mutual funds. The bulk of this book walks the reader through how this investment club evaluated and selected individual stocks.

Seto's book boasts, "Matt Seto manages a portfolio that consistently outperforms 99 percent of all mutual fund managers . . . and returns an annual average of 34 percent." In his book, this 17-year-old investing genius says to forget bonds, real estate, and mutual funds and grow rich by investing entirely in individual stocks.

Each of these books makes prominently displayed and marketed performance claims. The Beardstown club's and Seto's returns, compared with the market averages, place them shoulder to shoulder with the legendary Peter Lynch of the now famous Fidelity Magellan fund, and Warren Buffett, an investor who Peter Lynch described as "the Greatest Investor of them all." Problem is, neither book contains information as to how these investment gurus calculate their returns, nor are the authors able to substantiate their claimed returns when asked.

When Eric first wrote about the Beardstown book for *The San Francisco Examiner* in 1995, he offered to work with an accounting firm to calculate the club's returns if the club supplied the necessary information. He asked the same of Seto when he read his book. Neither of these authors could supply the documentation to prove their claims, and they back-pedalled when pressed.

Initially, the Beardstown club said it would send the information, but months passed, and it never arrived. The club's media spokesperson then told Eric that the club has "chosen not to make our return an issue . . . we're not out to be bragging." This statement was surprising, given the claims prominently plastered all over its book.

A 1998 piece in *Chicago* magazine proved that, although the Beardstown investment club claimed 23 percent per year returns versus 14 percent for the market, the club actually tremendously underperformed the market and earned only 9 percent per year. The publisher of the Beardstown book, Buena Vista Publishing (which was doing business as Hyperion and Seth Godin Productions), was ultimately sued. The book publisher settled the lawsuit in 2002. Do you think the Beardstown ladies would have gotten their book deal (and landed on best-seller lists) if the facts had been known? Seto, likewise, couldn't prove his claim of an astounding 34 percent return. Meanwhile, the printing presses crank away.

If a performance claim hasn't been independently audited, ignore it. Remember also that the stock market over the long term provides annualized returns of about 10 percent. View sceptically any prognosticator or author claiming substantially higher returns that sound too good to be true.

Investing Books Worth Reading

Exceptional investing books — ones that are readable, educational, and insightful — are rare. Some of the better investment books are technical in nature and are written by career investment folks, so don't be surprised if they require more than one read. Make the investment of time; it'll pay big dividends (and capital gains!). Following are our picks for books that are worth the trouble of tracking down and reading.

A Random Walk Down Wall Street

Now in its seventh edition, *A Random Walk Down Wall Street* (Norton), by Burton Malkiel, is a classic that was first published in 1973. Malkiel is an entertaining and intelligent writer. Drawing from examples from this century and others, Malkiel teaches how *speculative bubbles* (frenzied buying) and fear and greed, as well as economic and corporate fundamentals, can move the financial markets.

One fundamental premise of his book is that the financial markets can't be predicted, especially in the short term. Common sense confirms this premise: If someone could figure out a system to predict the markets and make a fortune, then that person wouldn't waste time writing a book, publishing a newsletter, and so on. Malkiel, in fact, is one of the pioneers and proponents of *index mutual funds,* which simply invest in a relatively fixed basket of securities in order to track the overall market performance rather than to attempt to beat it. (See Chapter 8 to find out about index funds and how to use them.)

Needless to say, many Wall Street types aren't enamoured of this book. As Malkiel says, the very term *random walk* is an "obscenity." But Malkiel presents a mountain of compelling arguments and data to support his case that most Wall Street firms and their investment research aren't worthy of an investor's hard-earned money. He also convincingly rebukes the whole field of technical analysis, which purports to be able to predict security prices based on charting and following past price movements. (See Chapter 6 for more about technical analysis.)

Malkiel explains how to look at some common-sense indicators — such as whether the stock and bond markets are fairly valued and your own personal goals and desire to take risk — to develop a thoughtful, successful investment plan. Instead of trying to predict the future, Malkiel explains how the level of risk an investor accepts will ultimately determine future returns.

Money Logic

The premise of this intriguing and illuminating book is that a key part of many investing decisions involves choosing between two or more alternatives of what to do with a sum of money. In other words, should you invest in this stock or that mutual fund? If you choose mutual funds, should it be fund X or fund Y? And does paying the extra management fees on segregated funds that guarantee you your principal back after a set number of years make financial sense? Surprisingly, there's often little research or advice available on how to approach such decisions and on what factors to consider.

Money Logic: Financial Strategies for the Smart Investor (Stoddart), written by Moshe A. Milevsky with Michael Posner, fills that void with a thoughtful discussion of many common investment quandaries. Milevsky, who teaches risk management at York University, uses historical data and mathematical logic to offer practical advice on what information to focus on in order to make sound choices. Among the common concerns he addresses are how to assess the value that managers bring to funds, whether the guarantee of getting your principal back after a certain number of years is worth the extra management expense fees charged by segregated funds, and how much international diversification is best.

While the authors have tried their best to avoid getting bogged down with numbers, there are many examples, some of which distract from the main message and sound as if they were originally designed to tantalize the minds of attentive students. Nonetheless, this is a worthy exercise in explaining a little-explored area — not just how you should make investment decisions, but the kinds of returns you should expect given the price you're willing to pay and the risk you're willing to take on.

Stocks for the Long Run

Finance professor Jeremy J. Siegel loves investing data, especially examining it over long time periods. In *Stocks for the Long Run: The Definitive Guide to Financial Market Returns and Long-Term Investment Strategies* (McGraw-Hill), Siegel presents an analysis of U.S. stock and bond returns since 1802! The book is packed with charts and graphs, some of which you won't readily comprehend unless you're the analytic, graphical sort. Even so, Siegel provides comprehensive discussion of the worldwide financial markets. The book focuses on stock market investing, although it also discusses bonds if for no other reason than to compare their returns and risk with that of stocks.

Built to Last and Good to Great

Given the title, some people may think that *Built to Last: Successful Habits of Visionary Companies* (HarperCollins) is just for the small number of people who want to build a large company. However, the book, written by management consultant James Collins and Stanford Business School professor Jerry Porras, is an excellent resource for all entrepreneurs and people who work in leadership positions in companies, as well as those interested in investing in individual stocks. Rarely does a great book make it to the business best-seller lists, but *Built to Last* did.

The book presents the findings from an extensive six years' worth of research into what's behind the success of such companies as 3M, Boeing, Ford, Hewlett-Packard, Motorola, Sony, and Wal-Mart, all of which have achieved great success in their respective industries over many years. The average company in the Collins and Porras study was founded in 1897. In all, the authors tracked 18 extraordinary companies (referred to as the gold medal winners in their industries) and compared their traits with those of similarly long-lived but less successful peer companies (in the same industries).

Collins's and Porras's findings not only yield insight into how to build or identify a great business in which to invest; they also destroy some commonly held myths. For example, some people feel that a great idea is behind every great company. This concept is wrong and, in fact, according to the authors' research, companies founded on the basis of a great idea can lead to focusing on the idea rather than laying the groundwork for building a great company. Sony's founder, for example, wrote a nine-page philosophical prospectus setting the stage for this great company, yet he had few product ideas in his firm's early days. Early products, such as a rice cooker, failed miserably.

Great, visionary companies are also rigid and unyielding when it comes to respecting their core ideologies and principles. On the other hand, such companies tinker and experiment to stimulate positive change and innovation. And despite their often stunning financial success, great companies usually have a higher or equal aspiration to that of maximizing profits: fulfilling a purpose and being driven by values. This book is packed with insights, information, and examples, so don't expect to absorb all its contents in one reading.

Collins more recently wrote another outstanding book, *Good to Great: Why Some Companies Make the Leap . . . And Others Don't* (HarperCollins), which he calls the prequel to *Built to Last*. In *Good to Great,* Collins presents the engaging and insightful results of another long-term study of numerous companies that over time moved from being average companies to outstanding companies. As with *Built to Last,* this newer book can assist readers with not only managing their own small businesses but also with selecting companies to invest in.

Can a book make you invest like Warren Buffett?

In recent years, Warren Buffett, considered one of the best investors of all time, has received lots of attention for his investing prowess. Numerous books about him have been published (none by Buffett himself). Most of them were written and promoted based on the philosophy embodied in the marketing slogan "He did it his way; now you can, too," for the book *The Warren Buffett Way*.

You can read every book ever written about Buffett, and the odds are about 10 million to 1 that you're going to be able to invest like he does. It's not that you're not an intelligent, willing-to-learn kind of person. But you can't invest like Buffett for the same reason that you can't become a professional basketball player by reading books about basketball greats Larry Bird or Michael Jordan, even if they themselves wrote the books.

One financial market commentator said of Buffett and the financial markets, "If making money in the market is so easy, why has only Warren Buffett made $14 billion picking stocks?" However, Buffett didn't make $14 billion picking individual stocks. It's true that Berkshire Hathaway, the firm he purchased in 1965 and still runs today, makes substantial investments in the stocks of individual companies. But Buffett built much of his great wealth through his buying and managing a variety of businesses, particularly insurance companies.

In addition to 13 insurance companies, Berkshire Hathaway owns divisions such as See's (candy manufacturer), *The Buffalo News* (newspaper), Nebraska Furniture Mart (home furnishings retailer), Borsheim's (jewellery retailer), World Book (encyclopedia publisher), Kirby's (home cleaning products manufacturer), Fechheimer Brothers (uniform manufacturer), and H.H. Brown and Dexter (shoe manufacturers).

The property and casualty insurance businesses that Berkshire Hathaway bought, most of which are located in Nebraska, afforded Buffett lots of low-cost money that his firm could invest in a tax-favoured way. Specifically, insurance companies collect premiums from policyholders and invest the money, called *float*, until insurance claims need to be paid. Unlike almost all other insurers, Berkshire Hathaway, which is in Nebraska, a state with loose insurance company regulations, can invest much of its float in riskier investments like stocks.

Although most other insurers invest no more than 20 percent in stocks, with the remainder in conservative, boring, low-return bonds, Buffett has taken full advantage of Nebraska's loose regulations, investing at times more than 95 percent of the float in stocks. Buffett likes to buy name-brand company stock and is attracted to almost anything that hooks consumers. Witness his investment in tobacco companies, of which he said, "I'll tell you why I like the economics of the cigarette business. It costs a penny to make. Sell it for a dollar. It's habit forming. And there's fantastic brand loyalty."

The float is also invested in a tax-favoured way, as these reserves compound tax free and the final capital gains are taxed at a reduced rate thanks to the protection afforded insurance companies. Buffett's insurance operations have also shrewdly kept their float reserved from claims at higher-than-needed levels to take full advantage of these tax benefits.

As Berkshire Hathaway grew over the years, acquired more businesses, and squirrelled away more money to invest, Buffett's wealth also ballooned, thanks to his 41 percent ownership stake in the outstanding stock of the company. So to say that Buffett built his wealth through stock picking and that you can replicate what he did simply by reading books is ludicrous!

Chapter 19

Internet and Software Resources

● ●

In This Chapter

▶ Choosing investing software

▶ Recognizing Internet pitfalls and opportunities

▶ Finding the best investing Web sites

● ●

Thousands of investing software packages and Web sites claim to enable you to more easily make profitable investments. As with most other advertising claims, the reality of using your computer for investing and other tasks falls short of the promises and the hype.

In this chapter, we show you ways that your computer may be able to help you with your investing challenges and chores. Throughout this discussion, however, please remember several important caveats:

✔ Many highly successful investors don't use their computers (or use them quite little) to manage their investments.

✔ You may subject yourself to information overload and spend a fair amount of money without seeing many benefits.

✔ Don't believe everything you read, especially in the online world, where filters and editors are often absent. (Of course, as we discuss elsewhere in this part of the book, filters and editors don't guarantee that you'll find quality investment advice and information when you read financial publications.)

Seeking Investment Software

Good investment software should be user-friendly and provide quality information for making sound decisions. Software that helps you make personal investment decisions also needs to provide, if applicable, well-founded advice.

Which software is best for you depends on what you're trying to accomplish, as well as your level of investment knowledge and computer savvy. Software can help you with a variety of investment tasks, from tracking your investments to researching, planning, and placing trades through your computer (a topic we discuss in Chapter 9). The following sections help you find the best software for your needs.

Investment tracking software

Many investors don't know how they're doing — that is, what returns their investments are producing. People usually know their GIC and bond yields, but ask most people investing in individual stocks and bonds what the total return was on their entire portfolio, and at best, you'll get a guess. It's the rare person who can quote you total returns or tell you whether her returns are on track to reach her future financial goals. If someone does know his investments' returns, he probably doesn't know whether that return is good, bad, or otherwise. Feel good about having made 22 percent on your portfolio of stocks last year? Maybe you wouldn't if an index of comparable stocks was up 35 percent over the same period. And beyond knowing what your returns are, wouldn't it be nice to know the total value of all your investments and where all your money is currently residing? The fact that Canadians leave millions of dollars lying idle every year in forgotten bank accounts is testimony to the disarray of some investors' tracking systems.

Many software makers produce programs that claim to solve these and other investment tracking quandaries. (Numerous financial Web sites offer tracking tools as well.) However, investment tracking software is not a painless panacea for investors who want to track their investments and returns.

Many people buy these programs thinking that the programs will, after a small commitment of time, simplify their investment lives. Our review of many investment tracking packages suggests that you should be prepared to make a substantial time commitment to find out how to use these packages and that other, less high-tech alternatives may be more efficient and enlightening. Also know that a good portion of program users tire of entering all the required data and then feel guilty for "falling behind."

One of the best benefits of these packages is that using them can help you get organized. If you enter your investments into the program, the software can help you make sure that you don't lose track of your holdings. (Keeping a current copy of each of your investment statements in a binder or file folder can accomplish the same purpose.) Of course, if your home burns to the ground and you don't have a back-up copy of your files or software off-site, you have to start your documentation from scratch.

In addition to organizing all your investment information in one place, investment software allows you to track your original purchase price, current market values, and rates of return on your investments. If you have accounts at numerous investment firms, using software can reduce some of the complications involved in tracking your investing kingdom. (You can accomplish the same things by consolidating your investments at one investment company. See our discussion of discount brokers in Chapter 9.)

Software that can help you with investment tracking falls into one of two main groups:

- ✔ Personal finance software that also includes investment tracking capabilities
- ✔ Software that focuses exclusively on investment tracking

The broader personal finance packages such as Quicken and Microsoft Money are more user-friendly and are probably more familiar if you already use these packages' other features (such as bill paying).

If you want to see what your investment returns have been over the years, beware that entering historical data from your account statements (if you can find them) is a time-consuming process regardless of which package you use. In order to calculate your returns, you generally need to enter each new investment you make as well as all your reinvestments of dividends, interest, and capital gains distributions (such as those made on mutual funds). Ugh!

Investment tracking software can be more useful for stock traders. In our experience, stock traders, the people who would most benefit from using these programs, often don't track their overall returns. If they did, they could calculate the benefit (or lack thereof) of all their trading.

If you're a buy-and-hold mutual fund investor, tracking software gives you limited benefits because of the time required to enter your data. Mutual funds and many other published resources tell you what a fund's total return was for the past year, so you don't need to enter every dividend and capital gain distribution.

As for calculating the return of your overall portfolio, there are fairly simple ways to estimate your return using an old-fashioned paper and pencil. Simply weight the return of each investment by the portion of your portfolio 'invested in it. For example, with a simple portfolio equally divided between two investments that returned 10 and 20 percent respectively, your overall portfolio return would be 15 percent ($10 \times .50 + 20 \times .50 = 15$).

People who make investments at various times throughout the year and want to know what their actual returns were during the year can use software to get answers. Unless you're a frequent trader and are trying to measure the success of your trading, knowing the exact returns based on the precise dates you fed money into investments has limited value. This is especially true if you're a regular, dollar-cost-averaging investor (see Chapter 3). If you're a frequent trader, using a financial calculator works as well as software in calculating your returns based on the timing of your investments. Also know that increasing numbers of investment companies are providing personal return data via their Web site and/or on account statements.

Investment research software

Investment research software packages usually separate investment beginners (and others who don't want to spend a lot of their time managing their money) from those who enjoy wallowing in data and conducting primary research. If you already have a plan in mind and just want to get on with investing, then go to it! But even if you don't want to conduct more specific research, some of the packages we discuss in this section can also help you conduct online investment transactions and track an investment's performance.

Investment software packages do not lack information and research data. In fact, you may have the problem of sifting through too much data and differentiating the best from the mediocre and the downright awful. And, unless cost is no object, you need to make sure that you don't spend too much of your loot simply accessing the information.

Before you plunge into the data jungle and try to become the next Peter Lynch or Warren Buffett and pick individual stocks, be honest about your reasons for wanting to research. Some investors fool themselves into believing that their research will help them beat the markets. Few investors, even so-called professionals, ever do. Witness the fact that over long time periods (ten-plus years), mutual funds that invest in a fixed market index, such as the Standard & Poor's 500, outperform three-quarters of their actively managed peers thanks to the index fund's lower operating expenses (see Chapter 8).

Researching individual securities

If you like to invest in individual securities, the Canadian Shareowners Association Stock Selection Guide software ($129) helps you research individual companies. You can enter the data yourself or purchase it in electronic form from the association. The association has information on over 6,000 Canadian and U.S. companies. The data, available on CD or online, costs $199 for an annual subscription. Subscribers get a new CD with updated data every two months. If you buy the Guide software and the data together, the package price is $299. You can also buy data on individual companies for about $1 each. You can order the software and data by calling the Canadian Shareowners Association at 800-268-6881, or by visiting its Web site at `www.shareowner.com`. We discuss the association in more detail in Chapter 6.

Another good choice is the Value Line Investment Survey for Windows, which helps you research individual stocks using the data that the Value Line Investment Survey provides. This software package lets you sift through Value Line's data efficiently. You can also use it to track your stock portfolio. A 13-week introductory offer for Value Line's software costs $65 (all prices for Value Line are in U.S. dollars), and an annual subscription costs $538 for monthly updates. The software is available from Value Line at 800-654-0508 or by visiting its Web site at `www.valueline.com`. We provide more information on Value Line in Chapter 6.

Understanding how software calculates returns

Most software programs calculate returns in one of two ways. First, the programs can calculate your effective or "internal" rate of return (IRR) by comparing your original amounts invested with the current market value. Of those programs that we've tested that calculate IRR — and some don't — the results were accurate. After you calculate your returns, knowing how they compare with relevant market averages would be nice. Unfortunately, not all programs allow you to compare your performance with various market indexes.

The tax or cost basis method is the second way software may calculate your returns. All the packages we've reviewed calculate your cost basis for accounting purposes. Your cost basis is your original investment plus reinvested dividends and capital gains for which you have already paid taxes in a non-registered plan. To get an accurate cost basis, you need to key in all your investments, including reinvested distributions. Time-starved investors can take solace in the fact that most investment companies, particularly larger mutual fund providers, provide cost basis information for you upon request or when you sell an investment.

Some packages provide only this cost basis information and don't report actual returns. Cost basis reports make your returns look less generous because reinvested distributions increase your original investment and seemingly reduce your returns. We know from talking with investors that many people often assume their cost basis reports tell them what their investment returns are. This happens partly because of the reports' misleading names, such as "investment performance" or "investment analysis."

The difference between the rate of return using the cost basis and internal rate of return methods is generally insubstantial. For the data we looked at, the cost basis method software calculated a 2.7 percent annual return, and the internal rate of return method software calculated a 13 percent annual return. The portfolio's actual total return was 13 percent, but an investor using a software package that calculates only cost basis is led to believe that her profit was just 2.7 percent (which is correct for tax purposes only for a non-retirement account).

Is all this calculation method mumbo jumbo too technical for your taste? Because they already have the data on your accounts, more investment firms can and hopefully someday will be able to send you your account's performance numbers. To date, surprisingly few investment firms provide personal investment returns.

Morningstar, which is better known for its mutual fund information, has followed in Value Line's footsteps in providing lots of data on individual U.S. stocks. Morningstar's Principia Pro for Stocks has data and features equivalent to what Value Line's Plus Edition offers. This program is intended for those with in-depth knowledge of how to analyze stocks and most definitely is not for beginners. An annual subscription to Principia Pro for Stocks with monthly updates costs $595 U.S.; a single update costs $125 U.S. You can reach Morningstar at 800-735-0700 or visit its Web site at www.morningstar.com. Morningstar offers a number of ways to tap into the more basic stock data it collects through its Web site, which we discuss in the next section.

Researching mutual funds

For mutual funds, the Canadian Shareowners Association, Value Line, and Morningstar all publish a number of software packages. These packages are geared toward more sophisticated investors who understand mutual funds and how to select them. For more on how to select winning mutual funds, see Chapter 8.

Investigating Internet Investing Resources

As people interested in managing their money surf the Internet, thousands of Web sites have sprung up to meet the demand. Although the low barriers to entry in the online world make it easy for scamsters and incompetents to flog their wares and flawed advice, this medium can offer some helpful resources if you know where to look and how to discern the good from the not so good.

The Securities and Exchange Commission (SEC) in the U.S. shutters numerous online scams, such as the one run by two individuals (Gene Block and Renate Haag) that bilked investors out of more than $3.5 million by promising to double investors' money in four months in a fictitious security they called prime bank.

Although you may be smart enough to avoid offers that promise pie in the sky, you're far more likely to fall for unsound financial advice. For example, at the stock-picking Motley Fool's site, an online scribe posted a column entitled "Paying your mortgage off early? Might as well put the money under your mattress." In the poorly reasoned piece, this person argued: "If you move before the mortgage is paid, the money you gave your bank actually saved you nothing. All your money did is reduce your principal amount by the exact extra amount you paid. Sounds like a mattress savings account to me."

Paying your mortgage balance off faster *can* be a good investment, regardless of whether you move. See Chapter 3 for a discussion of the merits and drawbacks of paying your mortgage off faster.

You can find plenty of self-serving advertorial content and bad advice online, so you should be wary. The next section offers tips for evaluating Internet resources.

Evaluating online resources

Fraud and bad financial advice existed long before the Internet ever came around. The SEC describes online scams as "new medium, same message." The tips in the following sections can help you find the nuggets of helpful online advice and avoid the land mines.

Checking out agendas

Get an idea of who's behind a site before you trust its information. When navigating the Net for investment purposes, remember that financial service companies that want to sell you something erect the vast majority of sites. Thus, the "free" entrance fee to these sites is driven by companies wanting you to buy what they're selling.

Some sites go to extraordinary lengths — including providing lots of information and advice and attempting to conceal the identity of the company that runs the site — to disguise their agendas. Therefore, don't turn to the Web for advice or opinions, which usually aren't objective. Similarly, approach online financial calculators with scepticism. Most are incredibly simplistic and biased.

Many Web sites have icons you can click to see some background on the site's sponsor and to find out whether the site solicits potential advertisers. With a simple click, you can quickly see that a site purporting to be a reference service for the best small-company stocks in which to invest may be nothing more than an online directory of companies that paid the site an advertising fee. Look for sites that exercise quality control in what they post and use sensible screening criteria for outside information or companies they list.

Just because every Tom, Dick, and Jane can easily and at relatively low cost set up an Internet site doesn't mean that their sites and advice are worthy of your time. Stake a lot on the reputation of the name. Not surprisingly, the financial companies with reputations for integrity offline are the ones that offer some of the best integrity online. For example, as we discuss later in this section, the leading and most investor-friendly investment companies often have the best education-oriented Web sites.

Soliciting grassroots customer feedback

The Internet can be a useful place to do consumer research. The more enlightening message board conversations we've encountered start with someone asking what others thought about particular financial service firms, such as brokerage firms. If you're investigating a certain financial service, the Internet can be an efficient way to get feedback from other people who've had experience dealing with that firm.

In order to find a dozen people offline who've done business with a given firm, you'd probably have to speak with hundreds of people. Online, finding customers is a snap. Those who feel wronged by a particular firm are more than willing to share their gripes. As in the offline world, though, don't believe everything you hear, and watch out for employees of a given firm who post flattering comments about their firms and dis the competition.

Verifying advice and information offline

You can enhance the value of the online information you gather by verifying it elsewhere. Do some fact checking both online and offline. For example, if you're contemplating the purchase of some stock based on financial data that you read on an investing site, check out those numbers at the library or at one of the Web sites we recommend later in this chapter before buying.

Lots of Internet investment advice (and most of the scams) focus on smaller companies and investment start-ups; unfortunately, these are often the most difficult businesses to locate information about. In the U.S., the SEC requires companies that are raising less than $1 million to file a "Form D." To inquire whether a company has filed Form D, call the SEC at 202-942-8090. Also check with the state's securities regulator; the contact information for all 50 regulators is on the SEC's Web site at www.sec.gov.

And, if something does sound too good to be true, check out and possibly report your concerns to Internet fraud-fighting organization sites. In addition to the SEC's Web site, check out the National Association of Securities Dealers Regulation Web site (www.nasdr.com) and the National Consumers League's National Fraud Information Center (www.fraud.org, 1-800-876-7060).

Unfortunately, here in Canada, we as yet do not have a national body overseeing the securities industry. Worse, our regulatory system is a patchwork, with a mix of federal and provincial bodies overseeing different aspects of the financial services and securities industries.

A good starting place for digging up information is the Ontario Securities Commission Web site at www.osc.gov.on.ca, as well as the regulators of the other provinces.

The best investment Web sites

Although you can live without the Internet and not suffer any ill financial or educational consequences, the quality of what's on the Net is gradually improving, and a handful of sites are setting a high standard. You can find the best sites by going directly to the Internet rather than through online service providers such as America Online.

In addition to the consumer advocacy sites that we recommend earlier in this chapter, here are our top picks for investing sites worthy of your online time.

Investorlearning.ca

Funded by the Canadian Securities Institute, this site offers a good basic overview of different types of investments and is a great source for financial links. The Money School section is also helpful. In its Focus section you can click on many different subjects — from annual reports to researching old stock certificates — and find links that offer basic information, suggested books, and the Web sites and addresses of related organizations and government bodies.

Globeinvestor.com

Globeinvestor.com (www.globeinvestor.com) is one of the few sites you'll visit and think, "Wow, somebody spent some time figuring out the sort of information investors want — and provided generally useful ways of retrieving it!" The site covers most publicly traded stocks in both Canada and the U.S. It's easy to get a quick snapshot of a company's stock, including a chart of its historical prices going back five years. You can also access quarterly and annual financial results, sift through the press releases archive, and search current news from *The Globe and Mail*. Like other good sites, globeinvestor.com makes intelligent use of technology by allowing you to search out stocks according to the price and company financial information you specify. If you're looking for undervalued stocks, for instance, you can search for stocks trading below a certain price/earnings level, or stocks whose prices dropped by 60 percent in the last year but that have started to recover. As well, you can sift companies according to how they're growing in terms of profits, sales, and earnings.

The site also has an in-depth section dealing with income trusts. In addition to quotes and charts for income trusts, there's a library of articles from *The Globe and Mail* along with ratings from the Dominion Bond Rating Service and Standard & Poor's.

Look who's talking

If you're at a cocktail party and you receive investing information and advice from someone you've just met, you would check him out to determine how much credence you should give to his words. No matter how wise he seems, you wouldn't judge him on the basis of just one conversation.

In the online world, you need to do the same thing, but you may have greater difficulty determining who's doing the talking and even why he or she is talking. On some Internet sites, visitors may post comments and opinions on message boards (the online equivalent of a big bulletin board).

As the National Association of Securities Dealers (NASD) says on its Web site, "In most instances, there is simply no way to uncover someone's true identity. Are you getting information from a broker, short seller, corporate insider, amateur investor, or stock touter?"

You have to use a little induction and a lot of intuition. Start by eliminating any advice from online posters who are totally anonymous. Pseudonyms are common online, and some salespeople try to hide their true identities. Aliases are especially easy to adopt on America Online, where users can have multiple self-chosen screen names.

Among the more popular message boards on the Net are those where people debate and discuss the prospects for individual stocks. The postings play fast and loose with the facts. "Investors need to understand that, although they may be reading honest conversations, they could just as easily be looking at the work of a corporate insider, stock promoter, or short seller using an alias to deceive the unsuspecting or to manipulate the market," warns the NASD Regulation unit.

CorporateInformation.com

CorporateInformation.com is owned and operated by Wright Investors' Services, which, in addition to primarily managing money for affluent individuals, publishes comprehensive reports on thousands of companies around the globe. Those who want to do Web-based stock research will enjoy the many links to other Internet investing information and research sites. This site also provides plenty of current business news.

Globefund.com

A companion site to GlobeInvestor, GlobeFund (www.globefund.com) is a straightforward and easy-to-navigate site for researching and screening funds. You can chart funds, compare them with others, look up ratings, and sift the Canadian fund world for those that meet your needs. In addition to profiles of funds and fund companies, you can look up data from the *Globe*'s 15-year fund review. This is an excellent resource, since looking at a fund's year-by-year performance for a decade and a half can offer you lots of insights into a fund's behaviour and up and down markets.

Morningstar.ca and Morningstar.com

The behemoth of the mutual fund data business in the U.S., Morningstar opened up a Canadian office several years ago and launched a free Web site (www.morningstar.ca) that provides information and tools for Canadian mutual fund and stock research.

The focus is on funds, and you can rank, research, and compare funds easily. What makes this site worthwhile, though, is its cache of important information that's not commonly available. Its QuickTake reports give you in-depth break-downs of a fund's tax effectiveness, critical for funds you're considering investing in outside of a registered plan. There are also useful valuation data, including a fund's price/earnings and price/book ratios. The U.S. site (www.morningstar.com) offers much more data, and analysis of stocks as well as funds. The basic stuff is free, but to access their analyst reports and stock research reports, among other premium content, you must pony up $115 U.S. per year. The site sometimes offers free trials of a few weeks. In addition to providing more data than you could ever possibly digest on funds and stocks, this site includes short articles that are insightful and useful to more educated investors.

Sedar.com

Sedar.com (www.sedar.com) is an excellent one-stop shop for the many different documents that publicly traded Canadian companies and mutual funds must file. The information at Sedar (which stands for System for Electronic Document Analysis and Retrieval) is made available by the Canadian Securities Administrators (CSA) and the Canadian Depository for Securities (CDS).

If you're researching individual companies, you can find all the corporate reports — annual reports and the like — that we discuss in Chapter 6 via this Web site. (Alternatively, of course, you may call the individual companies that interest you and have them mail you the desired material.)

All the files are in PDF format, meaning they each have to open in their own window, and scrolling can be a chore. But if you're tenacious, you may find something that's hard to come by on the Web: cold, hard facts and no spin.

Sec.gov

All U.S. publicly held companies and mutual funds must file annual and quarterly reports and other documents electronically with the U.S. Securities and Exchange Commission (SEC). In the past, the simplest way to access this information was to pay a private service. Now this information is easily accessible for free (paid for by U.S. tax dollars) on the SEC Web site (www.sec.gov).

The SEC site isn't pretty, and searching the Electronic Data Gathering, Analysis, and Retrieval system (EDGAR) database can be challenging, especially for the novice investor. If you find the SEC's search engine frustrating and tedious to use, surf on over to www.freeedgar.com for an easier-to-use search engine to access company documents filed with the SEC.

The Motley Fools: Online investing geniuses?

David and Tom Gardner, who launched The Motley Fool (www.fool.com), claim that novices can "nearly double the S&P 500 posting returns in excess of 20 percent per year" and that "you might be able to fish out greater than 30 percent per year on your own without assuming considerably greater risk." They also assert, "It's not an exaggeration to say that fifth graders can wallop the market after one month of analysis. You can too."

Although they claim to have walloped the market averages with their stock picks, according to research by Investorhome.com only one of their seven portfolios has actually performed better than the market averages — two of their portfolios were shuttered after poor performance (one of which plunged 50 percent during its brief six-month existence).

The Fool story is rich in lessons for all consumers of investment newsletters online (and off):

✔ Beware of promises of easy riches. To deter investors from mutual funds, the Fools say of their stock picking, "We hope to have put you in position to nearly double the S&P 500 . . . it'll demand little research per year, and present you little, if any, long-term risk." We've said it before, and we'll say it again: If investing were that easy, we'd all be rich! And as any professional money manager knows firsthand, successfully managing a portfolio of individual stocks takes time, not just a few hours per year.

✔ Beware of bloated performance claims. The Fools love to compare their integrity and accountability with the notoriously shady marketing practices of other financial newsletters. As the Gardners repeatedly point out, the Fool portfolio uses real money, and calculated returns account for trading commissions. However, their real-money portfolio is a non-retirement account, and the Fools fail to calculate and report their returns taking into account their greatest investment cost of all: taxes. In fact, because of trading, the Fools' one portfolio that looks like it's beaten the market averages has only performed on par with what an investor could have earned, with no ongoing research time required, in a low-cost index fund. Ironically, the Gardners say, "If you can't beat the index after all costs are deducted, you've blundered."

By 1996 the Fools were basking in the media spotlight. However, the deluge of newcomers to their online site soon found out about the perils of hitching your investment cart to a shooting star. Since that time, a stock they aggressively promoted — Iomega — has plunged from $27½ to less than $4, at which point they sold it. A buy recommendation for ATC Communications at $23 proved disastrous when the stock crashed to less than $4 just one year later, before the Fools threw in the towel. They bought Excite@Home for $28 and rode it all the way down to less than $6 per share before dumping it.

✔ Beware of actions that contradict the newsletter's stated philosophy. "We invest for the long term" is the Fool mantra, invoked in their portfolio report on a regular basis (almost daily when the portfolio performs poorly). They add, "Part of the enduring beauty of long-term equities investing is the advantage of buying and holding — never touching — stocks like General Electric, which rack up 20 percent annualized gains over a decade or more. We're talking compounded returns untainted by capital gains taxes."

The portfolio's trading history, however, tells another story. The Fools have sold an average of about six investment holdings annually (in a portfolio with typically just ten stocks) and have held just one stock — in fact just a portion of the original position — since their portfolio first started! Moreover, the Fools engage in risky short selling (and have lost money overall doing it), where you sell borrowed stock in the hope that you can buy it back later at a lower price. If this is long-term investing, then perhaps the Fools' definition of a long-term trader is anyone who doesn't day trade!

✔ Successful investing doesn't require following the market closely. Buying and holding index or other quality mutual funds for many years doesn't take much review time — perhaps as little as an hour once per year to read the fund's annual report. Although the Fools rightfully criticize the financial media's short-term reporting — "So many are lost in the day-by-day noise of stock moves" — the Fools themselves report on the biggest stock price changes of the day throughout the trading day. This daily tracking of stock prices leads investors to lose sight of the long term and the big picture (although it does draw more visitors to the site, which satisfies advertisers and enriches the Gardners).

The bottom line? Be sceptical of financial newsletters, online or off. Like politicians, they're out to make themselves look as good as possible, taking credit when things go well and blaming external forces when they don't. According to *Hulbert's Financial Digest,* during the period that Hulbert has tracked the Fools' stock picks they haven't performed among the best newsletters. See Chapter 17 for more about investment newsletters.

Part VI
The Part of Tens

The 5th Wave   By Rich Tennant

"The first thing we should do is get you two into a good mutual fund. Let me get out the 'Magic 8-Ball' and we'll run some options."

In this part . . .

The Part of Tens contains shorter chapters, each
including about ten items on important investing topics
that don't quite fit elsewhere in the book. The topics in
this part cover the psychological issues to overcome to
be a successful investor, what you need to know when
you're considering selling an investment, and advice for
investing during a down market.

Chapter 20

Ten Psychological Investing Obstacles to Conquer

In This Chapter

▶ Putting your faith in experts

▶ Letting your emotions guide your investment decisions

▶ Giving up when the market takes a plunge

▶ Ignoring your financial big picture

*J*ust as with raising children or in one's career, "success" with personal investing is in the eye of the beholder. In our view, a successful investor is someone who, with a minimal commitment of time, develops an investment plan to accomplish financial and personal goals and earns returns commensurate with the risk he's willing to accept.

In this chapter, we point out ten common psychological obstacles that may keep you from fully realizing your financial goals and share tips and advice for overcoming those obstacles on the road to investing success.

Trusting Authority

Some investors assume that an adviser is competent and ethical if she has a lofty title (financial consultant, vice-president, and so on), dresses well, and works in a snazzy office. Such accessories are often indicators of salespeople — not objective advisers — who recommend investments that will earn them big commissions — commissions that come out of your investment dollars.

Additionally, if you overtrust an adviser, you may not research and monitor your investments as carefully as you should. Figuring that Mr. Vice-President is an expert, some investors go along without ever questioning his advice or watching what's going on with their investments.

You should also question authority elsewhere in the investment business. Too many investors blindly follow analysts' stock recommendations without considering the many conflicts of interest that such brokerage firm employees have. Brokerage analysts are often cheerleaders for buying various companies' stock because their firms are courting the business of new stock and bond issuance of the same companies. And as the highly publicized accounting scandals at firms like Enron and WorldCom have highlighted, just because a big-name accounting firm has blessed a company's financial statements doesn't make them accurate or even close to accurate.

You can't possibly evaluate the competence and agenda of someone you hire until you yourself understand the lay of the land. Similarly, you can't possibly know for sure that an analyst's report or a professional service firm's recommendation or approval of a company is worth the paper it's printed on. Read good publications on the topic to master the jargon and how to evaluate investments. Seek independent second opinions before you act on someone's recommendations. If you're in the market for a broker, be sure to read Chapter 9.

Getting Swept Up by Euphoria

Feeling strength and safety in numbers, some investors are lured into buying hot stocks and sectors (for example, industries like technology, biotechnology, retail, and so on) after major price increases (see Chapter 5). Psychologically, it's reassuring to buy into something that's going up and gaining accolades. The obvious danger with this practice is buying into investments selling at inflated prices that too soon deflate.

For example, Robert Shiller, professor of economics at Yale University, conducted a survey of Japanese investors. He found that few (14 percent) expected a major correction at that market's peak in 1989 when Japanese stocks were selling at outrageous price/earning multiples (how high the stock prices were in relation to profits — see Chapter 5). By the mid-1990s, when tremendous damage had been done and the Japanese market was off more than 60 percent from its peak and selling at less risky levels, far *more* investors (32 percent) expected a crash.

In the Canadian and U.S. stock markets, by the late 1990s investors were getting spoiled with gains year after year far in excess of the historic average annual return of 9 to 10 percent. Numerous surveys conducted during this period showed that many investors expected to earn annual returns in the range of 15 to 20 percent annually, nearly double the historic average. As always happens, though, following a period of excessively high returns such as those of the 1990s, returns were below average in the subsequent period beginning in 2000.

Develop an overall allocation among various investments (especially diversified mutual funds), and don't make knee-jerk decisions to change your allocation based on what the latest hot sectors are. If anything, de-emphasize or avoid stocks and sectors that are at the top of the performance charts. Think back to the last time you went bargain shopping for a consumer item — you looked for value, not high prices. See Chapter 5 to find out how to spot good values in the financial markets and how to detect speculative bubbles to avoid.

Being Overconfident

As we discuss in Part V, newsletters, books, and even some financial periodicals lead investors to believe that you can be the next Peter Lynch or Warren Buffett if you follow a simple stock-picking system. The advent of the Internet and online trading capabilities has spawned a whole new generation of short-term (sometimes even same-day) traders.

Dr. Paul Linton is a marriage and family counsellor. Despite his expertise in psychology, Linton had to come to terms with his own relationship to money and the psychological obstacles he faced as an investor.

"I got overconfident with my stock picking when some of my technology stocks soared and from my work in benefits in a previous company where I was responsible for choosing investment funds, one of which returned 90 percent one year," says Linton. When the market crashed in 1987, Linton was "psychologically devastated" because he lost about two-thirds of the money he had saved over the previous 10 years.

Linton's challenge was that his early investment successes during a strong stock market misled him to believe that he had a magic investing touch. This resulted in excessive trading and risk taking and, eventually, losses when the market reversed its course. "I realized that if I was going to be a stock trader, I had to work at it full time and be prepared anxiety-wise to handle it," says Linton.

If you have the speculative bug, earmark a small portion of your portfolio (no more than 10 to 20 percent) for more aggressive investments. Linton traded in most of his high-risk, frequently traded individual stock portfolio for diversified mutual funds that he buys and holds. If overtrading is a problem for you, seek out Gamblers Anonymous. (See Chapter 5 for questions to help you decide whether you or someone you know has a gambling problem.)

Throwing in the Towel When Things Look Bleak

For inexperienced or nervous investors, it's tempting to bail out when it appears that an investment is not always going to be profitable and enjoyable. Some investors dump falling investments precisely at the times when they should be doing the reverse — buying more. Whenever the stock market drops more than a few percentage points in a short period, it attracts a lot of attention, which leads to concern, anxiety, and, in some cases, panic.

Investing always involves uncertainty. Many people forget this, especially during good economic times like Canadians enjoyed in the late 1990s. We find that investors are likely to feel more comfortable with riskier investments, such as stocks, when they recognize that all investments carry uncertainty and risk — just in different forms.

The Canadian and U.S. stock markets experienced a severe decline in the early 2000s — with some growth stocks, especially technology stocks, plunging like stocks do in a depression. Layoffs mounted, and the tragedy of September 11, 2001, undermined consumer confidence — the last prop holding the economy from a recession. The United States also experienced major accounting scandals at many companies, including large companies like Enron, WorldCom, and Global Crossing.

We see many similarities between the early 2000s and the early 1970s, when over several years a multitude of problems unfolded that could not have been predicted. The early '70s saw record trade and budget deficits; inflation was rearing its ugly head; U.S. troops invaded Cambodia; college students staged demonstrations against the Vietnam War; and four Kent State University students were killed by National Guardsmen during an antiwar protest. Here at home we had our own political and social turmoil with the FLQ crisis. Other events included the Arab oil embargo and that period's Arab–Israeli conflict — the Yom Kippur War. Then news of Watergate broke, and President Richard Nixon's impeachment hearings began. Meanwhile, inflation was going through the roof, and Trudeau introduced wage and price controls.

Following this string of events, and after flirting with the 1,000 level since 1966, the Dow Jones Industrial Average plunged below 600 after Nixon resigned in 1974. The Canadian stock market also plunged, falling some 38 percent. This severe stock market decline soured some investors on the market for many years, which was truly unfortunate, as most major stock markets, even with the major decline in the early 2000s, have risen more than ten-fold since the mid-1970s.

The string of unfortunate events in the early 2000s soured some investors on stock investing. History has repeatedly proven, however, that continuing to buy stocks during down markets increases your long-term returns. The worst thing you can do in a slumping market is to throw in the towel.

Financial earthquakes and media coverage

Eric remembers when a major earthquake struck the San Francisco Bay Area, his home, in 1989. He had just left an office building in San Francisco's financial district when the ground started to shake, rattle, and roll. His first panicked thought as he looked at all the glass-windowed skyscrapers towering over him was that someone would find him buried under piles of shattered glass. Although unpleasant, the thought wasn't original. He'd heard others explain this scenario. Although the quake was scary, the only thing he lost that day was a bit of his courage!

Immediately following the earthquake, some of his East Coast friends and family thought the entire Bay Area was in ruins, based on early TV coverage. Television news programs typically played a few minutes' worth of tape showing a collapsed freeway near the city of Oakland, several partially collapsed and fiery buildings in the Marina district of San Francisco, and a fallen portion of the upper deck of the Bay Bridge. The media played these segments over and over again.

Now we don't want to diminish the tragedy, loss of life, and damage the earthquake caused. However, watching these news programs throughout the week following the quake, you'd never have known that more than 99 percent of the Bay Area was just fine, except for people with shaken nerves and a few broken vases. Far fewer people died as a result of this earthquake than die every day from driving on U.S. roadways or from guns.

The media often report on stock market tremors the same way they do earthquakes. When the financial markets suffer earthshaking events, some investors worry that their investments are in a shambles. As we discuss in Part V, the media are often to blame because they hype short-term events and blow those events out of proportion to captivate viewers and listeners. History has shown that financial markets recover; recovery is just a question of time. If you invest for the long term, then the last six weeks — or even the last couple years — is a short period. Plus, a mountain of evidence and studies demonstrate that no one can predict the future, so you gain little from trying to base your investment plans on predictions. In fact, you can lose more money by trying to time the markets.

A big danger of larger-than-normal market declines is that they may encourage decision making based on emotion rather than logic. Just ask anyone who sold *after* the stock market collapsed in 1987 — the Canadian stock market dropped 31 percent and the U.S. stock market dropped 35 percent in a matter of weeks in the fall of that year. By the spring of 2004, even with the significant declines in the early 2000s, the Canadian market had risen almost three-fold and the U.S. market had risen more than five-fold!

Investors who are unable to withstand the volatility of riskier growth-oriented investments, such as stocks, may be better off not investing in such vehicles to begin with. Examining your returns over longer periods helps you keep the proper perspective. If a short-term downdraft in your investments depresses you, avoid tracking your investment values closely. Also, consider investing in highly diversified, less-volatile funds that hold stocks worldwide as well as bonds (see Chapter 8).

Investing Too Much to Quit

Although some investors realize that they can't withstand losses and sell at the first signs of trouble, other investors find that selling a losing investment is so painful and unpleasant that they hold on to it despite its poor future prospects. The late Amos Tversky, a Stanford psychology professor, and Daniel Kahneman of Princeton documented how people find accepting a given loss twice as painful as the pleasure of accepting a gain of equal magnitude.

Analyze your lagging investments to identify why they perform poorly. If a given investment is down because similar ones are also in decline, hold on to it. However, if something is inherently wrong with the investment — such as high fees or poor management — make taking the loss more palatable by remembering two things:

> ✔ If your investment is not held in an RRSP or other tax-sheltered retirement plan, you can use the loss to offset otherwise taxable gains you realize with other investments.
>
> ✔ Consider the "opportunity cost" of continuing to keep your money in a lousy investment — that is, what returns can you get in the future if you switch to a "better" investment?

Over-Monitoring Your Investments

The investment world seems so risky and fraught with pitfalls that some people believe that closely watching an investment can help alert them to impending danger. "The constant tracking is not unlike the attempt to relieve anxiety by fingering worry beads. Yet, paradoxically, it can increase emotional distress because it requires a constant state of vigilance," says psychologist Paul Minsky.

In our work, we see time and time again that investors who are the most anxious about their investments and most likely to make impulsive trading decisions are the ones who watch their holdings too closely, especially those who monitor prices daily. The proliferation of Internet sites and stock market cable television programs offering up-to-the-minute quotations gives these investors more temptation to over-monitor investments.

Restrict your "diet" of financial information and advice. Quality is far more important than quantity. Watching the daily price gyrations of investments is akin to eating too much junk food — doing so may satisfy your short-term cravings but at the cost of your long-term health. If you invest in diversified mutual funds, you really don't need to examine your fund's performance more than once or twice per year. An ideal time to review your funds is when you receive their annual or semi-annual reports. Although many investors track their funds daily or weekly, far fewer read their annual reports. Reading these reports can help you keep a long-term perspective and gain some understanding as to why your funds perform as they do and how they compare with major market averages.

Being Unclear about Your Goals

Investing is more complicated than simply setting your financial goals (see Chapter 3) and choosing solid investments to help you achieve them. Awareness and understanding of the less tangible issues can maximize your chances for investing success.

In addition to considering your goals in a traditional sense (when do you want to retire, how much of your kids' university costs do you want to pay) before you invest, you should consider what you want and don't want to get from the investment process. Do you treat investing as a hobby or simply as another one of life's tasks, such as maintaining your home? Do you enjoy the intellectual challenge of picking your own stocks? Don't just ponder these questions on your own; discuss them with family members, too — after all, you're all going to have to live with your decisions and investment results.

Ignoring Your Real Financial Problems

We know plenty of high-income earners, including more than a few who earn six figures annually, who have little to invest. Some of these people have high-interest debt outstanding on credit cards and auto loans, yet spend endless hours researching and tracking investments.

We also know many people who built significant personal wealth despite having modest-paying jobs. The difference: the ability to live within their means.

If you don't earn a high income, you may be tempted to think you can't save. Even if you're a high-income earner, you may think you can hit an investment home run to accomplish your goals, or that you can save more if you can bump up your income. This way of thinking justifies spending most of what you earn and saving little now. Investing is far more exciting than examining your spending and making cutbacks. If you need help coming up with more money to invest, see the latest edition of our book *Personal Finance For Canadians for Dummies* (published by Wiley).

Overemphasizing Certain Risks

Saving money is only half the battle. The other half is making your money grow. Over long time periods, earning just a few percent more makes a big difference in the size of your nest egg. Earning inflation-beating returns is easy to do if you're willing to invest in stocks, real estate, and small businesses. Figure 20-1 shows you how much more money you'll have in 25 years if you can earn investment returns that are greater than the rate of inflation (which is currently running at about 2 percent).

Figure 20-1:
Slightly higher returns compound to really make your money grow.

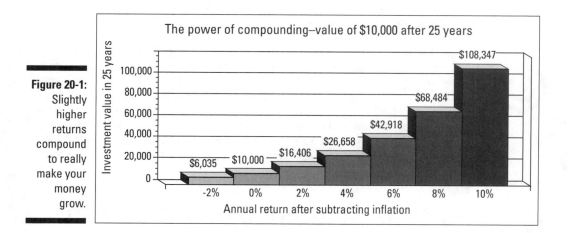

As we discuss in Chapter 2, ownership investments (stocks, real estate, and small business) have historically generated returns greater than the inflation rate by 6 percent or more, while lending investments (savings accounts and bonds) tend to generate returns of only 1 to 2 percent above inflation. However, some investors keep too much of their money in lending investments out of fear of holding an investment that can fall greatly in value. Although ownership investments can plunge in value, you need to keep in mind that inflation and taxes eat away at your lending investment balances.

Believing in Gurus

Stock market declines, like earthquakes, bring all sorts of prognosticators, soothsayers, and self-anointed gurus out of the woodwork, particularly among those in the investment community that have something to sell, such as newsletter writers. The words may vary, but the underlying message does not: "If you'd been following my sage advice, you'd be much better off now."

People spend far too much of their precious time and money in pursuit of a guru who can tell them when and what to buy and sell. Peter Lynch, the former manager of the Fidelity Magellan Fund, amassed one of the best long-term stock market investing track records. His stock-picking ability allowed him to beat the market averages by just a few percent per year. However, even he says that you can't time the markets, and he acknowledges knowing many pundits who have correctly predicted the future course of the stock market "once in a row"!

Clearly, in the world of investing, the most successful investors earn much better returns than the worst ones. But what may surprise you is that you can end up much closer to the top of the investing performance heap than the bottom if you follow some relatively simple rules, such as regularly saving and investing in low-cost, growth investments. In fact, you can beat many of the full-time investment professionals.

Chapter 21

Ten Things to Consider When Selling an Investment

In This Chapter

▶ Understanding your investment goals and other big-picture issues

▶ Selling for the right reasons

▶ Factoring taxes into your profit

*Y*ou can and should hold good investments for years and decades. Each year, people sell trillions of dollars' worth of investments. Our experience working with and instructing people about investments suggests that too many people sell for the wrong reasons and hold on to investments they should sell. In this chapter, we highlight some issues to consider when you contemplate selling your investments.

Remembering Your Personal Preferences and Goals

If you've inherited investments or your life has changed, your current portfolio may no longer make sense for you. The time that it takes you to manage your portfolio, for example, is a vital matter if you're starved for time or weary of managing time-consuming investments.

Leo, for example, loved to research, track, and trade individual stocks — until his daughter was born. Then Leo realized how many hours his hobby was taking away from his family, and that realization put his priorities into perspective. Leo now invests in time-friendly mutual funds and doesn't follow them like a hawk.

In his Me and My Money column in *The Globe and Mail,* Tony profiled Stephen, a puppeteer who really enjoys investing in real estate. By buying and renovating historical buildings, he helps preserve his small town's charm, attracts small businesses to the area, and gives the friends and neighbours he partners with a way to earn a healthy return investing locally. For Stephen, real estate isn't just a profitable investment; it's also a way of expressing himself and growing personally.

Maintaining Balance in Your Overall Portfolio

A good reason to sell an investment is to allow you to better diversify your portfolio. Suppose that before reading this book you purchased a restaurant stock every time you read about one. Now your portfolio resembles several bad strip malls, and restaurant stocks comprise 80 percent of your holdings. Or maybe, through your job, you've accumulated such a hefty chunk of stock in your employer that this stock now overwhelms the rest of your investments.

It's time for you to diversify. Sell off some of the holdings you have too much of and invest the proceeds in solid investments, such as those we recommend in this book. If you think your employer's stock is going to be a superior investment, holding a big chunk is your gamble. At a minimum, review Chapter 6 to see how to evaluate a particular stock. But remember to consider the consequences if you're wrong about your employer's stock.

Conservative investors often keep too much of their money in bank accounts, GICs, and the like. Read Chapter 3 to come up with an overall investment strategy that fits with the rest of your personal financial situation.

Reining In Your Emotions

We're all for people finding healthy ways to express their feelings. But selling an investment in a fit of impatience, frustration, or perhaps even anger over its lack of performance doesn't qualify. If you're prone to making decisions in the heat of the moment, be on guard against acting too quickly when it comes to selling investments.

As Tony has heard firsthand talking to investors for his *Globe and Mail* column, quite often this leads to short-term — and usually highly unprofitable — trading. You sell because the stock has fallen, but barring any significant developments, it may just be part of the natural up-and-down nature of the markets. Before you know it the investment may suddenly rise in value, leading to another knee-jerk reaction . . . this time to buy it back. Pretty soon you're doing the opposite of what you should be doing — buying high and selling low instead of the other way around.

Deciding Which Investments Are Keepers

Often, people are tempted to sell an investment for the wrong reasons. One natural human tendency is to want to sell investments that have declined in value. Some people fear a further fall, and they don't want to be affiliated with a loser, especially when money is involved. We think this reaction resembles the phenomenon of piling into the lifeboats when a ship springs a leak.

Step back, take some deep breaths, and examine the merits of the investment you're considering selling. If it's otherwise still sound, why bail out when prices are down and a sale is going on? What are you going to do with the money? If anything, you should be contemplating buying more of such an investment. Don't make a decision to sell based on your current emotional response, especially to recent news events. If bad news has recently hit, it's already old news. Don't base your investment holdings on such transitory events.

Use the criteria in this book for finding good investments to evaluate the worthiness of your current holdings. If an investment is fundamentally sound, don't sell it.

A better reason to sell an investment is that it comes with high fees relative to comparable investments. For example, if you own a bond mutual fund that's socking it to you with fees of 2 percent per year, check out Chapter 8 to discover high-performing, lower-cost funds.

Tuning In to the Tax Consequences

When you sell investments that you hold outside an RRSP or other tax-sheltered retirement plan, taxes should be one factor in your decision. (See Chapter 3 to find out about tax rates that apply to the sale of an investment as well as to the distributions that investments make.) If the investments are inside an RRSP or RRIF, taxes aren't an issue because the plans are sheltered from taxation, unless you're withdrawing money from the plans.

Just because you pay tax on a profit from selling an investment that's not sheltered from tax by an RRSP or RRIF doesn't mean you should avoid selling. With real estate, you can often avoid paying taxes on the profit that you make (see Chapters 10 and 11).

If you're selling stock, your capital gain is simply the difference between what you received less what you paid when you bought the investment, along with any fees or commission. The purchase cost, plus any extra fees you incur when buying and selling it, is called the *adjusted cost base*. If you've bought the same unit at different times, you'll need to do a little math to calculate your adjust cost base. Each time you make another purchase of the same investment, you have to add together your total number of shares or units, and divide them by your total cost to that point to come up with an average.

Say you bought 1,000 shares of Bombardier for $5.00 a share including any commissions. Now suppose the stock rose to $6.00 and you bought another 1,000 at $6.00 a share including associated costs. You would now own 2,000 shares for a total cost of $11,000. Here's how to determine your adjusted cost base.

(Initial purchase + commissions/fees) + (Subsequent purchase price + commissions/fees)

Total number of shares/units

Or, to apply it to the example

$$\frac{\$5,000 + \$6,000}{2,000} = \$5.50$$

Selling Investments with Hefty Profits

Of course, no one likes to pay taxes, but if an investment you own has appreciated in value, someday you'll have to pay tax when you sell it. Capital gains tax applies when you sell an investment at a higher price than you paid for it. As we explain in Chapter 3, your capital gains tax rate is different from the tax rate you pay on ordinary income (such as from employment earnings or interest on bank savings accounts).

Odds are, the longer you've held securities such as stocks, the greater the capital gain you'll have, because stocks tend to appreciate over time. If all your assets have appreciated greatly, you may resist selling to avoid taxes. However, if you need money for a major purchase, sell what you need and pay the tax. Even if you're in the top marginal tax bracket, you'll have lots left, since the approximate effective tax rate will be 22.5 percent (rates vary depending on the province you're in). Before you sell, however, do some rough figuring to make sure you'll have enough money left to accomplish what you want. Also, if you seek to sell one investment and reinvest in another, you'll owe tax on the profit unless you're selling and rebuying real estate (see Chapters 10 and 11).

If you hold a number of assets, in order to diversify and meet your other financial goals, give preference to selling your largest holdings with the smallest capital gains. If you have some securities with profits and some with losses, you can sell some of each in order to offset the losses with the profits.

If your circumstances allow, it may pay to sell your investment in two chunks, one near the end of the year and the second at the beginning of the next. By doing this, you spread your taxable capital gain over two years. This may help you keep your total taxable income in both years lower, potentially keeping you in a lower marginal tax bracket. Spreading your gain out in this way may also help you avoid being hit by the minimum tax. (When you calculate your tax bill, you have to do it both the regular way and using the minimum tax rules, which are aimed at ensuring that high-income users aren't able to pay little or no tax through the use of shelters and special credits.)

Cutting Your (Securities') Losses

Perhaps you own some turkeys in your portfolio. If you need to raise cash for some particular reason, you may consider selling some securities at a loss. You can use these losses to offset gains you've made — or will make in the future — on the sale of other securities.

Your actual loss when it comes to the tax department is the difference between what you paid for the investment — the adjusted cost base — and what you received when you sold it, after deducting commissions and other fees involved in selling.

Just as you take half of any capital gain before calculating any taxes due, only one-half of your loss can be used to offset these taxable capital gains. However, if you can't use some or all of your allowable capital losses in a given year, it's not wasted. In general, you can't use capital losses to reduce ordinary income. But you can apply a capital loss against taxable capital gains you had in any of the three prior years. You can also carry the allowable capital loss forward indefinitely, and use it to offset taxable capital gains in any future year. The current amount of allowable capital losses that you have yet to apply against taxable capital gains is known as your *net capital losses*.

If you own a security that has ceased trading and appears worthless (or you've made a loan that hasn't been repaid), you can likely deduct this loss. Peruse the latest edition of *Taxes For Canadians for Dummies* (published by Wiley) for more information on what situations are deductible and how to claim these losses on your annual tax return.

Selling an Investment with an Unknown Cost

You may not know what some investments originally cost you or the person who bought them and later gave them to you. If you can't find that original statement, start by calling the firm where the investment was bought. Whether it's a brokerage firm or mutual fund company, the company should be able to send you copies of old account statements, although you may have to pay a small fee for this service.

Also, increasing numbers of investment firms, especially mutual fund companies, can tell you upon the sale of an investment what its original cost was. The cost generally calculated is the average cost for the shares you purchased. See *Taxes For Canadians for Dummies* for more ideas about what to do when original records aren't available for other assets, such as real estate.

Recognizing That All Brokers Are Not Created Equal

If you're selling securities such as stocks and bonds, you need to know that some brokers charge more — in some cases lots more — to sell. Even if the securities you want to sell currently reside at a high-cost brokerage firm, you can transfer them to a discount brokerage firm. See Chapter 9 for the virtues of using a discount brokerage firm.

Finding a Trustworthy Financial Adviser

You aren't stupid. Before you picked up this book, you may have considered yourself an investing dummy. We didn't, and we still don't, but hopefully you feel less like a dummy after reading this book. If you delegate your investment decision making to an adviser, you may be disappointed.

Few financial advisers offer objective and knowledgeable advice. Many financial consultants work on commission, which can cloud their judgment. And among the minority of fee-based advisers, a good number manage money, which creates other conflicts of interest. The more money you give them to invest and manage, the more money these advisers make. If you need advice about whether to sell some investments, consider turning to a tax or financial adviser who works on an hourly basis.

Chapter 22

Ten Tips for Investing in a Down Market

. . . .

In This Chapter

▶ Keeping a level head amidst the doom and gloom

▶ Identifying and fixing flaws in your portfolio

▶ Understanding why value stocks have less downside risk

. . . .

*U*nless there's a lot of other breaking news, sharp drops in the stock market make headlines. No wonder — stock market gyrations are great media fodder. Every day the market environment is different, and new stocks are plunging and rising. And now with more individuals holding stocks through company and personal retirement plans, the media has a captive, concerned audience. In this chapter we discuss how to maximize your chances for investing success when stocks take a turn for the worse.

Don't Panic

No one enjoys turning on his car radio, clicking her television set on, or logging on to the Internet and getting this news: "Stocks plunge. The Dow Jones Industrial plummeted 400 points today." Don't panic — it's just one day's events. Just because a home burned to the ground recently in your town and the news is being broadcast all over the local media doesn't mean your home is next.

You wouldn't stop living in the neighbourhood upon hearing that news, but you might take some sensible precautions such as installing smoke alarms and repairing any malfunctioning appliances that might cause a fire to ensure that your home isn't likely to become the next fire department statistic. Likewise, don't shun stocks just because of the down periods. As we discuss in Chapter 2, risk and return go hand in hand. If you want wealth-building investments that provide superior long-term returns, you must be willing to accept risk (that is, volatility and down periods).

Do you see the media reporting on stories with headlines such as "Luxury home prices plunged $40,000 today in West Vancouver"? We didn't think so! Although other wealth-building investments, such as real estate and small business, go through significant declines, you generally see few headlines on their daily price movements. That's because no one reports on the pricing of real estate and small business minute by minute every business day, as is done with stock prices.

Keep Your Portfolio's Perspective in Mind

If you follow our advice, you should hold stocks worldwide along with some bonds. Here's a common quandary that you yourself may have experienced, particularly when the markets fell precipitously in 2002: "I just saw that the TSE is down 32 percent and the S&P 500 is down 28 percent. Should I sell?"

You may be quite surprised to find, even when the markets are dropping like this, that your particular portfolio of stocks and bonds is down much less, perhaps having fallen only 6 or 8 percent. Mind you, we aren't trying to minimize or trivialize the fact that you may have lost money. But you might have overlooked the fact that the bonds in your portfolio actually increased in value, as did some of your value-oriented stocks. (See Chapter 8 for how to build a diversified mutual fund portfolio.)

View Major Declines as Unadvertised Sales

Unlike retail stores, which experience bigger-than-normal crowds when prices are reduced, fewer investors, especially individual investors, rush to buy stocks after they've suffered a sharp decline. Stocks usually bottom when pessimism reaches a peak. The reason: Those who were motivated to sell have done so, and the major selling has exhausted itself.

When stock prices decline, don't get swept up in the pessimism. View declines as the financial markets' having a sale on stocks.

Now, we're not saying simply to buy any stock after any decline. For example, as we discuss in Part II, we're not generally big fans of buying individual stocks, especially focusing on a specific industry (such as technology or auto manufacturing). When technology stocks started declining in 2000, some investors made the mistake of buying more of them after prices dropped 10 or 20 percent. What such "buy on the dip" investors didn't realize was that the technology stocks they were buying were still grossly overpriced when measured by price/earnings ratios and other valuation measures (see Chapter 5).

You're generally best off buying stocks gradually over time through well-managed, diversified mutual funds. When the broad stock market suffers a substantial decline, you can step up your buying when stocks are at reduced prices — on sale.

Identify the Real Problems with Your Portfolio

Stock market declines can be effective at more quickly exposing problems with your portfolio. For example, when technology stocks tumbled in 2000 and 2001, we started hearing from lots of investors who had loaded up on technology stocks and wondered what they should do with their holdings. Most of these investors kept thinking about how much more their technology stocks were worth at their peak before the decline set in.

We urged such investors to acknowledge the huge risk they were clearly taking by putting so many eggs in one basket. We also highlighted the dangers of chasing after a hot sector, and pointed out that today's hot sector often becomes tomorrow's laggard.

In addition to poorly diversified portfolios, a declining stock market can expose the high fees you may be paying on your investments. Fewer investors care about getting whacked with fees amounting to, say, 2 percent annually when they're making 20 percent year after year. But after a few years of low or negative returns, such high fees become quite painful and more obvious.

Avoid Growth Stocks If You Get Queasy Easily

In a sustained stock market slide (bear market), the stocks that get clobbered the most tend to be the ones that were most overpriced from the period of the previous market rise (bull market). Like fads such as hula hoops, pet rocks, and Cabbage Patch dolls, in each bull market, particular types of growth stocks, such as Internet or biotechnology companies, can be especially hot.

Predicting the duration and magnitude of a bear market is nearly impossible. Consequently, wouldn't it make sense to focus your stock investing on those stocks that produce solid long-term returns and that tend to decline less in a major market decline? So-called value stocks tend to be among the safer types of stocks to hold during a bear market. Value stocks generally have less downside risk because they generally pay higher dividends and have relatively greater underlying asset values in comparison with their stock valuations.

As happened in some past bear markets, numerous value-oriented stocks actually appreciated during the bear market that began in 2000. See Chapter 8 for our discussion of the different types of stocks and mutual funds that practise value stock investing.

Tune Out Negative, Hyped Media

When the stock market is crumbling, subjecting yourself to a daily diet of bad news and conflicting opinions about what to do next makes most investors do the wrong things. When major stock markets were really getting clobbered during the summer of 2002, we heard remarks like this: "It seems the civilized world as we know it is coming to an end. We have all this tension and conflict in the Middle East, there's a war in Afghanistan, the news media are talking about the U.S. going after Iraq next, no one can believe company financial statements, and stocks are too risky to hold. All I keep hearing is bad news when I turn on my television or go online. Shouldn't I just sell my stocks and buy something else?"

Our advice to the many who felt the same way was simple: Stop watching and focusing on bad news. Just like a steady diet of junk food is bad for your physical health, a continuous stream of negative, hyped news is bad for your financial health. In our observations, dwelling on bad news doesn't do such great things for people's emotional health either.

Conflict is always occurring somewhere in the world. The business world will always have unethical and corrupt company executives. Holding stocks always carries risk. That's why those who see the glass as half full build wealth by holding stocks, real estate, and small business over the long term.

Ignore Large Point Declines — Consider the Percentages

It drives us crazy when the news media show a one-day chart of a major stock market index, such as the Dow Jones Industrial Average, on a day when the index drops a large number of points. In recent years, 200- and 300-point drops in the Dow happened fairly frequently.

It's important to look at the percentage decline in an index rather than at a point decline. Although 200 to 300 points sounds like a horrendous drop, when the Dow was around 10,000 it amounted to a move of 2 to 3 percent. No one likes losing that portion of their wealth invested in stocks in one day, but the percentage of change sounds less horrifying than the point change.

Don't Believe That You Need a Rich Dad to Be a Successful Investor

A young man wrote to Eric about an interview he had read about with Robert Kiyosaki, author of the *Rich Dad, Poor Dad* series. In the interview, Kiyosaki said that the rich are different from the rest of us because "they teach their children how to be rich. . . . These get-rich techniques include investing with leverage . . . and staying away from mutual funds . . . which are way too risky."

The young man came from a humble background and had been salting money away in mutual funds through his company retirement plan. But he thought he might be doomed to a lifetime of poverty after reading what the Rich Dad guru had to say.

Here's our response: We've known plenty of people over the years who came from non-wealthy families who built substantial wealth by living within their means and by investing in the three wealth-building assets we focus on in this book: stocks, real estate, and small business.

With regard to mutual funds and retirement plans, as well as saying they're way too risky, Kiyosaki says that "those vehicles are only good for about 20 percent of the population, people making $100,000 or more." We couldn't disagree more. In fact, our experience is that mutual funds are tailor-made for non-wealthy people who don't have the assets to properly create a diversified portfolio themselves.

Kiyosaki also says that he doesn't like mutual funds because they "have got no insurance from a stock market crash. To me, that's sad, and I am concerned." As we discuss in Parts I and II, the best way to reduce the risk of investing in stocks is to be diversified, not only in a variety of stocks but also in other investments that don't move in tandem with the stock market.

Kiyosaki claims that when investing in real estate he does so with the benefit of insurance because "my banker requires me to have insurance from catastrophic losses." This is nonsensical, since such an insurance policy would cover losses from, say, a fire, but not a decline in market value of the real estate due to overall market conditions.

(Re-) Read Chapters 4 and 5

When the going gets tough in the stock market, you can easily lose perspective. Even if you've already read them before, please go back and read again Chapters 4 and 5 of this book. These chapters explain how the stock market works and what influences stock prices in the short term versus the longer term. Make sure you have the long-term perspective you need to succeed with stock investing and that you really understand how the financial markets work.

Talk to People Who Care about You

Life's challenging events can be humbling and sometimes depressing. Holding an investment that's dropped a lot in value — whether it's a stock, mutual fund, real estate, or a small business — is one such event.

But you don't have to carry the burden yourself. Talk about your feelings with someone who understands and cares about you. Be clear about and communicate what you're seeking — empathy, good listening, a sounding board, or advice.

Index

Notes

Notes